In Search of New Scales

Eastman Studies in Music

Ralph P. Locke, Senior Editor
Eastman School of Music

Additional Titles in History and Theory of Music from 1870 to 1920

*The Poetic Debussy: A Collection of
His Song Texts and Selected Letters*
(Revised Second Edition)
Edited by Margaret G. Cobb

*French Organ Music from the
Revolution to Franck and Widor*
Edited by Lawrence Archbold
and William J. Peterson

*Analyzing Wagner's Operas: Alfred Lorenz
and German Nationalist Ideology*
Stephen McClatchie

*Music's Modern Muse: A Life of
Winnaretta Singer, Princesse de Polignac*
Sylvia Kahan

*"Claude Debussy As I Knew Him" and
Other Writings of Arthur Hartmann*
Edited by Samuel Hsu,
Sidney Grolnic, and Mark Peters
Foreword by David Grayson

*The Pleasure of Modernist Music:
Listening, Meaning, Intention, Ideology*
Edited by Arved Ashby

*Debussy's Letters to Inghelbrecht:
The Story of a Musical Friendship*
Annotated by Margaret G. Cobb

*Explaining Tonality:
Schenkerian Theory and Beyond*
Matthew Brown

*The Substance of Things Heard:
Writings about Music*
Paul Griffiths

*Musical Encounters at the
1889 Paris World's Fair*
Annegret Fauser

*Schubert in the
European Imagination, Volume 2:
Fin-de-Siècle Vienna*
Scott Messing

*Pentatonicism from the
Eighteenth Century to Debussy*
Jeremy Day-O'Connell

*French Music, Culture, and
National Identity, 1870–1939*
Edited by Barbara L. Kelly

*Beethoven's Century:
Essays on Composers and Themes*
Hugh Macdonald

*Variations on the Canon:
Essays on Music from Bach to
Boulez in Honor of Charles Rosen on
His Eightieth Birthday*
Edited by Robert Curry, David Gable,
and Robert L. Marshall

*Analyzing Atonal Music:
Pitch-Class Set Theory and Its Contexts*
Michiel Schuijer

A complete list of titles in the Eastman Studies in Music Series,
in order of publication, may be found at the end of this book.

In Search of
New Scales

Prince Edmond de Polignac,
Octatonic Explorer

Sylvia Kahan

UNIVERSITY OF ROCHESTER PRESS

First published 2009

University of Rochester Press
668 Mt. Hope Avenue, Rochester, NY 14620, USA
www.urpress.com
and Boydell & Brewer Limited
PO Box 9, Woodbridge, Suffolk IP12 3DF, UK
www.boydellandbrewer.com

ISBN-13: 978-1-58046-305-8
ISSN: 1071-9989

Library of Congress Cataloging-in-Publication Data

Kahan, Sylvia.
 In search of new scales : Edmond de Polignac, octatonic explorer / Sylvia Kahan.
   p. cm.—(Eastman studies in music, ISSN 1071–9989 ; v. 63)
 Includes bibliographical references and index.
 ISBN-13: 978-1-58046-305-8 (hardcover : alk. paper)
 ISBN-10: 1-58046-305-3 (alk. paper)
 1. Polignac, Edmond, prince de, 1834–1901. 2. Musical intervals and scales.
3. Music—19th century—History and criticism. I. Title.
ML410.P764K34 2009
780.92—dc22
[B]
                                                              2009020124

A catalogue record for this title is available from the British Library.

This publication is printed on acid-free paper.
Printed in the United States of America.

To Noah and Carly

Edmond de Polignac, page 3 of the *Study on the Sequences of Alternating Whole Steps and Half Steps*, showing the three scales A, B, and C. Used by permission.

Contents

Musical Examples

Musical examples in the Treatise are not listed separately

Illustrations

Figures

Acknowledgments

My interest in octatoncism began during my doctoral studies at the Graduate Center of the City University of New York, when I took a course on the music of Stravinsky with Professor Joseph Straus. It was Joe who first encouraged me to write this book and who provided generous help in shaping the theoretical language of Edmond de Polignac's octatonic treatise.

As I pursued my research and grappled with the intellectual challenges of nineteenth-century octatonic theory, I was fortunate to have the help of colleagues and friends who offered suggestions, comments, and critiques, and who provided thoughtful readings of earlier drafts of this essay. For their invaluable contributions, I would like to thank L. Poundie Burstein, Carlo Caballero, Catrina Flint de Medicis, John Graziano, Roy Howat, Andy Jaffe, Ralph P. Locke, François Luguenot, François de Médicis, Charles Palermo, Maria Rose, and Frédéric Saffar. I am especially grateful to Richard Taruskin, whose brilliant writings on octatonicism have served as a beacon light through my years of research. His insightful comments were invaluable in crafting the language of the final draft of this book.

I wish to thank Catherine Massip and the staff of the Département de la Musique of the Bibliothèque nationale de France and Pierre Vidal of the Bibliothèque de l'Opéra for facilitating my research in Paris. Jann Pasler and Anne de Rambuteau provided valuable help with my research on the Comtesse Greffulhe. Equally helpful were Anne de Beaupuy and Guy Selva, who generously provided access to archival material on, respectively, René de Castéra and Blanche Selva. Special thanks go to Alexandra Laederich and John Shepard, who generously provided eleventh-hour practical help. I am grateful to Duc Antoine de Gramont for his permission to publish material from the Fonds Greffulhe, located in the Archives nationales, Paris. I am grateful to Natalie Mauriac-Dyer for her permission to include excerpts of the letters from Marcel Proust to Edmond de Polignac. I thank the Dance Division of the New York Public Library for allowing me to reproduce material from the Isadora Duncan Papers.

In the transcription and the decoding of Edmond de Polignac's octatonic treatise, I was fortunate to have the indefatigable and thoughtful help of David Smey, computer-graphics/music-examples wizard and music theorist *par excellence*. As we worked together as an editorial committee of two, Mr. Smey progressively became pulled into the eccentric world of Edmond de Polignac's octatonic thinking and composition. It is thanks to David Smey's intellectual acuity, imaginative and interpretive leaps, collaborative spirit, and endless patience that I was finally able to make visual and musical sense of the Polignac treatise. Without his help, this book would have never come to fruition.

I am so grateful to the staff at University of Rochester Press—Suzanne Guiod, Tracey Engel, Katie Hurley, Susan Smith—for making the production of this book a genuine pleasure. I am especially grateful to Ralph P. Locke, who, in his position as Senior Editor of the series Eastman Studies in Music, guided the book throughout its preparation. Special thanks go to Louise Goldberg, whose eagle eye and encyclopedic knowledge of all things musical and francophone rendered the copyediting process a thing of beauty. This book is my second with the Rochester team, and I am proud that this volume bears its imprint.

William Harris very kindly supplied the translations of the Latin texts that appear in this volume. Duncan Bray of Sovereign Ancestries provided assistance with genealogical matters.

Finally, I wish to express my gratitude to Prince Edmond de Polignac—great-grandnephew and executor of the musical estate of the composer, godson of Winnaretta Singer-Polignac, and *grand mélomane*—and to his wife, Princesse Edmond de Polignac, née Valéria Bohringer. I hope that, with this book, I have repaid their faith in my scholarly work and the generosity with which they opened their home and their hearts to me. Through them, the beautiful and forward-thinking music of their illustrious forebear lives on.

Parts of this book first appeared in other publications. Nathalie Mauriac-Dyer and I collaborated on an article, "Quatre Lettres inédites de Proust au Prince de Polignac," which appeared in the *Bulletin Marcel Proust* 53 (December 2003). Earlier versions of chapter 9 and excerpts from the Polignac treatise first appeared in the article "'Rien de la tonalité usuelle': Edmond de Polignac and the Octatonic Scale in Nineteenth-Century France," published in the journal *19th-Century Music* (2005). I am grateful to Patrick McCreless for his wisdom and careful editing of the article.

My research was supported by a Presidential Fellowship in the Humanities and Social Sciences from the College of Staten Island, City University of New York. I am equally grateful for the generous award of a publication subvention from the Society for Music Theory.

Abbreviations

AN	Archives nationales, Paris
AP	Archives privées, Archives nationales, Paris
BnF-Mss	Bibliothèque nationale de France (Département des Manuscrits)
BnF-Mus	Bibliothèque nationale de France (Département de la Musique)
CaP	Prince Camille de Polignac, Edmond de Polignac's brother
ChP	Princesse Jules de Polignac, née Charlotte-Maria Parkyns, Edmond de Polignac's mother
EG	Comtesse Henri (Élisabeth) Greffulhe
EP	Prince Edmond de Polignac
FSP	Fondation Singer-Polignac
LMLV	"Le Monde et la Ville," *Le Figaro*'s society column
LP	Prince Ludovic de Polignac, Edmond de Polignac's brother
MP	Comte Melchior de Polignac, Edmond de Polignac's nephew
NAfr	Nouvelles acquisitions françaises, Bibliothèque nationale de France, Paris
NLa	Nouvelles lettres autographes, Bibliothèque nationale de France, Paris
RGMP	*Revue et Gazette musicale de Paris*
RM	Comte Robert de Montesquiou
WP, WSP	Winnaretta Singer, later Winnaretta Singer-Polignac, Edmond de Polignac's wife

Introduction

Edmond de Polignac and the Discovery of Octatonicism

It was less than fifty years ago, in 1963, that composer and theorist Arthur Berger's article, "Problems of Pitch Organization in Stravinsky," was published in the journal *Perspectives of New Music*. This landmark scholarly essay reveals a fundamental organizational device underlying the pitch structure of extensive passages in works such as *Petrouchka*, *Le Sacre du printemps*, and *Les Noces:* a series of eight alternating half steps and whole steps, which Berger dubs, for the first time, "the octatonic scale." Berger identifies a number of characteristic features of the scale: its symmetrical structure, its bisection at the tritone, its emphasis on minor third relations, its construction from two diminished seventh chords a semitone apart, and interaction with diatonic elements.[1]

Since 1963, scholars have continued to shed light on the functional and formal uses of the octatonic scale, also referred to in post-tonal music theory as the octatonic collection.[2] Pieter van den Toorn demonstrates the pervasive use of the octatonic collection in over forty of Stravinsky's works and creates a vocabulary to account for harmonic and structural events within an octatonic framework; Richard Taruskin systematically traces the genesis of the scale back first to Schubert, then to Liszt, and finally to a large number of Russian composers, principal among whom was Nicolai Rimsky-Korsakov.[3] Taruskin credits Rimsky with the reification of the collection, which the latter described in a letter to Balakirev (1 August 1867) as "a descending scale of semitone, whole tone, semitone, whole tone"[4]—a scale that, during the composer's lifetime, came to be known as the "Rimsky-Korsakov scale." In the aforementioned letter, Rimsky describes a passage from his symphonic poem *Sadko*, which features in the upper voices a descending octatonic scale, supported harmonically by chords related by minor third;[5] this passage becomes an important leitmotif throughout *Sadko*. The mediant harmonies in *Sadko*, which include harmonic relations not only in the octatonic scale but also in the whole-tone scale, denote what Taruskin calls "evil sorcery."[6]

Today, the post-Berger generations of scholars have unearthed the scale in music ranging from Weber to Webern.[7] Several studies in the last two decades have focused on the role of octatonicism in French music, especially that of

Debussy and Messiaen (who listed the octatonic scales among the "modes of limited transposition"[8]), and, most recently, that of Ravel.[9] The octatonic collection is now widely regarded as one of the principal organizational devices of twentieth-century music.

However, while theory often lags behind practice, the lag between the use of the octatonic collection in composition and its articulation in theory seems to have been particularly long. The fact that Rimsky-Korsakov never wrote down in any systematic way the theory underlying the scale that bore his name—as he did, however, when he codified his theories of orchestration—meant that its presence in early modernist compositions, although used frequently and conspicuously by his followers, remained obscure to those outside his circle.[10] Consequently, many composers in the succeeding generation, both Russian and non-Russian, used the collection in a manner that Taruskin describes as "a fortuitous veneer on the surface on the surface of common practice," that is, as an embellishment of diminished or diminished seventh chords.[11] "True octatonicism," defined by Taruskin, is identified as the supplanting of functions generated by movement within the circle of fifths by a rotation of thirds or by a tonally stable diminished harmony.[12] Who, before Stravinsky, was the first composer to write "truly" octatonic music?[13]

Interestingly, it appears that an important historical link between nineteenth- and twentieth-century octatonic composition—a link with particular implications for the presence of octatonicism in early modernist French music—is found in the music and theoretical writings of Prince Edmond de Polignac (1834–1901), an aristocrat and amateur French composer who, around 1879, penned not only the first pervasively octatonic compositions, but also what appears to be the first treatise on octatonic theory.

*   *   *

This volume is written in two parts. Part one is at once a biography of Edmond de Polignac and a history of Polignac's invention of the octatonic scales. It provides an overview of the social and cultural forces at play at the time of Polignac's invention, an examination of the reception given Polignac's octatonic music and theories by late nineteenth- and early twentieth-century French musicians, and an analysis of Polignac's octatonic compositions. Part two contains a preface to the composer's octatonic treatise-sketchbook; a complete transcription and analysis of his octatonic treatise, "Étude sur les successions alternantes de tons et demi-tons" (A Study on the Alternating Sequences of Whole Steps and Half Steps), the text of which is given in English translation with transcriptions of the music by David Smey; and a transcription of the treatise's original French text, without the music.

The organization of the book's material, a mélange of biography, history, and theory, is somewhat unorthodox; however, it reflects both my belief that Polignac's interesting life and creative/theoretical work are all of a piece and my hope that a cross-disciplinary approach to this material will be useful to music scholars in both the musicological and theoretical domains. While Polignac may be a minor figure in music history, and while the influence of his octatonic music on his contemporaries can only be speculated upon, his life and octatonic explorations might serve as exemplars for an examination of music in Second-Empire France and the place that interest in new and "alternative" scales occupied in that particular cultural moment. In this study, Polignac's remarkable invention of octatonicism is posited as both a reflection of the aesthetic ideas, musical developments, and theoretical discussions swirling around him in Belle-Époque Paris and as a precursor of things to come—when Parisians were introduced to Stravinsky's ground-breaking music—more than thirty years later. An entire chapter is devoted to the years 1875–79, the period during which Polignac embarked on his octatonic explorations and wrote his first compositions based on the octatonic collection. The year 1878, during which time Paris hosted a World's Fair, is singled out as an exceptionally fertile breeding period for new and unusual ideas. Here the discussion of the influences on Polignac's octatonic invention is limited mostly to musical influences. A more in-depth study of this amazing period—one that might include lengthier discussions of the social, political, and artistic upheavals in play, as well as the influence of Symbolist and Decadent literary figures such as Huysmans, Mallarmé, Verlaine, and Moreau—must be left to another scholar.[14]

It is not my intention to use this study as a defense of Edmond de Polignac as an "unjustly neglected composer"—although some of the tonal music (the music for string quartet and some of the vocal and choral music), all discussed only briefly in this study, might justify the appellation. The octatonic music itself is, regrettably, not much more than a historical curiosity. Nonetheless, the thorough analyses offered here demonstrate interesting parallels between Polignac's octatonic compositions and the octatonic works that both precede and follow them by greater composers.

* * *

As a theoretical study, this work seeks to provide a link between Rimsky-Korsakov's first foray into octatonic writing, in 1867, and late nineteenth-century octatonicism. Readers conversant with the pedagogical writings of Rimsky-Korsakov, or with Richard Taruskin's studies and transcriptions of these materials, will recognize in some of Polignac's examples an uncanny resemblance to the concluding section of Rimsky-Korsakov's harmony textbook, which contains exercises outlining "false progressions" written both on the "circle of major thirds" and the "circle of minor thirds."[15] Here, too, a comparison of the similar exercises and chord progressions of the two men demonstrates clearly Rimsky's superiority as both a composer and a pedagogue: the progressions in the musical examples of Polignac treatise are obviously weaker and the voicings and voice leading less skillful than those of the Russian. But, as Taruskin notes, Rimsky's students are able to discover the complete whole step/half step scale only if they complete the exercises, whereas Polignac's treatise overtly exposes basic principles of octatonic procedures. And, it is likely that Polignac's work predates that of Rimsky: the first edition of this latter's harmony textbook was not published until the mid-1880s.

This study might also usefully be included in the discussion of several questions:

- What exactly constitutes "octatonic music"?

- What are the most likely influences on octatonic and proto-octatonic composition in late nineteenth-century France?

- What does "octatonic music" sound like?

- Which nineteenth-century works can justifiably be considered to be precursors of twentieth-century octatonic works?

As I did the research for this project, I was struck by the fact that, even almost a half century after the publication of Berger's article, there is still a surprising diversity of opinion on the answers to these fundamental issues among some of academic music's most eminent scholars. For some reason, octatonicism and the historical questions surrounding its origins have inspired some exceptionally heated arguments in the scholarly literature. Have there been such fierce battles over the meaning of the word "tonal"? It is my hope that the perspective of one obscure nineteenth-century musician will help shed some light on the subject of the history of octatonicism and provide some clarity. The greatest dichotomy of opinion appears to exist in what I shall call "collectional" versus "structural" utilizations of the scale in the literature. It is not clear whether the presence alone of the eight pitch classes of one of the three collections (or a subset of a collection) is sufficient to warrant the appellation "octatonic," any more than the presence of the diatonic collection in a piece (say, the "Russian Dance" in Stravinsky's *Petrouchka*) renders the work "tonal" just because it is constructed from the white-key diatonic collection. Allan Forte is the leading proponent of the "collectional" definition of the octatonic collection. In his 1991 article, "Debussy and the Octatonic," Forte takes an expansive view of octatonicism, defining it to include "not only . . . the octatonic scale, but also and more generally . . . any [ordered or unordered] subset of that scale that contains from three to seven notes."[16] He identifies the octatonic collections as a group of ordered segments within "a system of lexical designations often used in contemporary studies of non-traditional pitch structure."[17] Under this rubric, asserts Forte, portions of Hector Berlioz's *Symphonie fantastique* (1830)—especially a tritone-related passage from the work's fourth movement (mm. 152–161), in which a D-flat-major triad is followed by a G-minor triad—might be identified as octatonic.[18] While Forte's application of set theory to octatonicism provides a useful classification of whole-step/half-step pitch content on the surface level, it does not provide any framework for discussing its special—indeed, astonishing—sonic qualities: the audacious third-related progressions of proto-octatonicists such Schubert, Liszt, and—perhaps—Chopin; the pervasive associations with magic and sorcery in nineteenth-century Russian music; and the identification of the collection with exoticism and barbarism in the twentieth century.[19]

In regard to current octatonic theory, it is hoped that the current study might prove useful in discussions of terminology associated with the collection. For example, there is no standard nomenclature in the theory literature for the octatonic scales. Van den Toorn (in *The Music of Igor Stravinsky,* pp. 50–51, and in "Octatonic Pitch Structure in Stravinsky," in Pasler, *Confronting Stravinsky,* pp. 130–56) identifies the three collections as Collection I (ascending half-step/whole step from C♯/D, descending whole step/half step from C♯/B), Collection II (ascending from D/E♭, descending from D/C), and Collection III (ascending from E♭/E♮, descending from E♭/D♭). Polignac's three scales, in ascending form only, would thus correspond to van den Toorn's in the following manner: Scale A = Collection III, Scale B = Collection II, Scale C = Collection I. Taruskin (in "Stravinsky's Angle," p. 73) uses a Collection I, II, III system whereby the collections begin with the semitones C/C♯, C♯/D, and D/D♯, corresponding with Polignac's Scales A, C, and B, respectively. Joseph N. Straus, in his *Introduction to Post-Tonal Theory,*[20] p. 144, labels each of the three octatonic scales in its half-step/whole-step form according its numerically lowest semitone, using integer notation (C=0, C♯=1, D=2, etc.) to identify the pitch classes that begin each collection; the three collections are thus named Scale OCT0,1 (contains C/C♯), OCT1,2 (contains C♯/D), and OCT2,3 (contains D/E♭). Given the confusion generated by these multiple naming systems, Polignac's "Scales A, B, C" nomenclature might be a useful alternative.

As a composer and theorist, Edmond de Polignac was a precursor to the Berger–Van den Toorn–Taruskin model: his octatonicism was based on the supplanting of circles of fifths and the substitution of mediant-related writing. In his 1985 article "Stravinsky's 'Angle,'" Taruskin writes, "A large chapter in the as-yet-unwritten history of nineteenth-century harmony will show how composers increasingly availed themselves of these new harmonic paths that tended to short-circuit the traditional key system."[21] I hope that this study might occupy a small corner of that large chapter.

A Note on the Translations

All translations into English, from both original and secondary sources, are my own unless otherwise noted.

Part One

Edmond de Polignac (1834–1901): Man, Prince, and Composer

Prince Edmond de Polignac, ca. 1893. Collection of Prince Edmond de Polignac. Used by permission.

Chapter One

Childhood and Education (1834–1859)

"I was the last one born," recounted Prince Edmond de Polignac to his amused nephews, "the bottom of the barrel, and I got all the ancestral muck: eczema, gout, probably VD as well." Older looking than his sixty-plus years, Polignac huddled in his armchair, gloomily warming his feet, his tall thin frame wrapped in plaid shawls, his bald pate covered with a little knit cap. With a few curt phrases and witty gestures, speaking to no one in particular, he conjured up a lively caricature of some recent, well-meaning visitors. "'How're you doing, Prince?' they say. 'Rotten,' I say. 'Come now, dear Prince. . . . ' 'Ah, you don't believe me! Jokers, just like the others.' 'But everything's just fine. You're looking well, you're strong as Hercules. Come on, now, stop worrying . . . uh-oh!—he's dead!'"[1]

* * *

Edmond de Polignac was born on 19 April 1834 in his parents' apartment on the Grande Rue de Chaillot, in what was then the 1st (now the 8th) *arrondissement* (district) of Paris; he was baptized the next day in the nearby Church of Saint Pierre de Chaillot. Legally speaking, the newborn child did not exist: almost four years earlier, his father, Prince Jules de Polignac had been condemned by the French courts to *mort civile,* a total privation of his civil rights.[2] As a consequence, the baby's birth certificate and baptismal record identified him as Edmond-Melchior-Jean-Marie de Chalançon, son of the Marquis de Chalançon, "currently away on a trip," and his wife, Dame Marie-Charlotte (in English-language sources, Maria Charlotte) Parkyns.

Edmond was the seventh and youngest child born to Prince Jules de Polignac (1780–1847) (see Fig. 1.1), best known as the minister to France's King Charles X and author of the notorious Ordinances that brought down the Bourbon monarchy. Jules's father, Duc Jules-François de Polignac (1746–1817), held various posts at the courts of Austria and Russia during the "exile" of aristocrats that followed the French Revolution; his mother, born Gabrielle de Polastron (1749–1793), had been the notorious intimate friend of Marie-Antoinette and governess to the royal children. Jules spent his young years at the court of Versailles, but during the Revolution, when the name of Polignac became one of the most despised in France, the family was forced to flee. The Polignacs eventually became part of the "émigré" community that settled in London and remained

Figure 1.1. Prince Jules de Polignac, artist and date unknown. Used by permission of Prince Edmond de Polignac.

there for the next twenty years. After choosing a military career, Jules allied himself with Charles, the Comte d'Artois, Louis XVI's ultraconservative younger brother. Arrested in 1804 as part of a plot to overthrow Napoleon (known as the Cadoudal conspiracy), Jules spent the next ten years in prison. He escaped in 1814, and, in 1816, he married Barbara Campbell, a young Scotswoman. After giving birth to two children, Barbara died.

Jules was given a princely title by Pope Pius VII in 1822. From 1823 to 1829, he served as French Ambassador to England. While living in London, Prince Jules married Maria Charlotte Parkyns (1792–1864), most commonly called Charlotte, the daughter of Thomas Boothby-Parkyns, Lord Rancliffe, and of Elizabeth Anne James. The youngest of six siblings, Charlotte was described in family memoirs as a pretty, quiet woman with a gentle, placid manner. Married first to Comte César de Choiseul, she was widowed at age thirty. She met Prince Jules at the British Embassy while she was renewing her passport; they were married in 1824. Two sons, Alphonse and Ludovic were born during Jules's ambassadorship.

Meanwhile, back in France, the Comte d'Artois had become more influential in court circles; his archconservative views were viewed favorably by those opposed to the liberal government of his brother Louis XVIII. The "Ultras" (ultra-Royalists) disavowed the new constitution, the Charter of 1814, and worked to sweep away the democratic reforms of the Revolutionary and Napoleonic eras. Upon the death of Louis XVIII in 1824, Artois ascended to the monarchy as Charles X; he would become the last member of the Bourbon monarchy to rule France. His reign began an era of extreme reaction. In his six years on the throne, Charles undermined the middle class while promoting the clergy and the aristocracy, and curtailed educational reform, electoral fairness, and freedom of the press. In 1829, to bolster his position, rendered vulnerable by the moderate and liberal deputies in his government, Charles recalled Jules de Polignac from England and appointed him Prime Minister.

Like the king to whom he was blindly devoted, Jules de Polignac believed in the absolute power of the throne and the Church. His charming manners and strong sense of honor had served him well as ambassador, but, as prime minister, he lacked the forceful character necessary to lead the divided and recalcitrant Chamber of Deputies. As one of the original Ultras, he had refused to recognize the 1814 Charter. Just at the moment that the moderate opposition was gaining more power, he began to draft a series of decrees that would place ultimate power firmly in the hands of the King. The resulting "Thirty Ordinances," announced on 25 July 1830, dissolved the newly elected Assembly, established a electoral system that deprived the wealthy bourgeoisie of the right to vote, and imposed rigid censorship on the press. The fury of the public was instantaneous and violent: an insurrection erupted on 26 July and lasted for three days—what the French call "les trois glorieuses." When the fighting ceased, the Bourbon monarchy was replaced by the constitutional monarchy of Louis-Philippe. The deposed Charles managed to flee safely to England, but Prince Jules and his cabinet members were arrested on charges of treason; they were tried and sentenced to death. Due to international pressure, the sentences were revoked; instead, Jules and the ministers were sentenced to *mort civile*—complete deprivation of their civil rights—and incarcerated in the Fortress of Ham, in the flat, gray northern region of France called La Somme.

According to family chronicles, Charlotte bore the difficulties created by her husband's trial and sentence "with great courage and quiet calm."[3] After Jules was incarcerated, Charlotte moved with her children—including a newborn daughter, Yolande—to the village of Ham, where she settled in a house just outside the prison gates. Even though he was an "enemy of the state," Jules was allowed liberal privileges in prison, including conjugal visits from his wife. It was thus that a son, Camille, was born in 1832, and, two years later, the seventh and last child: Edmond.

The year of Edmond's birth, 1834, was fraught with political unrest and insurrection. The July Revolution of 1830 had represented the triumph of the upper bourgeoisie over the nobility. Hailed for his unpretentiousness and his sympathy for the common person, Louis-Philippe ascended the throne as a "king of the French nation." In the early days of his reign, he did away with the rigid press censorship that had prevailed under the July Ordinances. Economically, he undertook an expansion of industries and factories, thus creating a new urban working class. However, his *laissez-faire* attitude towards regulation of conditions in the factories and the mines led to subsistence wages, deterioration of living conditions for the urban working class, and a cholera epidemic. Economically squeezed, the workers resorted to demonstrations and riots. As Louis-Philippe and his government became the butt of criticism and satire in the liberal press that he helped to create, the "Citizen King" became progressively more conservative and monarchical, limiting freedom of association and expression. In 1834, new reductions in factory workers' wages resulted in widespread uprisings. The government's reaction to the insurrections was increased military repression of civil disorder, culminating in the National Guard's brutal slaying of a dozen innocent people in the Marais district, infamously immortalized by Alphonse Daumier's lithograph *Massacre in the Rue Transnonain*. Edmond's birth on 19 April coincided with the arrest of a thousand citizens in Paris. It was surely more than the *mort civile* of her husband that caused Charlotte de Polignac to enter the name of "Prince de Chalançon" on her baby's birth certificate and baptismal record. It was not a propitious moment to be born into a family whose very name was associated with the repressive government of the *ancien régime*.

The political upheaval of the mid-1830s coincided with the flowering of Romanticism, a word first used during the Napoleonic era. Victor Hugo, Alphonse de Lamartine, and Stendhal led the vanguard of a new wave of creative thinkers, writers, and artists who dared to express the drama and unfettered passions of those who helped to bring down the Bourbon government. "The nation is thirsty for its national tragedy," declared Stendhal. "Romanticism is the art of offering the public literary works which, given their present habits and beliefs, are capable of giving them the greatest possible pleasure; classicism, on the contrary, presents to them literature that gave the greatest possible pleasure to their great-grandparents."[4] The bold colors of the canvasses of Delacroix depicted the artist's vision of romanticism, terrible and stormy. In the 1830s, musical composition entered what posterity would regard as a golden age. It was represented in France by works as different as Berlioz's "narrative" *Symphonie fantastique* and Chopin's poignant and harmonically daring mazurkas. The flamboyant piano virtuoso Lizst and his violinist counterpoint Paganini had taken Paris by storm. In Germany, Mendelssohn and Schumann were infusing music with a new kind of poetry; the young Richard Wagner had just written his first opera.

Edmond de Polignac passed his earliest years in this era of rebellion against established authority, in an atmosphere of moral disillusionment created by the strife between liberals and monarchists. During the reign of Louis-Philippe, the name of Polignac continued to connote ignominy, and the stain on the family's reputation was felt by Charlotte and the children on a daily basis. The family was taunted in the streets; for the older children, school life became a battleground. Nonetheless, public opinion was leaning towards clemency for Prince Jules and the other prisoners who had been part of Charles X's ministry. Although refusing to revoke the *mort civile* of Prince Jules and his ministers, the court agreed to end their incarceration, on the condition that all of them leave France. In November 1836, Jules de Polignac was released from the Fortress of Ham. He went first to England, where he was joined later by his wife. The couple's marriage having been annulled by the French Chamber of Peers, Jules and Charlotte renewed their vows before the French consul in London in March 1837. The following year, after receiving a second princely title from King Ludwig I of Bavaria, Jules decided to resettle with his family in Germany. He bought a property in Lower Bavaria; there he built a château, which he named Wildthurn. It was at Wildthurn that Edmond de Polignac passed his childhood.

The zeal and sense of exactitude that Prince Jules had brought to his ministry was now redirected towards the upbringing of his children. He insisted that they receive a classical education, and supervised their studies closely. The Polignac children grew up in a lively intellectual environment. Jules and his sons were all gifted in mathematics, and it was not uncommon for the brothers to entertain each other with mathematical challenges in the way that other young boys might dare each other with feats of strength. The household was multilingual: French, German, and English were all spoken and read regularly; additionally, the children were schooled in Latin and Greek. The rigor and breadth—and consequent success—of the educational regime imposed by Prince Jules can be ascertained in extant letters exchanged by the siblings, which are peppered with quotations of Schiller's poems and Latin wordplay.

Intellectually curious and a natural-born show-off, Edmond was a lively presence in the household. Jules had had a small theater built at Wildthurn for his children and, by age six, Edmond was performing in the original theatrical pieces written by his siblings to entertain the adults; sometimes those performances included musical solos.[5] At age eight, he was writing his own plays and comedies, creating characters named "Baron Chamber-pot" and "Monsieur *Casse-Assiette* (Mister Broken Dish)."[6] His father's fervent religiosity influenced him as well: not only did Edmond show an early, even exaggerated interest in spirituality and the afterlife, he also put his performance talents to use by becoming the self-appointed household "preacher." One such oration had as its theme: "God is the dyer of men."[7] His father wrote to one cousin, "He is the most unusual child that one could ever meet; he amuses us more and more every day."[8]

It was fortunate that Edmond possessed artistic talent: since birth he had been a frail, sickly little boy, and was never able to participate in the rough-and-tumble play of his athletic older siblings. His brothers teased him mercilessly, calling him names like "rattling skeleton."[9] To console him, his parents, cognizant of their son's nascent musical talent, hired a professor from Munich to give their youngest son lessons in piano, counterpoint, and harmony.[10] Edmond was fortunate in having the encouragement of two music-loving parents. Charlotte had grown up in a musical household and had studied the pianoforte.[11] Jules, while not trained to play an instrument, had a cultivated gentleman's interest in music; according to one biographer, "he would spend long solitary hours sitting at the piano, trying out different combinations of complicated chords."[12]

The Polignac family spent eight happy years in Bavaria. But as one son after another departed for Paris to pursue formal education, Prince Jules decided that it was time to return to France. The Polignacs left Bavaria in 1845; as Jules was forbidden to dwell within the Paris city limits, the family settled in the suburb of Saint-Germain-en-Laye. Young Edmond frequently accompanied his mother on trips to Paris to visit the older Polignac children; all together, they attended musical *soirées* in the home of their maternal cousins the Delmars. Some of the greatest composers and artists in the capital, including Rossini, came to perform in the Delmar salon, and Edmond gained an invaluable education in hearing masterworks performed in a refined and intimate setting.[13]

The years spent in prison had compromised Jules's health. After years of illnesses, he died in 1847. The death of her husband freed Charlotte de Polignac from the obligation of living outside the Paris city limits. Within months she moved herself and her family into pleasant, roomy apartments in a townhouse at 3, Rue Neuve de Berry (today called Rue de Berri), just off the Champs-Élysées. It was a neighborhood where the aristocracy, the upper bourgeoisie, and well-established artists lived side by side. Balzac was their neighbor.

Thirteen-year-old Edmond was the only child left in the household: his older siblings were either married or boarding away while they pursued their studies. Like his older brothers, he received private instruction in the classic disciplines with a tutor named Abbé Legrand. However, his education was not limited to academic subjects. The Champs-Élysées neighborhood was in close proximity to the opera, theaters, and concert halls. Edmond frequently attended musical and theatrical performances, often in the company of his brother Camille, an equally ardent music lover and Edmond's closest confidant. Numerous passages in the brothers' correspondence affirm the veneration that both felt for the classic composers and their works, as well as the strong emotional bond that their mutual love of music created between the brothers.[14]

Edmond was in Paris during the bloody uprising of February 1848 and the subsequent "June days" four months later. He and his family were fortunately spared the loss of life and spoliation of property that befell so many Parisians. If fourteen-year-old Edmond was too young to understand the agitated political events taking place around him, he was certainly receptive to the fevered *zeitgeist* of his era. He was an avid reader; in addition to the classic Latin texts that he studied under the tutelage of Abbé Legrand, his collection of books included the writings of the great writers and poets of the period, including Goethe, Vigny, Balzac, Lamartine, Gautier, and Musset. He also began to build a personal music library, filling his bookshelves with scores of the string quartets and symphonies of Haydn and Beethoven, the songs of Schubert, and the operas of Auber, Berlioz, Boieldieu, Gluck, Hérold, Meyerbeer, and Mozart. Polignac's collection also included scores of J. S. Bach's *St. John Passion* and *St. Matthew Passion,* works that he may have heard during his early years in Germany. The family's frequent trips to England to visit Charlotte's relatives may also have provided the young man with opportunities to hear music not frequently heard in France; it is likely that he attended performances at St. James Hall and the Crystal Palace, where he would have come to know Mendelssohn's symphonies and chamber music and Handel's oratorios and operas.[15] By time he reached adulthood, Polignac would have a conversance with Baroque music that was unusual for most French musicians and music-lovers of his era.

Sometime after his family's relocation to Paris, Polignac began composition lessons with Alphonse Thys (1809–1879). Winner of the Prix de Rome in 1833, Thys had built a modest reputation in Paris as a composer of *romances,*[16] popular songs, easy pieces for piano, and incidental music for light theater pieces; when his hoped-for career as an opera composer failed to materialize, he turned to teaching.[17] Polignac was presumably an attentive pupil; his earliest extant compositions reflect his teacher's simple, charming compositional style. An 1851 "Choeur de buveurs" for men's voices is appropriately rollicking; a lovely 1852 "Romance pastorale" for contralto and piano, on a text attributed to Charles IX, was apparently the first of his works to be printed, in a private edition.[18]

Another important influence in Polignac's early musical development was Charles Gounod. Gounod, a kind, spiritually inclined man, had not yet achieved the fame that would follow the successful premiere of his most famous opera, *Faust* (1859). In 1852, Polignac's eighteenth year, Gounod assumed the directorship of the Orphéon de Paris. This populist choral institution recruited the majority of its members from the male working class, the goal being to bring the ennobling art of music to the common person. In the post-1848 political climate, the belief told hold that "the culture of fine arts is one of the most powerful rings in the political chain,"[19] and, in 1853, Gounod became director of the public education program that undertook the teaching of vocal music and music literacy in the municipal music schools. Once or twice a year, he would lead the group in a performance in a large Parisian concert hall such as the Cirque Napoléon. Polignac was present at a number of these "séances solennelles," listening with rapt attention as 1500 young choristers, under Gounod's baton, sang works written for the ensemble by the most highly esteemed composers of the era—Adolphe Adam, Ambroise Thomas, Fromenthal Halévy, Léo

Delibes, Daniel Auber, Giacomo Meyerbeer—before a capacity audience, in the presence of the Emperor.[20] The experience surely left an indelible impression on the young musician. The extent of Polignac's association with Gounod is not well documented, but the little evidence that exists—coupled with the large collection of that composer's scores in his library—suggests that Gounod was a source of encouragement for the fledgling composer, as well as a source of Polignac's lifelong passions for early music and choral composition.

The restoration of the empire in December 1852 began a period of enormous economic and social upheaval in France. Louis-Napoléon transformed himself into Napoléon III; his 1853 marriage to Eugénie de Montijo resulted in the establishment of a dazzling new court, made up of the newly rich: the bankers, stockbrokers, and industrial magnates of the upper bourgeoisie. These empire builders changed the financial landscape of Europe and France: taking advantage of the new government's easy credit policy, they built a new network of railway lines, turned the nation's harbors into massive centers of import and export, and expanded the mining and metallurgic industries. In doing so, they ultimately improved the standard of living for both rich and the working middle class, and created a spirit of renewal and optimism in a France weary of revolution and bloodshed. The lifting of restrictions on civil liberties and the reinstatement of freedom of the press and freedom of intellectual thought gave rise to a healthy cross-fertilization of cultures and classes. Through the enlightened vision of Baron Eugène Haussmann, Paris was transformed into a light, airy city of wide boulevards, punctuated by graceful traffic circles and stately squares. The upper bourgeoisie, increasingly and confidently on the rise in this new culture, built sumptuous mansions alongside those of the oldest families and began to participate more fully in cultural life, creating a counterpoint to the somewhat moribund aristocratic society.

During this fertile creative period, Edmond de Polignac was living with his mother and an English female cousin in the Rue de Berri apartment, his brothers having left France for military assignments in Algeria and the Crimea. In a perennial state of ill health, bereft of fraternal companionship, and lacking direction, Polignac cultivated his ennui. Even so, he kept up his creative efforts, filling a composition notebook with songs, duets, and short instrumental compositions.[21] Apparently at some point he showed the notebook to Charles Gounod; a vocal "Nocturne" for tenor, soprano, and piano, received the comment of "très bon" from the celebrated composer.[22] Encouraged by the praise, Polignac submitted his composition notebook to the entrance committee of the Conservatoire de Paris, and was accepted for admission.

However, Edmond was not admitted as a composition student: the Conservatoire's rules dictated that students needed to have at least one first prize in music theory before they could enter composition classes proper. It was thus that in the fall of 1855, Edmond de Polignac entered the harmony class of composer-theorist Napoléon-Henri Reber (1807–1880). Reber had composed works in every genre, including chamber music, symphonies, and ballet. One light opera had been performed at the Opéra-Comique; a future work, *Les Dames capitaines* (1857) would be performed at the Opéra. Reber became a professor of harmony at the Conservatoire in 1851; a decade later he would succeed Ludovic Halévy as professor of composition. His 1862 *Traité d'harmonie* would remain the standard text on the subject well into the twentieth century.[23] Edmond de Polignac's notebook from this class, extant in family archives, reveals that students were given a thorough and rigorous grounding in harmony, counterpoint, and the classical forms.[24] Polignac's relatively undisciplined home life may not have fully prepared him for the serious atmosphere in which he now found himself. In 1856, at the end of his first year of study, he received a Second Prize in Harmony, a respectable, if not brilliant, commendation. The following year, however, his diligence flagged: in the spring of 1857 his prize was only *Deuxième accessit* (second honorable mention).

During his years at the Conservatoire, Polignac continued to compose. In 1856 and 1857 he wrote two lengthy, serious works for choir. The first, a vocal quintet in F minor for baritone solo, men's chorus, and piano (titled "Majestiosi" in one source and "O Dieu puissant" in another[25]) is a lament by the Biblical Jacob, who mourns in impassioned strains the death of his youngest son Joseph; the baritone solo is following by a choral refrain, in which the older brothers express anguished culpability for Joseph's presumed murder. A year later, Polignac wrote "Prière à la Mecque" for mixed chorus and piano.[26] The work is a paean to the god Allah and the prophet Mohammed; the subject matter may have been suggested by the recent departure of his brother Ludovic for military service in northern Africa.[27] Both works, in which the influence of Gounod is evident, feature a $\frac{12}{8}$ meter; rich, somber harmonies in the chorus; and throbbing triplets in the accompaniment.

His student years also marked the beginning of two lifelong trends that would follow Polignac through his life. The first was a dramatic aggravation of his medical problems and chronic illnesses, especially gastroenteritis and other stomach irritations. As the illnesses increased, so too did Polignac's propensity for indolence and self-pity. Moreover, nothing in his home life or his aristocratic milieu helped him to maintain the discipline needed for his studies. The social calendar of the aristocracy, with its balls, hunting season, and visits to country houses, was frequently in direct conflict with the academic calendar, and it was often the rigors of Reber's class that Polignac chose to forego. Whether it was because his health obliged him to spend many weeks at a fashionable spa to "take the waters," or because the creation of an amateur theatrical piece required an extended stay at a friend's country house, family letters demonstrate the diverse ways in which Polignac was able to neglect his musical studies.[28]

It is possible that both the illnesses and Polignac's undistinguished career at the Conservatoire were the result of family pressures. Becoming a professional composer was out of the question for a member of the aristocracy. Dabbling in music (composition or performance), or poetry, or painting, were perfectly acceptable hobbies, but, as far as professions went, very few were acceptable for a young aristocratic man: he could oversee a family property or the family's other investments, or join the clergy, or join the military, or—the favorite of most—remain "without profession." Above all, he must marry and produce male heirs. Edmond de Polignac seemed predisposed to do none of these, and he surely felt the disapprobation of his mother and other members of his family. Only Camille continued to encourage his compositional endeavors. It is also likely that during this period, especially given his exposure to the artistic milieu of the Conservatoire, that Polignac was forced to confront his nascent homosexuality. To be a "delicate" son in a family of strong, brilliant older brothers, each of whom had distinguished himself in military action, surely caused him great anguish. The additional turmoil of his sexual uncertainty, coupled with the pressure to keep those feelings repressed, may very well have exacerbated both his stomach ailments and his need to escape. Self-awareness—or self-denial—may literally have made him sick.

A mediocre showing at the conclusion of his third year at the Conservatoire in the form of a *Troisième accessit* prize may have convinced Polignac to adopt a more abstemious and disciplined routine, both for the sake of his health and his art. In January 1858, his mother wrote to Ludovic, "Edmond really studies his music and has requested his young friends not to visit him, which I am glad of, as they idled him sadly."[29] That April, one of Edmond's choral works was presented at a charity concert sponsored by the Oeuvre de la Miséricorde; its organizer was the Prince de Talleyrand-Périgord, one of Charlotte's relations through her first marriage to the Comte de Choiseul. On that occasion, Polignac had the satisfaction of hearing his work sung by a hundred-voice choir.[30] But better health did not mend the composer's tendencies towards indolence: in February 1859, his mother wrote: "Edmond is at last I think quite well tho' *il se dorlote* [*sic*, i.e., *dorlotte;* he mollycoddles himself], which does not prevent is going to Balls and concerts."[31]

In Spring 1859, Edmond de Polignac finished his fourth year of study with Reber with a prize of *Premier accessit*. This "first honorable mention," while a respectable achievement, was not sufficient to win Polignac admission into composition classes at the Conservatoire. And thus his formal study of music ended. The young prince left behind the rigors of the Conservatoire to embark on the only career for which he was fit: that of a gentleman composer.

Chapter Two

A Young Composer (1859–1877)

After leaving the Conservatoire, Edmond de Polignac found himself at loose
ends, musically speaking. The most frequent performances of Polignac's music
took place in the salon. The music salon was a fixture in the aristocracy and
the high bourgeoisie. Members of the high bourgeoisie who had become newly
wealthy during Napoleon III's Empire built sumptuous mansions in the 8th
arrondissement, and in many of these palaces of high finance could be found
rooms built specifically for music making. Piano music by Chopin, Schumann,
and Liszt and all variety of songs and arias were staples of the salon, but, in these
intimate surroundings, contemporary composers such as Charles Gounod,
Ambroise Thomas, Léo Delibes, Théodore Dubois, and Camille Saint-Saëns,
were also provided elegant and socially visible venues for the presentation of
their new works. Many musicians formed their own salons. New pieces were created expressly for performance in the home, creating a new genre: salon music.
Polignac fit perfectly into these surroundings. Tall, thin, handsome, elegant and
witty, he cut a fine figure in society (see Fig. 2.1). The men found him charming,
the women found him handsome. His ability to improvise waltzes at the piano
frequently made him the life of the party.

Despite the amount of time that he spent as a social and musical gadabout,
Polignac remained determined to pursue a career as a professional composer.
Such aspirations were deemed unacceptable by his milieu, and, although she
did not interfere with his activities, were a source of dismay for his mother. At
his death, Prince Jules had left his widow and children comfortable, but hardly
wealthy. Alphonse, Ludovic, and Camille de Polignac had chosen military and
engineering careers in part out of economic necessity. Edmond clearly was not
going to follow suit; he then had but one choice: to marry a wealthy woman. He
did his best to oblige: from 1858 onward, family correspondence is filled with
mentions of Polignac's various quests to find a bride in Paris, in the south of
France, and in England. Camille de Polignac, traveling in the Americas in 1859
to study political economy and geography, encouraged his younger brother to
consider wedding an American heiress: if she was from the North, her fortune
could be figured in dollars; if she was a Southern belle, wrote Camille, her worth
would be calculated in balls of cotton![1] The constant rumors about Polignac's
imminent marriage to this or that beautiful and wealthy young woman never
materialized. As in previous years, the sense of familial and societal pressures felt
by Polignac became manifested in the form of chronic illnesses.

Figure 2.1. Edmond de Polignac, artist and date unknown. Used by permission of Prince Edmond de Polignac.

The first of Charlotte's sons to marry was her oldest. Alphonse de Polignac, a mathematician and engineer,[2] had a reputation of being as mercurial as he was brilliant.[3] In June 1860, he married a young woman from Marseilles named Jeanne-Amélie Mirès. The union was a controversial one: Alphonse's new father-in-law, Jules Mirès, was a newspaper magnate and a venture capitalist closely tied to Second Empire political circles. In the early 1850s, taking advantage of Napoleon III's liberal economic programs and loosening of regulatory policy, Mirès and his partners bankrolled the enormous expansion of the French railroads; Mirès subsequently used his ownership of the newspapers to generate public interest in his financial ventures. His investment in the new Bank of Turkey garnered him the reputation of being a "second Rothschild." The financier and his daughter moved to Paris's Faubourg Saint-Honoré in the late 1850s, and it was there that Alphonse met his future wife. Their engagement was commonly viewed as a cynical exchange of money for a title. The royalist members of the Polignac family abhorred everything that Jules Mirès represented: his Republican allegiances, his questionable financial dealings, and his Jewish faith; they were outraged by what they regarded as Alphonse's shameful misalliance. And yet this kind of marriage—the merging of the old (and often cash-poor) aristocracy, on one hand, and republicanism and literary and artistic circles, on the other hand—had become quite the fashion in the Second Empire. The alliance netted Alphonse a certain degree of celebrity. Reports of the Polignac-Mirès marriage ceremony were printed not only in the society columns, but also in the literary, theatrical, and musical press. The marriage also yielded some publicity for Edmond, who had composed a setting for the nuptial mass. The piece was sung by members of the chorus of the Opéra and accompanied on the organ by Camille Saint-Saëns. One music journal praised Polignac's music as being "at once sober and skillful";[4] another hailed Polignac as "a young composer of talent with a future."[5]

Just prior to the marriage, Alphonse and Edmond were involved with the organization of a new music club, the Cercle de l'Union artistique, also known as the Cercle des Mirlitons. Founded by Prince Josef Poniatowski,[6] the goal of the Cercle was to establish an artistic fusion between artists, writers, and musicians, and society men outside the cadre of professional theaters.[7] Poniatowski was named the first president, and Charles Gounod, Comte Melchior de Vogüé, and Alphonse de Polignac were named vice presidents.[8] The music budget of the Cercle was considerable, thus permitting the organization of weekly concerts; the programming, too, was of high quality. Consequently, contemporary composers eagerly joined, glad for the chance to have their music heard by an elite and appreciative audience. In addition to performances of works by J. S. Bach, Beethoven, Schumann, and Wagner, many first performances of works by Berlioz, Bizet, Chabrier, Delibes, Gounod, Massenet, and Saint-Saëns took place at the Cercle's private music room on the Rue de Choiseul. It was one of the few concert venues in Paris where chamber music performance was vigorously championed—this, during an era when opera reigned; among the offerings heard at the Cercle was a cycle of the late string quartets of Beethoven, performed by the appropriately named "Société des Derniers Quatuors de Beethoven."[9] The orchestral and opera performances were of no less high quality; their execution was entrusted to conductor Jules Pasdeloup (1819–1887), whose Cercle concerts were often warm-ups for public performances of the same programs with his newly created music society, the Concerts Populaires, inaugurated in 1861. Performances of compositions by the aristocratic and *haut bourgeois* membership were scheduled alongside those of their better-established professional colleagues; some of these composers were dilettantes, but others, like Polignac, were men of exceptional talent who were just as grateful as the "professionals" for the chance to have their music heard in a milieu of serious music lovers (notable among this group were Marquis Paul d'Ivry and Comte Alexis de Castillon).

A number of Edmond de Polignac's works in many genres were performed under the Cercle's auspices. One of the first of these was a String Quartet in F Major, written in 1860 for the Cercle's inaugural season.[10] It ranks among Polignac's most successful works, and evokes, in its ebullience and elegance, the spirit of the Razumovsky Quartets of Beethoven. The four movements (in the keys of F major, D major, E major, and D minor, respectively) include some unusual, protomodernist features. Mediant relations are featured in every movement. The opening theme of the first movement (Allegro) passes quickly from F major to A minor. Additionally, Polignac's approach to writing in sonata-allegro form is iconoclastic: the exposition's first and second themes are both written in the tonic F major in the exposition, but in the recapitulation the second theme is written in B-flat major, and the final return to F major is delayed until the coda. The third-movement Scherzo, in E major, moves quickly into the mediant-related key of G-sharp major (Ex. 2.1a) and subsequently to a pizzicato section in E minor (not shown).[11] A surprising arrival at the end of the section emphasizing the flat supertonic (F) acts as a bridge to the Trio, in B-flat major, a tritone distance from the tonic E of the scherzo (Ex. 2.1b). This foregrounding of minor-third relations foreshadows future harmonic movements in Polignac's octatonic compositions.

Polignac's initial forays into harmonic and formal unconventionality may have been influenced by the presence in Paris of Richard Wagner. After a frustrating, financially precarious first sojourn in Paris (1839–42), Wagner returned in early 1860 to conduct three concerts of excerpts from his operas at the Théâtre Italien. While the French music press regarded the German composer with suspicion (the reviewer in *Le Ménestrel* wrote: "M. Wagner seems to strive for the title of *Prophète sonore*,"[12]) Polignac's early and ardent love of Wagner's music may have been inspired by these concerts. In negotiation to have *Tannhäuser* performed at the Opéra, Wagner remained in Paris through the remainder of 1860, and during this period he joined the Cercle des Mirlitons. He met Edmond de Polignac at the home of Comte Osmond d'Osmond, a young noble who, after losing an arm in a duel, became active in amateur music societies, and often hosted performances sponsored by the Cercle.[13] Polignac invited Wagner to lunch at Rue de Berri, and the German, who had read Alphonse de Polignac's translation of *Faust*, accepted the younger Polignac's offer. Wagner retained a vivid recollection of their meal together: "I heard him emit fantastical ideas that music inspired in him. For example, he wanted to convince me of the accuracy of his conception of Beethoven's [Seventh] Symphony in A Major: in the last movement, he claimed to recognize all the stages of a shipwreck."[14] Regrettably, no other documentation provides accounts of Polignac's interactions with Wagner. Polignac was present on 13 March 1861 for the notorious first performance of *Tannhäuser* at the Opéra, when a claque from the Jockey Club—a club to

Example 2.1a. String Quartet No. 2 in F Major, mvt. 3, mm. 1–14

which Polignac and his brothers belonged—disrupted the performance with catcalls, boos, and whistles, ultimately preventing the performance of the opera from reaching a conclusion.[15] After three nights of such antics, coupled with tepid reviews from the press, all remaining performances of *Tannhäuser* were canceled. For the next decade, the scheduling of an opera by Wagner in Paris frequently gave rise to public demonstrations.

The *Tannhäuser* debacle coincided with Polignac's own misadventures with Paris's opera establishment. Through Alphonse, Polignac was able to meet a wide range of literary and artistic figures with whom he might not necessarily

Example 2.1b. String Quartet No. 2 in F Major, mvt. 3, mm. 58–74

come in contact in more conservative aristocratic circles. One such figure was Roger de Beauvoir (1806–1866). Beauvoir was a prolific and successful writer of poetry and light dramatic works, a number of which had been set to music.[16] In 1860 Polignac set to music Beauvoir's "prière bretonne," "Notre Dame au peigne d'or" (Our Lady of the Golden Comb); the song, in an arrangement for solo voice, chorus, and piano was included in a set of six vocal works by Polignac published by Flaxland.[17] Beauvoir was present at the Polignac-Mirès marriage, and was apparently impressed with the music that Edmond had composed for the nuptial mass. The writer had recently submitted a libretto for a one-act opera to the Opéra-Comique, and apparently mentioned Polignac's name to the artistic management as a potential composer for the work. In mid-July, on the very day that he was to depart for a health spa in the Pyrenees, Edmond de Polignac received word from the Opéra-Comique that Beauvoir's libretto had been accepted for production—and that Polignac was being invited to provide the music.[18] The theater's new director, Alfred Beaumont,[19] was committed to expanding the company's repertoire and to featuring works by new, young composers. Although untried as an administrator, Beaumont was an experienced opera director. He was apparently convinced that, even with the music not yet composed, the libretto for *Un baiser de duchesse* showed great potential for success; he told Polignac that the work would be included in the 1861 season, and could perhaps be put into rehearsal as early as November of that year.[20] At that time, the Opéra-Comique linked a composer's fee to each evening's receipts; therefore, a successful new production could draw large audiences and garner substantial fees for the composer and the librettist.[21] Polignac left for the Pyrenees with composition notebooks and buoyed spirits. On 3 September he wrote to Ludovic from his mountain hideaway:

> For a month and a half . . . I've been living in a deep retreat, which I love. I'm working very hard. . . . [The opera] is a little piece in one act, the subject is very simple: the intrigue takes place in Flanders (circa 1760). There are Flemish choruses, there are millers, a French captain, an English major . . . and, finally, a *grande dame*. Finally, there's what to do for the music, and I'm content. A novice [like me] can't ask for a Middle-Ages scenario, Don Juanesque, full of Duels, serenades, barcarolles, etc. etc., which, I confess, would better suit the character of my music.[22]

Polignac's mother had a less than enthusiastic view of these musical endeavors. "Edmond's Opera was accepted at the Opéra Comique the very day of his departure," she wrote to Ludovic. "He [received] advice of it which made him set off in excellent spirits. I don't believe it will be lucrative."[23]

Polignac met with Beaumont at the Opéra-Comique in November 1860.[24] Presumably Beaumont was pleased with the arias and ensemble pieces that the composer had completed thus far, for Polignac kept writing; the last of the thirteen musical numbers was completed on 8 January 1861.[25] In February, Charlotte wrote to Ludovic, "Edmond's opera finished, not yet "en repetition";[26] in June, she wrote that "Edmond . . . is gone to Uriage for the Waters, which are said to be good for the nerves. Poor fellow, he cannot sleep well: his music absorbs him too much."[27] Here, the trail of the opera's history becomes cold: *Un Baiser de duchesse* was never produced by the Opéra-Comique. The reasons appear to be economic, not artistic. The financial difficulties that had plagued the Opéra-Comique's previous administrator, Nestor Roqueplan, were hobbling the current administration as well. Beaumont's appointment had been a political one, and the Minister of State was clearly not happy with his management of the coffers. On 27 January 1862 Beaumont arrived at his office only to be met by a representative of the Ministry, who informed him that his mandate had been revoked; henceforth the Opéra-Comique would be directed by veteran artistic administrator Émile Perrin.[28] Absent any documentary evidence to explain the situation, it would appear that the Beauvoir/Polignac production was a casualty—probably only one of many casualties—of the behind-the-scenes financial debacle at the Opéra-Comique. It furthers appear that Polignac, out of shame or embarrassment, did not tell his family or friends about the collapse of the opera project for quite some time after Beaumont's ouster. Even Camille, his closest confidante, was kept in the dark: in a letter dated December 1862 posted from America (where he was fighting for the South in the American Civil War[29]), Camille writes: "I'm astonished to have heard nothing more of your first opera. If the delay is due to laziness it would be unforgivable."[30]

Edmond's professional woes were overshadowed by a family tragedy. On 30 June 1863, Alphonse, who had suffered ill health for some time, died at the age of 37. Alphonse's last years had not been happy ones. In March 1861, only weeks before his wife Amélie gave birth to a baby girl, his father-in-law Jules Mirès was accused of embezzlement, and was subsequently arrested and ordered to stand trial for "forgery, swindling, and abuse of public trust."[31] The scandal rocked Napoleon III's Empire and caused financial and political reverberations throughout Western Europe. Alphonse had been working on a bridge engineering design for the French government, the contract for which was procured through Mirès's help. Even though the financier was ultimately exonerated of all wrongdoing, the court of public opinion had already condemned him. Alphonse apparently could not withstand the psychological blow that came from social humiliation. Mounting debts and an overwhelming sense of shame contributed to his physical and mental disintegration, leading to his death.

The loss of her oldest son took its toll on Charlotte's health. She became increasingly preoccupied with the hopes of seeing her three bachelor sons settled into financially advantageous marriages. Over the next two years, Edmond de Polignac made periodic trips to England, where he resumed his courtship campaign. In London he was brought into contact with any number of attractive candidates: one such charming young lady, in full evening attire, was immortalized in a pencil sketch, which Polignac tucked into the pages of his score of Mendelssohn's oratorio Saint Paul.[32] He did not neglect the opportunity to make publicity for his own compositions as well. On 7 May 1864, Charlotte wrote to Ludovic: "Edmond is very well pleased in London, has 3 balls every night and intends to go thro' the Season there, he however returns here for a few days to fetch some manuscript music of his own which he thinks of having executed at some musical society there."[33] Soon afterwards, however, Polignac was recalled to Paris. His mother had begun to suffer from severe heart palpitations and was no longer able to go up and down the stairs.[34] On 1 September 1864 Charlotte de Polignac passed away, at the age of 72. There is no documentation of Polignac's reaction to his mother's death. He continued living with an English cousin, Bessy Levinge, in the Rue de Berri town-house; after Bessy's departure in 1873, he remained in the family house by himself for another ten years.

After the failure of the Opéra-Comique project, Polignac concentrated on writing *melodies* and works for chorus that could be performed at the Cercle des Mirlitons. Many were simple, unaccompanied choral works, for women's and men's chorus; larger works for mixed chorus were accompanied by piano, chamber ensemble, or orchestra. While some of the texts were secular, Polignac's most noble creations were based on the scriptures, such as the beautiful "Martha et Maria" (1863), on texts from the book of Luke.[35] On 15 January 1864, Polignac's choral work "Les Dryades" was included in a group of "modern" works performed at the Cercle, sung by the Choeur de la Société du Conservatoire and conducted by Pasdeloup. *Le Ménestrel* described Polignac's work as "elegant," and added a note of thanks to the Cercle "for what it's done for living composers, whom we so love to neglect in favor of the dead ones."[36]

In the 1860s, the populist all-male *orphéon* was enjoying its heydey. This grass-roots musical movement had become especially attractive as a symbol to local politicians, because it represented a cultural framework through which the simple worker could unite with composers and professional musicians through their common love of music. A consummate symbol of egalitarianism, the *orphéon* eschewed making any distinction in its membership because of birth, education, or social milieu. By 1861, there was not a *département* in France that did not have its own *orphéon*. Nationwide, three hundred popular musical clubs had a total membership of 100,000 singers; by the end of the decade that number had almost tripled.[37] Simple but well-crafted choruses were needed to fill the concert programs of hundreds of municipal *orphéons* from the big cities to the farthest-flung villages. Polignac produced a substantial number of simple, unaccompanied works for men's voices, on appropriately masculine subject matter, bearing titles such as *chœurs de buveurs* (drinkers), *chœurs de chasseurs* (hunters), and *chœurs de poltrons* (cowards).

The Orphéon de Paris stood somewhat apart from its counterparts elsewhere in France. As opposed to the educational "associations" organized for working people—primarily adult men—in the provinces, the Paris *orphéon* was more closely aligned with the municipal coeducational singing schools for children and young adults. It was not nearly so class-blind, and therefore remained philosophically aloof from the "associative ideal" practiced by its provincial counterparts.[38] However, it offered more potential for variety to composers because of the inclusion of children and females. And, traditionally, its artistic directors—and the composers whose works were performed—were great musicians: Gounod led the group until 1861, at which point it was taken over by no less a conductor than Jules Pasdeloup.[39]

In order to bring new choral works before the public, the Orphéon de Paris mounted annual composition competitions in conjunction with the City of Paris.

Polignac had never forgotten the thrill he experienced, as a young man, hearing the 1,500–voice Orphéon de Paris perform at the Cirque Napoléon under Gounod. In 1865 he entered the Paris Orphéon's competition, hoping for the chance to have his music heard in similar circumstances. Contestants were invited to submit up to three compositions based on a small number of predetermined poetic texts. There were to be three first prizes, five second prizes, five third prizes, and six honorable mentions awarded; only the gold-medal pieces would receive public performances. The folders containing the pieces were identified only by a number and by a phrase or motto of the composer's choosing. Polignac submitted compositions on three poems: "Le Myosotis," "Respect à la Vieillesse," and "Hirondelles (Où est le bonheur!)." Altogether, 545 pieces were submitted. On 5 March 1865, the jury, which included composers Gounod and Ambroise Thomas, and conductors Pasdeloup and François Bazin, published its results. The pieces in folders 135, 137, and 136 were the three gold-medal-winning compositions. Upon opening the folds that concealed the names of the authors, it was revealed that the three first prizes had all been won by the same composer: Edmond de Polignac.[40] This coincidental triple victory was unprecedented, but the jury viewed the singular result as proof positive of its own "high impartiality." The commissioner who submitted the jury's report had this to say of Polignac's music:

> These three pieces, in different genres, possess equally elevated ideas that were not found to the same degree in the other compositions. No. 137, on the theme *Respect à la vieillesse*, is happily inspired. . . . No. 136, on the theme *Où est le bonheur!* is a chorus conceived in the manner of Mendelssohn; it is charming and will please when performed. No. 135, on the words *Le Myosotis*[41] seems superior still to the two preceding compositions; it recalls the school of Meyerbeer; it's just a bit long and contains a few [passages] that are difficult, but not insurmountable, even for [the level of the singers in] the Orphéon of the Municipal Schools of Paris.[42]

This unprecedented success seemed to vindicate Polignac's hopes and aspirations. Two public performances of the choruses were given, one at the Cirque de l'Impératrice, conducted by Bazin, on 14 May 1865, and the second a week later, at the Cirque Napoléon, under the baton of Pasdeloup. The critic of *La Revue et Gazette musicale de Paris* wrote, "In [Polignac's] compositions one finds the most delicate feeling, a melodic and harmonic instinct of exquisite distinction."[43] And the critic of *L'Art musical* wrote, "['Le Myosotis'] is written with as much grace as distinction. Its refrain is really charming, and won an ovation for the young prince, who, as an artist, has debuted with a great success."[44] Two years later, Polignac won another first prize in the Paris Orphéon competition with a charming work for mixed chorus a cappella, "L'Abeille" (The Bee).[45] Inexplicably, a different one of Polignac's choral works, "Adieu montagnes!" was substituted for the prize-winning composition when the Orphéon performed its "séance solennelle" at the Cirque Napoléon in May 1867. One music critic who reviewed the concert found Polignac's "Scotch chorus" to be "beautifully colored, elegantly shaped, and keenly inspired"—although it did seem to him a bit strange "to hear 1,200 little schoolgirls from every quarter of Paris singing, at the top of their lungs, a text that included the words 'Chassons! En chasse! Vive la chasse!'" ("Let's hunt! To the hunt! Long live the hunt!").[46]

Unfortunately, Polignac's uncertain health did not allow him to enjoy his victories: he would work himself into such a nervous state before the competitions that he would make himself ill. Polignac's periods of productivity and success alternated with frequent physical crises and retreats to various health spas to "take the waters."[47] Much of his time in Paris was spent lounging around the men's social clubs, where he could nurture his lassitude. Like his brothers, he was a member of the Jockey Club, the gathering place of choice for the aristocracy. In 1867 he joined another club, the Cercle de la Rue Royale, which seemed to have no particular aim other than to provide young masters of the universe with another venue in which to sit around, smoke cigars, and discuss politics and the stock market. The indolent lifestyle of the group is captured in James Tissot's panoramic masterpiece, *Le Balcon du Cercle de la rue Royale* (1868). Commissioned by the Comte Robert de Miramon, the enormous canvas presents a group portrait of twelve young aristocratic and other high society gentlemen.[48] Polignac is depicted as a long, lean, bearded figure, lounging in a chair, staring off into space as a pen and notebook lay idle in his hands. However, despite these bouts of inactivity, Polignac was regarded by many Paris composers to be "one of them"; the esteem in which he was held by his colleagues may be assessed in a letter from Georges Bizet to Carcassonne composer Paul Lacombe: "When you come to Paris," wrote Bizet, "I'll put you in contact with several musicians: *Gounod, Reyer, Saint-Saëns, Guiraud, le prince Polignac,* etc. . . . and thus you'll be among peers."[49] An estimable group of peers!

In 1867, an opportunity arose for Polignac to realize his hopes for a career as an operatic composer. In August of that year, during the Exposition Universelle, the Ministry of the House of the Emperor and Fine Arts, in conjunction with the committee of General Theater Management, created a competition for librettos and musical scores, with the goal of awarding and presenting a newly written three-act opéra comique at the Théâtre de l'Opéra.[50] In April 1868 the winning libretto was announced: *La Coupe du Roi de Thulé,* written by Édouard Blau and Louis Gallet.[51] Forty-two composers now competed for the grand prize: the performance of the winning score at the Opéra in the spring of 1870. The names of the contestants were not known to the jury; the scores were identified only by a number accompanied by an epigraph chosen by the composer. Edmond's choice of epigraph was "Sic vere, non valet mellificator"[52] (So, in truth, [my work] is not worthy of the honey-maker), an allusion to Virgil, who was called "Mellificator," the honey-maker; self-deprecatingly, Polignac is saying, in effect, "Here's my work, even if it's not Virgil." When the results of the contest were announced on 21 November 1869 by the president of the jury, Émile Perrin, the winner was revealed to be Eugène-Émile Diaz de la Peña, a young, inexperienced composer, and the pet pupil of juror Victor Massé, who (it was rumored behind the scenes) had written most of the score.[53] The remaining forty-one scores were ranked in order of merit, and those which had been ranked second through fifth were singled out as worthy of special mention. Polignac's score ranked fifth.[54] He was in good company among those composers who did not win the prize: Jules Massenet placed second, and Georges Bizet placed seventh.[55] The jury commented that the score "stood out through its excellent construction and the skillfulness of its orchestration"[56]—although, ironically, Polignac found out later that the score was removed from consideration for the grand prize because some judges found the orchestration "too complicated": the orchestra included *two* bass clarinets, "an unpardonable monstrosity!"[57] As it turned out, the laureate winner of the competition, Eugène Diaz, never achieved any success as a result of his (possibly rigged) victory. The premiere of his work, scheduled for the Opéra's 1870 season, was cancelled because of the outbreak of war. When the production was finally mounted, in January 1873, the reviews were far from favorable: the critics denounced the manifold weaknesses in Diaz's score and the inexperienced composer's inability to handle the Opéra's massive vocal and orchestral forces.[58]

As for Polignac, finishing fifth in a field of forty-two contestants was certainly an honorable achievement, but the ranking was not high enough to bring him the public recognition and fame that he had hoped for. Nonetheless, there was one consolation: in late 1869 or early 1870, a number of Polignac's *mélodies* were accepted for publication by the renowned Paris music publisher Georges Hartmann. Hartmann had reciprocal agreements with London and Berlin publishers J. McDowell and D. Fürstner, respectively, and thus was able to offer the possibility of foreign sales of Polignac's music.[59]

Artistic matters were soon superseded by the incendiary political situation. Napoleon III's inability to achieve assurance of nonagression from mighty Prussia, especially after Bismarck's 1866 defeat of Austria, had progressively inflamed French sentiments. In 1870, Napoleon III was goaded into declaring a war for which his country was ill prepared. Quickly overwhelmed by the superior Prussian army, French forces capitulated after only six weeks of battle; Napoleon III was captured, and the Second Empire came to an end. In January 1871, an armistice was signed. The formation of a National Assembly, whose goal was to make peace with Germany, created a furor among the starving citizens of Paris, who had suffered long months of privation during the German siege. When troops were sent in to quell insurgency, the Parisians resisted; supported by the soldiers of the regular army, they repudiated the authority of the National Assembly and formed their own government, the Commune. Six months later, the National Assembly suppressed the Commune in a bloody and definitive coup. After the cessation of hostilities, it took another year or so for Paris to emerge from psychological ravages that had the accompanied the physical devastation of the city. Edmond de Polignac was in Geneva when the war broke out in 1870; after the formation of the Commune, he made his way to the south of France, staying for nearly a year with Alphonse's widow Amélie, who had a home outside of Marseille.

With the establishment of the Constitution of the Third Republic in 1873, the residents of the capital made a miraculous collective recovery from the recent sad, bloody chapter of their history. A kind of collective amnesia overtook the citizenry, as if the bloody Commune had never existed. Parisians seemed to feel a keen desire to forget their sorrows. The new and beautiful urban landscape designed and realized by Baron Haussmann in the 1850s and 1860s, with its wide, tree-lined boulevards and expansive gardens, became the background, during the Third Republic, for a new era of pleasure, sociability, and beauty: a "belle époque."

It was also at this moment that the worldly Parisians accorded music a new place of honor, especially in the most visible salons in the capital. In the new mansions of the upper class, the music rooms were often built to the size of a small theater; those of more modest proportions could still comfortably seat over one hundred people. In these salons, some of the greatest artists of the age could be heard; in fact, the greater the artist, the greater the prestige and social standing that was accorded to the hostess of the musical event. Almost all of the great singers of the era—veritable stars like Adelina Patti and Jean de Reszke—performed in the salons, as did internationally known pianists and violinists such as Franz Liszt, Pablo de Sarasate, and Henri Vieuxtemps. Many salons had their own organ, and the great organists who performed in private performances included Eugène Gigout, Alexandre Guilmant, Charles-Marie Widor, Gabriel Pierné, and Louis Vierne. In the larger salons, full orchestras were conducted by eminent symphonic and operatic conductors. The society hostesses vied like tigresses to be able to say that they had been the first to present the greatest diva or virtuoso of the hour at their musical gathering. The social wealth spilled over to composers as well. It was not just established composers like Gounod, Delibes, and Thomas whose music was performed in these circles: young newcomers like Jules Massenet and Gabriel Fauré who might be struggling to make a name for themselves in public venues could be assured of refined surroundings and a somewhat knowledgeable audience in the salons.

The salons also gave the talented performers of the nobility a chance to demonstrate their musical gifts, often in collaboration with professional musicians. It was often the master or the mistress of the house who was the featured composer or performing artist in intimate gatherings of elegant music-lovers. Thus when virtuoso pianist Princesse Rachel de Brancovan hosted a *matinée musicale,* she herself was the soloist, performing works of Chopin and Paderewski, or Mozart concertos, accompanied by the orchestra of the Concerts Colonne. When the soprano Comtesse Marie-Thérèse de Guerne or the baritone Comte Arthur de Gabriac sang the latest songs of Fauré, it was frequently the composer himself who accompanied at the piano. Compositions by members of the aristocracy received enthusiastic hearings in such venues as well, before a ready-made audience of supporters. Those aristocrat-composers who could afford to do so hired the greatest artists in Paris to perform their works for their guests. The press began to report the details of these salon gatherings, devoting almost as much space to the private concerts as to those in public theaters and concert halls—the notable difference being that it was the society columnists who wrote the articles, not the music critics; therefore, the "reviews" had nothing but laudatory things to say: the Comtesse d'X or the Duchesse d'Y hosted a musical soirée, welcoming "the most elite members of society"; the hall was "the most elegant"; the works performed were "the most original/interesting/brilliant"; the performers were "heartily applauded."

When Polignac returned to Paris, he was immediately swept into the whirl of salon activity. In this vibrant atmosphere, Polignac was constantly busy: here was a milieu where he could apply both his social charm and his musical talents. In addition to performances in the homes of his relatives—including intimate soirées hosted by his stepbrother the Duc de Polignac at the Hôtel Crillon,[60]—he was now sought after in the most brilliant salons of the nobility, where his newly published *melodies* surely found receptive audiences. One song, "Lamento," set to Théophile Gautier's haunting poem, is arguably one of Polignac's most beautiful, poignant works in any genre.[61] Written in the archaic-sounding key of A natural minor (called by nineteenth-century French theorists the "Diatonic Oriental Latin" scale), the song features a melody that foregrounds minor thirds (Ex. 2.2a) and series of modulations through mediant-related keys: from A minor to C minor, and from G minor to E major (Ex. 2.2b).

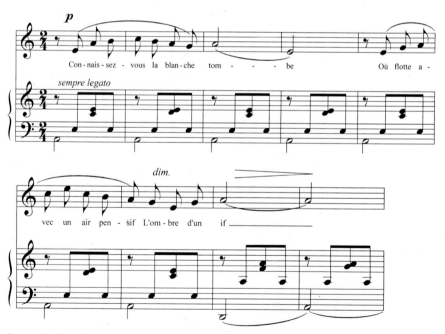

Example 2.2a "Lamento," mm. 8–16

Example 2.2b "Lamento," mm. 28–52

While "Lamento" was written in an intimate style, other songs were composed in a more extraverted *arioso* style, like the *bel canto* "Cavatine" for tenor and piano (Italian text by J. Zaffirà) and an English-language song (the text presumably by Polignac), "Remembrance."[62] "Remembrance" was dedicated to Adelina Patti,[63] and it is not implausible that the great diva, who (like many a great artist of the era) graced the Paris salons with her brilliant voice, paid Polignac the supreme compliment of performing his song at an aristocratic soirée.

Polignac was in the audience for the first performance of Eugène Diaz's *La Coupe du Roi de Thulé* in January 1873.[64] After the reviewers panned the production, Polignac was emboldened to reintroduce excerpts of his own score in the salons. One such performance took place in April of that year at the home of Comte Osmond d'Osmond. The society press reported on the event.

> This salon, much sought after by both high society members and artistic luminaries, was more brilliant than ever. There was particular interest in two pieces, excerpted from the score that the Prince de Polignac wrote on the libretto *La Coupe du Roi de Thulé*, the Overture and "Queen Claribel's Aria" (act 2), delightfully performed by Mademoiselle Montesini, a rising star. The success of these two pieces was very great, and makes us regret that the score of M. le Prince de Polignac has never been performed at the Opéra.[65]

For a concert sponsored by the Cercle de Mirlitons at the Palais Royal, Polignac wrote a farcical "oratorio-opérette," *Rallye champdouillard* (1873), on a libretto by Pierre de Boisdeffre. The performance whetted Polignac's appetite for a return to theatrical music. When he was invited to compose a piece for a charity concert at the newly reopened Salle Ventadour (part of the Théâtre des Italiens), he turned to the work of a favorite poet and playwright, Alfred de Musset (1810–1857). Musset was still considered to be the *enfant terrible* of Romanticism. Polignac was attracted to Musset's independent and fantastic spirit, and his ability to mold his love of classicism with the soulful Romantic style. The piece that he chose to set was Musset's 1832 "dramatic poem" *La Coupe et les Lèvres* (The Cup and the Lips). The plot revolves around the misadventures of Frank, a hot-headed young hunter who becomes involved in a love triangle; the story finishes tragically as Frank inadvertently causes the death of his young and innocent fiancée Deïdamia. Musset's text lent itself to the creation of rousing hunting choruses and impassioned love duets. The excerpt performed at the Salle Ventadour, "Les Adieux de Deïdamia," comes from act 5, scene 1 of Musset's play.[66] Set for soprano solo and female chorus, the *scena* is an epithalamium, in which Deïdamia expresses to her friends her hopes that Frank will find her beautiful and her regrets at soon being separated from her maiden companions. A reporter who was present at the charity concert described Polignac's work as "one of the principal attractions of the program."

> This piece . . . is remarkable by the veracity of the expression, the natural and happy turn of its melody, its interesting harmony and instrumentation. It is written a bit in the manner of Mendelssohn. M. le Prince de Polignac no longer has to offer his proofs as a musician. Mademoiselle Heilbronn performed the solo

in a charming manner; the solo, sung in reprise by the women's choir, [create a fine] effect. The total raised at this charity soirée was 10,000 francs.[67]

In 1874, Ludovic and Camille de Polignac both married.[68] Edmond, who turned forty that year, found himself bereft of the company of his brothers. He consoled himself with a trip to London and the trienniel Handel Festival, held at the Crystal Palace. That year the renowned festival enlisted a monumental force of nearly six thousand musical executants to perform both the famous and lesser-known works from the Handel canon. Polignac, familiar since childhood with Handel's music, already knew the composer's music well. He was unprepared, however, for the overwhelmingly powerful impression made by the music as performed by a gigantic chorus and orchestra. Years later, he would describe the Handel Festival as "the Elysium of eternal music," recalling the "sublime" performance of "God Save the King" from *Zadock the Priest*, "where the peoples sing . . . with the luminous fringe embroidered by the sopranos, and, later, the prodigious scrolls rolled out by the Basses."[69]

In January 1875 Polignac left the cold of Paris for an extended stay with his niece Yolande, the Duchesse de Luynes, at her villa in Cannes. Madame de Luynes presented her uncle's music at soirées held in her salon; on one evening, when the distinguished audience included Queen Sophie of Holland, Polignac sang a newly composed song, "Adieu, France," on a text by Mary, Queen of Scots, accompanied by renowned harp virtuoso Alphonse Hasselmans.[70]

It was during his southern sojourn that Polignac made the acquaintance of a man who, for the next two decades, would have a far-reaching influence on his emotional and artistic life. Born in 1855, Comte Robert de Montesquiou was related by marriage to just about every important family in the aristocracy. He was beautiful: tall, dark-haired, and delicately thin. His cousin Élisabeth Greffulhe would describe him as "proud, arrogant, disinterested, not accepting compromise just to please others . . . [he was] enthusiastic, impassioned by poetry, reciting from all the old poets . . . mad about music, a great art lover, intoxicated by rhythms, impressed by beauty in all its forms."[71] After completing his education, Montesquiou moved into his father's mansion, where he decorated his attic apartment with extraordinary furniture and objects, painting the walls in exotic hues of crimson, pink, grey, and green, turning the space into something resembling a tale from the Arabian nights.[72] Foreshadowing Oscar Wilde's dictate, he endeavored to make his person into a work of art. In subsequent years he would become a consummate symbol of Decadent artificiality, calculating every aspect of his physical appearance—clothing, hair, moustache, speech, and motions—"to inspire admiration and desire."[73] The count's profound vanity and artificiality inspired a number of literary characters: Des Esseintes in Joris-Karl Huysman's Decadent novel *À Rebours* (Against the Grain; 1884), the Comte de Muzarett in Jean Lorrain's novel *Monsieur de Phocas* (1902), and, especially, the vain, pretentious homosexual Baron de Charlus in Marcel Proust's masterwork *À la Recherche du temps perdu* (1913–27).

Proust biographer George Painter summed up Montesquiou as "a hollow man. The terrifying, impenetrable facade of his vanity, his insolence, his perversity, covered nothing but the frightened small boy with whom he had irrevocably lost touch."[74] A decade after the fact, Montesquiou would describe the walks he took with Polignac soon after their meeting in Cannes:

> . . . from Cannes to Menton, with their too-yellow roads, their too-violet moun-tains, their too-blue Mediterranean, their unfamiliar sea, without ebb or flow, a prude who never permits access to her bed, in the whole of this countryside, too hard, too rude, too raw, and too cruel, and too accredited with defined contours, almost as leaden as windows, and similar to the crockery made by an inexperienced demoiselle.[75]

Of that same period, Polignac would write:

> I look back on our walks in Cannes, on the roads dug out between the two low garden walls, near the sea, and you come back to me as you were then, in a checkered jacket: it was our first meeting; you read me passages from "Letters from a Traveler." You seemed to me to be lost in a strange world, and also a little bit like one abandoned.[76]

These two recollections serve to illustrate the differences between the two men. In his description, Montesquiou revels in the sensual wordplay that forms the basis of his poetry. He reveals himself as the consummate pre-Raphaelite, depict-ing the hues of the surrounding countryside as almost perversely brilliant, more brightly colored than life. This acolyte of Decadence describes the walk along the simple country road as a fantastic, illusory series of metaphors, gilding nature to make the idea of the walk more desirable than the real event. The description is empty of feeling, more of a tribute to the poet's agile manipulation of language than a testament to friendship. In contrast, Polignac's recollection reflects his directness and emotional sincerity—and his tendency to project his own melan-choly onto other people and situations: his perception of Montesquiou's aban-donment reflected his own isolation.

The importance to Polignac of Montesquiou's friendship cannot be over-stated. The prince had always felt out of place with the other men of his class. With the twenty-year-old Montesquiou he was able to open up and reveal his imagination, his insecurities, his creativity, and his longings; he felt that his new friend saw his true worth as a lonely artist in a way that others could not. The impassioned tone of his letters reveals a man who finally feels the relief of being understood. Equally importantly, Montesquiou was a homosexual from his own class. Like other homosexuals in nineteenth-century Paris, Polignac surely feared societal ostracism and legal recrimination; unlike the many who married woman to cover up the truth,[77] Polignac preferred lonely solitude.

Now he could draw comfort, and hide in plain sight, knowing that there was another homosexual man in his own milieu—one who circulated comfortably in society, suavely concealing his sexual preferences, thanks in part to the level of denial among the people who frequented his milieu.[78] And even though Polignac continued to suffer from chronic illnesses (which he dubbed "the sinister teasings of irritable gods"[79]), he felt better knowing that Montesquiou seemed to enjoy listening to him suffer.

The two men also expanded and enriched each other's cultural tastes and circles. Montesquiou introduced Edmond to writers and poets that he admired, such as d'Annunzio, Mallarmé, Leconte de Lisle, Verlaine, Hérédia, and Régnier, and artists Helleu, La Gandara, Moreau, Degas, Lobre, and Gallé. On many evenings, Edmond and Montesquiou would dine together and then read to each other the works of their preferred poets and writers (Gautier and Musset were particular favorites) over a glass of sherry. Edmond looked forward to these evenings, where he could avail himself of the "battalion of cooks" at 41 quay d'Orsay.[80] In turn, Edmond shared his insights into the music of the masters that he venerated, writings his thoughts and explanations in letters stuffed with English proverbs and Latin quotations. Montesquiou attended performances of Polignac's music, including a 1875 performance at the Cercle des Mirlitons of the vocal quartet from *La Coupe du Roi de Thulé*.[81]

Montesquiou's encouragement gave Polignac much-needed creative confidence. In 1877, Polignac won a competition sponsored by the Société Académique of the town of Saint-Quentin open only to French composers; the required contest piece was a cantata for three voices. Polignac collaborated with librettist Edmond Delière to write *Don Juan et Haydée,* nominally a cantata, but, in reality an *opéra comique.* The work carried off the first prize (the runner-up was André Messager), which included a gold medal and the guarantee of a performance at the Theater of Saint-Quentin. All of the town's artistic resources and personnel—including the local choral society and a combination of the Saint-Quentin Philharmonic and theater orchestra—were put at Polignac's disposal; acclaimed singers, including star tenor Jean-Alexandre Talazac, were hired to sing the principal roles.[82] The solitary performance, which took place on 26 November 1877, was lauded in the press as a great success.

> One feels the touch of a master in several of the cantata's constituent pieces, and the ensemble is distinguished by a true originality and by a remarkable sonority. . . . The poetic and turbulent work of M. Delière lends itself completely to the interesting developments and successively sweet, melodious, and pathetic colors that the composer gives to his music.[83]

This was the last tonal composition that Polignac would write for some time. He would devote the last years of the 1870s to an even more "interesting" musical development: the discovery of octatonicsm.

Chapter Three

Scales A, B, C: Polignac's Invention of Octatonicism (1877–1879)

In his sixty-year correspondence with his brother Ludovic, Edmond de Polignac routinely kept him apprised of his musical activities: new compositions, upcoming performances of his works, concerts attended, books read, scores studied. However, no letters from Edmond to Ludovic survive for a one-year period between April 1878 and April 1879. Parenthetically, there are no extant letters written dating from this period to Robert de Montesquiou, another person with whom Polignac maintained a lengthy and important correspondence that includes frequent mentions of musical matters.

The first letter written to Ludovic after a year of epistolary silence, dated 18 April 1879, includes the following paragraph:

> . . . I continue to dream about some musical works. I have begun to set the beautiful and dramatic scenes of the Passion according to the Gospels. I've already almost finished two numbers, one including "Pilate hands over Jesus— *tolle, crucifigatur,* etc." I played this number for Pasdeloup, who seemed very interested in hearing the effect. Perhaps he'd be willing to have it performed, if I pushed him a bit, but I'm not very good at pushing others; I have enough trouble pushing myself. I'm also planning to do the scene at the palace of Caiaphas, the high priest, but I'll have to judaize and arabize hard; I'm going to try to bring in a ferocious fugue on the [text] "Prophesy unto us," when the abuse and the blows rain down from all sides.[1]

The full meaning of this text will be discussed in due course, but what can be said now, by way of introduction, is that it is a marker of crucial importance for the present study: it attaches a date to the composition of Polignac's first octatonic works, the aforementioned settings of New Testament texts. However, the letter documents only the imminent completion of the works; frustratingly, it reveals nothing of the process that caused the composer to begin his long journey down this new creative path. It will therefore be necessary to examine cultural trends and musical events that may have contributed to Polignac's octatonic invention, and to speculate about the most likely sources of influence.

Polignac might have been influenced by important early nineteenth-century composers whose music is regarded today as proto- or crypto-octatonic:

Schubert, Liszt, and Chopin, all of whom were progressive harmonists who sidestepped traditional harmonic procedures and key relationships. As a highly educated musician whose instrument was the piano, not only would Polignac been familiar with the works of these composers, he would have been alert to their experimentalist tendencies; he might even have identified procedures that have recently been analyzed by modern octatonic scholars.[2]

However, the most important earlier nineteenth-century composer to influence Polignac would have been Richard Wagner. Polignac, as we know, revered Wagner, and would have heard as many performances as possible of his idol's music, both in Paris (thanks especially to Pasdeloup's indefatigable championship of the composer[3]) and in other major music centers visited during his travels. He was sophisticated enough to recognize and understand, through score study, Wagner's innovative harmonic vocabulary, especially his expanded approach to triadic movement and the resultant destabilization of diatonic harmony. Passages such as the opening of act 1, scene 5 of *Tristan und Isolde* or act 2, scene 1 of *Siegfried,* both of which contain sustained use of diminished-seventh harmonies and mediant-related or tritone-related key centers may very well have influenced Polignac's own innovative approach to triadic atonality and, subsequently, his octatonic compositions.[4]

His interest in composing music on scales other than major and minor might have come from the writings of Franz Liszt. In 1859, Liszt's ethnographic study *Des Bohémiens et de leur musique en Hongrie,* dedicated to his gypsy forebears and friends, appeared in installments in the journal *La France musicale* and was published as a book that same year. Polignac would have had easy access to this work (coauthored in certain passages by Lizst's mistress, Carolyne Sayn-Wittgenstein), in which Lizst makes an explicit connection between the exoticism of Hungarian gypsy music and the affective qualities in Greek scales—particularly the medieval and modern Phrygian scale, which begins with a half step between scale degrees $\hat{1}$ and $\hat{2}$.[5] The book contains a discussion about the distinctive use of semitones and even quarter tones,[6] followed by a spelling-out of one of the two collections commonly known as "gypsy scales": *verbunkos,* the so-called Hungarian minor scale, with an augmented second in each tetrachord between scale degrees $\hat{3}$–$\hat{4}$ and $\hat{6}$–$\hat{7}$ (for example, C–D–E♭–F♯–G–A♭–B♮–C).[7] Even if these writings offer no direct assertions that feed into Polignac's invention of octatonicism, Lizst's writings on Gypsy music indicate a mid-nineteenth-century fascination with manipulation of the major and minor scales to produce "exotic" music, a fascination that clearly continued to engage musicians a quarter century later.

Polignac's interest in "alternative" scales might also have come from Gregorian chant. The prince's engagement with chant is notable, especially since most nineteenth-century musicians did not consider chant to be "real" music, but another practice altogether. Polignac's library included an 1875 edition of the *Graduale Romanum,* as well as the *Canticle Psalms,* and the *Chants ordinaires.* It is not known whether he had read Louis Niedermeyer and Joseph d'Ortigue's 1856 *Treatise on Plainchant*,[9] or whether he was aware of the monumental work on Gregorian chant taking place at the Benedictine monastery at Solesmes that would culminate in the 1880 publication of a historically correct anthology of the Gregorian melodies.[10] Like his contemporary Joris-Karl Huysmans, he may have been attracted to the music because it appealed to his mystical side.[11] The role that chant might have played in Polignac's octatonic invention shall be revisited later in this chapter.

Another influence upon Polignac's octatonic composition may have been his encounters with (to use a complicated term loosely) musical "exoticism" and other forms of cultural "alterity," such as art and dance. There was no lack of possibility for such encounters in 1878: beginning in May of that year, Polignac had only to travel a kilometer or so to the Champs de Mars, home of the Paris World's Fair, where music and visual spectacles emanating from every corner of the globe could be heard and seen on a daily basis. The Paris music press gave widespread coverage to the sonic goings-on at the Fair. Noted musicologist and journalist Émile-Mathieu de Monter wrote twenty-two articles for the *Revue et Gazette musicale de Paris* on the subject, providing an overview of the various national musics and instruments, as well as an introduction to some of the major composers from the individual countries.[12] Of particular interest during this period was music from "The East"—Near, Far, and Middle. Evidence suggests that sonorities from the Arab countries—the "Islamic Orient"—captured Edmond de Polignac's imagination as well. From an 1894 octatonic sketch entitled "Après des Airs arabes entendus chez la Belle Fatma," we know that the composer was familiar with the performances of "La Belle Fatma," the stage name of Tunisian dancer Rachel Bent-Eny. Bent-Eny was only seven years old when she performed at the 1878 Fair; she so captivated audiences that she stayed on in Paris for the next eleven years to perform in the popular *café-concerts* that sprang up in Paris in the Fair's aftermath.[13] While we cannot know whether it was in 1878 or long afterward that Polignac heard the Arab music that accompanied the beautiful Fatma's dances, it is nonetheless notable that this "exotic" repertoire served as a basis for octatonic composition.

Another body of "exotic" repertoire that captured public attention during the 1878 World's Fair was Russian music. Here, the lack of evidence of what Polignac heard and when he heard it is particularly frustrating, for it is in mid-nineteenth-century Russian music that the octatonic collection was first widely exploited as both a melodic and structural element. The first chronicled description of the scale appears in a letter from Nicolai Rimsky-Korsakov to Mily Balakirev, written on 1 August 1867, in which he describes writing a "descending scale of semitone, whole tone, semitone, whole tone"[14]—a scale that, during the composer's lifetime, came to be known as the "Rimsky-Korsakov scale." In the aforementioned letter, Rimsky describes a passage from his symphonic poem *Sadko,* which features in the upper voices a descending octatonic scale, supported harmonically by chords related by minor third;[15] this passage becomes an important leitmotif throughout *Sadko*. The mediant harmonies in *Sadko*, which include harmonic relations not only in the octatonic scale but also in the whole-tone scale, denote what Taruskin calls "evil sorcery," a staple of musical exoticism.[16]

Neither letters nor other documentary materials give any indication that Polignac was aware of the existence of Rimsky-Korsakov's music or the "Rimsky-Korsakov scale"—or any Russian music, for that matter—at the time that he was formulating his own octatonic ideas. Nonetheless, the possibility of some influence cannot be entirely ruled out, as there were numerous opportunities for engagements with Russian octatonic music in the late 1870s. In 1878, anyone who followed closely musical events and trends would have been hard-pressed to ignore the prominence place given to Russian music in the Paris music journals. The most important of these was a series of articles in the *Revue et Gazette musicale de Paris* by Russian composer and writer César Cui, published in six installments between May and December, which introduced the French musical public to "all the genres and all the eras of musical art in Russia."[17] Cui gave special prominence to the works of Mikhail Glinka, the "father" of modern Russian music, whose 1842 opera *Ruslan and Ludmila* was the first Russian work to feature a whole-tone scale.[18] The fact that the first installment of Cui's series was published in May, contemporaneously with Monter's coverage of the opening of the World's Fair, guaranteed a large readership; Monter's own articles on Russian music appeared in late June, so there was almost continuous coverage of this country's music over a six-month period. Perhaps these articles caused some composers to visit the Paris Conservatoire and consult the twenty-seven scores of Russian music—including two partially octatonic scores, Rimsky's *Sadko* and Musorgsky's *Boris Godunov*—that had been sent to the Conservatoire's library in 1874.[19] The constant coverage of Russian music may explain, in part, why, in September, Parisians and visitors to the city flocked to the newly built Trocadéro Palace to hear three concerts of orchestral music by modern Russian composers (beginning with "Father" Glinka) performed under the baton of pianist-conductor Nicolai Rubinstein. Russian art music was virtually unknown to French audiences, as it was almost never programmed in French concert programs (Berlioz's *séance russe* of 16 March 1845, built around the works of Glinka, being the rare exception[20]). French visitors to the previous (1867) World's Fair would have heard no Russian art music—only folk music was presented.[21] The richness of this repertoire was thus a revelation to the 1878 concert-goers: Rubinstein and his musicians enjoyed "packed houses and great success"; Glinka's music especially—including the whole-tone-inflected Overture to *Ruslan and Ludmila*—"occupied the place of honor" in the first program.[22]

Rimsky's partially octatonic symphonic poem *Sadko* was performed at the third concert, on 21 September. The work received a tepid reception both by audiences and the press: while acknowledging the brilliance of Rimsky's orchestration, the critics from both the *Revue et Gazette musicale* and *Le Ménestrel* complained about the lightweight quality of program music in general and the laxity of *Sadko*'s form in particular.[23] It is not known if Polignac attended the Russian concerts, or if he heard *Sadko*. However, two highly esteemed musicians of Polignac's acquaintance were enraptured by Rimsky-Korsakov's music. One was Jules Pasdeloup, who programmed *Sadko* on the 1 December installment of his "Concerts populaires" series; when *that* performance garnered less-than-favorable reviews of the work itself from the audience and the press,[24] Pasdeloup, "a man of firm convictions," issued a musical retort by programming the piece yet again on the 29 December concert.[25] Thus, Polignac would have three occasions in as many months to hear this octatonic music—and to hear it described and debated by various professional musicians and experienced concertgoers. Hearing Pasdeloup utter once sentence about *Sadko*'s interesting progressions and modulations, for example, could have been as much of a galvanizing force as hearing the work itself.

Another contemporary of Polignac's who ardently championed Rimsky-Korsakov's music was composer and musicologist Louis-Albert Bourgault-Ducoudray (1840–1910), whose laudatory review of Rimsky-Korsakov's newly published harmonization of Russian folk melodies would appear some months after the *Sadko* performances.[26] Bourgault-Ducoudray entered Reber's harmony class at the Conservatoire in 1859, just as Polignac was completing his course of study.[27] As the 1862 laureate of the Prix de Rome, he spent the next several years in Italy, where he was introduced to the music of Palestrina. It is not clear when he and Polignac first crossed paths after his return to Paris, but the two had much in common, including their mutual love for early music, Renaissance polyphony, and Baroque music, especially that of J. S. Bach. (It is conceivable that it was Bourgault-Ducoudray who interested Polignac in plainchant in the first place.) Surely the prince would have attended performances of his younger colleague's choral society, founded in 1868, which sponsored numerous performances of the rarely heard Bach cantatas. By 1892 the two men would be in constant contact as founding members of the Schola Cantorum.

Bourgault-Ducoudray was an early practitioner of the discipline today known as ethnomusicology. Breton by birth, Bourgault-Ducoudray began investigating the music of his heritage while he was still a student. In 1874, during a vacation in Greece, he discovered that country's folk and ecclesiastical music; a year later, he parted on an official mission, funded by the French government, to study and document Greek music. The first publication resulting from these studies was *Trente mélodies populaires de Grèce & d'Orient*, published in 1876—a book that came to be included in Edmond de Polignac's library. In a preface to the book, chiefly devoted to the modern notation and harmonization (in Western style) of Greek folk melodies, Bourgault-Ducoudray gives an overview of the modal scales of Greek Orthodox chant, and the application of their theory to the study of Greek folksong. He divides the scales into two tetrachords, each containing two whole steps and a half step and spanning a perfect fourth. He discusses, in succession, (1) the use of diatonic scales in early music; (2) the comparison, first, between the use of modes in ancient Greek music and in Gregorian plainchant, and, next, between ancient music and Greek ecclesiastical music; and (3) the "Oriental chromatic" scale (that is, a scale—like the gypsy/Hungarian *kalindra*—that contains two augmented seconds between scale degrees $\hat{2}$–$\hat{3}$ and $\hat{6}$–$\hat{7}$).[28] Considerable discussion is devoted throughout to the affective result of different placements of the half step amongst the whole steps in various scales, a subject to which we shall return in due course.

Bourgault-Ducoudray followed up his monograph of Greek folk music with one on Greek ecclesiastic music.[29] In 1878 he was invited to give a lecture-recital lecture at the Trocadéro Palace on "Modality in Greek music."[30] The talk, which drew from all the musicologist's previous publications, attracted a large audience and was the subject of long articles in the major music journals. *La Revue musicale* noted:

> The hall was full, which is quite rare for a [scholarly] lecture, and the most complete success crowned the perseverant efforts of M. Bourgault to promote understanding of Greco-Oriental music and to show the varied and precious resources that it holds in reserve for our composers. [He] cited several musical phrases, demonstrated by his able performers, conceived in the spirit of this modality, consciously or not, by Rossini, Berlioz, Gounod, Ambroise Thomas and all the rest.[31]

The writer for *Le Ménestrel* was struck by the affective diversity of the different modal scales, noting that "we're not accustomed to hearing a scale start with a half step followed by a whole step. This scale existed, however, in the Greek musical system, and we find it in plainchant under the name of the 'phrygian mode.' . . . The able lecturer thinks that perfect knowledge and active practice of the ancient Greek modes will rejuvenate [musical] art and give it, by new means, a virility that, to him, seems currently to be lacking."[32] To quote Bourgault-Ducoudray directly,

> No element of expression existing in a tune of any kind, however ancient, however remote in origin, must be banished from our musical idiom. All modes, old and new, European or exotic, insofar as they are capable of serving an expressive purpose, must be admitted by us and used by composers. I believe that the polyphonic principle may be applied to all kinds of scales. Our two modes, the major and minor, have been so thoroughly exploited that we should welcome all elements of expression by which the musical idiom may be rejuvenated.[33]

One last word on possible influences on Polignac's octatonic invention: it is interesting to note the visual proximity—accidental or otherwise—of some articles in the 1878 issues of the *Revue musicale;* these accidental "pairings" may have inspired some readers to make synthetic connections of seemingly unrelated ideas. In the 12 May issue, Cui's opening article on Russian music was immediately followed by the first installment of a two-part article by librarian and Greek historian Charles-Émile Ruelle, "Histoire de notre gamme" ("History of our Scale"), which traced the origins of the diatonic scale to Pythagorean theory.[34] The continuation of Ruelle's article was published in the 23 June issue, whose first page featured Émile-Mathieu de Monter's article on Russian music at the World's Fair, and a second article, "Les Tziganes de Moscou" ("The Gypsies of Moscow").[35] Finally, the 15 September contained the review of the first "Russian concert"; the same page contained the long article on Bourgault-Ducoudray's lecture-recital on modality in Greek music.[36]

To recapitulate: in 1878, the Paris musical cognoscenti could have read about the following topics in music magazines: scales and their history; exoticism; rejuvenation of modern music; Russian music; and Gypsy music. Writings on ancient and medieval modal scales, Middle-Eastern scales, and Gypsy scales could have been especially influential on Edmond de Polignac: they might have put him in a frame of mind to think about collections with a flatted second degree, or, more specifically, a $\hat{1}$–b$\hat{2}$–b$\hat{3}$ succession—which, extrapolated conjunctly upwards, yields the octatonic scale; any or all of these could have inspired him, in 1878, to tinker with the notion of "new scales"—to try, perhaps, to be the first to heed Bourgault-Ducoudray's exhortation to revitalize European music by "drawing from newly combined elements and as-yet unexploited means of expression in the adaption of harmony to the ancient modes."[37]

The first product of Polignac's experiments is a "Fantaisie-Tanz," a wistful, mazurka-like piece for piano in ternary form.[38] In a preface to the piece, which the composer refers to as a "little study with a conclusion [written] on a new Scale," Polignac writes, "The constitution of this new Scale could cause it to belong to the Greek Dorian mode,[39] in which the sixth degree is raised by a half step; but it parts company from this mode by virtue of its more modern tonality, which easily takes on an aspect that is bizarre, disconnected, quasi-macabre."[40] Above Polignac's preface, a motto is written: "Rien n'est vrai que le faux, le faux seul est aimable" ("Only the false is true; the false alone is kindly"). It bears pointing out that the French word *faux* (false) can also be translated as "out of tune."

The first section (Ex. 3.1a) is written in the key of B minor, with varying alterations of scale degrees $\hat{6}$ and $\hat{7}$. The more energetic Trio section (Ex. 3.1b) is written on a so-called Hungarian major scale—that is, a major scale with a lowered 6th degree: D–E–F♯–G–A–B♭–C♯–D.[41] As the section progresses, the music centers, for brief periods, in unusual keys: first E-flat major and then C major. A conventional return to the A section and the tonic key is signlaed

Example 3.1a. "Fantaisie-Tanz," mm. 3–10

Example 3.1b. "Fantaisie-Tanz," mm. 32–35

by a stepwise chromatic descent in the bass that arrives on F♯, the dominant of B minor. Suddenly, Polignac extends the bridge, introducing a pedal point on C♮ and adding the pitches C♮ and G♯ to the melodic line (Ex. 3.1c). Over the next fifteen measures, the juxtaposition of F♯ in the melody and C♮ in the bass is emphasized.

When the first theme returns (Ex. 3.1d), the pitch collection changes: the C♯ in the melody—and the key signature—has been replaced by a C♮, and the sixth degree of the scale has been raised to G♯. The result is the scale below; the pitches are listed on the first line; the second line denotes the distances between one pitch or another: either half steps (½) or whole steps (1).

B	C♮	D	E	F♯	G♯	A♮	B
½	1	1	1	1	½	1	

Polignac's "bizarre, disconnected" scale both begins and ends with a half-step/ whole-step pattern. Let us imagine that Polignac consulted Bourgault-Ducoudray's writings as he composed. On pages 11–13 of *Trente mélodies populaires de Grèce et d'Orient,* Bourgault-Ducoudray explains that all diatonic scales are composed of two tetrachords spanning a perfect fourth, plus one whole step. First he shows

Example 3.1c. "Fantaisie-Tanz," mm. 74–81

Example 3.1d. "Fantaisie-Tanz," mm. 91–97

three configurations of tetrachords, with the half step placed at the beginning, middle, and end of the tetrachord (Fig. 3.1, p. [11]), then the scales derived from these arrangements (Fig. 3.2, p. 13).

Let us further imagine that Polignac was struck by the palindromic configuration of the "third species" tetrachord, 1–½–1, which, when replicated and connected by a "complimentary" 1 produced the ancient-Greek Phrygian scale. For someone who grew up playing mathematical games as a kind of sport, further manipulation of the pattern would not have been much of a stretch. Perhaps Polignac looked at his "Fantaisie-Tanz" again, and thought about another possible reconfiguration: an alteration of the middle three scale degrees would create a scale of eight—rather than the customary seven—pitches, whose half steps and whole steps would produce a repeating pattern:

B	C	D	E♭	F	F♯	G♯	A	B
½	1	½	1	½	1	½	1	

and two transpositions of the same pattern, beginning on C and C♯. Polignac would have discovered quickly that there were, in fact, only three possible transpositions—a fact that, some seventy years later, would cause Olivier Messiaen to include the collections among what he called the "modes of limited transposition."[42] Polignac named the collection beginning on C "Scale A"; the one beginning on C♯ was called "Scale B," and the one beginning on D "Scale C." He grouped the three collections together under the name "chromatico-diatonic scales"—what we call today the octatonic scales. The more Polignac explored the constructive possibilities that lay within these scales, the more convinced he became that he had taken an important germinating first step towards a "rejuvenation" of modern musical idioms.

These scales became the basis of Polignac's next creative project, a group of musical settings of texts from the Gospels. The powerful texts of the New Testament had been set countless times, by great and lesser composers, in any number of forms and styles. For his own interpretation of the immortal words, Polignac used his newly invented scales as the basis of a compositional language that could approximate, if not replicate, the music heard in Jesus's Jerusalem; a language that could evoke the "ancient Orient," a place that, to the Romantic nineteenth-century imagination, connoted "exoticism" and "barbarism"; a musical language that could, above all, represent in a new way the dramatic and spiritual power of the Gospel texts. Polignac would not be the first Western composer to reimagine and represent Orientalist music—but he would arguably be the first to set the music outside the context of Western common-practice tonality.[43]

In addition to the Gregorian chant anthologies already in his library, Polignac added new volumes that would his further his research into "Oriental" scales. One of these was a collection of liturgical chants from the Armenian Church.[44] In 1879 he acquired a collection of settings of the *Psalms of David* and the book of synagogue chants used by the Paris Consistory of Israelite Temples.[45] If he was hoping to find that his experiments with new scales had precedents in Judaic tradition, Polignac would have been disappointed; however, although there was no octatonicism to be found in the tropes of the traditional *nusach* (the practice of singing chant in a particular Jewish community according to liturgical function and local tradition), he would ultimately appropriate the shape and style of the chants for use in octatonic and later Orientalist compositions.

In the aforementioned letter of 18 April 1879 to his brother Ludovic, Polignac writes that he has "already almost finished two numbers" based on "the beautiful and dramatic scenes of the Passion in the Gospels."[46] The unnamed first "number"

INTRODUCTION

DE LA FORMATION DES GAMMES DIATONIQUES

Pour comprendre la formation des douze gammes diatoniques, il faut avant tout
e rendre compte de la composition de la *quarte*.

Toute *quarte juste* (1) est composée de deux *tons* et un *demi-ton*, par exemple :

Le *demi-ton* peut occuper dans la quarte trois positions différentes.

Il peut être au commencement ; ce sera la *première espèce* de quarte :

Il peut être à la fin ; ce sera la *seconde espèce* de quarte :

Il peut être au milieu ; ce sera la *troisième espèce* de quarte :

(1) Il est question ici du genre *diatonique*.

Figure 3.1. Bourgault-Ducoudray, *Trente mélodies populaires de Grèce & d'Orient*, p. [11].

dans le second, on aura :

Considérons les trois octaves génératrices comme divisées en *quarte* et *quinte*, cela nous fournit les gammes suivantes :

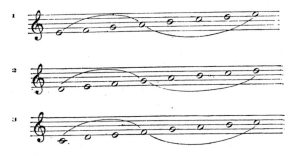

Intervertissons l'ordre de succession de la *quarte* et de la *quinte* dans chacune de ces gammes, nous obtiendrons trois nouvelles gammes :

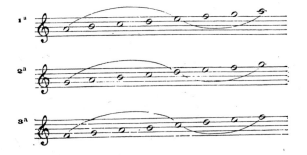

Nous voici déjà en possession de six gammes dont les trois premières (octaves *génératrices* sont divisées en *quarte* et quinte, et les trois autres (gammes *engendrées*) sont divisées en *quinte* et *quarte*.

Dans la gamme n° 1 (première octave génératrice) et dans la gamme 1ᵃ (première gamme engendrée), le *mi* et le *la* conservent leur caractère respectif; dans les deux gammes, *mi* joue le rôle de dominante, et *la* celui de tonique.

Figure 3.2. Bourgault-Ducoudray, *Trente mélodies populaires de Grèce & d'Orient*, p. 13.

referred to in the letter is most likely Polignac's "Ruine du Temple prédite" (Ruin of the Temple Foretold), on texts from Matthew 23 and 24 and Luke 11 and 21.[47] In this piece, Jesus speaks to the crowds and his disciples, condemning the beliefs and practices of the Pharisees. Conceived (according to a note by the composer in the published version) in the Phrygian mode, the music becomes purely octatonic when Jesus utters the excoriating phrase "Woe unto you, scribes and Pharisees, hypocrites!" This phrase may be the first octatonic music written by Polignac. The second work, explicitly named in the letter, is "Pilate livre le Christ" (Pilate hands over Jesus). This piece employs the octatonic collection for more extended passages, and in bolder ways. Scored for baritone solo, mixed chorus, and orchestra, the work evokes, through gritty, tritone-infused harmonies, the noisy barbarity of the Jewish mob clamoring to Pontius Pilate for the crucifixion of Jesus. Clearly, Polignac heard something in the octatonic collection and its resultant harmonies that could depict the exoticism of the locale and the savagery of the mob. It was apparently the dramatic, biting "effect" of music based on the octatonic collection that he believed would be interesting to Pasdeloup. It is equally clear that he ascribed to the collection—at least as it was employed in "Pilate"—an essentialist meaning: years later he would describe "Pilate" as "an essay in the application of naturalism in music, consisting of adapting the known character of the music of a people to the interpretation of a dramatic scene depicting this people."[48] Both "Ruine du Temple prédite" and "Pilate livre le Christ" will be discussed and analyzed further in chapter 9.

Polignac continues in his letter: "I'm also planning to do the scene at the palace of Caiaphas, the high priest, but I'll have to judaize and arabize hard; I'm going to try to bring in a ferocious fugue on the [text] 'Prophesy unto us,' when the abuse and the blows rain down from all sides."[49] Here we are presented with a new mystery, which, to date, cannot be solved. Apparently, Polignac did indeed begin to sketch a prelude and fugue for a "scene at Caiaphas's palace" (presumably Matthew 26:64–68), as well as a "march to the Calvary" (presumably Matthew 27:27–31), which he jotted in a notebook of sketches based on "Scales A, B, and C." None of these sketches seem to have made their way into completed compositions. But we know about them and their inclusion in what Polignac called "Cahier de Gammes A. B. C. ("[First] Notebook of Scales A, B, and C") because Polignac makes allusion to both the notebook and the "Caiaphas" sketches in a *second* notebook, written sometime after April 1879, the date of the letter to Ludovic. In this second notebook, Polignac sets forth an exposition of octatonic theory, which he supports with musical examples and longer compositional sketches based on the octatonic collections. The notebook was given the title "A Study on the Sequences of Alternating Whole Steps and Half Steps."[50]

Polignac's 98-page treatise-sketchbook (whose organization and style, not surprisingly, are similar in some ways to Reber's *Treatise on Harmony*) seems to represent the composer's attempt to develop a comprehensive theory of the "chromatico-diatonic" scales. (As Polignac's treatise-sketchbook will be analyzed and translated in part two of the book, only a brief resume of its contents will be offered here.) Polignac begins by theorizing the octatonic collection, then later offers octatonic-based chord progressions and procedures that can be applied directly to composition. First he spells out the three scales, which he calls "Series A, B, and C." Next, he shows that the collection generates major and minor triads on the first, third, fifth, and seventh scale degrees. On tr-p. 6, the three collections A, B, and C are officially given the name "chromatico-diatonic scales." A few pages later Polignac notes the importance of the tritone as a focal point in the collection. He then begins to experiment with melodic and contrapuntal figures, as well as harmonic progressions derivable from the scale, even including "modulations" from one form of the scale to another. By the end of the treatise's 98 pages he has reached an impressively detailed and complex level of compositional application of the octatonic collection.

About a third of the way through the treatise-sketchbook, Polignac begins to note specific affective qualities applicable to certain of his octatonic motives. His identification of the octatonic collections with Orientalist, semitic, and exotic subjects is manifested by the titles and commentary on the various pages of the document. One sketch is described as being of a "serious, noble, sad, mixed with fright, good for Dante's *Inferno*"; "this example," he writes, "could also be employed for a large celestial choir, Catholic style, because of the dominant sevenths that have none of the Hebraic or Oriental character."[51] In addition to references to the scene with Caiaphas and "a march to the Calvary," "already tried [in the first notebook]," as well as numerous allusions to "Hebraic" and "Judaic" music in general, there are also specific references to music for "the Passover," the "phalanxes of harps and cherubim, and "'the vision' of Christ." The final musical sketch in the treatise is described as "a motive incited by the melody of Pilate—sickly, desolate, sad."[52] On the last page of the notebook, Polignac writes a philosophical afterword, defiantly asserting that his "tests [and] experiments" were "not done to please the public."[53]

And yet the negative consequences of "not pleasing the public" were very much on his mind. Polignac closed his letter to his brother with a melancholy musing:

Berlioz has been very much in style for some time with our Paris audiences. A festival in his memory, for the anniversary of his death, was put on at the Hippodrome, and had a great success.[54] The beautiful Septet from *Les Troyens* was encored. This piece breathes with poetry of the highest order—but also what weaknesses, what confusion, what inextricable bad taste. It explains, despite this posthumous success, why he had so much trouble getting his music played during his lifetime. Finally, *voilà,* he has arrived [i.e.: he has achieved success]; and it seems that, in this life, we can arrive only after we're gone.[55]

Chapter Four

"Nothing of the Usual Tonality"
(1880–1888)

Polignac began the next decade with a series of new medical crises: pulmonary attacks followed by strong chest colds, nervous fever, and chronic dizzy spells. He despaired of "the all-too-frequent days when I'm wounded, dribbling, and woozy" (*écloppé, baveux et vaseux*).[1] Ordered to a health spa in the Pyrenees by his doctor, he submitted with fatalistic resignation to a long regime of drinking the mineral waters. The abysmal state of his health did not prevent him from enthusiastically reporting to Ludovic a "very interesting piece of news for supra-lunar minds like mine": the discovery, on the planet Mars, "of rectilinear canals, 1,000–1,500 kilometers long, putting into communication all of the Red Planet's interlocking walls."[2]

Polignac's tendency towards introversion became more pronounced during the 1880s. Nonetheless, he was obliged, as a matter of social survival, to keep up his cycle of visits to relatives and friends. The frail prince especially dreaded the necessary sojourns to country homes, so often cold and drafty; "too much air for me," he would complain.[3] Other aspects of country life proved terrifying as well. One night, while Polignac was visiting relatives in Brittany, he was awakened by a strange noise. His nephew Melchior de Polignac heard him stumbling around in the hallway, calling desperately, "Melchior, it's Waterloo, it's Waterloo!" and thought he had gone mad. He found his uncle in the corridor, wrapped in his plaid shawls and clutching his mattress. It turned out that Edmond's light sleep had not withstood the hoof-taps of the horses, whose stables were just under the windows of his room.[4]

Usually, when visiting the homes of nonfamily members, Polignac would simply hide in his room for most of his stay, solitude being preferable to having to put on a forced smile with the guests, whom he referred to as "The Others." Often, he would entreat Montesquiou to accompany him on these outings, as a buffer. Montesquiou was a socially agile creature, and could easily keep up his end of the conversation, even while mocking his hosts behind their backs. Polignac was grateful for his friend's presence, although he deplored the very hypocrisy that lightened his own social burden. "I know that you always welcome my complaints with solicitude," he wrote to Montesquiou, "although you proscribe it during *mondain* rituals. . . . But why, like the Others, do you prefer the [artificial] "Jolly Good Humor" to the spontaneous sad cry? By any calculation I would prefer the cry."[5]

One country house where Prince Edmond's antisocial behavior was indulged with humor and affection was the Villa Bassaraba (often called "Amphion" for the town in which it was situated), the estate of pianist Princesse Rachel de Brancovan overlooking Lake Geneva. Every year, the princesse welcomed a large group of writers, musicians, and political and cultural figures to the villa, and Polignac was often among them. Prince Edmond's fantastical manner—considered by most, even the artistically inclined, to be "eccentric," provided no end of fascination for the Princesse de Brancovan's young daughters, Anna and Hélène. Little Anna—who would grow up to become the celebrated poet Comtesse Anna de Noailles—recalled the remarkable prince-musician, who seemed to the girls to be "invisibly crowned by Parsifal's angels."

> One sensed that the Prince de Polignac was bound by love with Carpaccio's Saint Ursula and Mozart's Dona Elvira. . . . His English blood gave to the curious person that was our friend his elegant height, a thinness that seemed to be made of ivory, an inperceptably disdainful ease, an attentive correctness, a negligently refined appearance that revealed an article of clothing of uncommon color, a vast and silky Indian handkerchief, deployed in the British manner, as if he were throwing a discus. . . .
>
> At Amphion, we saw him, in October, before lunchtime, pacing up and down the garden path lined with plantanes . . . and, in the whirlwind of falling leaves, both of us attached to his every step, we listened respectfully to this voice with the bitter and magical laugh, from whence emanated wisdom, like an enchanted fantasy.[6]

In 1883, the Polignac brothers relinquished the lease on the Rue de Berri apartment. Edmond rented an apartment one block west, at 39 Rue Washington. Apparently he found the change liberating. He made a concerted effort to promote his operatic works through performances at the Cercle de l'Union artistique.[7] In April 1884, he attempted once again to interest Jules Pasdeloup in performing "Pilate livre le Christ" at the Cercle (Pasdeloup apparently found particularly striking a short passage of the work featuring the whole-tone scale).[8] During the same period, Polignac brought a number of his piano pieces, songs, and choruses to Henri Heugel, editor of the weekly music magazine *Le Ménestrel* and director of a reputable music-publishing house specializing in educational texts and modern music. Heugel agreed to publish Polignac's music, with the proviso that the composer assume the design and printing costs.[9] Two volumes, *Mélodies et pièces diverses* and *Pièces diverses à 2 et à 4 mains pour piano*, were released in September 1884.

The year 1884 also marked the beginning of Polignac's friendship with Robert de Montesquiou's cousin, Vicomtesse (later, Comtesse) Élisabeth Greffulhe (1860–1952). Daughter of Belgian diplomat Prince Joseph de Caraman-Chimay and his wife Marie, née Montesquiou (Comte Robert's aunt), Élisabeth was as cultivated as she was beautiful. She was passionate about music, a trait inherited from her mother, who had studied piano with Clara Schumann and played chamber music with Franz Liszt. However, Élisabeth's parents lacked the financial means to provide their daughter with a suitable dowry. It was thus that, when the ultra-rich Vicomte Henry Greffulhe proposed marriage, the eighteen-year-old Élisabeth had no choice but to accept the offer. The match assured her financial future, but it trapped her in a stultifying milieu with a philandering, hot-tempered husband and his family, whose rigidly conventional mores were matched only by their total ignorance of the arts. And there was no escaping Henry's family: his mother lived with them in a gigantic mansion on the Rue d'Astorg in the 8th *arroundissement,* and his sisters and their spouses lived in adjacent, communicating townhouses.

Hungry for intellectual and artistic outlets, the young Vicomtesse established a salon in her palatial home, attracting the leading minds and talents of the literary, political, and musical worlds with her beauty and charm.[10] Its refinement and its exclusivity made the Greffulhe salon one of the most sought-after in the aristocracy. By dint of will, the Vicomtesse Greffulhe continued to educate herself artistically. She took up the piano again, and also learned the guitar; she studied photography with Paul Nadar and read voraciously the volumes suggested to her by her cousin Robert de Montesquiou, whom she regarded as her "cultural mentor."

It was through Montesquiou that she was introduced to Edmond de Polignac. Even though the prince was "so old" (over fifty), Élisabeth thought him charming, found his imagination "devilish" and his youthful flights of fancy "astonishing."[11] Polignac was equally captivated, and, thus, when Élisabeth invited him to join a large group of guests at her summer home in Dieppe, he accepted. Ordinarily, young women—even married women—were not allowed to spend time in the company of bachelors without a chaperone. But the prince and the vicomtesse so enjoyed each other's company that they dared to flout convention: they lunched alone, they dined alone, they went for long walks alone, they spent whole days together—alone. He read to her, they played four-hand piano music. They were both aware of the strangeness of the situation, but, while neither crossed the line of discretion, both pursued with ardor this platonic intimacy, for each recognized the other as a "soulmate."[12] Evidently, Henry Greffulhe was not bothered by his wife's new friendship; on the contrary, in an expansive moment, he offered to help Polignac financially to secure a performance of his music with the Orchestre Colonne in the forthcoming season, a prospect that filled the composer with joy.[13]

Polignac idealized Élisabeth Greffulhe; in his writings, he describes loving her in an exalted, spiritual way. Inevitably, he suffered disappointment: when engaged in earthly pursuits, the Vicomtesse was nothing like the girl of Polignac's fantasies. Like her cousin Robert de Montesquiou, she was a creature of society; she knew how to play to the hilt the role of *grande dame,* especially when entertaining a house full of guests. In an unusually frank letter, Polignac admitted to her that he disliked the "false self" that she presented in the "communal life" at Dieppe—"these lunches, these dinners . . . the endless daily social round"; he could not bear the fact that, in altering herself, chameleon-like, she became like the "Philistines" who surrounded her. "This permanent public exhibition of your persona . . . wounds me, wears me out."[14]

He did not refuse, however, when, in November, Élisabeth invited him to Bois-Boudran, the Greffulhe's country estate south of Paris, where Henry Greffulhe traditionally invited a large group of friends to spend the hunting season. Élisabeth never enjoyed these annual fall gatherings: when not attending to the needs of her husband and his cronies, she inevitably found herself lonely and without sufficient occupation. That autumn of 1884 she had the happy idea of inviting Polignac to keep her company. Anticipating the prince's aversion to being trapped in a country house amidst a pack of hunters, she enticed him with the promise of "a piano in his room and [being left in] peace." Polignac's visit proved salutary for both of them. "The presence here of Edmond de Polignac has changed Bois-Boudran for me," wrote Élisabeth to her mother. "He doesn't hunt; he works [on his compositions]. We go out from 9:30 to 5; we make music; we play the fugues of Bach, each of us playing one hand."[15] A few days later: "It seems as if I had already known him on some other planet. I like him very much; he is so rare."[16] And: "The Prince is charming and does well with the personal freedom accorded to him. Between us we have a language that excludes the others, who understand nothing at all."[17]

Polignac eventually made peace with his feelings of unrequited love for his "dream girl." He saw Élisabeth Greffulhe frequently, at her city and country homes and in public. But in his heart, he yearned to relive the moments of intimate spiritual and musical communion that they had shared at Bois-Boudran. In one letter, in which he sends regrets at not being able to join her at the Opéra for a performance of *Faust,* he writes, "Thank you for having thought of me, I who think so often of you, in my very precious and selective cerebral receptions, in which you appear in a beautiful gown: a vision, passing by, all alone, no longer closed up in a matrix of senseless social niceties, and thus receptive to good counsel and healing effusions."[18]

During this same period, Montesquiou became particularly attentive to Polignac, sending him a series of short notes with thinly veiled erotic undertones. The notes, penned in purple ink and often accompanied by newly written poems, were written in a nearly illegible, flowery script, as visually decorative as the language itself.[19] Copious references to music were often sexually suggestive: "Music sometimes drenches me like an ocean."[20] In one note, Montesquiou invited Polignac to accompany him to a performance of Wagner's *Meistersinger* in Brussels; not receiving an immediate response, Montesquiou sent another note mixing two languages, creating suggestive wordplay between the German "mund" (mouth) and the French "monde" (world)—and, at the same time, feminizing the name Edmond: "*Munde Edmunde,* haven't you taken my Wagnerian proposal seriously? It's for the beginning of next week. Reply quickly, so that I can provide myself with another companion in [the absence of] my *Edmonde monde.* Tuus meus, MF"[21]

Polignac was ill during that period, and travel was out of the question. But, that spring, his health improved, and, in June 1885, he and Montesquiou, in the company of their friend Dr. Samuel Pozzi, set sail for London. They attended the Handel Festival at the Crystal Palace, where they heard the oratorio *Israel in Egypt,* presented in honor of the bicentennial of the composer's birth. "The performance made a gigantic effect," wrote Edmond to Ludovic. "The 4,000 executants royally feted *le grand* Haendel."[22] Later that week, the three Frenchmen met writer Henry James, who squired the trio around the city, introducing them to Pre-Raphaelite poet Dante Gabrielle Rossetti and "aesthetic" artists Edward Burne-Jones and William Morris.[23] Polignac and company subsequently dined with celebrated painter James McNeill Whistler, who showed them the "Peacock Room" that he had designed for the home of Frederick Leyland.[24] They were also received at the home of Lady Brooke, where poet Algernon Charles Swinburne was present. Polignac was flabbergasted when Swinburne said, "I believe that my family is slightly related to you, and I'm delighted," to which the prince, who sincerely believed that talent always trumped a noble name, responded, "Believe me, between the two of us, the more honored by this relation is myself!"[25]

Polignac's friendship with Montesquiou deepened upon their return to Paris. The letters that fall between the two men affirm a strong, intimate friendship, cemented by their shared love of music, art, and poetry, and other possible bonds left unspoken. They used titles and phrases from their favorite poems as a coded language. Thus, when Polignac wrote that "you have understood my ambiguous phrases, from the beginning, by the efficacious grace of our secret affinities,"[26] he was making reference to Théophile Gautier's poem "Affinités sécrètes."[27] When traveling, Montesquiou would send the prince long, newsy letters, filled with witty wordplay and double entendres. Polignac cherished these letters from his "very precious Friend . . . my smile and my comfort in the bad days through which I pass."[28] In Montesquiou's absence, Polignac spent idle hours at the Jockey Club listening to the other men of his class engaging in mindless discussions about their two favorite topics: hunting and women. After overhearing one particularly odious conversation about the whores of Amsterdam, Polignac wrote to Montesquiou (on Jockey Club letterhead), "I'm blinded by the atmosphere, heavy with smoke and made heavier by the astonishing tone of the conversations. I'm up to my neck in this cesspool."[29] Some of Polignac's friends found his constant railing against the members of his class to be hypocritical. Baronne Annette de Poilly wrote to Montesquiou, "This animal Polignac . . . cries about the stupidity of worldly people, but he never refuses a dinner at the home of those whom he finds annoying in theory. Decidedly the stomach is a bad guide."[30]

The spring of 1886 brought some upturns of Polignac's musical fortunes. He was asked to contribute a choral work to a collection being offered to Pope Leo XIII; his offering was a simple but moving "Litanie de Notre Dame."[31] His "Les Adieux de Deïdamia" received a warm reception at the Cercle des Mirlitons.[32] And, in May of that year, Élisabeth Greffulhe hosted a full-length concert of Polignac's songs, arias, and choral music in her salon, a gesture of friendship and encouragement that surely thrilled the composer. It is possible that this salon concert had been offered as a form of recompense: Henry Greffulhe's promise to secure a performance of Polignac's music by the Orchestre Colonne had come to naught. It appears that no expense was spared to engage the musicians. The two vocal soloists, soprano Rose Caron and tenor Edmond Vergnet[33] were two of the Opéra's leading stars; they were accompanied by the chorus of the Société des Concerts du Conservatoire, two pianists,[34] and an organist. The program's eight pieces included first performances of two a cappella choral works on religious texts and "Queen Claribel's Aria" from *La Coupe du Roi de Thulé,* whose pyrotechnic cabaletta would have been a perfect diva vehicle for Caron.[35]

Polignac's modest musical successes had no impact on his precarious financial state. He continued to live on the meager income from his inheritance, receiving the occasional loan from his brothers. In July 1886 he almost committed to making an enormous expense that he could ill afford, when he bid at an auction at the Galerie Georges Petit on a new painting by Monet, *Champs de tulipes en Hollande.* To his astonishment, he was outbid by a young American woman, Miss Winnaretta Singer, an heiress to the Singer Sewing Machine fortune. He watched in helpless rage as she left with "his" painting.[36] Polignac's family and friends were astounded to hear of such a dramatically impractical action on Edmond's part, and raised once again the issue—indeed, the necessity—of Polignac's making a financially advantageous marriage. Shortly thereafter, the prince began courting a wealthy Brazilian woman named Madame Texeïro. Friends and family waited with anticipation for a happy announcement.[37] To facilitate the hoped-for alliance, Princesse Rachel de Brancovan invited the two parties to join a large number of guests at the Villa Bassaraba in September. As usual, the marriage "campaign" came to naught.[38]

However, the stay at the Brancovans' proved important to Polignac for other reasons: though he returned to Paris without a fiancée, he did come back with an idea for a new octatonic composition—inspired by a different woman altogether. While at the Villa Bassaraba, the prince had the occasion to hear the "unforgettable, ineffable voice" of one of the other guests, lyric soprano Comtesse Marie-Thérèse de Guerne (1859–1933). One of the outstanding musicians of the aristocracy, Madame de Guerne was renowned for her silvery voice and artistic mastery. She was one of Fauré's favorite interpreters of his works; Marcel Proust would some years later be so moved by her voice that he would immortalize it in a full-length article.[39]

The Comtesse became the inspiration for Polignac's next octatonic work, a "Prayer to Tanit," ultimately renamed "Chant à la lune" (Song to the Moon). The text was excerpted from Gustave Flaubert's steamy 1862 novel *Salammbô*, a work that had caused an uproar in Parisian literary circles when it was first published.[40] Flaubert's story of Salammbô, fictional daughter of the Carthaginian general Hamilcar and priestess of Tanit, is full of incense and color, idol worship, bloody battles, and smoldering sexuality.[41] The French fashion for "exotic" and Orientalist music within the context of Western composition had been well established through the popularity of operatic works like Halévy's *La Juive* (1835), Meyerbeer's *L'Africaine* (1865), and Saint-Saëns's *Samson et Dalila* (1877).[42] However, the music in these works fits squarely into French Romantic idioms, albeit with touches of modality and the occasional distinctive use of orchestral color. The spectacular subject matter of *Salammbô* lent itself easily to an over-the-top musical treatment,[43] and Polignac considered that his octatonic scales would be ideal in evoking both the ferocious barbarism and the steamy sensuality of the story. While still at the Villa Bassaraba, he sketched out plans for a musical setting, in seven sections, of several pages from chapter 3 of Flaubert's novel, envisioning "a musical production with a new accent . . . historic, ethnological, literary."[44] By time Polignac left the villa, he had completed the vocal line of one section (apparently the only section to reach completion): Salammbô's incantation, which depicts the priestess (as the composer described in a letter to Montesquiou)

> . . . praying at night on the terrace of the Palace of the Barea, prostrate before the Moon. Taanach, her servant-nurse, accompanies her on the nebel.[45] "The sounds follow, muffled and hurried, like a buzzing of bees, and, becoming more and more sonorous, they fly in the night with the sobs of the waves and the shivering of the tall trees, to the summit of the Acropolis." The nebel, here, will be replaced by a simple Pleyel [piano].[46]
>
> The voice, carried on the sacred names "Tanit, Baalet, Rabbetna, Derceto, Mylitta," etc., soon wafts plaintively, muffled from afar, then a terrible heart-rending outburst, in a monody (borrowed from my scales) that contains nothing of the usual tonality [*rien de la tonalité usuelle*].[47]

The manuscript of the octatonic "Chant à la lune" reveals a virtuosic vocal line, with frequent metric changes, long stretches of chromatic melisma, arabesque-like figurations, and daunting intervallic leaps, all derived from the octatonic scales.[48] Polignac wrote to Montesquiou that, after he had presented the soprano with her solo, "Madame de Guerne, at first startled and thrown off, wasted no time in applying her flexible and implacably accurate voice to the difficult and wide intervals of my musical canvas, which she will soon brilliantly ornament and illustrate."[49] And, indeed, by November 1886, when Polignac came to visit her estate near Douai, the Comtesse had already mastered the fiendishly difficult vocal line.[50] The composer began writing the orchestral accompaniment in December and continued his work through August 1887.[51]

The year 1887 marked the beginning of Polignac's friendships with two composers who would play an important role in Polignac's professional life, including the public dissemination of his octatonic music. The first was Eugène d'Harcourt (1859–1918), an aspiring composer from a distinguished aristocratic family. Twenty-five years younger than Polignac, he had studied composition with Massenet at the Conservatoire, and had continued his studies at the Berlin Conservatory. Recently he had received his diploma of Professor of Voice from the City of Paris. Harcourt was part of a younger generation of aristocratic composers such as Vincent d'Indy and Pierre de Bréville, who were less daunted by the constraints of their noble upbringing in the pursuit of their professional aspirations. That same year, Polignac also began what would become a warm lifelong friendship with Gabriel Fauré. Fauré had been engaged by Élisabeth Greffulhe—an ardent admirer of the composer and his first important patron—to organize and perform in her music salon programs, which were given throughout the spring on alternate Wednesday evenings. Polignac was a regular attendee of these soirées, where he and Fauré formed a mutual admiration society, both musical and personal.

On 2 July 1887, Polignac, Harcourt, and Fauré presented a joint concert of their works at a place called "La Châtaigneraie" (The Chesnut Grove).[52] Three of Polignac's orchestral works were performed, including *Robin m'aime,* an orchestral transcription of Adam de La Halle's 1240 pastoral, *Le Jeu de Robin et Marion.*[53] While the exact location of this bucolic-sounding grove—or the financial underwriters of the event—cannot be ascertained, the concert given that evening might have been the one that allowed Polignac to fulfill one of his greatest artistic dreams: to have his music heard outdoors. A curious notion, given Polignac's well-known dread of the country and its cold drafts! Nonetheless, a number of the composer's writings mention his wish to create a "musique de plein air"—an "open-air music"—that, in its freshness, naturalness, and color, took its cues from the "plein air" school of painting.[54] Polignac's "musique de plein air" would be mentioned in a 1903 article by Marcel Proust commemorating Polignac and his compositions. "Concert halls horrified him," wrote Proust. "Fresh air suited him better. The idea of music in the woods was beautiful to him. 'My motto in music is *plein-champs*' [out in the fields],' said the Prince de Polignac, even if he wasn't writing '*plain chant.*'"[55] Here, Proust is making a play on words: in French, "plein-champs" is homophonous with "plain chant."

Polignac and Fauré were together again later that summer, at the Dieppe estate of the Comtesse Greffulhe.[56] In his memoirs, painter Jacques-Émile Blanche recalled Greffulhe's extraordinary collection of guests that summer: "a royal court of art lovers in the outdoors: Helleu, Walter Sickert, Montesquiou, Gabriel Fauré; Edmond de Polignac, wrapped in blankets, watching them."[57]

Polignac and Fauré continued to see each other and encourage each other after their return to Paris. In December, Fauré wrote to Greffulhe, "I went recently to pay my respects to the very charming Prince de Polignac, still muffled up, still feeling the cold, and still full of enthusiasm. I found him in front of [the score of] the 'Siegfried Idyll'"[58] It may have been Fauré who encouraged Polignac to pursue the reissue of some of his songs.[59] Polignac was present at the Church of the Madeleine for the first performance, on 16 January 1888, of Fauré's new Requiem. Polignac described the music to Montesquiou as being "deeply moving."[60] A few months later, Polignac and Greffulhe joined forces to underwrite another performance of the work; the prince contributed a third of the funds.[61] With this financial aid, Fauré's Requiem was indeed performed again at the Church of the Madeleine on 4 May—this time, with additional instruments: two horns and two trumpets.

Around that time, Polignac made the acquaintance of Nélie Jacquemart-André, a society painter and the wife of Édouard André, a wealthy Protestant banker and arts patron. Members of the upper bourgeoisie, the couple lived in a sumptuous mansion, built on the then-new Boulevard Haussmann and completed in 1875. The Andrés decorated their home with gilt walls, tapestry panels, and Louis XVI furniture. Enthusiastic art collectors, they accumulated a breathtaking collection of Italian Renaissance and eighteenth-century French and paintings and objects.[62] In the spring of 1888 they decided to expand their artistic activities during the "season" by hosting a series of soirées, consisting of a banquet, followed by an after-dinner concert, and concluding with a *tour de valse*. Madame André asked Polignac to organize the concerts. Polignac wasted no time in involving Harcourt and Fauré. With the bountiful resources that Madame André put at his disposal, he was able to engage for the inaugural concert two celebrated soloists—tenor Emmanuel Lafarge and violinist Martin Marsick—and assemble an instrumental ensemble that conformed to his somewhat eccentric theories of orchestration. As he wrote to Montesquiou,

> We will have three pianos and around twenty stringed instruments. The orchestra is constituted according to my intentions and following my views, settled on long ago. Fauré will play one of the pianos . . . Eugène d'Harcourt is in charge of recruiting the players from among the young students of the Conservatoire. At the head of this young and docile phalange, we can see in these weekly gatherings the point of departure for some curious musical expressions."[63]

Among the "curious musical expressions" intended for presentation at the inaugural concert at the Jacquemart-André mansion was a new setting that Polignac had made of an excerpt from chapter 10 of Flaubert's *Salammbô*, based on two of the octatonic scales and entitled "La Danse du Serpent." Ultimately, Polignac incorporated the *Salammbô* music into an Orientalist suite in three movements: the work began with a "Hebraic" movement called "Marche des

Pasteurs d'Ephraïm—Chant du Hazzan"; next came an incantatory "Charmeur des serpents," followed by the serpent's dance that ended the work. The suite was scored for the aforementioned three pianos and string ensemble, plus tenor solo, two E-flat trumpets, two chromatic trumpets, four horns, and harmonium. On the back covers of the instrumental scores, Polignac wrote out the two octatonic scales used in the "Danse du Serpent"; this was probably for practice purposes, so that the instrumental players could better acquaint themselves with these strange scales. The text sung by the "hazzan" ("le chef des Pasteurs") combined phrases from Hebrew scripture ("Ani Adonai Eloechem") with others written in a curious *faux* Hebrew ("Barouch enbama chanéa Amnorayarou"). The three pianos were no doubt intended to approximate the jangling sonority of Oriental percussion instruments and chimes.[64] This entire Hebraic-Orientalist-Carthaginian mishmash was grouped under the general title *Échos de l'ancien Orient*. The printed program would call attention to the fact that the "Danse du Python" was based "on a new scale" (see Fig. 4.1).

For the same program, Polignac also decided to present his own orchestration of Wagner's *Kaisermarsch*, written in 1871 in honor of Wilhelm II. This was an audacious move on Polignac's part: for many French people, the nation's defeat at the hands of the Germans was still a fresh wound. Despite Wagner's championship by French musicians and the growing presence of French music lovers at the Bayreuth Festival, the German master and his music were still viewed with suspicion, and attempts to present the music of Wagner in concert usually resulted in whistling and booing in the hall and demonstrations outside.[65] As recently as 1887, a group of forty hecklers had disrupted a performance of *Lohengrin* by throwing stones and jostling the operagoers at the Eden Theater. Montesquiou advised his friend against arousing a "feuror Teutonicus,"[66] but Polignac decided to follow his own muse: "Your observations on the danger that I run in performing the Marche Teutonica are very sensible and judicious. I've thought it through, but am going on anyway. . . . I've already half-finished my work on the arrangement, which I've done too conscientiously not to have the benefit of the performance. And, when I look closely at Wagner's orchestration, I am completely overwhelmed by the logic and the sincerity of this work—and what clarity in this richness!"[67]

The night of the first concert, 14 May 1888, the audience was seated in the large music room; the guests must have had to crane their heads to watch the musicians, who performed from the balcony that ringed the music room on three sides. The Andrés' *soirée* had been publicized as one of the high points in the spring society calendar, and thus, the morning after the event, an article describing the evening's festivities in detail appeared on the front page of *Le Figaro*. The society columnist who wrote the article described the Jacquemart-André mansion as a "palace of high finance." As for the music, the columnist especially enjoyed violinist Marsick's rendition of Polignac's "Andante," as well as Harcourt's songs, which he found "fresh, dreamy, inspired." But he didn't

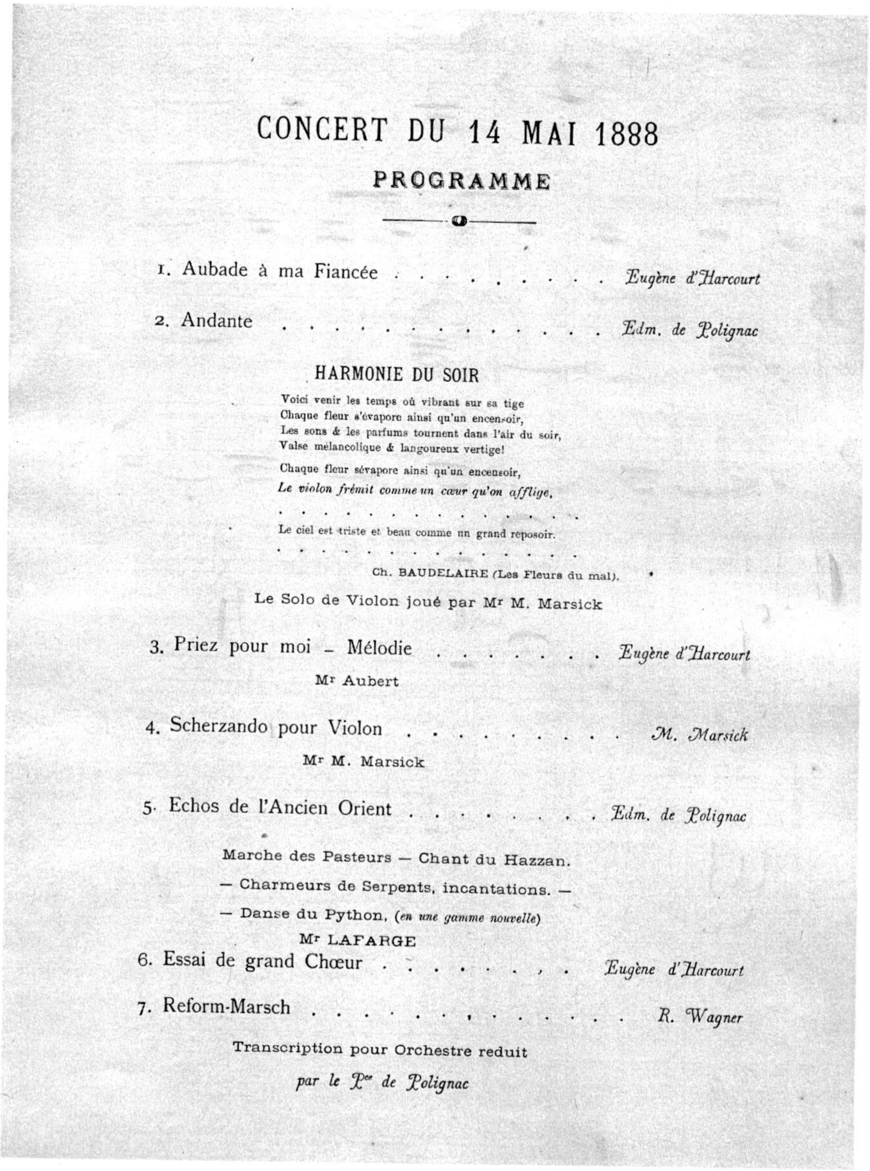

CONCERT DU 14 MAI 1888

PROGRAMME

———⬤———

1. Aubade à ma Fiancée . . . . *Eugène d'Harcourt*

2. Andante . . . . *Edm. de Polignac*

HARMONIE DU SOIR

Voici venir les temps où vibrant sur sa tige
Chaque fleur s'évapore ainsi qu'un encensoir,
Les sons & les parfums tournent dans l'air du soir,
Valse mélancolique & langoureux vertige!

Chaque fleur s'évapore ainsi qu'un encensoir,
Le violon frémit comme un cœur qu'on afflige,

. . . .

Le ciel est triste et beau comme un grand reposoir.

. . . .

Ch. BAUDELAIRE (Les Fleurs du mal).

Le Solo de Violon joué par Mr M. Marsick

3. Priez pour moi – Mélodie . . . . *Eugène d'Harcourt*

Mr Aubert

4. Scherzando pour Violon . . . . *M. Marsick*

Mr M. Marsick

5. Echos de l'Ancien Orient . . . . *Edm. de Polignac*

Marche des Pasteurs — Chant du Hazzan.

— Charmeurs de Serpents, incantations. —

— Danse du Python, *(en une gamme nouvelle)*

Mr LAFARGE

6. Essai de grand Chœur . . . . , . *Eugène d'Harcourt*

7. Reform-Marsch . . . . *R. Wagner*

Transcription pour Orchestre reduit

par le Pce de Polignac

Figure 4.1. Program featuring the works of Edmond de Polignac performed in the Jacquemart-André salon, Paris, 14 May 1888. Private collection. Used by permission.

quite know what to make of Polignac's compositions. Of the Orientalist suite, the columnist wrote, "It's sometimes great art, always original art. The *Échos de l'ancien Orient* contain the same hallucinatory intoxications that fill the books of Loti."[68] The columnist did not see fit to mention the Wagner transcription.

A more enthusiastic reaction to Polignac's music—and to the octatonic music in particular—was published by critic Alfred de Lostalot after a repeat performance of Polignac's work at the Conservatoire two weeks later. "*La Danse du Python* is written on a new scale where a whole step is invariably followed by a half-step," wrote the critic. "The artist had to overcome some almost insurmountable technical obstacles," he continues, "but the effort was nowhere apparent, and we took the greatest pleasure in listening to it."[69] Lostalot's review is important to the history of music theory, for not only does it introduces to the French readership "a new scale," but it records, for the first time in print, a description of the octatonic collection.

In June 1888, Polignac's "La Danse du Serpent," in a version for solo piano, was published in a music album of short works for piano offered by the daily newspaper *Le Gaulois* to its subscribers.[70] The editor of the volume, entitled *La Danse*, at a loss to describe Polignac's eccentric contribution, wrote in the introductory note, "Be certain that banality will never fall from his pen. He has audacity, even strangeness, and he is someone."[71] The equivocal praise of Polignac and his music notwithstanding, the publication of "La Danse du Serpent" is historically important: the "explanatory note" at the end of the piece introduces two of the three octatonic scales; it is the first appearance of these collections in print[72] (Fig. 4.2). A concluding "remark" reaffirms Polignac's linking of the scales with Orientalism: "The desired systematic exclusion, throughout the piece, of every conventionally tonal harmonic device can be justified by a logical bias towards avoiding, in the adaptation of a scene from the ancient Orient, our modern tonality, which took hold only after the fifteenth century of our era."[73]

The *Gaulois* album also included Gabriel Fauré's "Pavane," with *ad libitum* verses by Robert de Montesquiou, dedicated to Élisabeth Greffulhe. Montesquiou was in London at the moment that the album came out. The prince wrote to his friend, "I'm happy that we are together for the first time in the same pages"; remembering their stay together in London in 1885, Polignac waxed sentimental:

If you go to the Handel Festival, think of your old concert comrade. I think that it will *de rigueur* to go hear, in *The Messiah*, the "Hallelujah Chorus," a musical monolith; a mind such as yours, open to the vast horizons, should [be able] to take in the gigantic triangulations. . . .
Your present stay will probably not have the same perspective as the old one. However, in the midst of your current impressions, new but reflexive, you will recall, no doubt, our joining as partners and our nights at the hotel and your long tales of school life, and our joyful encounters with esthetic women. Your departure has brought all these events back to me as a sweet evocation. Memories, as they become more distant, become more poetic. . . .[74]

NOTE EXPLICATIVE

Ce morceau, conçu en dehors de la tonalité usuelle, ne comportant point d'armure connue à la clef, nous donnons ici, sur un intervalle d'octave, et pour éviter toute hésitation devant les accidents de notes, l'échelle fixe des sons employés à l'exclusion de tous autres (depuis le début marqué par (C) jusqu'à la lettre (A), **Sol** étant pris ici comme point de départ arbitraire ou tonique fictive) :

Échelle des sons: ou leurs identiques enharmoniques comme : pour etc.

Nous appelons cette série fixe de sons : Série ou Gamme C.

La lettre (A) marque un virement subit par l'entrée en une nouvelle série fixe de sons dont voici l'échelle pour une octave, **Ut** étant pris comme point de départ arbitraire sur l'échelle complète :

Échelle des sons: avec les enharmoniques : pour etc.

Cette nouvelle série fixe constituée symétriquement à la précédente, et sa congénère, sera désignée par : Gamme ou Série A, pour la distinguer d'une troisième série B, la dernière réalisable sur notre échelle tempérée, et non employée ici.

La lettre (B) marque une succession d'accords ascendants dont la partie supérieure procédant par tons entiers, s'écarte par conséquent du processus constitutif de l'une ou l'autre des deux séries fixes précédentes, C ou A.

Puis, en (C') retour à la Gamme C du début, en laquelle le morceau conclut.

(REMARQUE). L'exclusion systématiquement voulue de toute formule harmonique tonale usuelle, au cours de ce morceau, pourra se justifier par un parti-pris logique d'éviter, en adaptation à une scène de l'ancien Orient, notre tonalité moderne qui ne prend date guère antérieurement au XVᵉ Siècle de notre ère.

Figure 4.2. Polignac, "La Danse du Serpent," solo piano version (*La Danse*, 1888), explanatory note at the piece's conclusion.

Chapter Five

The Unexpected Woman (1889–1894)

J'étais triste et pensif que je t'ai rencontrée;
Je sens moins aujourd'hui mon obstiné tourment.
O dis-moi, serais-tu la femme inespérée,
Et le rêve idéal poursuivi vainement?
O, passante aux doux yeux, serais-tu donc l'amie
Qui rendrait le bonheur au poète isolé?
Et vas-tu rayonner sur mon âme affermie,
Comme le ciel natal sur un cœur d'exilé?

—Charles Grandmougin

In 1889, Polignac took up a new avocation: politics. Inexplicably, he became involved in Boulangism, a popular movement whose hero was General Georges Boulanger. Boulanger had been a hero of the Franco-Prussian War and the Paris Commune; however, in subsequent years, as Minister of War, his extreme anti-German attitudes (which included instigating a ban on performances of *Lohengrin* in France) put him afoul of the pragmatist government, which was trying to maintain a shaky peace with Germany. After being dismissed from the Army, Boulanger formed his own conservative political movement, which advocated revenge on Germany, restoration of the monarchy, and revision of the Constitution. Boulangism gained the support of various factions of the collective Right wing: the Church, conservative members of the business and financial community, the dispossessed aristocracy, and the royalists—in short, all those who had opposed the Republic and yearned for a strong figure who could stand up to Bismarck. But Boulanger was even attractive to some people with more liberal penchants, like Polignac. Many intellectuals and members of the disenfranchised younger generation had lost confidence in the political regime, and felt themselves to be living in an intellectually and spiritually bankrupt society. Boulanger was able to acquire the dimensions of a national savior, a sort of modern-day Joan of Arc. National elections were being held in 1889, and *boulangiste* candidates were present in every region of France.

It is not clear how Polignac came to join forces with Maurice Barrès (1862–1923), the writer–political philosopher who was at the origin of the "Culte du Moi," (1889–1891), and Paul Adam (1862–1920), a novelist and one of the founders, in 1884, of the Decadent movement. But somehow these gentlemen, new converts to Boulangism,[1] managed to convince Polignac to run on the Boulangist ticket for the third constituency in Nancy in the elections of the Chamber of Deputies. The campaign was not easy for Polignac. Answering public questions about his political positions caused some embarrassments. In Lorraine, on the campaign trail, his name was misunderstood by the crowd, and caused someone to yell, "Vive la Pologne!"[2] On another occasion he made a speech at a public gathering where he was forced to espouse some rather insincere platforms. One worker demanded to know if he was a socialist, to which he replied, "Why, how could you have doubted it for an instant?"[3] Finally, the whole ordeal became too fatiguing for Polignac, and he renounced his participation for the Deputy seat. Barrès, who went on to win the election (he would serve as Deputy of Nancy until 1893), wrote a good-humored letter to the prince: "I just want to thank you and to tell you that, perhaps, probably, if you hadn't abandoned the struggle, we would have been three revisionists in Nancy. . . . I won't forget what we owe you."[4]

His political career behind him, Polignac returned to composition. He continued to experiment with octatonicism, filling a notebook (labeled "Cahier No. 3") and dozens of loose pices of staff paper with themes and "études" employing the three scales. These jottings reveal Polignac's continued creative linking of octatonicism with Orientalist themes.[5] A substantial number of these pages include sketches for a project whose subject was the mythological Pan. Polignac apparently was attempting to develop a "Hellenic" sound by harmonizing octatonic melodies with dyads consisting solely of perfect intervals. these experiments were placed in an envelope bearing the title "Harmonies de 2 sons de 5tes et de 4tes, Genre 'Grecques'—Thrénies PAN Orgiastiques et processus Hébraïques" (Harmonies of Two Sounds [i.e. dyads] in Fifths and Fourths, 'Greek' style—Orgiastic Threnodies of Pan and Hebraic Progressions").[6]

Polignac continued to seek out performance venues for his works. In early 1890 he conceived the idea of proposing *La Coupe du Roi de Thulé* to Italian opera houses. He seems to have reasoned that if he changed the subject and altered parts of the original French libretto, and then had the altered libretto translated into Italian, the Italian companies would not be obliged to pay foreign authors' rights to the French Ministry of Fine Arts, thus making it more attractive for production. To that end, he engaged Marquis Achille de Lauzière de Thémines, a renowned libretto translator and one of the most respected music journalists of the late nineteenth century,[7] to translate *La Coupe du Roi de Thulé* into Italian. The translation was completed in May 1890.[8] Apparently, nothing came of the project.

Every so often Polignac's works were played in the salons and at the Cercle des Mirlitons. Probably encouraged by Fauré, Polignac joined the Société Nationale de Musique, founded in 1871 by Camille Saint-Saëns and Romain Bussine with the goal of promoting the music of French composers; in addition to Fauré, the original membership included Chausson, Duparc, Chabrier, Dukas, Franck, and Massenet; in the late 1880s and 1890s, younger composers like Debussy and Ravel joined the ranks of the organization. Through the Société Nationale de Musique, Polignac got to know Vincent d'Indy, an ideological firebrand of a musician, who suffered none of Polignac's conflicts about being of noble birth *and* a professional composer. D'Indy became president of the Société Nationale de Musique in late 1890;[9] the following February, he notified Polignac that his "Chant de Blancheflor (complainte gothique)" a chamber work for mezzo-soprano, two violas, cello, and piano, had been accepted by the organization's program committee for performance on its March concert. The Société Nationale de Musique would provide the string players; Polignac could choose his singer and pianist.[10] Fauré agreed to play the piano part, and recommended a singer, the mezzo-soprano Rachel-Pascaline Leroux-Ribeyre. Polignac, in a tizzy at the thought of his music being performed publicly for the first time in years, thanked his friend in a self-deprecating letter:

> Dear friend, I was afraid to ask you to perform the kind service of accompanying my Romance. I was quite touched . . . shall I say even a bit overcome with emotion (these are decidedly the first symptoms of the senility and stupidity that encroach). I was able to get myself *completely* back together only at the thought of all the embellishments [that you would make] at the piano, and I found the vision really majestic and marvelously upstart-like!!! So thank you—you will be the fish that will make my lousy sauce palatable. I'm touched and honored.[11]

The performance of the "Chant de Blancheflor" took place on 9 March 1891 at the Salle Érard, on a program that also included works of J. S. Bach, Fauré, Chausson, Paul Vidal, and Franck.[12] Polignac's work received a guardedly positive review from Julien Tiersot in *Le Ménestrel:* "While the form is not readily apparent upon first hearing, the composition is not without character. Mme Leroux-Ribeyre sang it with a great deal of charm and talent."[13]

In the early 1890s, Polignac became involved in two important new musical organizations. The first was the brainchild of the Comtesse Greffulhe. In 1889, on the advice of Montesquiou,[14] she had organized a performance of excerpts from Handel's *Messiah,* under the auspices of the Société Philanthropique (a charity presided over by her brother-in-law, Prince d'Arenberg). The event was an artistic and financial success, and awakened Greffulhe to her capabilities as an active force in the realm of public *mécénat* (patronage). The next year she founded the Société des Grandes Auditions Musicales de France, whose goal was "to assure in our country the primacy of French works, an honor too often reserved for foreigners."[15] She enlisted the participation of conductor Charles Lamoureux, whose name brought prestige to the enterprise. Edmond de Polignac was invited to join the administrative committee of the new organization, a role that he accepted with pleasure. In fact, the new Société was, for all intents and purposes, a one-woman operation; Polignac's role was limited to talking up the new enterprise and attending the performances, beginning, in 1890, at the Théâtre de l'Odéon, with the first French performance of Berlioz's opera *Béatrice et Bénédict.*

Polignac played a more active role as a member of the founding committee of the Société des Chanteurs de Saint-Gervais, created by choral conductor Charles Bordes in 1892; the other committee members were d'Indy, organist Alexandre Guilmant, and musicologists Bourgault-Ducoudray and André Pirro. Bordes had been a student of César Franck. In 1890 he was appointed *maître de chapelle* at the Church of Saint-Gervais. That same year, inspired by the Abbé Perruchot, who held the post of choirmaster at Notre Dame des Blancs-Manteaux, he began an exploration, through study and performance, of the works of Palestrina. His passion for this music grew to include all the great polyphonic liturgical music of the fifteenth and sixteenth centuries. Bordes sought to revive public interest in this music so that it could take its rightful place in the Catholic liturgical repertoire of Holy Week, and to dispel the notion that it was antiquated and arcane, something to be relegated to the domain of historians. To this end, and with the excellent choir of Saint-Gervais at his disposal, he and the committee planned an ambitious program of sixteenth-century a cappella music for Holy Week 1892, including works by then-forgotten composers Palestrina, Victoria, Josquin, and Orlando de Lasso.[16] If Polignac had not been previously acquainted with these composers, he was surely eager to know their music, and his deep knowledge of Baroque music surely made him a valuable member of the Committee and an ardent spokesperson for the Société in the aristocratic community.

His involvement with these worthy musical endeavors allowed Polignac to avoid serious examination of his precarious financial state. In the past, his brothers had kept an eye on his finances; now that they were both living abroad (Camille in Austria and Ludovic in Algeria), and with no income resulting from the occasional performance of his compositions, Polignac fell into a descending spiral of debt. His nephew Melchior recalled that his uncle's upright nature "*swallowed* very easily, *hook, line, and sinker,* whatever some fast-talking types might say to him, and he was often the victim of his own rectitude and credulity. It was thus that, little by little, he ate up his small fortune in *excellent investments,* recommended by the *cleverest* people."[17] It is not clear that Polignac was actually receiving poor financial advice; it seems more probable that he was simply incapable of managing his money, even the small sums necessary for quotidian upkeep. By 1892, he was living hand-to-mouth, relying on the occasional check from Camille to pay for the bare necessities.[18] Naively, he apparently hoped that the wealthier members of his family might offer their financial support. "But nothing—silence and zero," Polignac wrote in despair to his nephew Guy,

> not even the vaguest allusion in the middle of my tiring struggles and unjust worries; [instead,] manifold dippings into holy water from court, or tactlessly

calling attention to their luxury with "my ease comes before your needs," coldly underlined. . . . They should have understood or should understand, however, that, even more than them, I've brought honor to my name, by myself, and added to it.[19]

It would not have occurred to him that many of his conservative relatives viewed his musical activities as an embarrassment, and viewed him, personally, as a hopeless eccentric.

Help did come, from an expected quarter. Polignac's nephew, Comte (later Marquis) Guy de Polignac, was eighteen years younger than his uncle. His marriage to Louise Pommery, who had ascended to the directorship of her family's celebrated champagne-producing house, brought the couple an enormous fortune. Guy was a warmhearted family man, and a great music lover. He too had suffered from the disdain and hypocrisy of the close relations who had disapproved of his marriage with a woman from the bourgeoisie, and could sympathize with Edmond's ostracism by those closest to him.[20] By chance he and his brother Melchior paid a visit to Edmond in the last days of January, just at the moment when the latter was living through his darkest moments. Melchior recalled the visit:

> One day we found him huddled in his armchair, his forehead covered with a knitted cap. He was warming his feet in a melancholy fashion. Not one piece of furniture in the antechamber, the paintings in the salon were gone, and there was not one chair for us to sit in! We inquired gently . . . he made a circular gesture: "Gone!" and another quick horizontal one: "Seized!" Then, in a deep voice with two fingers squeezing his neck: "Strangled by the creditors!" And then he began to laugh.[21]

Guy's heart went out to his impoverished uncle, and he sent him an unsolicited check for five hundred francs, with a promise to loan him a total of 125,000 francs. The money enabled the elderly prince to reclaim his possessions, and assured him a decent nest egg on which to live.[22] To show his appreciation, Edmond de Polignac offered his nephew the one thing that he still possessed: a ticket to a choral concert of fifteenth- and sixteenth-century music, one of a series of concerts to be sung during Holy Week by the Chanteurs de Saint-Gervais, under the direction of Charles Bordes.[23] This turned out to be a "hot ticket," historically speaking. Bordes's ambitious program—a full concert of a cappella music by Palestrina, Victoria, Josquin, in addition to two motets by J. S. Bach—was the culmination of 150 rehearsals with the choir (a responsibility shared with d'Indy) and an indefatigable campaign to attract subscribers and publicity.[24] Thanks to the support of *Le Figaro*'s editor-in-chief, François Magnard, the Holy Week concert received front-page newspaper articles. The press coverage generated excitement and word-of-mouth publicity in both avant-garde and high-society circles. Suddenly, Bordes's enterprise and Bach's music had "snob appeal." The Holy Week concert series enjoyed sell-out crowds. This unprecedented success garnered Bordes and the Chanteurs an enthusiastic following for their future endeavors. The Société des Chanteurs de Saint-Gervais would evolve, two years later, into the Schola Cantorum, directed by Vincent d'Indy.[25]

Polignac probably discussed his financial crisis with Robert de Montesquiou, who in turn related the details to Élisabeth Greffulhe. The cousins echoed the exhortations so often pressed upon him by his family: in order to stave off future financial calamities, he must marry a wealthy woman. The name proposed to Polignac was that of ultrarich Singer Sewing Machine heiress Winnaretta Singer.

Daughter of American sewing-machine industrialist Isaac Singer and the Parisian-born Isabella Boyer, Winnaretta was the twentieth of her father's twenty-four children.[26] She had led a peripatetic childhood, living first in the suburbs of New York, then in Paris, followed by eight years spent on a sumptuous estate in Devonshire, England, and finally back in Paris following her father's death in 1875. The household, filled with Winnaretta's five siblings and numerous stepbrothers and stepsisters, was a lively center of music making and artistic activity. The young girl studied piano and painting from an early age, and often participated in family musicales and theatrical productions. She adored her imaginative, boisterous father, but found herself in constant conflict with her vain, social-climbing mother. The death of Isaac Singer left his widow and all the Singer children spectacularly wealthy. Isabella Singer moved her minor children back to her hometown of Paris, hoping for financially advantageous connections for her sons and socially advantageous marriages for her two daughters—and for herself. In 1879 the still-beautiful Madame Singer remarried a handsome and charismatic Belgian violinist, Victor-Nicolas Reubsaet. Reubsaet had always claimed that a lapsed aristocratic title existed in his family background. With his wife's fabulous wealth at his disposal, he "rediscovered" *two* titles; in 1879 he reinvented himself first as the Vicomte d'Estenburgh and, in 1881, as the Duc de Camposelice.

Now a full-fledged duchess, Isabella pursued social ascent in Paris society. She and Victor bought a double quartet of Stradivarius and Guarnerius stringed instruments, and created a music salon in their home that featured repertoire for those instruments, played by Paris's finest musicians. As a consequence, Winnaretta became familiar during her teenage years with the great works of the chamber music literature. She studied piano with a respected teacher, Émile Bourgeois (who, coincidentally, had been among the performers at the 1886 performance of Polignac's works at the home of the Comtesse Greffulhe). Often Winnaretta was called upon to accompany her vocalist mother and her violinist stepfather when they performed in home concerts. In the 1880s Winnaretta and her family began to spend part of each summer in Normandy, in the environs of fashionable Deauville. The region was home each summer to a group of friends, all artists and musicians, which included painter Ernest Duez and composers Gabriel Fauré and Roger Jourdain. The studios and salons of this group were often the settings for performances of Fauré's songs, piano pieces, and piano quartet, and Winnaretta was present as some of these recitals. From the first time she heard Fauré's works, Winnaretta was full of enthusiasm for this music "worth comparison to the analogous works of Chopin and Schumann."[27] During the same period she added a new composer-hero to her personal pantheon: Richard Wagner. In 1882 Isabella took her daughter to the Bayreuth Festival, at a time long before the mania for Wagner's music had seized hold of the French. From the moment she first heard the music of *Parsifal,* Winnaretta became a confirmed Wagnerite.

As attracted as Winnaretta was to music, it was the decision of her mother that she make art her main focus. Winnaretta was sent to study painting with Félix Barrias, a Prix de Rome winner and a respected faculty member at the École des Beaux-Arts. Another visual artist in the Camposelice social circle was caricaturist Jean-Louis Forain, whom Winnaretta accompanied on his frequent trips to the Louvre. Open to new artistic discoveries and trends, the young woman came to greatly admire the works of "avant-garde" artists like Édouard Manet and members of the new Impressionist school, painters who found few advocates during that period. The influences of these cutting-edge artists found their way into Winnaretta's well-made, compositionally interesting canvasses, some of which were accepted in the spring Salons des Beaux-Arts.[28]

Winnaretta's involvement in art and music became a psychological shelter from the tensions in her homelife. The Duc de Camposelice was a man with a volatile temper. Rumors circulated about the possibility of violence within the opulent mansion on Avenue Kléber. It is quite possible that Winnaretta suffered sexual abuse at the hands of her stepfather. She did not tarry in her mother's home any longer than necessary: as soon as she reached the age of majority, she seized control of her Singer inheritance—at that time worth more than a million dollars—and moved out. Shortly thereafter she purchased a large property, upon which were situated two houses, at the corner of Avenue Henri-Mandel and Rue Cortambert.

Winnaretta knew that she could not circulate in polite society as a single, unchaperoned woman. She had to worry about her safety, her fortune, and her reputation. Few choices were open to her, and she opted for the most obvious one: she married. Her choice of mate was Prince Louis de Scey-Montbéliard, the third son of a respected Protestant aristocratic family. Beginning in the Second Empire, it had become more commonplace for the daughters of rich bankers and industrialists—including American industrialists—to marry young European noblemen. Everyone profited from these marriages of convenience: the coffers of the impoverished aristocrats were refilled, and the young women, known as "dollar princesses," added titles to their names. If Winnaretta had thought that she could put up with a marriage of convenience, she soon realized that she had erred in her belief. The 1887 marriage of Winnaretta Singer and the Prince de Scey-Montbéliard was not a success. For whatever reason, it seems that Winnaretta was not willing to fulfill the traditional connubial obligations of a young wife. It is quite possible that the abuse that she suffered from her stepfather permanently rendered heterosexual relations impossible for her. Whether she had yet acknowledged the attraction to women that made her a "famous" lesbian in her later years is not clear. In any event, for the sake of appearances, she and her husband kept up socially imposed appearances for four years.

Shortly after her marriage, Winnaretta established a music salon in her home. During the Belle Époque, when public concert programs featured predominantly the work of German composers,[29] the promotion of contemporary French music owed much to salon culture. Gabriel Fauré is an example of a composer who could directly attribute his success with the larger public to the reputation that he gained as composer and pianist in the musical salons. As a consequence, it was not unusual for many of the hostesses to feel a proprietary interest in the artists and composers whose music provided the sheen and the sparkle in these brilliant gatherings. As both friend and composer-pianist, Fauré was a familiar presence in Winnaretta's salon, and their correspondence indicates that she took a proprietary interest in "her" composer.[30] Fauré introduced her to his other musical friends from the Société Nationale de Musique, including d'Indy, Franck, Pierre de Bréville, and Emmanuel Chabrier. It was this last whose sparkling personality, and equally sparkling music, especially charmed Princesse de Scey. Chabrier, who earned his living as a functionary in at the Ministry of the Interior, had struggled mightily to make his works known to the public, but had enjoyed only intermittent success; with the exception of his 1883 orchestral work, *España*, Chabrier's music was thought to be too modern and advanced for most tastes.[31] His most recent opera, *Gwendoline*, had been rejected by the Opéra de Paris, but Winnaretta was attracted to the work's voluptuous, almost Wagnerian, harmonies. To Chabrier's delight, she offered her salon for a presentation of excerpts of his opera, and further offered to invite her contacts in the opera world to the performance.[32] This "backer's audition" of *Gwendoline* took place in Winnaretta's salon in May 1888, with the vocal parts sung by stars from the Opéra; the chorus and the orchestra from the Concerts Lamoureux, accompanied the singers, joined by Chabrier at the piano, Fauré at the harmonium, and d'Indy and Messager playing the timpani.[33] A sizable number of women from the nobility were in attendance, and *Le Figaro* reported the soirée of 22 May as being "*très brillante*."[34]

By 1889 the Princesse de Scey-Montbéliard had gained a reputation not only as a woman of fortune with sophisticated musical tastes, but also as an enlightened *mécène* (patron) of music. In addition to supporting organizations such as the Société Nationale de Musique,[35] she also made her home available to individual composers, such as Vincent d'Indy, whose new piano trio was performed in her salon in July 1889.[36] In 1890, having decided to devote a substantial portion of her fortune towards the promotion of modern art and music, she commissioned the first of a series of artistic projects that she intended to be associated with her salon. The first commission was given to ceramicist Jean Carriès, who was asked to create a monumental vault for the interior of the *atelier,* which—rumor had it—would house a manuscript of Wagner's *Parsifal.* The entrance to the vault was to be called "La Porte de Parsifal."

After four years of an unhappy marriage to the Prince de Scey-Montbéliard, Winnaretta decided that she could not remain in that situation. In 1891 she left her husband; in March of that year she obtained a civil divorce, and left Paris to spend several months in Venice. Gabriel Fauré, who had become a cherished and trusted friend, was among the visitors who stayed in her rented *palazzo* in May and June. At that point still unknown to the Paris music public, and exhausted by his stressful life as a Parisian free-lance musician, Fauré found much-needed repose in Venice. The convivial atmosphere of the Piazza San Marco and the seductive qualities of the lagoons inspired the composer to to write a series of *mélodies* on poems by Paul Verlaine. Although three of the songs were completed only after Fauré's return to Paris, the cycle, one of the composer's most beloved, came to be known as the *Cinq Mélodies de Venise.*

It would soon become clear that, like the Comtesse Greffulhe, Winnaretta viewed patronage and organization of musical and artistic events as a calling.[37] During the period between her separation and her annulment, Winnaretta remodeled her two adjoining houses on the corner of Avenue Henri-Martin and Rue Cortambert in Paris's 16th *arrondissement.* The reconstruction included the creation of an *atelier* designed for painting and music making, equipped with a custom-built organ from Paris's premier organ builder, Aristide Cavaillé-Coll. Winnaretta intended the new space to become the heart of the house, a center for the most up-to-date manifestations of art and music, brilliant enough to attract the cultured elite of Paris society. She offered Fauré a commission of 25,000 francs for a new work on an (as-yet unwritten) text by Verlaine to be performed for the inauguration of the *atelier.*

Even as she planned to relaunch herself in society, Winnaretta understood that her divorce had put her in a precarious social position, and that it was necessary to form new and powerful alliances to bolster her reputation. To that end, she engineered an introduction to the socially powerful Comtesse Greffulhe. The Comtesse found Winnaretta to be intelligent and musically sophisticated, her questionable social rank notwithstanding.[38] Winnaretta expressed a keen interest in attending the performances of the Société des Grandes Auditions Musicales, and, with a contribution of 10,000 francs (the same amount as Greffulhe), she became a "lifelong member"[39] of the Société. She was subsequently invited to attend the Comtesse's party on the island in the Bois de Boulogne on 21 July 1891.[40] A concert given that evening included works by some of Winnaretta's favorite composers—J. S. Bach, Wagner, and Fauré (including the Fauré-Montesquiou *Pavane,* arranged specially for the occasion for dancers, chorus, and orchestra)—as well as a charming orchestral piece, *Robin m'aime,* by a composer at that time unknown to her: Edmond de Polignac.[41]

Winnaretta attracted Montesquiou's attention through her attendance of the performances of the Société des Grandes Auditions Musicales and some of the music salons of the aristocracy. Montesquiou came to see her as an ideal spouse for his friend Polignac: she was wealthy, she was as passionate about music as the prince—and she was not sexually interested in men. Polignac realized that he and Winnaretta had already met on an occasion that he would have preferred to forget: it was she who, several years earlier, had outbid him at auction for the purchase of Monet's *Champs de tulipes en Hollande;* that day, he had been forced to watch in helpless frustration as the canvas was carried from the room.[42] However, that was the past. Given his current impecunious state, the potential benefits of the match were not lost on Polignac. He went to discuss the matter with the Comtesse Greffulhe, who recalled his visit in her memoirs. "Turning his back to the fireplace, he said to me: 'I have something very important to say to you. Could you present my marriage proposal to Madame Singer, whom you know? It's understood that, in this plan, she doesn't have to expect anything but a *mariage blanc* (nonsexual marriage)— that is to say, I'll have my room and she'll have hers; but our artistic interests will help us both mutually, and I hope to make her happy through the admiration that we both have for the arts.'"[43] Greffulhe accepted her friend's request to act as go-between with Madame Singer. The following strategy was devised: Polignac should try to speak to Winnaretta alone when they both happened to be attending the same musical salon, and make at least some tentative forays into the subject of matrimony. Polignac, who had still not completely come to grips with the idea, was dubious about his own ability to bring about the desired conclusion. He had been a single man his whole life, he wrote to Montesquiou, and "the age arrives when, in female questions, it's wise to say to myself: 'quieta non movere [don't upset the peace].'"[44]

As it happened, the prince-composer found an approach that, unbeknownst to him, was probably the surest way to this particular woman's heart: he engaged her intellectually and musically. A performance of his song "Lamento" (discussed previously in chapter 2) was scheduled for 5 April 1892 at the Cercle de Mirletons. Polignac sent Winnaretta an invitation to the performance; with his letter he sent a copy of the score, accompanied by a note:

I hasten to send you an entry card for tomorrow's Tuesday's concert, very happy that you will honor me with your benevolent presence. . . . I permit myself to send you the piece that you will hear, sung by Madame Caron. This is the original version, which I was obliged to ornament with embroidery in the accompaniment, according to the spirit of the day. There is, noticeably, in the third verse, "Les Belles de Nuit demi-closes," an artifice that I believe to be almost unique in the Music Literature, consisting of having heard, underneath the melody, the initial motive, in the chorus (*bouche fermée*) and the orchestra simultaneously, in . . . four different note values.[45]

As is suitable for suggestive and simple words, the musical color lends itself rather to the Diatonic Oriental Latin [scale],[46] rather than German romantic chromaticism, which is perhaps too exclusively practiced today, and, all things being equal, the Diatonic Latin will always work better. Excuse me, Madame, for this very pedantic digression. I risk passing before you as a "professional," as I know you avoid them.[47]

What might have been regarded as an odd kind of seduction letter by any other woman worked perfectly for Winnaretta. And how could she have failed to be moved by the beauty of this song, with its haunting text by Théophile Gautier, one of Polignac's most perfect compositions? Perhaps the mysterious connection between the two was established from that moment.

By coincidence, Winnaretta happened to contact Montesquiou during this period, seeking his advice on the decoration of her new *atelier*.[48] He agreed to help her, and as a consequence, the two saw each other frequently in the spring months of 1892. During this period, Montesquiou expressed his keen desire that Winnaretta speak with the Comtesse Greffulhe, whose as-yet unidentified "ideas" were, he assured Winnaretta, in complete concordance with his own.[49] Winnaretta was intrigued, but also amused, by the secrecy in which this "important" meeting was shrouded. Because of her summer travels, the tête-à-tête with Greffulhe was postponed until late in the fall of 1892, when the two women met at Montesquiou's house on Rue Franklin.[50] Here, Greffulhe presented Polignac's proposal. She laid out all the reasonable arguments in favor of the match: Winnaretta needed to consider her social position, which had been compromised by her divorce. Even though Polignac was much older—thirty-one years separated them—a marriage to the prince would ally her with one of the oldest and most distinguished aristocratic families in France. And, Greffulhe surely hinted (discreetly), Winnaretta could continue to lead her personal life as she wished, without the imposition of sexual demands that she had had to endure from the Prince de Scey-Montbéliard.

Slowly, tentatively, Winnaretta and Polignac got to know each other better. To their shared amazement and delight, a bond of friendship and affection quickly grew between them. Their common musical tastes—the operas of Wagner, Renaissance and Baroque music, music of the avant-garde, like that of Debussy—were only a jumping-off point. For Winnaretta, Edmond de Polignac was an equally imaginative, but a frailer and sweeter version of her father. She loved his fantastical tendencies, his eccentricity, and his inventiveness—but there was nothing to fear from his sexuality. In Winnaretta, Polignac found a true equal, a strong and level-headed woman who could understand him and support him—intellectually, emotionally, and musically. Perhaps he showed her his latest octatonic experiments: sketches with titles such as "Greco-Oriental Threnody" and "Funereal Theme (a bit Egyptian)."[51] For Winnaretta's twenty-eighth birthday, he presented her with a solemn "Exercise for organ," composed on octatonic scales.[52]

Figure 5.1. Winnaretta Singer, Prince Edmond de Polignac, and Comte Robert de Montesquiou, ca. 1893. Private Collection. Used by permission.

And yet, in spite of this important new attachment—or perhaps because of it—Polignac revisited with great nostalgia his intimacy with Montesquiou: letters to the Comte written during the same period that he was courting Winnaretta indicate that Polignac was still in the younger man's thrall.[53] (See the portrait of Polignac, Montesquiou, and Winnaretta [with back turned], Fig. 5.1). And it also seemed that, despite his role as marriage broker for his friend, Montesquiou had no intention in releasing his emotional hold on Polignac. In 1892 and 1893 he plied his friend with letters and books of his poetry, newly published. One volume, *Le Chef des suaves odeurs*, appeared in early 1893. The title is itself a paean to Polignac: the phrase "le chef des odeurs suaves" comes from Flaubert's *Salammbô*. One of the poems, entitled "Effusions" (Bursts), is dedicated to Edmond de Polignac. It describes a beautiful flower that can bloom only in darkness, and whose intoxicating odor allows the moon to illuminate the night sky.

Confidence d'odeurs, aveu de l'aromate
Dans l'obscurité bonne et l'éveil ténébreux,
Vous ressemblez au coeur qui point ne s'acclimate
Qu'à la douceur tranquille, ombrageux et peureux

Mais qui s'ouvre tout grand sous l'invite de l'ombre
En parfums plus flagrants s'il furent contenus
Loin de l'après-midi bruyante et qui s'encombre
De vaporisateurs trop indiscontenus.
. . . .
Quand la Lune aux bords blancs, le grand vase d'albâtre
Qui fume de nuage et brûle froidement
Versant de sa paroi, votre ardeur violâtre
Lui permet d'encenser enfin le firmament
Quand tout est solitaire, invisible et dormant . . .[54]

(Confidant of odors, confession of the spice
In the good darkness and the cloudy awakening,
You resemble at heart that which can never be acclimated
Except in tranquil, cloudy, and fearful sweetness

But which opens wide under the invitation of the shadow,
In perfumes more flagrant for having been contained
Far from the noisy afternoon, and which obstructs itself
From too-continuous sprays.
. . . .
When the Moon with white borders, the great alabaster vase,
which smokes with clouds and burns coldly,
[is] spilling past its surface, your purplish ardor
permits it, finally, to shower praises upon the firmament,
when all is solitary, invisible, and sleeping . . .)

Montesquiou's thoughts may have revolved around Polignac's sexuality, but by time the volume of poems appeared, Polignac was already moving away from his complicated friendship with the Comte. Perhaps he saw in his relationship to Winnaretta a chance to achieve a kind of emotional and spiritual purity that could never be achieved with Montesquiou. That summer, while Winnaretta was in Bayreuth, Polignac wrote to her:

> You flatter me excessively in according to me this exceptional certificate of Goodness. I don't know if I deserve it. Perhaps I'd prefer a spike of perversity, which is always less banal. Now it's perhaps you who inspires this goodness in me; in any case, I fervently hope that you will always keep close to you (in the middle of torrents and ravines, blue lakes and society parties, across time and distance) the memory of an attachment (reasonable and unreasonable) that nothing can attenuate.[55]

In November 1893, fifty-nine-year-old Edmond de Polignac proposed marriage to twenty-eight-year-old Winnaretta Singer, and she accepted him.[56] The reactions of the families were mixed: Polignac's brothers found Winnaretta delightful, but the more conservative members of the Polignac family were unhappy about Edmond's alliance with an American divorcée, even an ultrarich one: she was not one "of their people." (They did not hesitate, however, to warn Winnaretta that she was marrying an "unbearable maniac." [57]) As for the Singers, they found the prince charming, if a bit incomprehensible; Winnaretta's sister, Duchesse Isabelle Decazes, wrote, "I'm dying to get to know him better, but he intimidates me so much that I shall never dare to speak to him."[58] Edmond de Polignac and Winnaretta Singer were married on 15 December 1893 by the Abbé Broglie in the Chapelle des Carmes, with only a small number of family members from both sides present.[59] As the Polignac princely title had originally been granted by the Vatican, Pope Leo XIII sent his blessing to the couple.

Paris society was fascinated by the notion of this match. Painter and diarist Jacques-Émile Blanche recounted the reaction of his mother when Polignac came to announce his engagement. "To prove that he was still 'marriageable,' [Polignac] galloped around the terrace; his clothes swam on him—checked pants and a Second Empire alpaca vest. Feet together, he jumped over a chair, crowing, 'You can say that you saw me jump like a racehorse.' [Said Blanche's mother,] 'So now we shall have the marriage of the sewing machine and the lyre.'"[60] Writer Edmond de Goncourt, who visited Edmond and Winnaretta some months after their marriage, wrote that Polignac had "the air of a drowned dog," and that Winnaretta had a cold, cutting beauty, the beauty of the daughter of a sewing-machine manufacturer."[61] He wrote, "They say that the marriage between these two was arranged on the condition that the husband not enter his wife's bedroom, netting him a sum of money that will permit him to mount performances of his music, which the opera houses don't want."[62]

The greatest malice, however, spewed forth from Robert de Montesquiou, who was dismayed when the cynical marriage of convenience that he had orchestrated evolved into true affection. Much worse a betrayal was the fact that the couple apparently did not demonstrate enough *gratitude* to him for making possible their newfound happiness. Although he had been one of the very few nonfamily members invited to the wedding, he claimed to have never received the invitation. Élisabeth Greffulhe reported the purported slight of her cousin to Polignac, who wrote to Montesquiou, "I affirm that the letter bearing your name was sent by the person in charge of delivering it. I wanted to inform you of this *right away*, so that you don't suppose any negligence on my part, and that you will receive—as it suits you and as it suits me—the assurance of all my regrets."[63] Upon the reception of such a cool, impersonal response, Montesquiou was enraged. From that point on, he took every opportunity to cut down the couple as publicly as possible. A malicious story began to circulate (later recounted by writer André Germain): Montesquiou and Polignac had made a bet as to whether the Comte could successfully arrange a match with Winnaretta Singer. The loser would pay the sum of 100,000 francs to "the greatest poet of our time, Verlaine," who, during this period, was suffering from his addiction to absinthe and was frequently hospitalized. "The deal—or rather, the marriage— was made, to the great stupefaction of the two parties. . . . The Prince paid the agreed-upon sum. And, [said Montesquiou], 'Naturally I kept the 100,000 francs, but I gave Verlaine a very beautiful Charvet scarf.'"[64] Upon hearing the story, the Polignacs cut off relations with the Comte. Montesquiou continued to make mischief, attempting to turn their common friends against the couple.[65] Among his *Quarante Bergères* (Forty Shepherdesses), a collection of satirical poems about the ladies of the aristocracy, one of the most scathing verses is entitled "Vinaigrette,"[66] a take-off on the name Winnaretta. How much of this vengeful attitude was wounded pride, and how much an actual sense of loss and regret, can never be known: Montesquiou was so narcissistic and so committed to an ethos of artificiality that it is not clear whether he could have ever admitted to himself how much Polignac had meant to him. Thirty years later, in his memoirs, he would recall their 1885 trip to England in this way: "I had dragged along with me an old traveling companion, who I thought loved me (and who has since proved to me that I was quite wrong.)"[67]

As for Polignac, if he had any regrets about leaving the companion of his "*affinités secrètes*" behind, he never revealed them, at least in any form left to posterity. He loved Winnaretta, and was probably relieved by the patina of "normalcy" that marriage afforded him. How proud of him his mother would have been: he had finally succeeded in marrying a rich woman! In public, Edmond joked that now that he had married the American woman who had walked off with "his" Monet canvas, he could sit and look at the painting to his heart's content.[68] What Montesquiou had conceived of as a marriage of convenience blossomed into a true love match between two kindred spirits.

Figure 5.2. Gabriel Fauré, Edmond de Polignac, and Winnaretta Singer-Polignac. Private collection. Used by permission.

During their seven-year marriage, the Prince and Princesse Edmond de Polignac created a loving home, a manifestation of their deep bond, consecrated through music. The most powerful symbol of their union was the music salon they created together; the nonstop music-making that took place in their house was the daily expression of their vows. Within weeks of their marriage, the Polignacs began to host musical gatherings in the *atelier*. The first of these were "organ evenings," during which Paris's great organists (Alexandre Guilmant, Charles Widor, Louis Vierne, and Eugène Gigout, among others) came to perform on Winnaretta's Cavaillé-Coll organ. In the months that followed, vocalists and instrumentalists came to offer songs and chamber music. Contemporary French music was performed as frequently as the standard classical and Romantic repertoire.[69] Fauré, as both family friend and "house musician," was often on hand to play his own works and participate in the general festivities (see Fig. 5.2). The *atelier* gradually gained a reputation as an ideal place for composers to present first performances of their new pieces. Early music was given a prominent place in the Polignac salon as well: the *atelier* was equipped with a harpsichord that Edmond had inherited from his parents, and Paris's foremost early-music performers were engaged to perform rarely heard treasures of the Renaissance and Baroque eras.[70]

The Polignacs' championship of early music extended beyond their salon: in early 1894, they underwrote a series of performances of Bach cantatas by Charles Bordes, organist Guilmant, and the Chanteurs de Saint-Gervais.[71] The performances took place at the Salle d'Harcourt, built in 1892 by Polignac's old friend Eugène d'Harcourt. The enterprising young composer had had the hall constructed at his own expense and subsequently mounted a series of popular concerts of diverse and unusual repertoire, conducted, for the most part, by Harcourt himself.[72] The Polignacs' Bach cantatas series was successful from every standpoint: it attracted large audiences, eager to hear this rarely performed repertoire, and garnered praise from the press.[73] In gratitude and friendship, Harcourt included Polignac's music in his Wednesday night "popular concerts" series at the Salle d'Harcourt; one such program, performed in March 1894, included Polignac's lively *Tarentelle* for orchestra.[74]

Polignac's music often took center stage in the "intimate" surroundings of the Rue Cortambert *atelier*, where, with one hundred guests in attendance, the composer heard his music performed by top-rank singers and musicians. Madame de Saint-Marceaux, Winnaretta's old friend, and doyenne of the music salons, was present one night when "Winnie accompanied a chorus by Polignac on the organ. She was delightful and very kind in the way she brings her husband's best qualities to light."[75] And it was not just Winnaretta who accompanied her husband's music: Fauré, a longtime friend of both Polignacs and a sincere admirer of the prince's compositions, often served as a collaborator in performances of his friend's music.

Winnaretta assiduously courted the editors of both *Le Figaro* and *Le Gaulois*, to promote both her salon and her husband's music. The *Figaro*'s editors, François Magnard and Gaston Calmette, became the Polignacs' social friends, attending their dinner parties and musical gatherings.[76] Soon both *Le Figaro* and *Le Gaulois* were reporting these gatherings as being "highly sought out in Parisian high society."[77] Polignac's compositions were described as the "highlights" of many Polignac gatherings. In the next—and last—seven years of his life, Polignac would find himself lauded in the press as "a composer who honors musical art."[78]

Chapter Six

Alexandre de Bertha and the Guerre des gammes (1894–1896)

The happiness that Polignac had been enjoying during the first two months of his marriage came to a grinding halt on 24 February 1894. On that day he happened to open the January 1894 issue of *La Nouvelle Revue*, a magazine devoted to literature and the arts. Perusing its pages, he came upon an article entitled "Un Système de gammes nouvelles" (A System of New Scales), written by a Hungarian composer-musicologist, Alexandre de Bertha.[1] The text was based on a lecture on the same subject that Bertha had given at his home three months earlier, on 27 November 1893—just as Edmond de Polignac and Winnaretta Singer were making preparations for their wedding—before an erudite audience of composers, performers, musicologists, and critics.[2] In the texts of both the lecture and the article, the author revealed and described his recent invention: three scales, which he dubbed "the enharmonic scales," where a whole step invariably follows a half step. Despite their misleading nomenclature—for Bertha does not use the term "enharmonic" according to the commonly understood definition of the term—Polignac recognized Bertha's "invention" to be *his* "chromatico-diatonic scales," that is to say, the octatonic scales.[3]

A fringe figure in Paris music circles, and a zealous Hungarian nationalist, Alexandre de Bertha was born Sándor Bertha in Pest in 1843. Much of what is known about him comes from a long and astonishingly inflated, self-serving article in three parts devoted to Liszt.[4] At age thirteen Bertha was so inspired by hearing Liszt conduct two symphonic poems at the National Theater of Pest that he decided to devote himself to Hungarian music. After studying "modern piano music" (Moscheles, Chopin, Alkan, Thalberg, Liszt, etc.) with Antoine Feley, he took up the study of harmony in 1859 with Michael Mosonyi, a Liszt disciple. In 1860 he published two "popular Hungarian songs" in *Zenészeti Lapok* (Feuilles musicales), Hungary's first music journal. In 1863 Bertha moved to Germany, where he studied with Franz Richter and Hans von Bülow. The following year he arrived in Paris, but his antipathy towards French music led him to confine himself to Hungarian circles. In Paris, he was presented to Liszt; he later accompanied the older composer to Rome and joined his group of students. Despite his newfound proximity to his idol, Bertha was wounded to discover that he was not among the master's favorites; worse, Liszt's willingness to frequent high-society German and Austrian "oppressors" revolted Bertha's ultranationalist sensibilities. The more

Liszt appeared to "exalt the neo-German aesthetic," the more disillusioned Bertha became. At least in part, this was sour grapes: Bertha was evidently insulted by the fact that Liszt was not particularly interested in him as a musician, evinced by the fact that Liszt was doing little to advance the younger man's career as a composer or pianist.[5] The final blow came when Liszt voted against him in 1878 during the Exposition Universelle when Bertha sought to participate in the jury for the Hungarian section. Polemic articles were exchanged. The two men did meet up again in Paris in 1886 and, according to Bertha's article, they reconciled only a few days before the death of Liszt on 31 July of that year. Despite the professional setbacks mentioned above, Bertha enjoyed some success as a musicologist. He wrote numerous articles on Bohemian and Hungarian music, two of which were included in Lavignac's *Encyclopédie de la musique*.[6] His compositional output was less distinguished: it consisted mostly of short piano works: *airs hongrois*, waltzes, polonaises, an "Andante religieux," and similar pieces.[7] While most of these works were diatonic, a handful of them, especially the several *csárdáses*, were written on the "Hungarian scale" and incorporated the two augmented seconds that were trademarks of the scale.[8]

While no documentation exists to explain the process that led Bertha to *his* octatonic epiphany, it can reasonably be assumed the influence of Liszt and Liszt's harmonic procedures played a major part in the process. Some manipulations of the Hungarian scale could very easily produce the whole-step/half-step pattern. Unlike Polignac, Bertha did not view his octatonic discovery as radical, but as a middle ground between the diatonic and chromatic scales. Rather, it was his frustration with what he perceived as "a halt in the development of harmonic progression" and "the abuse of the modern use of dissonance"[9]—especially in the music dramas of Wagner—that inspired him to create "special scales" that could "marvelously express the floating psychological state of our era."[10]

In January 1894, Bertha's lecture was published, in slightly modified form, in *La Nouvelle Revue*. Bertha's article, in a sense a treatise, covers much of the same ground as Polignac's from fifteen years or so earlier, and in a manner that is more fleshed out and written with more polish (Figure 6.1 reproduces the page on which he introduces the new scale).[11] If Polignac's treatise was intended to be a handbook for composers, Bertha's apparent goal was to reach scholars of musical aesthetics and pure theory. (Although Bertha writes a few chord progressions demonstrating the harmonic use of the collection in his treatise, these never ended up, apparently, in any full-length compositions.) From a theoretical standpoint, there are several important differences between the two treatises. First, Bertha deals more extensively with the two different forms of the scale, the one beginning with a half step/whole step and the other beginning whole step/half step (Fig. 6.2), and he provides useful names for them, *première homotone* and *deuxième homotone* (*homotone* meaning "same tonic").[12] Bertha discusses at length the shared pitch content among the three transpositions of each form—four common tones between scales A and B, and the remaining four between scales

nous familiariser autant avec les demi–tons que nous le sommes aujourd'hui. On peut même prétendre qu'ils expriment à merveille l'état psychologique si flottant de notre époque. Donc les prendre à leur tour comme unité pour la construction des gammes nouvelles nous semble être tout indiqué. En tenter au moins l'essai doit séduire tout homme tourmenté par l'idéal.

II

On compte cinq tons et deux demi–tons dans une gamme diatonique majeure et trois tons, une seconde augmentée et trois demi–tons dans une gamme diatonique mineure. Si l'on divise maintenant chacun de ces tons en deux demi–tons, la seconde augmentée en trois, on obtient pour chaque gamme un total de douze demi–tons, qui se retrouvent ensemble dans la gamme chromatique.

La division de ce total en parts égales est depuis longtemps usitée dans l'harmonie, comme le prouvent les accords de *septième diminuée* et de *quinte augmentée*, le premier ayant un quotient de trois et le second de quatre demi–tons. Il en résulte que chaque note dont ils se composent peut être considérée comme basse fondamentale par suite de changements enharmoniques subis. Étant identiques dans plusieurs tonalités, il n'existe du premier accord que trois formes et du second que quatre.

Avec des précédents semblables, si l'on conclut à la possibilité d'une gamme symétrique, on ne peut pas être taxé d'aberration. Car ayant des demi–tons tempérés entièrement à notre disposition — comme il a été dit plus haut — grâce à l'habileté de nos exécutants et à la perfection de nos instruments, et reconnaissant que leur répartition actuelle n'a rien de régulier, qu'est-ce qui nous empêche de les grouper dans une progression arithmétique, en alternant les demi–tons seuls avec la réunion de deux demi-tons en un ton et *vice versa*, c'est-à-dire :

$$\frac{1}{2} + 1 + \frac{1}{2} + 1 + \frac{1}{2} + 1 + \frac{1}{2} + 1$$

$$\text{ou } 1 + \frac{1}{2} + 1 + \frac{1}{2} + 1 + \frac{1}{2} + 1 + \frac{1}{2}$$

combinaisons, qui donnent également un total de douze demi-tons? Et effectivement des gammes pareilles, construites sur

Figure 6.1. Alexandre de Bertha, excerpt from "Un Système de gammes nouvelles" (*La Nouvelle Revue* 86 [1 January 1894]): 128

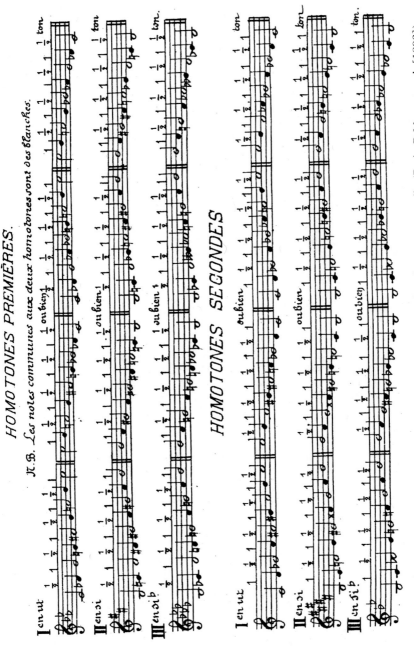

Figure 6.2. Alexandre de Bertha, excerpt from page 3 of *Essai d'un système de gammes nouvelles* (Paris: P. Mauret, n.d. [1893])

A and C, and the consequent implications for harmonic relationships: "It's not only because of their mixed sonority that we have assigned a place to the 'enharmonic scales' between the diatonic scales and the chromatic scales; their theoretical structure borrows their constituent elements equally from both."[13]

When Polignac read Bertha's article in *La Nouvelle Revue*, he recognized Bertha's "enharmonic scales" as his own "chromatico-diatonic" scales. Outraged, he sent a letter to the editor of *Le Figaro*, railing against what he considered to be theft of his artistic property.

> I assert my rights of absolute priority regarding the invention and the application of these same scales, recalling that the 1888 Musical Album of the *Gaulois* published a piece by me, entitled "Danse du serpent," composed using these scales. An explanatory note following the piece gave two noted examples their mode of formation and their designation by the letters A, B, and C, a designation borrowed from my study notebooks on the theory of these scales and their application, studies dating well before the publication of the *Gaulois*. Also, as the *Gazette des Beaux-Arts* of 1 June 1888 confirms, in its "Musical Chronicle," signed A. de Lostalot, the employment of these scales was heard in diverse concerts, and I judge, by this fact, the public to have been sufficiently informed.[14]

Bertha did not see the situation from Edmond's point of view, and his acerbic response was published in *Le Figaro* some days later:

> It was through mathematical combinations that I found the enharmonic scales and I've never heard of the signer of the letter. My ignorance is shared by Messieurs Ambroise Thomas, Marmontel *père*, Joncières, Pougin, Mangeot, Marchesi, de Dubor, etc., who paid me the honor of attending my lecture on 27 November 1893, as well as Messieurs Diémer, Eymien, Lavignac, and Soubie [*sic*], to whom I showed my publication at a later date.
>
> It is strange that no musician before me noticed the possibility of arranging tones and semitones symmetrically. It is a fact that is within reach of everybody.
>
> It's quite another thing to deduce a complete system, determining the resources that this new arrangement of intervals furnishes to melody, harmony, and counterpoint. I have under my eyes neither the *Gaulois* album nor the article by M. de Lostalot, but I'm sure that nothing similar is found there; this specialized kind of work cannot be found in the framework of either a society album or a newspaper article. My essay . . . is devoted particularly to these scales and is the fruit of several months of research.
>
> So, if the signer of the letter in question was lucky enough to recognize the possibility of a new arrangement of intervals as long ago as 1888, I am very proud, since this proves that I was not wrong. But he should also grant that the system of enharmonic scales belongs to me entirely and that I have the right to disseminate information about it, just as he had the right not to follow up on his inspiration of 1888.[15]

The two men faced off that spring in a battle of dueling treatises, presented before the prestigious French Académie des Sciences and subsequently published in the proceedings of the Académie as new discoveries in the field of "Musical Acoustics."[16] Bertha's paper was read first, in May 1894; he presented concisely the basic qualities of the scales in their two forms.[17] Polignac, as respondent, was put in the unhappy position of defensively reclaiming his right of priority, harking back once again to the 1888 publication of the scales in *Le Gaulois.*[18] To Polignac's frustration, Bertha was permitted to have the last word: in a follow-up presentation to the Académie des Sciences, he conceded that, indeed, Polignac had been the first to publish two of the scales in 1888, in their half-step/whole-step (*première homotone*) form; however, asserted Bertha, the fact that he had been the first to study and expose the *second homotone* (i.e., whole-step/half-step) form of the scale gave him the right to claim authorship of "the entire property."[19]

Some months earlier, Winnaretta had made a pragmatic proposal to her husband: as a live performance would make a deeper impression than any amount of theoretical debate: why not let the public hear the octatonic compositions, and let the power of the music speak for itself? She organized the performance of a charity concert (to benefit an orphanage) at the Salle d'Harcourt, the centerpiece of which would be Edmond de Polignac's octatonic music. The date was set for 17 May 1894—four days before Bertha was to present at the Académie des Sciences. *Le Figaro* reported in its advance publicity that "the program is very interesting, and contains an extremely curious work by the Prince de Polignac: 'Pilate,' written on a new scale that makes a very gripping effect."[20] The names of all the "dames patronesses" and artistic notables (d'Indy, Tissot, Bréville, Barrès, Forain . . .) who had already reserved their seats were listed on the front page.

The concert program, which included works by Clément Janequin, Fauré, and Wagner, opened with "Pilate."[21] The reporter for the society column of *Le Figaro,* while noting that "the concert obtained the huge success deserved because of this good [*charitable*] work and the superb program," made no particular mention of any of the music.[22] But at least one composer in the audience was impressed by Polignac's work: four months later, Gabriel Fauré wrote to Princesse de Polignac, "What is the Prince doing? Is he working? I don't know if he is aware of the real impression that his 'Pilate' has made on people who are not *imbeciles!*"[23]

The prince was indeed working: enthused by finally having heard "Pilate" performed by a large chorus and full orchestra, he was in the process of revising and correcting that score and the score of the other (partially) octatonic movement from 1879, "Ruine du temple prédite," with an eye towards having the two works published as part of a complete Passion oratorio. Apparently he had decided to scrap the idea of setting to music the "Caiaphas" and "March to the Calvary" texts for which he had also made sketches in 1879, and was looking for material for a third, concluding movement. Sketches dated July 1894 indicate that one possible inspiration was an octatonic motive based on "Arab songs heard at La Belle Fatma."[24] The final product ended up being not nearly so interesting: the movement composed to complete the oratorio was a rather bland, non-octatonic work entitled "Christ à Gethsemani" (The Garden of Olives), based on Matthew 28. The three movements were gathered together as an oratorio for baritone solo, chorus, and orchestra. Borrowing from the title *Échos de l'ancien Orient*, under which three of his Orientalist pieces had been performed at the André salon in 1888, Polignac gave the oratorio the revised title *Échos de l'Orient judaïque*. It was apparently Polignac's wife who financed the first, private printing of the three pieces; the works are dedicated to "Madame la Princesse Edmond de Polignac."[25]

Meanwhile, Alexandre de Bertha had also been working. In 1895 he expanded his octatonic treatise into a three-article series in *Le Ménestrel*.[26] "Experiments have demonstrated," wrote Bertha, "that the scales enrich melody and harmony with new colors. . . . The real harmonic originality of the new scales stems from the surprising manner in which one can group together . . . all the eight major and minor chords on the second degree, thus producing a logical and agreeable bringing together of the most distantly related chords, disconcerting the wisest harmonist . . . so attractive and unforeseen is the sonority."[27] In the third installment of the article, Bertha makes an important connection with the past:

> Citing the finale of Beethoven's F-major *Variations on a Theme of Süssmayer*, where the main theme is reproduced on the four major chords from the common notes from the two *homotones* (F–Ab–B–D), and recalling an identical progression that Rossini uses in the finale of *Guillaume Tell*, it proves . . . that unconscious allusions to the new system are not lacking in the music of the great masters.[28]

After the publication of this article, Bertha seemed to abandon the octatonic argument in public forums. None of his later compositions bears any trace of his "discovery." After Bertha's death in 1912, Henri Heugel, editor-in-chief of *Le Ménestrel*, wrote in the "Nécrologie" column, "Bertha had dreamed up, thirty years or so ago, a new musical system, the details of which I no longer remember, although he spoke to me about it at length on diverse occasions."[29]

Polignac, on the other hand, would continue advocating for and composing sketches based on "his" scales right up to his final days. And, from 1894 until the last months of his life, he would have the good fortune of hearing his octatonic experiments made audible.

Chapter Seven

Years of Plenty (1894–1899)

Part of what drew Edmond de Polignac and Winnaretta Singer together when they first met was their mutual love of the music of J. S. Bach and Wagner, both of whom were considered "cult" musicians in late nineteenth-century France.[1] But their marriage also made possible a fruitful expansion of their knowledge of musical repertoires previously unknown to each of them, as well as introductions to musicians in Paris associated with those repertoires. In particular, Polignac introduced his wife to early music, and Winnaretta introduced her husband to the music and musicians of the younger generation. As a consequence, the musical taste and sophistication of each one grew. Throughout the almost eight years of their marriage they managed successfully to form friendships and useful alliances in conservative and progressive artistic circles alike. Individually and collectively, Edmond and Winnaretta would serve as important mediators between the various musical camps in Belle Époque Paris.

Polignac was deeply involved with the founding of the Schola Cantorum. It may have been the prince who, in 1893, introduced Bordes to Eugène d'Harcourt; Harcourt subsequently provided his concert hall and musicians to Bordes and Paul Dukas for a series of twelve "historical concerts," at generously reduced rates.[2] On 15 June 1894 he joined d'Indy, Bordes, Alexandre Guilmant, and Bourgault-Ducoudray in announcing a platform that supported the "restoration of Gregorian chant . . . [and] honoring so-called Palestrinian music as a model of figured-bass music that could be associated with Gregorian chant," as well as "the creation of a modern religious music repertoire, respectful of the text and the laws of the liturgy, inspired by the Gregorian and Palestrinian traditions."[3] Polignac served first as a member of the founding and organizing committee, and then as a vice president.[4] During the first year, he was involved with finding a building suitable to house the program's new school, as well as participating in concert programming, competition juries (for "Gregorian, Palestrinian, and modern music"), and fundraising.[5] Between 1895 and 1901, the Schola provided numerous opportunities for performance of Polignac's sacred choral music, written in the contrapuntal style and modal orientation favored by the society. Abbé Perruchot, the choirmaster at Notre-Dame des Blancs Manteaux who had introduced Bordes to the music of Palestrina, was impressed with Polignac's incorporation of plainchant style into his compositions, and asked him to compose "a little 15th-century-style chorus for the distribution of prizes to the young female music students."[6] During those same years, Charles Bordes became a de facto contractor for the Polignac salon. As a result, many

Figure 7.1. Edmond de Polignac and his niece, composer Armande de Polignac. Private collection. Used by permission.

performances by the Chanteurs de Saint-Gervais and faculty and students of its school took place in the Polignac salon. Surely the most significant presentation of major early-music repertoire in the *atelier* took place on 23 April 1895, when Bordes led soloists and the Chanteurs de Saint-Gervais in performances of Schütz's *Dialogo per la Pasqua* and Rameau's 1739 opera *Dardanus*.[7] At that time, the Schola Cantorum's building lacked a performance space, and the Polignacs invited composers associated with the Schola to perform their pieces in the *atelier*. There were familiar reasons as well as musical ones to support the Schola: Polignac's niece Armande de Polignac (Camille's daughter), a talented musician, was receiving musical training there, studying composition with d'Indy.[8] Since childhood, Armande had maintained a special bond with her composer uncle. The photograph (Fig. 7.1) shows them together in the Polignac *atelier*.

Polignac's alliance with a musical organization that represented everything conservative, patriotic, and pro-clerical did not impede him from associating with the "other side." Since her young adulthood, Winnaretta had frequented the circles of the avant-garde, and was nonplussed by the less-than-refined behavior of some of its denizens. It was thus that Polignac came to meet some extraordinary creative individuals that he would never have encountered in the more genteel aristocratic salons. By the end of 1894, the Rue Cortambert *atelier* had already come to be known as a bastion of musical progressivism. Winnaretta also introduced her husband to the artistic and musical salons of her friends. Her favorite of these were the "Fridays" of Marguerite "Meg" de Saint-Marceaux on Boulevard Malesherbes, where the atmosphere was decidedly casual and where admittance was based on artistic, musical, or scientific achievement—not social standing.[9] In the comfortable, unpretentious Saint-Marceaux living room, friends were free to break up into groups, while the hostess herself sat absorbed in her reading. The artists would huddle in a corner to engage in a friendly "painters' quarrel"; Fauré would sit at the piano, playing for no one in particular; tenor Maurice Bagès might ask whatever pianist was available to accompany him in the songs of Schumann or Pierre de Bréville; Emma Calvé would sing without ever leaving her chair.[10]

In February 1894, the Polignacs were introduced in the Saint-Marceaux salon to Claude Debussy, whose striking appearance and "faunlike features" were accentuated by the small plain hooped earrings he wore during that period.[11] It is highly likely that, on that same evening, Debussy played before an audience for the first time excerpts of his new opera, *Pelléas et Mélisande,* based on the symbolist play by Maurice Maeterlinck. Meg de Saint-Marceaux noted in her diary that Debussy's music "is a revelation. Everything is new. The harmony, the writing, and everything remains musical."[12] It is disappointing that no account exists of Edmond's reaction to this seminal modernist work. At the Saint-Marceaux salon, the Polignacs also made the acquaintance of Fauré's brilliant young student, Maurice Ravel. Ravel was subsequently invited to attend musical gatherings in the Polignac salon; in 1899, he would surprise Winnaretta by dedicating to her his newly written *Pavane pour une infante défunte.*[13] Ravel was one of the first French composers to write octatonic music (his 1901 *Jeux d'eau* is the first of many compositions to feature prominently the octatonic collections—including a C-major/F♯-major juxtaposition of triads that foreshadows the "Petrouchka" chord).[14] While it is known that Ravel had come into contact with contemporary Russian composers using the "Rimsky-Korsakov scale," it is also tempting to speculate that the young composer might have been inspired to delve into octatonicism after spending an evening in the Polignac salon, listening to the prince hold forth on the subject of "his" scales.

Another regular at those Fridays was a shy young writer named Colette, newly married to the brilliantly witty arts journalist Henry Gauthier-Villars, known as Willy. As the wife of the best-known music critic in Paris, Colette served her "apprenticeships" in the city's concert halls, salons, and literary and artistic cafés, often taking notes of her experiences.[15] Both Polignacs appear in her recollection of the Saint-Marceaux salon. Colette found Winnaretta, with her high-necked dress and "character of indestructibility" intimidating. But she found Edmond de Polignac "charming, young in spirit, like a big ironic bird." Colette noted how, in order to stave off his habitual chilliness, he would seek out the best-heated corner of the room and wrap himself in a beige vicuna shawl that served to warm, alternately, his thin shoulders and knees. While the musicians gathered around the piano, Polignac would ensconce himself in the sofa cushions and draw. Colette would always regret losing "the flattering little sketch" that Polignac made for her on one such occasion.[16]

Meg de Saint-Marceaux paid her first visit to the Polignac *atelier* in May 1894; that evening she and tenor Maurice Bagès sang some of Fauré's songs, with the composer at the piano. The soirée allowed Meg to observe Edmond de Polignac at close range. Her impressions were mixed: "The old prince happily tolerates his role of young husband. He was wearing a cardigan, a skullcap on his head. Seated beside his wife, young and in the pink of health, the contrast was quite unpleasant. But he's intelligent and very kind. He made us laugh by mimicking the sermons of the protestant pastors in the London parks."[17]

A more positive impression of Polignac was formed by a young, unknown writer named Marcel Proust, who was probably introduced to the Polignacs by Robert de Montesquiou just prior to their marriage in December 1893.[18] Proust had met Montesquiou earlier that year. A budding esthete, he became a "disciple" of the elegant count, whom he called his "*professeur de beauté.*" In 1894 Montesquiou introduced Proust into the elite salons of the aristocracy. By that time the rift between Montesquiou and the Polignacs had already occurred, but Proust managed to maintain independent contact with the couple. Within the first few months of his marriage, the Prince de Polignac invited Proust to accompany him and his wife to the Théâtre Libre, a showcase for the "naturalist" plays of Hugo, Strindberg, and Ibsen.[19] Polignac probably felt a natural affinity for the young man with the soulful eyes and a constitution as fragile as his own. Proust attended the Polignac salon for the first time on 6 February 1895; he was accompanied on that occasion by his lover, the composer-singer Reynaldo Hahn. Since meeting Montesquiou and Hahn—and, subsequently, Fauré, whose music he adored—Proust had become a serious and sophisticated music lover, and was eager to broaden his knowledge of new repertoire. The night of 6 February, in addition to hearing works by Fauré and Schumann, Proust was also introduced to the music of Edmond de Polignac. The next day, he wrote to his host:

> Prince, I was delighted by "Au pays où se fait la guerre," which my friend Hahn, who accompanied it the other night at the Trompette, sang for me, and which I heard again [sung] by Mme. Remacle. It has an exquisite Gothic color. The persistence of the [pitch] "mi" (it is "mi," isn't it—the note on [the syllable] "re" in "guerre"?) is a real find, and gives to the harmony, in addition to an extreme distinction, a very faithful Middle-Ages color. It's music of princely elegance, which doesn't mean "the music of a prince" (in the malevolent seventeenth-century sense), but the music of a rare musician, not of a musician-nobleman, but of a noble musician."[20]

The song to which Proust refers, "Au pays où se fait la guerre," is a setting of a poem by Théophile Gautier. The date of its composition is unknown, but it is included in Polignac's *Mélodies et pièces diverses* (1884), and ranks among the most beautiful of his songs. The lilting $\frac{6}{8}$ meter and delicate counterpoint contribute to what Proust describes as "an exquisite Gothic color."[21] Proust was in the audience for the *Dardanus* performance in April, and also for a performance of the octatonic "Pilate" on 16 June.[22] He would immortalize the Polignac salon in a long, effusive article written in 1903, two years after the prince's death. In it, he would recall with enthusiasm

> the original and fervent performances of all the latest songs of Fauré, the sonata [in A major for violin and piano] of Fauré, the [Hungarian] dances of Brahms. . . . Often held during the day, these musical feasts were illuminated by the sun's rays, which, when filtered through the prisms of the window panes, creating in the studio a thousand sparkling lights. It was a delightful thing to see the prince lead to her place, which was that of the discerning judge and fervent supporter, that of the beauty queen, the splendid and laughing Comtesse Greffulhe.[23]

After the performances, Polignac would often improvise at the piano. "Under his fingers, the waltzes never ceased." Proust remembered that, even on warm evenings, the prince was always wrapped in shawls and travel blankets. "'What can you expect?' he would say to those who teased him about his covers. 'As Anaxagorus said, life is a voyage!'"[24]

Like Proust, Claude Debussy had also become an admirer of the prince and his music. On 23 February 1895 he wrote to Pierre Louÿs, "I couldn't, to my great regret, go to hear 'Chilpéric,'[25] but this evening I'm going to hear the music of E. de Polignac, and I hope that that will replace the other."[26] The musical event that Debussy attended was a concert presented by the Société Nationale de Musique at the Salle d'Harcourt; Polignac was represented by his *Robin m'aime*.[27] Polignac's quirky orchestration of the work's lovely, lilting little melody did not find favor with the critics. While *Le Siècle* found the work to be "gracious,"[28] the critics of the other papers were not so gracious. *Le Monde musical* wrote: "Good heavens! What orchestration! This harp-horn duo—where the devil could one come up with these ideas?"[29] *Le Journal* concurred: "*Robin m'aime . . .* begins with a badly written horn solo, from which the horn soloist had the greatest trouble . . . extricating himself."[30] *Le Mot d'Ordre* was terse: "Robin loves me, says the Prince de Polignac; as for me, Robin bugs me."[31] Polignac had always wanted to be regarded as a "professional" composer; now he was forced to lick his wounds like other colleagues who had suffered the merciless bite of public criticism. Unlike the rest of his colleagues, however, if he found the negative consequences of critical scrutiny unbearable, Polignac had only to retreat back to the closed and secure world of the salon, where the society reporters deemed all the music performed therein to be "supremely elegant" and "very successful, much applauded."

Polignac had related to Proust his ideas about "musique de plein air"; he still dreamed of presenting another outdoor concert similar to the one given at La Chataigneraie a decade earlier. He approached Charles Bordes with the idea of having the forty-voice Chanteurs de Saint-Gervais sing his music outdoors, standing behind trees illuminated by projection lights.[32] As choirmaster, Bordes was not at all happy about the idea of his singers standing out in the open and possibly catching cold. Tactfully but firmly, Bordes squelched the plan, pointing out that "so few voices would not make a good effect outdoors."[33] A compromise was reached: thirty members of the choir would sing in the *atelier*, behind screens instead of trees. For this event, Polignac decided to indulge his interest in mixed media. The article in *Le Figaro* that publicized the event attempted to describe the composer's technological intentions:

> At a concert at the home of the Princesse de Polignac, announced for tomorrow, a completely new method of listening will be included. It will consist of music [accompanied by] a projected text, illuminated, and arranged in such a way that the audience can take in, in one glance, the plan of the piece. Reminders of the musical motives will be inscribed on cartridges, as reference points, while the piece is played. An illuminated "pointer beam" will follow, word by word, the sung text; another "pointer beam," placed on the corresponding cartridges will indicate the motives.
>
> It's a sort of "visual hearing." This initiative on the part of M. de Polignac is a new effort, along the lines of an analytical concert program, to concentrate the attention of the audience and to guide it safely in the course of a performance.[34]

If the journalists of *Le Figaro* had some difficulty articulating what was to be presented, the modern reader will easily recognize precursors of the "bouncing ball" from 1920s movie musicals, or of today's "supertitles" in modern opera houses.

Edmond, whose improved morale since his marriage was not matched by an amelioration of his physical woes, still spent a portion of each summer taking "the waters." His health spa of choice was the Hôtel du Mont-Blanc in the Haute-Savoie region. While Winnaretta went to visit her family in England, Edmond spent two weeks drinking and bathing in the mineral waters, taking long walks for exercise, and following a strict Spartan diet.[35] The greatest privation for Polignac, however, was the absence of his wife, to whom he addressed a constant stream of adoring love letters. This excerpt is typical: "I read the first pages, the very beautiful first pages of your letter; at the risk of seeming ridiculous, I [tell you that] they moved me deeply, and, full of devotion, I kissed the last word. . . . Goodbye, my beloved and dear, unique Friend. I kiss you very tenderly and put in this kiss all the joy that Fate has brought me, and all the happiness that I have finally found so late in life. [36]

In February 1896 a number of Polignac's a cappella choral works on religious texts were performed in the couple's salon by the Chanteurs de Saint-Gervais. Conductor Charles Bordes knew how to evoke in performance the quality of naturalism that Polignac strove to incoporate in his music; he promised the composer that his choir's performance of "Salve Regina" would be "'in the prairie'—light and charming." Composer Ernest Chausson was present for the performance; he was so moved that he wrote that night in his diary, "'Salve Regina' . . . [is] not a religious piece from church, but a religious hymn chanted by the angels in Dante's *Purgatory*. A lovely mélange of mysticism, poetry, and the picturesque."[37] Polignac's works were performed again by Bordes and the Saint-Gervais choir in the spring of 1896 in the Schola Cantorum's new headquarters on Rue Stanislas, a building that Polignac, as a member of the Schola's founding committee, had helped to procure.[38] During the same period, Polignac's "Chœur d'Esther" for women's voices and organ, on a text by Racine, was showcased at a concert organized by organist Eugène Gigout for his students (including Winnaretta) at his home at the Rue Jouffroy;[39] of the event, *Le Ménestrel* wrote, "Artists and amateurs were mixed together on the same program, which contained only the names of masters, and all shared equally in the success."[40]

In May 1896, four of Polignac's works—the song "Lamento" (text by Gautier), the "Andante" for violin and orchestra dedicated to the Comtesse Greffulhe, and the orchestral works *Robin m'aime* and *Tarentelle*—were presented in the Polignac salon.[41] Composer-pianist Reynaldo Hahn wrote to the prince following the performance, "Everything I heard astonished me: the fine and brilliant coloration of your orchestra, the nervous distinction of your style, the sophistication of your tonalities. . . . [Among the works] *Robin m'aime* holds a special place among my favorites. It [represents] musical humanism, or musicological poetry, whichever you prefer."[42]

That summer, after Edmond took his annual mountain "cure," the Polignacs attended the Bayreuth Festival together for the first time.[43] Winnaretta had been attending the festival since her teenage years, and, for the last decade, she had rented "Schloss Fantaisie," an enormous estate outside the town limits that had been the former summer residence of the margraves of Bayreuth. In order to accommodate her husband's need for solitude, Winnaretta prepared for him a comfortable room where he could retreat and compose.[44] The couple welcomed guests that summer as well, including the Saint-Marceaux family and Gabriel Fauré.[45] Together the friends attended the performance of the complete *Ring* cycle, presented that summer in its entirety for the first time since 1876 and conducted by noted Wagner conductor Felix Mottl. The long, enraptured hours spent listening to the *Tetralogy* did not diminish the Polignacs' desire for additional and frequent music making in their summer home. On one occasion pianist Édouard Risler, British soprano Esther Palisser, and some of the Bayreuth orchestra members joined Fauré and Meg de Saint-Marceaux in performing excerpts from Wagner's operas and Fauré's chamber music and songs for the Polignacs and some post-opera guests.[46]

After Bayreuth, the Polignacs continued their travels, first to Venice and from there to Monaco. It was in Monaco that they received news of the sudden death from a heart ailment of Winnaretta's sister Isabelle, the Duchesse Decazes.[47] Winnaretta's mourning period removed the couple from public life during the first half of 1897. As a result, they were shielded from the much of the societal rancor and division caused by the unfolding of the Dreyfus Affair. Families and friends engaged in violent arguments as they chose to ally themselves with the pro- or anti-Dreyfus camps, and those near and dear to the Polignacs were no exception. Years later, Winnaretta would recall this politically charged period as one which "developed hatred of every kind in Paris; families were split up, husbands and wives parted, and it was not unusual at a dinner to see guests leave the room if anyone appeared of an opposite opinion from their own."[48]

During this period Edmond returned to an old hobby which had fascinated him since his youth: furniture design. Inspired by Art Nouveau design and by the Arts-and-Crafts designs of William Morris,[49] he engaged a cabinet maker to realize some of his furniture designs. The results were so successful that some of Polignac's pieces—end tables made of lemonwood or black lacquered, with unusual twisting legs—were accepted for exhibition in the Salons des Beaux-Arts in the years 1897 and 1898. Polignac also continued to compose, mostly short pieces: a "Cantique à la vierge" for Bordes; a "Choeur de buveurs" for men's voices a cappella, based on the minuet from Mozart's String Quartet, K. 428; and a "Grande Marche" for two pianos, dedicated to his nephew Louis Decazes.

The Polignacs recommenced their musical soirées that spring; on 17 May they hosted the first concert of the Schola Cantorum, featuring the works of the school's composition students.[50]

That summer they returned to Bayreuth, this time accompanied by Edmond's niece Armande. Together the three attended performances of *Parsifal* and a reprise of the complete *Ring* cycle. After each performance, the trio would return to Schloss Fantaisie and dash to the piano to replay Wagner's music, "in order to prolong the ecstasy of what they had heard."[51] After the festival, they toured several German cities. Polignac's legs were so frail that often, during the couple's evening walks, Winnaretta was obliged to carry her frail husband on her back as they passed through the peaceful, empty cobblestone streets.[52] On the way back to France the trio stopped at Wildthurn, the Bavarian estate where Polignac had spent happy childhood years. Memories came rushing back to the 63-year-old prince as he rambled through his childhood home and revisited the woods where he and Camille had played as boys.[53]

Camille encouraged his brother to revive his operas. Apparently, in a letter that is lost, Edmond enumerated his lifelong insecurities. Camille was undaunted in his encouragement, and responded: "I see clearly that I will have to give up publicly listening to the suave melodies of your youth; for this pleasure, I assure you, I'd be less picky than you and less preoccupied with finding the exquisite conditions that you're looking for.[54] In his next letter (apparently lost), Edmond seems to have indicated that, having just come from Bayreuth, where he saw and heard Wagner's operas presented in ideal conditions, he was unwilling to settle for anything less. Camille countered, "Does this mean that you're not going to write anymore? . . . You need to think about pleasing others rather than satisfying yourself in the quest for an [unrealizable] Ideal. . . . Follow the advice of Rossini: always have your music played in public. Fauré does it, everybody does it. Why wouldn't you do it?"[55]

If the trip to Bayreuth did not inspire Polignac to revive his operas, it did return his creative thoughts to octatonicism. A dozen sketches written between July and December 1897 employ not only the three octatonic scales, but also whole-tone scales; the sketches reveal a general preoccupation on the part of the composer with the use of major and minor thirds and ways to use the various trichords formed by them as structural entities. A sketch from July 1897 ("good [example] of a 'trouble' effect for orchestra") features a "male chorus [for or from] PAN" accompanied by violas and brass; an "Incantation" (August 1897) includes a triplet ostinato in the bass described as a "tumultuous ritual," followed by a "Sort of Threnody" with a A-to-C bass ostinato in octaves meant to recall the "Bells of Parsifal"; yet another sketch (December 1897) is called "Violent effect of majors 3rds."[56]

In 1898, Polignac returned to the composition of choral music. In June of that year, two new a cappella choruses were performed by the Chanteurs de Saint-Gervais under Bordes's direction in the Rue Cortambert *atelier*. As he had in 1895, Polignac had his music accompanied by projected images. The first, "Effet de lointain," had as its background the image of a sunset in a Flemish village; a second, "Le Vallon," on a text of Lamartine, featured a bucolic landscape. These two pieces were written in a modernist style, employing nontonal harmonies and the unusual effects produced by the chorus singing "à bouche fermée." A third choral work, "Ave Maris Stella," inspired by the beauty of the Cathedral of San Marco in Florence, was written in the style of a sixteenth-century motet, and accompanied by an image of Fra Angelico's *Annunciation*, which is housed in the San Marco convent. *Le Figaro* hailed this last piece as "the hit of the program."[57] Once again, Proust was in the audience; afterwards, he wrote to Polignac:

Prince, I have the habit of sending you admiring letters after concerts where I've heard your music. But it seems to me that poets should be thanked, and I felt the other night, more than ever, what a serious, vast, and sweet poet you are. These sonorous waves blend like the waves of the "vessels" of "Le Vallon," these vast spaces measured by the music between these distant chants in the mountain, the differences of altitude and distance rendered palpable, and the great and sad majesty of these spaces and these hearts, all that touched me very much."[58]

Some years later, Proust would write in *Le Figaro* of the astonishing impression left by the composer's audiovisual experiments: "All of today's innovations uniting music and projected images, or music and the spoken word—Polignac promoted these trends. And no matter what [musical] progress has been made or whatever imitations have followed, the decoration, not always harmonious with the music, at the Rue Cortambert house, has remained entirely 'new.'"[59]

In June, the Polignacs traveled to London to hear the first public performance, on 21 June, of Maurice Maeterlinck's *Pelléas et Mélisande* and of Fauré's accompanying incidental music, dedicated to Winnaretta.[60] The next month Polignac's music was included in a concert in the *atelier* performed by the faculty and students of the Schola Cantorum, directed by Bordes and accompanied at the organ by Guilmant. The program featured music of the Renaissance and Baroque eras and modern religious works written in Palestrinian style.[61] At the beginning of August the Polignacs traveled to Podwein, Austria, to visit Camille and his second wife, Rita. Edmond was inspired by the peaceful mountain forests. "Above me, millions of flies are buzzing in the high summits, bathed with sunlight and filling the forest with a perpetually held note, invariably a "do," as if sitting on the string of an enormous invisible violin."[62] The beauty of the place inspired him to write *Am Thüringerwald*, a work for chorus and orchestra on a text of Goethe.

In February 1899, Polignac's "Chœur d'Esther" was included in a lecture-recital given by André Hallays on modern literary and musical works inspired by Scriptures.[63] His songs were presented alongside those of Chausson, d'Indy, and Bréville at a soirée hosted by the Comtesse de Saussine.[64] In March, string quartets by Edmond de Polignac and Armande de Polignac were presented in the *atelier*.[65] It was at this performance that Proust learned that the plucking technique utilized in the Scherzo of the prince's quartet was called "pizzicato." After the performance, he wrote to Polignac: "I *insist* on telling you how beautiful I found this quartet, in which, after strains of celestial charm, there was an ardent spirit of terrestrial joy, and finally, in the last measures, the eloquence of a concise and grandiose response."[66] These lines prefigure Proust's evocation of the quartet—which becomes, eventually, a septet—by the composer Vinteuil in the author's *The Prisoner;* in this work, Proust makes reference to a "celestial musical phrase," and to orchestrations that seem "render material . . . the deepest joy."[67]

In September, Edmond and Winnaretta joined a group of friends for an extended visit to the Princesse Brancovan at the Villa Bassaraba.[68] The Polignacs were lodged in a guesthouse some distance from the princesse's sumptuous château. Edmond was too sick to leave his little chalet, and so, every day, the other guests took the car from the château to come and pay him visits. Among his frequent guests were Marcel Proust, who was staying with his parents in nearby Évian, and fellow writer Abel Hermant. Hermant was charmed by the "singular wit" and "old-fashioned courtesy" of the "very elderly valetudinarian."[69] A frequent topic of conversation was Dreyfus's retrial, which had begun a month earlier and had given rise to demonstrations and an assassination attempt against Dreyfus's lawyer.

Figure 7.2. Edmond de Polignac in the summer of 1899 with members of the Brancovan family and guests at the Villa Bassaraba, Amphion. Collection of the author. Edmond de Polignac stands to the far left in the top row. The others are (top row) Madame Marie Bartholoni, Marcel Proust, Constantin de Brancovan, Jeanne Bartholoni, pianist Léon Delafosse; (middle row) EP's cousin Joséphine de Monteynard, Winnaretta Singer-Polignac, poet Anna de Noailles; (bottom row) Hélène de Caraman-Chimay, writer Abel Hermant.

These events were followed closely by the inhabitants of Amphion, who were devastated when, a few days later, the Military Court found Dreyfus guilty of high treason and condemned him to ten years of seclusion and a second degradation. Hermant marveled at the fact that, despite his physical frailty, Polignac expressed his views on the Affair with a "violence of opinion that would make the youngest ones jealous."[70] The prince joked mischievously with Proust about his Jewish heritage: "So what's the old Syndicate been up to now?"[71]

Towards the end of the summer, Dreyfus was pardoned. Polignac's health improved sufficiently to allow him to leave the chalet. He was even able to compose a little: a melody in shifting meters (including quintuple meter) accompanied by descending 4ths derived from octatonic scale B is entitled "Schema rythmique du Chœur PAN" (Rhythmic schema from the PAN chorus.)[72] A celebrated photograph (Fig. 7.2) shows the assembled group of guests at the Villa Bassaraba at the time of the announcement of Dreyfus's reprieve, relaxed, smiling.

Chapter Eight

Endings and Echoes (1900–)

At the beginning of the new century, Edmond de Polignac, sixty-five years old and increasingly frail, was preoccupied with thoughts of death. Walking in a crowd one day with Maurice Barrès, he exclaimed, "How sad it is, all this flesh on the way to the cemetery!"[1] His morbidity made its way into his music: a densely chromatic new work, *Imprécations,* for chorus, brass instruments, and organ (described to the Comtesse Greffulhe as "a curious new experiment in sonority"[2]) opens with the following text, presumably written by Polignac:

À ma voix, venez mots terribles!
Fatales douleurs, éternels sanglots, clameurs désespérées,
Éclatez vers les lieux impossibles!

(To my voice, come, terrible words!
Fatal woes, eternal sobs, desperate clamors,
Burst forth towards the impossible places!)

The prince's family and friends engaged him in activities that kept him busy, musically and socially. Winnaretta organized a first performance of *Imprécations* in the *atelier* on 13 January 1900; Fauré was at the organ.[3] Many of the musical soirées given in the Polignac salon during the 1900 "season" included the prince's music; in turn, his friends featured Polignac's music in their salon programs.[4] On 29 June 1900, "Les Adieux de Deïdamia" was performed at the home of the Comtesse Greffulhe; the guest list of thirty-eight overlaps with the names of the aristocratic women who sang in the chorus (Fig. 8.1).[5] Despite his frailty, Polignac could entertain a crowd as well as ever; if anything, his sense of humor became increasingly mordant with age. Eventually, Winnaretta started to write down her husband's words—both his charming, fine thoughts and his saltier witticisms—and compiled them in a little book (apparently no longer extant). One of the funnier ones is a "music dictionary" entry, impossible to translate: "Sara bande: tant mieux pour elle."[6]

Winnaretta encouraged her husband to look through his old manuscripts with an eye toward future publications and performances. The Schola Cantorum had been discussing the establishment of its own publishing house to promote the compositions of its members, and Winnaretta probably offered the Schola a substantial subvention to underwrite the publication of her husband's works. (The plan would materialize in 1902, after Polignac's death, when the Schola

Soirée du 29 Juin 1900

PROGRAMME

1. **Cantilène de Sapho**.............. GOUNOD

2. **Mors et Vita** (Fragments)............ GOUNOD

3. **Les Adieux de Déïdamia,**
   Paroles de MUSSSET (Chœur) .... Prince ED. DE POLIGNAC

Soliste : Madame la Comtesse DE GUERNE.

Choristes : Mesdames : Marquise de CHAPONAY, Baronne DE L'ESPÉE, Vicomtesse DE GALARD, Vicomtesse DE GAIGNERON, Comtesse GREFFULHE, Mademoiselle GREFFULHE, Baronne H. HOTTINGUER, Marquise DE LOŸS-CHANDIEU, Mademoiselle DE LASTOURS, Princesse MURAT, Marquise DE MUN, Comtesse LOUIS DE MONTESQUIOU, Duchesse DE NOAILLES, Comtesse DE PÉRIGORD, Mademoiselle DE PERTHUIS, Comtesse PAUL DE POURTALÈS, Madame RIDGWAY, Mademoiselle DE ROHAN, Duchesse D'UZÈS.

Chef d'Orchestre : Le Prince EDMOND DE POLIGNAC.

Pianiste : Le Comte HENRI DE SÉGUR.

Figure 8.1. Program of a soirée given in the salon of the Comtesse Greffulhe, 29 June 1900. Private collection. Used by permission.

created Édition Mutuelle.) Polignac made corrections and added improvements to his manuscripts. The three movements of the *Échos de l'Orient judaïque* were the first to be revised, in 1899; the 1860 String Quartet and "Les Adieux de Deïdamia" were corrected in 1900.[7]

That same spring, facsimiles of two Polignac manuscripts were included in a special collection of musical autographs being assembled for the 1900 World's Fair. Three hundred "contemporary composers" from eighteen countries submitted pages of their works, each of which was "framed" on the page with an Art-Nouveau-style border along with a portrait of the composer (Polignac's portrait is Figure 8.2). The collection ran to twenty handsomely bound volumes.[8] Polignac contributed two pieces: the first was his youthful "Prière à la Mecque" from 1857. The second work was a recent work for a cappella mixed chorus entitled "Aubade." Its thirty measures exemplify perfectly the freshness, clarity, and tunefulness of Polignac's "musique de plein air."

In mid-April, just as the multitudes began arriving in Paris for the opening of the World's Fair, the Polignacs departed to spend three weeks in Venice.[9] It was the couple's favorite city; the prince loved to say that "Venice is the only city where you can hold a discussion in front of an open window without having to raise your voice."[10] They were joined by a group of Paris friends that included Reynaldo Hahn, Marcel Proust, and poet Henri de Régnier and his wife. The Polignacs hosted moonlight sails in their gondola; on some occasions, Hahn would sing his songs, accompanying himself on Winnaretta's little five-octave piano, small enough to fit in the gondola.[11] During the day, Edmond de Polignac visited the music library of San Marco, reveling in "the glorious works of Monteverdi, and of Rossi, the great Venetian."[12] Sometimes he would walk along the Grand Canal with Madame de Caraman-Chimay and Proust, admiring the facades of the various *palazzos* and fantasizing about owning one or the other of the magnificent buildings. Since Polignac's sixty-sixth birthday would fall during the period of their Venetian sojourn, Winnaretta decided to surprise him with the present of a lifetime: she bought him a palazzo, a magnificent fifteenth-century edifice in pink marble that had belonged to the Montecuccioli family;[13] henceforth it would be known as the Palazzo Polignac. The couple's new palazzo became the subject of much talk of Parisian society.[14] Among the purveyors of gossip was Robert de Montesquiou, whose rancor towards the couple was undiminished. In his diary-scrapbook, he wrote, "The awful Polignacs just bought a palazzo in Venice that had belonged to the Montecucullis [*sic*]. . . . The twice-repeated syllable [*cu-cu*] at the heart of the name is a good-luck charm for the owners, since it refers to them by their name."[15] Appropriating a verse from Théophile Gautier's poem "Affinités secrètes"—the title formerly a code phrase of sympathetic understanding and complicity between himself and Edmond—Montesquiou compared the Polignacs to "two white wood-doves" whose "pink feet" were perched on the cupolas of Venice.[16]

Figure 8.2. Portrait of Prince Edmond de Polignac in the anthology *Musiciens contemporains*, published for the 1900 Exposition Universelle

The Polignacs spent much of the summer apart: while Winnaretta enjoyed the spas in Bad Kreuznach, Germany, Edmond visited Amsterdam. He spent his mornings in the Rijksmuseum, famous for its collection of Rembrandts and Vermeers, and discovered the paintings of Dutch skaters in quaint costumes by Henrich Avercamp. In the afternoons he went to the zoo, where he visited "the white bears, the Java peacock with wings of sapphire and an enormous tail with splendid gold feathers and . . . some other beast-friends."[17] When he returned to Paris, he looked into the purchase of a painting that his wife had wanted to buy for the Venice palazzo. Polignac, usually content to cede financial matters to his wife, insisted that he must contribute a portion of his small personal fortune to the purchase of the painting. "This will lighten the [financial] burden," he wrote to his millionaire wife, "and will represent a communal effort. . . . I owe it to you and to myself . . . in honor of our future Palaces."[18]

On 27 March 1900, Polignac's music was performed at a musical and literary soirée organized by the Société artistique des Amateurs, in a program "entirely comprised of works by amateurs, performed by amateurs." According to the advance publicity for the event, Montesquiou was to have read his poems that same evening. Ultimately, the Comte did not participate in the event; perhaps he did not like the idea of being on the same program as Polignac.[19]

Several performances of Polignac's music took place in 1901. Three of Edmond's unaccompanied choruses were presented in a program given in the Polignac salon on 18 April as part of a celebration of Edmond's sixty-seventh birthday; that the program also included works by Handel, Fauré, and Brahms. In place of the usual Chanteurs de Saint-Gervais, the Polignacs engaged a different choral ensemble, "L'Euterpe," conducted by Abel Duteil d'Ozanne.[20] Le Figaro's society column gave the program its typical uncritical praise.[21] However, a more thoughtful assessment of Polignac's music appeared in the magazine La Vie parisienne.

> The Euterpe Chorus, chez the Princesse de Polignac, sang choral music by the Prince de Polignac. It would have been much better if, as it says in the song, this excellent artist was named "Just-like-everybody-else."[22] Better to be able to express freely the subtle and rare intelligence that is the basis of [Polignac's] talent! His music has a curious power to burst the walls and create a feeling of the outdoors; listening to it, with its ardent and ambitious sensuality, one breathes in the summer evenings, with a passionate desire to savor all the aromas of the atmosphere. There was among the choral works sung the other day a certain "Ave Maris Stella." . . . [I]n the hold of this sophisticated and satisfying music, one can see emerging a Florentine countryside, ringed with mountains, in pensive style, with the svelte black line of cypresses, under a silky, immobile sky. It was beautiful, and infinitely strange. . . .[23]

One month later, an "all-Polignac" charity concert, organized by Winnaretta and sponsored by the Société Philanthropique (presided over by the Comtesse

Greffulhe's brother-in-law, Prince d'Arenberg), was presented at the height of the "season." With the help of the Minister of Fine Arts, Winnaretta was able to rent the beautiful Salle des Concerts du Conservatoire, the only medium-sized hall in Paris equipped with an organ, and normally unavailable for non-Conservatoire concerts. The concert took place on Ascension Thursday, 16 May 1901. Camille Chevillard conducted the Orchestra of the Concerts Colonne; two well-known opera stars, soprano Jane Hatto and baritone Paul Daraux, were the vocal soloists. Discussions regarding performances of Polignac's compositions were already in the works with a major conductor, Camille Chevillard. Since 1897, Chevillard had been been functioning as unofficial conductor of the Concerts Lamoureux; upon the death in 1899 of Charles Lamoureux (Chevillard's father-in-law), he was named director of the Lamoureux concert society. By 1900 Chevillard was regarded as one of Paris's most esteemed conductors, hailed equally for his performances of Wagner and his championship of modern French composers. Despite the fact that the music had to be put together during the busy Easter season with very few rehearsals, the event was a triumph for Polignac. The hall was packed with luminaries of high society and the artistic world. The ten works on the program represented the diversity of his compositional styles: the light orchestral works *Tarentelle* and *Robin m'aime;* the *Lamento* for soprano and orchestra on Gautier's haunting poem—the work which had drawn Winnaretta to Edmond; the recently composed a cappella choruses "Ave Maris Stella" and "Aubade"; the Mendelssohnian "Les Adieux de Deïdamia" and the melancholy "Derniers Rêves du bal," a choral work set to waltz rhythms evoking the dreams of a dying young woman about her last ball; the brilliant "Queen Claribel's Aria" from *La Coupe du Roi de Thulé;* and finally, works on scriptural texts: the magnificent "Martha et Maria," and the octatonic *Échos de l'Orient judaïque* (on this occasion called *Récits évangéliques*). Charles Joly, the critic of *Le Figaro*, ordinarily severe in his judgments, wrote of the variety and wealth of Polignac's ideas, admiring—while not completely understanding—his "modern" music.

> The *Récits évangéliques,* which produced the most striking effect on the audience are precisely those where the union of the word and the melody seemed to be the most perfect. I'm not quite sure that the audience savored the harmonic grittiness and the diatonic novelties that distinguish "Pilate livre le Christ"; on the other hand, all the pages of this interesting work, where the music and the poetry seem indissolubly united, made the greatest impression on them. . . . We see the composer, master of his talent, employ with the greatest ease the most recent conquests of modern music.[24]

Friends and colleagues showered Polignac with praise and letters of congratulations.[25] But it was Marcel Proust, who had not been able to attend the concert because of an asthma attack, who best described the prince and his music. He wrote to Polignac, "It's fortunate that I couldn't leave my bed. For if I had gone to the Conservatoire, my hacking and coughing would have added sonorities to your orchestration that undoubtedly would not have been to the public's taste."[26] He then went on to muse on the special quality of Polignac's music:

> It's through the juxtaposition of the works of one master that, in music, as in painting or literature, I'm able to grasp his personality. As objective as the works are, and as different are their subjects, they have . . . something in common, which is the essence of genius of their author. As different as two works like *Robin m'aime* and *Ave Maria* [sic] are from each other, they have, even so, an air of being part of a family, which is their resemblance to the soul of the Prince de Polignac. . . . Prince, you are young and I am old. Enumeration doesn't apply to age, and even if you had been ill before . . . you are now in the bloom of springtime.[27]

Two days after the concert, the "Literary Supplement" of *Le Figaro,* which published a weekly "Musical Page," featured Polignac's most recent song, "La Chanson de Barberine," on a poem by Alfred de Musset. This late *mélodie* affirms the words of Proust: it has the energy and the ardor of a young man, coupled with the musical know-how of an older, accomplished composer. Of Polignac and his music, *Le Figaro's* René Lara wrote:

> One is generally inclined, when, by chance, a noble sire takes up the noble fantasy of devoting his leisure hours to artistic matters, to qualify him immediately with the somewhat ironic epithet of "amateur," and consequently to consider his artistic output with merely an indulgent curiosity. This rather severe appraisal is often excused, admittedly, because it is justified. But sometimes that appraisal is misplaced. Thus, while the author of the "Chanson de Barberine" is a noble sire, I don't think that anyone would dream of calling him an amateur: the wealth of his musical knowledge, the beautiful quality of his works—the great value of which was revealed to us by his recent concert at the Conservatoire—his erudition, and his technique place him among our most appreciated and interesting composers. M. le Prince Edmond de Polignac is a true artist: he has the temperament and at the same time the modesty. . . . His "Chanson de Barberine" discreetly evokes the perfume of the lovely *romances* of the eighteenth century.[28]

That spring, Polignac initiated another artistic collaboration. The previous year, at the home of Meg de Saint-Marceaux, the prince was present for a dance recital performed by a young American, Isadora Duncan, who performed barefoot and astonished her audiences with her "recreations" of the dances of ancient Greece. Completely dazzled by Duncan's artistry, Polignac longed to meet her. At Winnaretta's invitation, Duncan came to the *atelier* to make the acquaintance of the elderly prince. In her memoirs, Duncan recalled Polignac as "a fine musician of considerable talent. . . . He hailed me a vision and a dream for which he

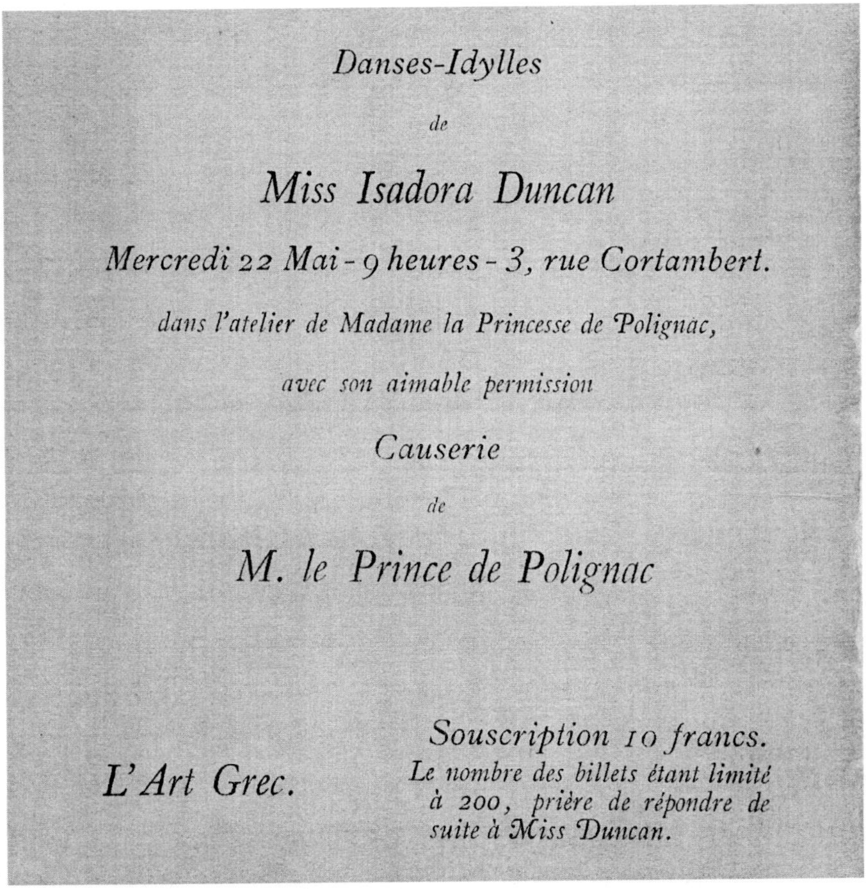

Danses-Idylles

de

Miss Isadora Duncan

Mercredi 22 Mai - 9 heures - 3, rue Cortambert.

dans l'atelier de Madame la Princesse de Polignac,

avec son aimable permission

Causerie

de

M. le Prince de Polignac

L'Art Grec.

Souscription 10 francs.
Le nombre des billets étant limité à 200, prière de répondre de suite à Miss Duncan.

Figure 8.3. Invitation card to a program of "Danses-Idylles" by Isadora Duncan, performed in the Polignac salon, 22 May 1901. Dance Division, New York Public Library. Used by permission.

had long waited. He played for me delightfully on a charming old harpsichord. . . . And then we envisaged a collaboration."[29] The collaboration took place on the evening of 22 May 1901 (Fig. 8.3), barely a week after the concert at the Conservatoire, when a program of Isadora Duncan's "Danses-Idylles" was given in the Polignac *atelier;* the dance recital was preceded by a talk given by Edmond de Polignac on the subject of "Greek Art."[30]

The last performance of Polignac's music during his lifetime took place on 27 June 1901. The occasion was a large-scale charity fair held at the Hamlet of the Versailles Palace, the proceeds from which would be used to restore the grounds and landmarks in the palace park.[31] It was a grand high-society event: without a hint of irony, the Republican newspapers reported the plan of the aristocratic "dames patronesses" to host the day's activities garbed in the dresses of their grandmothers, pretending to be milkmaids.[32] Visitors to the palace grounds that day were treated to artistic diversions of yesteryear: in the mill, minuets and rigaudons were being played; outdoors, gavottes were being danced; in the rustic theater, eighteenth-century songs were being sung; in the guardhouse, a painter was making portraits of the women in the style of Marie-Antoinette.[33] Winnaretta had organized a concert at the Maison de la Reine;[34] Polignac's contribution was his first "published" composition, the 1852 "Romance pastorale" with words by Charles IX. Originally written in contralto range, Polignac transposed the *romance* a third higher for the afternoon's soloist: the silvery-voiced soprano Comtesse de Guerne, for whose "ineffable voice" Polignac had written Salammbô's "Song to the Moon."

That was the last time that Polignac would hear his own music performed. Two weeks later he fell ill, and from then on never left his bed.[35] He had made plans to return to Amsterdam that summer, and had already booked the same rooms as last year, "because," wrote Proust to his mother six weeks later, "in his eccentric manner, when he had been in a hotel, he noted down the numbers of the rooms and the direction that the windows faced to be sure to have the same ones [next time]."[36] When it became clear that her husband could not travel, Winnaretta wanted to telegraph the Dutch hotel to cancel the reservations. Polignac became upset, crying out, "So that's it, you want to make me look like I'm skipping out on them—they'll think I was never really going to take those rooms!"; he then exhausted himself writing an eight-page letter of explanation to the director of the hotel.[37] As his condition worsened, Winnaretta engaged an English nurse to take care of him. But the nurse, with her little white collar, upset Edmond so much that he kept sending her out of the room, yelling "I have nothing to say to the Princess of Wales at three in the morning."[38] Finally, Winnaretta took to nursing her husband herself. She would stay awake with him until the wee hours, talking about Mark Twain.[39]

Edmond de Polignac died at 3 o'clock in the morning on 8 August 1901. In the death certificate and all the notarized acts written in connection with the settling of his husband's estate, Winnaretta insisted that her deceased husband be referred to as "Prince de Polignac, composer of music."[40] On 9 August, *Le Figaro* carried on its front page an obituary, "Un prince musicien," written by Eugène d'Harcourt, newly appointed as the paper's music critic. "My master and friend just died," wrote Harcourt. "He followed, step by step, the musical evolution of this last half-century. Always in search of novelty, he invented a scale, a succession of whole tones [*sic*], for which one could reproach him for a certain hardness [of sound], but which gave to his works an astonishing originality. . . . [H]e was interested in all new ideas and strove to be an artist, in whatever form that took."[41]

The funeral services took place on 12 August at the Église de l'Annonciation. Despite the fact that it was the height of the vacation season, a large number of family members and friends returned to Paris to be present at the ceremony.[42] Fauré, who played the organ for the ceremony, arranged a beautiful program of music, ranging from Gregorian chant (sung by the Chanteurs de Saint-Gervais) to Ravel's *Pavane pour une infante défunte;* after the funeral, he wrote to Winnaretta, "I couldn't do even one-thousandth of what I had wanted to do, as the organ was worthless and I only had a small number of the Chanteurs."[43] A month later, upon learning that Edmond had left him a bequest of 10,000 francs, Fauré wrote, "I was very proud that he counted me among his best friends, and I am so unhappy to have lost him!"[44] Marcel Proust, in attendance at the funeral, felt the loss of more than just a friend that sad day: in viewing the black velvet drape that covered the prince's casket, adored in scarlet with a crown and the letter "P," he felt that "the spiritual fire that inhabited the Prince Edmond de Polignac" had been extinguished, "his individuality had been effaced, he had returned to his [aristocratic] family. He was no more than a Polignac."[45]

According to Edmond de Polignac's wishes, his body was transferred to the Singer family crypt in Devonshire, England, so that he could be "buried alongside my dear wife."[46] On the stone Winnaretta had inscribed an epitaph that quoted a line from *Parsifal* and a line from Corinthians II:

> Edmond-Melchior-Jean-Marie, Prince de Polignac
> Born 1834, Died 1901
> Composer of Music
> Selig in Glaube, Selig in Liebe
> For the letter killeth, but the spirit giveth life

A year later, Winnaretta organized a memorial service for her husband in Venice. She borrowed the Palazzo Vendramin, Richard Wagner's former residence on the Grand Canal, one of the most beautiful specimens of Renaissance architecture in the city, now the home of the Duca della Grazia. On a bright October afternoon, Winnaretta and her friends gathered in the courtyard of the Palazzo, while the Banda Municipale de Venezia played the Funeral March from Wagner's *Siegfried* underneath the windows of the room where the German composer had died.[47]

That year, 1902, the Schola Cantorum realized its plan to create a music publishing association, Édition Mutuelle, which would promote the music of its composer members, both faculty and students.[48] Polignac's works were among the first to be published. The virtuoso pianist Blanche Selva, a faculty member of the Schola, was engaged by the princesse to oversee the editing and the correction of the manuscripts.[49] Ten of Polignac's works in diverse genres were released in spring 1903.[50] The proceeds from sales went to support the Schola's public performances of the published works. In 1905, two of Polignac's works, the song "Sur les Lagunes" and the choral work "Hirondelles" were published by impresario Gabriel Astruc, who had founded his own publishing company.[51] Winnaretta also solicited Astruc's help in organizing an "Edmond de Polignac Composition Contest" for young French composers, but the idea never came to fruition.[52]

To keep her husband's music before the public, Winnaretta sponsored concerts in his memory. In 1903 she collaborated with Élisabeth Greffulhe in organizing the first such event: a "concert of modern French music," produced under the auspices of the Société des Grandes Auditions Musicales de France.[53] The performance took place on 13 May 1903 in the thousand-seat Salle Humbert-des-Romans (16th *arrondissement*). Camille Chevillard conducted the program, which consisted of Polignac's *Tarentelle* and *Lamento,* the latter sung by the Comtesse de Guerne, all three movements of the *Échos de l'Orient judaïque,*[54] d'Indy's *Symphonie sur un chant montagnard français,* and the overture from Eugène d'Harcourt's opera, *Le Tasse.*[55]

On 18 April 1905, the *Échos de l'Orient judaïque* was performed at the Nouveau Théâtre on a program directed by pianist-conductor Alfred Cortot.[56] Baritone Paul Daraux, who had sung the role of Pilate at the Conservatoire four years earlier, was re-engaged for this concert. The next day, 19 April (Edmond de Polignac's birthday) a long article by Fauré, now serving as music critic for *Le Figaro,*[57] appeared in that paper.

> The social condition of the Prince de Polignac facilitated for him the most immediate as well as the most constant successes. . . . His worship for true art, however, inspired in him the will to scale the summits, just as his conscience commanded him to speak his own language, even at the price of not only not being readily understood, but also of being somewhat mocked. Undiscouraged, he undertook works that were considerable in their proportions, in their thought, and in the loftiness of the goal. . . .
>
> Among his numerous works, there is, however, none that characterizes so vividly his estrangement from the "easy" and the "convenient," none that causes the value of his personal conceptions to stand out more brilliantly than the *Échos de l'Orient judaïque,* which was honored yesterday among the illustrious works on the program of the Concerts Cortot. . . .
>
> Here, the eloquence of the text and the emotion of the scenes are enveloped in a truly far-off atmosphere, tinted with a truly Oriental color. . . .
>
> From this music, which recounts so well and which translates with such gripping accuracy, and which creates, at the same time, such vivid images, emanates an impression too real to escape.[58]

It was especially in the Polignac salon that Edmond's compositions remained alive. For the next thirty-six years, until just before World War II, Winnaretta organized performances of her husband's music in the *atelier* alongside the works of the great composers;[59] the last of these performances took place in June 1939. Nadia Boulanger was among the conductors who led performances of Polignac's music. And every summer in Venice, Winnaretta hosted a musical gathering in August to commemorate the anniversary of her husband's death.

In one way or another, Winnaretta Singer-Polignac spent the rest of her life honoring the memory of her husband. From 1910 to 1914 she sponsored an "Edmond de Polignac Prize" through London's Royal Society of Literature; the winners of the prize in each of the four years of its existence were Walter de la Mare, John Masefield, James Stephens, and Ralph Hodgson.[60] She financed the construction of a homeless shelter for the Salvation Army, and named it the "Edmond de Polignac Foundation."[61] To commemorate her husband's love of technology, she underwrote the development of the wireless telegraph by scientist Édouard Branly.[62] In September 1918 Marcel Proust wrote to Winnaretta, asking permission to dedicate the second volume of À la Recherche du temps perdu, À l'ombre des jeunes filles en fleurs, "to the dear and venerated memory of Prince Edmond de Polignac; homage from one to whom he showed so much goodness, and who still admires, in the reverence for memory, the remarkable nature of his delightful artistry and mind."[63] Fearing that this dedication might be construed by the public as an illusion to her husband's homosexuality, Winnaretta refused the dedication in the strongest terms. Proust pressed the point: the princesse had misunderstood his intentions; no one in the book resembled either of the Polignacs, and so forth.[64] Winnaretta repeated her refusal. The book was published without a dedication. "And that," Winnaretta would recount wryly years later, "is how I succeeded in *not* having Edmond's name appear on the first page of a masterwork."[65]

However, Winnaretta was successful in insuring that the name of "*Princesse Edmond de Polignac*" would appear on masterworks. Until the end of her days she fostered modernist music composition, commissioning almost two dozen works by twentieth-century composers, many of whom were young and struggling. The spirit and memory of Edmond de Polignac generated the creation of new compositions by his beloved niece Armande de Polignac, and by others who would become household names: Kurt Weill, Erik Satie and members of the "Groupe de Six," and most especially, Igor Stravinsky, who became Winnaretta's particular favorite. It is tantalizing to imagine that Winnaretta discussed her husband's "chromatico-diatonic" scales with the brilliant young Russian—who had learned these scales from his teacher Rimsky-Korsakov and had made them the cornerstone of many of his compositions. In addition to supporting and championing composers, Winnaretta helped the careers of many emerging (and often struggling) musicians, artists, and writers, including Arthur Rubinstein, Clara Haskil, Vladimir Horowitz, Paul Valéry, Léon-Paul Fargue, Colette, and Nadia Boulanger, to name just a few. She supported modernism in other genres as well, becoming a major patron of Serge Diaghilev and his Ballets Russes.

Winnaretta died in London in 1943, during the Blitz. In her will, she bequeathed her husband's music manuscripts and printed scores to her great-grandnephew and godson, Edmond de Polignac, born in 1914 and named for the composer. It had been Winnaretta's hope that "after I'm gone, some pious hands will gather up the manuscripts that he left, and that one of his own family will take care of his admirable musical works." [66] Prince Edmond, an ardent music-lover, now in his nineties, has devoted years of time and energy to the fulfillment of Winnaretta's wish, actively championing the performance and publication of the music of the composer for whom he was named. As a result, Edmond de Polignac's compositions and theories, including his octatonic inventions, are slowly becoming known in our own time.

Chapter Nine

Edmond de Polignac's Octatonic Music

Edmond de Polignac began writing octatonic music in either 1878 or 1879, and continued to do so until 1900, slightly more than a year before his death. His output, in addition to the treatise-sketchbook "Étude sur les successions alternantes de tons et demi-tons (et sur la gamme dite majeure-mineure)" (A Study on the Alternating Sequences of Whole Steps and Half Steps [and on the Scale Known as Major-Minor]), which will be discussed and translated in part two of the book, includes five complete compositions, the first two of which feature octatonic-diatonic interaction, and the latter three of which are predominantly octatonic.

In additional, more than one hundred pages of exclusively or predominantly octatonic sketches are still extant, in two sources: (1) a "Cahier [notebook] No. 3," twenty-four pages in length; and (2) approximately one hundred loose pages of staff paper and note paper, many of which are gathrered into an envelope bearing the title "Harmonies de 2 sons de 5tes et de 4tes: Genre 'grecques'—Thrénies PAN Orgiastiques et processus Hébraïques" (Harmonies of two sounds of 5ths and 4ths: "Greek" genre—Threnodies [on the theme of] PAN and Hebraic Progressions).[1] Some of the sketches are only a few measures in length; others might be considered complete pieces of music. Not all the sketches are dated; of those that are, the earliest date is May 1890 and the last is April 1900. A preponderance of the sketches involve the combination of intervals of perfect 4ths and 5ths (derived from the three octatonic scales) to form various sonorities. The sketches add nothing of theoretic value to the octatonic vocabulary, and most are not particularly interesting or original, musically speaking; therefore, they are not reproduced or analyzed in the current study. It is interesting, however, to note some of the sketches' titles, which reaffirm Polignac's preoccupation with the connection between octatonicism and Orientalist/exotic subject matter. A sampling of five titles give a clear indication of this connection:

- "Sorte de thrénie greco-orientale, avec plaintes de chœur" (Sort of Greco-Oriental threnody, with moans of the chorus), November 1892
- "Sorte de thème funèbre (un peu Egyptien) avec chœur" (Sort of funereal theme [a bit Egyptian] with chorus), November 1892

- "D'après et surtout après des airs arabes entendus chez la Belle Fatma" (According to and especially [derived] from Arabic tunes heard chez 'La Belle Fatma'), July 1894
- "Fouillis et appels hellènes" (Hellenic hodgepodge and calls), January 1897
- "Schema rythmique du Chœur PAN" (Rhythmic schema from the PAN chorus), August 1899.

From a historical standpoint, Edmond de Polignac's music may be seen as an immediate successor to the octatonic passage in Rimsky-Korsakov's 1867 tone poem *Sadko*, Op. 5. As Taruskin writes, "True octatonicism preempts functions normally exercised by the circle of fifths, whether by a rotation of thirds or, more radically, by a tonally stable diminished harmony."[2] In other words, a melodic or motivic element that features the semitone/tone collection[3] is supported by verticalities that find their stability in all or part of the (0,3,6,9) backbone of the collection. Polignac's octatonic compositions meet that standard. They manifest elements associated with Stravinsky's octatonic compositions in the writings of Berger, Van den Toorn, and Taruskin:

- tone centers do not function as "tonics" emanating from a tonal context;
- minor 3rds and tritones are emphasized as structural elements; the tritone often acts as an "axis" between two symmetrical iterations of all or part of the collection, or creates a polarity between one section and another;
- there is a high degree of interaction and correlation between diatonic passages and the octatonic collections, and the common pitch-class content of the two systems creates both stability and tension; major and minor triads and "dominant 7th" chords can be extracted from the collections; while these may refer to tonality, they do not "function" tonally, and they do not "resolve";
- the form of the scale beginning with the semitone (0,1,3,4) is used more frequently to create harmonic structures, while the form of the scale beginning with the whole step (0,2,3,5) is used to create melodies, specifically diatonically referential tetrachords that evoke the first four pitch classes of a diatonic minor scale.[4]

The five pieces of octatonic music analyzed in this chapter are presented in chronological order. Every attempt has been made to consult the largest possible number of sources, both in manuscript and published form.

Two Movements of the *Échos de l'Orient judaïque* (1879, revised 1899 and 1901)

A. *"Ruine du Temple prédite" (1879, revised 1894, 1899, and 1901)*

"Ruine du Temple prédite" (The Destruction of the Temple Foretold) is an aria for baritone solo, (brief) soprano solo, chorus, and orchestra (or piano reduction). The work is undoubtedly one of the two Gospel-based pieces mentioned in Polignac's letter to his brother, and, for reasons discussed later, may have been the first of the two movements written.[5] The orchestral version is scored for B♭ bass clarinet, four horns in F, three trumpets in C, three trombones, violin solo, and strings.[6]

The musical examples from "Ruine du Temple prédite" included in this study are collations of the following sources:

(a) an autograph manuscript of the piano-vocal score, undated (probably 1879);

(b) two other (presumably later) autograph manuscripts of the orchestral score, undated;

(c) a copy made from the manuscript of the orchestral score, in the hand of a professional copyist, Ch. Schnéklud, Paris, 13, Rue des Abbesses, undated;

(d) choral parts and stringed-instrument parts, numbered and corrected, printed by Chaimbaud, Paris, 18, Rue de la Tour-d'Auvergne;

(e) orchestral parts, in the hand of a professional copyist, Ch. Schnéklud, Paris, 13, Rue des Abbesses, undated;

(f) piano-vocal and vocal-orchestral scores, published by Édition Mutuelle, 1906; reprinted, Geneva: Henn, undated (after 1906);

(g) an autograph manuscript of the work's text, in Latin and French, written on graph paper in Polignac's hand, undated.

"Ruine du Temple prédite" has three sections: an introductory "Préface tonale," a central "Ruine du Temple," and a concluding choral peroration, "Écho d'Occident en séquence" (based on the Ambrosian hymn "Jam lucis orto sidere"), which serves as an extended coda. The text comes from Scriptural excerpts: Jesus's prediction of the destruction of the Temple (Matthew 24, Luke 21) and his condemnation of the hypocrisy of the Pharisees (Matthew 23, Luke 11); the text of the coda-like "Écho d'Occident" concerns Jesus's thoughts about his impending death (John 12). The baritone sings the roles of both the narrator and Jesus. It may be recalled that, in the research that he conducted before he wrote the first two Gospel movements, Polignac obtained the book of synagogue chants used by the Paris Consistory of Israelite Temples, perhaps hoping to find that his experiments had precedents in Judaic tradition.[7] Although there was no octatonicism to be found in the tropes of the traditional *nusach* (the practice of singing chant in a particular Jewish community according to liturgical function and local tradition), Polignac would appropriate the shape and style of the chants for use for this work and later octatonic and Orientalist compositions. In this piece, the baritone solo bears a striking resemblance to the synagogue chants in its melismatic approach to text setting, the use of one pitch for rapid textual passages (a practice also used for psalmodic recitation in Gregorian chant), and the frequent beginnings of phrases with perfect intervals. An example of a typical chant from the synagogue *nusach* is shown in Example 9.1.

Example 9.1. Synagogue chant, "Tefilat Geshema" (Prayer for Rain), opening, from *Chants en usage dans les Temples Consistoriaux Israelites de Paris* (Paris, 1879), p. 61

In an explanatory note preceding the "Écho d'Occident," Polignac writes:

The general tonality of ["Ruine du Temple"], excluding the passages "Væ vobis" and "Pater nunc anima," is conceived in the Phrygian mode. The harmonic overview is contained in the following bass progression, with its figured bass:

5 6 5 6 5 5

[Example 9.2.]

By "Phrygian mode," Polignac refers not to the medieval and modern form of the mode—with half steps between scale degrees $\hat{1}$–$\hat{2}$ and $\hat{5}$–$\hat{6}$—but to the ancient-Greek Phrygian mode, which corresponds to the medieval/modern Dorian scale, with half steps between scale degrees $\hat{2}$–$\hat{3}$ and $\hat{6}$–$\hat{7}$. Polignac's choice of the Greek version of the mode surely reflects his interest in Bourgault-Ducoudray's research in the late 1870s, the same perio d as the composition of this work (see Chap. 3); it may be remembered that ancient-Greek Phrygian scale was based on two ascending "third species" tetrachords, each one comprising a 1 ½ 1 configuration and linked by a whole step (see Chap. 3, Fig. 3.1, p. 48).

Conforming with Polignac's note, most of the movement is based on a pentatonic subset of the ancient-Greek Phrygian scale, beginning on B♭; the pentatonic collection—presented as a hexachord, with the B♭ repeated at the octave—dominates the "Préface tonale" (mm. 1–23, not shown) and the A sections of the ternary "Ruine du Temple" (mm. 24–66; mm. 127–150, not shown). There are three principal motives derived from the pentatonic hexachord. The first is the series of ascending whole steps illustrated in Polignac's note, representing Greek-Phrygian scale degrees $\hat{1}$–$\hat{2}$, $\hat{4}$–$\hat{5}$, and $\hat{7}$–$\hat{1}$; these pairs of pitches appear both in the bass line and in the melody. The second motive is a descending perfect 4th, first presented as a B♭/F dyad (F is almost as strong a pitch center as B♭) and appearing subsequently as descending E♭/B♭ and A♭/E♭. Perfect 5ths and octaves are employed throughout, both melodically and harmonically, creating a sonic environment of "quartal harmony." Despite the frequent occurrence of leaping bass motions in fourths and fifths, the "tonic-dominant" or "tonic-subdominant" functions implied by these motions are subverted by the almost-total absence of minor or major 3rds that would create triads. Thus, while the music makes specious allusions to potential pitch centers (emanating from the pentatonic hexachord), the absence of triads or any sense of "progression" keeps the music unmoored from functional harmony. Polignac's nonfunctional employment of the diatonic scale is a precursor of modernist procedure associated especially with Stravinsky; equally "modern" is the atmosphere of stasis that pervades the "Préface tonale" and the first forty-two measures of "Ruine du Temple"—what van den Toorn refers to as a "deadlock." That sense of stasis is broken only by the first iteration of the octatonic collection in the B section that follows—the first octatonic music in Polignac's creative output.

The B-section music (mm. 67–126) is divided into two large parts, "Væ vobis" (B1, mm. 67–111) and "Pater juste nunc anima" (B2, mm. 112–126). The first part, "Væ vobis" (presented here in both the original Latin and in translation) breaks down into four musical subsections. (The verses of the text, which include repetitions of certain phrases inserted by Polignac, do not always conform to the musical subdivisions):

B1.1 ("Recitando," mm. 66.3–74): "Væ vobis Pharisæi hypocritæ serpentes"

Woe unto you, Pharisees, hypocrites, you serpents

B1.2 (mm. 75–84): "Genimina viperarum; Væ vobis Scribæ et Pharisæi hypocritæ"

You offspring of vipers; Woe unto you, Scribes and Pharisees, hypocrites,

B1.3 (mm. 85–94): "Quia diligitis primas Cathedras in synagogis et salutations in foro; genimina viperarum, quomodo fugietis ajudicio gehennae?"

For you seek out the best seats in the synagogues and the greetings in the marketplaces; offspring of vipers, how will you flee the judgment of hell?

B1.4 (mm. 95–111): "Væ vobis Pharisæi, quia clauditis regnum cælorum ante homines! vos enim non intratis, nec introëuntes sinitis intrare. Væ vobis scribæ et pharisæi hypocritæ serpentes."

Woe unto you, Pharisees, because you shut the kingdom of heaven against men; for you yourselves do not enter in, and those that are going in, you suffer not to enter. Woe unto you, Scribes and Pharisees, hypocrites, you serpents.

Subsection B1.1 (Ex.9.3), an unaccompanied baritone recitative, presents in its opening measures all three motives from the "Préface tonale" and the A section of "Ruine du Temple": the descending perfect 4th (B♭ to F), the ascending whole step (A♭ to B♭) and the minor 3rd (C♭ to A♭). It is the C♭ that "modulates" the collection into octatonicism. In a passage that wriggles like the serpent of the text (Ex. 9.3, mm. 71–74), the Greek-Phrygian collection—B♭–C–D♭–E♭–F–G–A♭–B♭—is replaced by another collection with which it shares five pitches classes. This new collection, which forms a repeating half-step/whole-step pattern—B♭–C♭–D♭–D♮–E–F–G–A♭—is one of the three octatonic scales, called, in Polignac's nomenclature, "Scale C."

The recitative, which began on a B♭, ends in measure 74 on E♮, a tritone away. At this point the four flats of the key signature are rendered natural. The next section, B1.2 (Ex. 9.4, mm. 75–84), which also begins on E♮, features a metered canonic motive exchanged between the trumpet and the voice. The motive in Example 9.4 introduces two of the partitionings available in the octatonic collection: (1) the division of the collection into two symmetrical tetrachords, each tetrachord spanning the distance of a major 3rd; and (2) its division into four minor 3rds comprising a half step followed by a whole step. The motive formed by the first three pitch classes, E–G♮–G♯ (0,3,4)—creates a "cell" (much utilized by Stravinsky) that is transposed three times, at G (3), A♯ (6), and C♯ (9).

The canonic passage ends with an unaccompanied measure marked *recitando ad lib.* (m. 84); the most frequently repeated pitches, B and G♯, are used as "common-tone" pivots, leading to the next section (B1.3, mm. 85–94; Ex. 9.5).

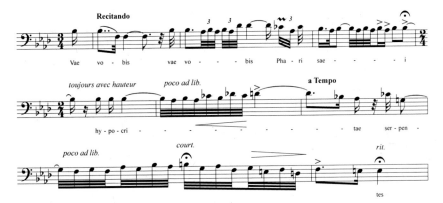

Example 9.3. "Ruine du Temple prédite," mm. 67–74

Example 9.4. "Ruine du Temple prédite," mm. 75–84

The pitch content of measures 85–89 derives from a second octatonic collection, Polignac's "Scale B": B♮, C♮, D♮, E♭, F♮, G♭, A♭, A♮. In this section, all four pitch classes common to both Scales B and C—B, D, F, and A♭—are foregrounded in both the melody and the accompaniment. The passage features rigid dotted rhythms, possibly denoting the prideful attitude of the Pharisees "in the synagogue and in the marketplace." In measures 89–91, pitches F and A♭ in the vocal line serve as "common-tone" links between Scale B and the Greek-Phrygian (modern Dorian) diatonic collection that returns in measures 90–94. In these final measures of B1.3, thunderous ascending thirty-second notes in the

Example 9.5. "Ruine du Temple prédite," mm. 85–94

bass powerfully underscore the text "Offspring of vipers, how will you flee the judgment of hell?" In measures 90–94, Polignac gradually reintroduces on strong beats the pitches from the pentatonic hexachord: first F and A♭, then B♭, C, and E♭.

In section B1.4 (mm. 95–111, not shown), the key signature of two flats, the meter ($^9_8$), the perfect-interval motives, and the rolling texture of the A section return, and the clear pitch-centricity of the passage on E♭ (the last pentatonic pitch reintroduced) strongly suggest a return to ancient-Greek Phrygian diatonicism. However, Polignac has tricked us: this section is also octatonic—although only six of the eight pitches are sounded. Here, the third octatonic collection, Polignac's "Scale A," is utilized: C–D♭–E♭–E♮/F♭–[G♭–G♮]–A/B♭♭–B♭. By omitting two of the pitch classes, Polignac has deftly crafted a parallel to the work's opening A section: the absence of G♭ and G♮ prevents the tonal implications that would have resulted from the filling in of the many E♭/B♭ dyads with major and minor thirds.

The text of non-diatonic Section B2 (mm. 112–127/1, not shown) consists of excerpts from John 12:

"Pater juste, nunc anima mea turbata est. . . . Venit hora, ut clarificetur Filius hominis."

(Just Father, now is my soul troubled. . . . The hour is come that the Son of man should be glorified.)

The E♭/B♭ dyad, continued over from the previous section and now used to open B2 (mm. 112–117, not shown), gives way to an astonishing descent by whole tones; the first four pitches (E♭–D♭–C♭–B♭♭) are presented in the vocal line, followed, in the accompaniment, by A♭–G♭–F♭/E; this line (mm. 118–23, not shown) is accompanied by a continuously changing assortment of scalar collections that aptly conveys the image of the "troubled soul." Suddenly, as Jesus declares "The hour is come that the Son of Man should be glorified," the music is filled with radiant major and minor triads scored in the upper registers. At once the sonic and spiritual atmosphere is cleansed, as it were, of the viperous Pharisees—so vehemently railed against in preceding text—and of the gritty octatonicism used to portray them musically.[8]

Interestingly, in his note, Polignac identifies both the "Væ vobis" and "Pater juste" music as "excluded" from the Phrygian mode in which the rest of the movement was conceived. He neglects, however, to identify the pitch collection—or any other organizational scheme—upon which these two sections are based. There is certainly no mention of a repeating pattern of half steps and whole steps. Perhaps, when writing this piece, the composer had not yet consciously identified or reified his "new scales." It suggests, as well, that this was the first of the two pieces written. However, as the text of "Ruine du Temple" makes clear, Polignac links his use of the octatonic collections—whether employed consciously or unconsciously—to the depiction of the Pharisees, Semitic men whom Jesus describes as "hypocrites, serpents, a brood of vipers."[9] The octatonicism of "Ruine du Temple" is only the first instance of what would become Polignac's lifelong association of octatonicism with Orientalist/semitic, barbaric, magical, and exotic subjects—an uncanny parallel to the use of the collection by Rimsky-Korsakov and other members of the New Russian School.

B. "Pilate livre le Christ" (1879, revised 1894, 1899, and 1901)

"Pilate livre le Christ" (Pilate renders up Jesus) is scored for baritone solo (Pilate), chorus SATB ("Choir of Jews"), solo violin, solo organ, and full orchestra (or piano reduction).

The musical examples from "Pilate livre le Christ" included in this study are collations of the following sources:

(a) an autograph manuscript of the piano-vocal score, undated (probably 1879);

(b) a second autograph manuscript of the full vocal-orchestral score, subtitled "Tolle," dated "Mars–Avril 1894";

(c) a manuscript copy of the piano-vocal score marked "Répétiteur" in the hand of a professional copyist, Ch. Schnéklud, Paris, 13, Rue des Abbesses, undated (possibly 1894);

(d) a set of choral parts in the hand of a professional copyist, with corrections in Polignac's hand, undated (probably 1888);

(e) a set of orchestral parts, in the hand of a professional copyist, with corrections by Polignac;

(f) a printed copy of the orchestral score, private printing, dedicated "A Madame la Princesse Edmond de Polignac," with corrections in Polignac's hand and notations on the front cover: "avec corrections 1899 et 1901" and "partition ayant servi à C. Chevillard";

(g) published piano-vocal score (Paris: Édition Mutuelle, 1906);

(h) published vocal-orchestral score (Paris: Édition Mutuelle, 1906).[10]

Like "Ruine du Temple," "Pilate livre le Christ" was probably written in 1879. The text is based on excerpts from Matthew 27, Mark 15, Luke 23, and John 19. As in "Ruine du Temple," Polignac has chosen the octatonic collection for music that could depict the Pharisees' demand that Pilate condemn Jesus to crucifixion: like Rimsky-Korsakov's use of the collection to denote "evil sorcery," here it is used to depict what might be called "evil, exotic others" (i.e., Pharisees). Years later, Polignac would describe this work as "an essay in the application of naturalism in music, consisting of adapting the known character of the music of a people to the interpretation of a dramatic scene depicting this people."[11] In other words, Polignac ascribes an essentialist meaning to the octatonic scales: the dramatic depiction of the Passion through music that the composer describes as "fervent, sad, Judaic"[12] reflects the "natural" qualities inherent in the three collections and the sonorities generated by them.

"Pilate" begins with a loosely imitative orchestral introduction (no key signature). All the notes of which are derived from Polignac's octatonic scale B (Ex. 9.6, a transcription of the manuscript of the piano-vocal score, mm. 1–28). The entries of first three instrumental voices on the pitches A, E♭, and C, respectively (mm. 1–3) spell out three of the four pitches of the diminished seventh chord that in this passage forms the backbone of octatonic "Scale B"; the missing fourth pitch, F♯/G♭, is added in entrances of voices in measure 11 and measure 13.

Example 9.6. "Pilate livre le Christ," mm. 1–28

Example 9.6.—*(cont'd)*

For the entry of the chorus, representing the Pharisees, Polignac adds a key signature of two flats, anticipating the music's sudden turn, a few measures later, to a purely diatonic G natural-minor collection. The chorus, intoning the text, "Raise him up! Crucify him!" (Ex. 9.7, mm. 31–43), begins with imitative entries on Eb and A, in keeping with the introduction's octatonic scale B, but soon moves to G-centric music. The pitch content of Pontius Pilate's long solo, which follows, consists mostly of scalar lines in the high baritone range, the scalar collection changing as his point of view shifts.

Example 9.7. "Pilate livre le Christ," mm. 31–43

Example 9.7.—(cont'd)

Example 9.7.—*(cont'd)*

At first, when he doubts Jesus's culpability, Pilate's vocal line is set on various modal scales: "I find no proof" on a Lydian scale on A♭ (mm. 54–68, not shown), and most of the following text (mm. 69–135, not shown) on the G-natural-minor collection with changing pitch centricity. Through much of this section he sings against the angry cries of the chorus; but when they drop out for a few measures, and Pilate comes to the words, "nullam causam invenio in homine isto ex his in quibus eum accusatis" (the people turn away, and behold that it is I, interrogating him before you; I find no proof in this man of the things of which you accuse him), the music instantly turns back to collection B of the introduction (Ex. 9.8, mm. 135–162).

Example 9.8. "Pilate livre le Christ," mm. 135–162

Example 9.8.—(cont'd)

A transitional passage follows (mm. 162–184, not shown), in which the chorus demands, "Sanguis ejus super nos, et super filios nostros! Dimitte nobis Barrabam!" (Let his blood be on us and our children! Release Barabbas to us!). For the next sixteen measures, the vocal and orchestral lines ascend in perpetual crescendo on sequential augmented triads. The passage appears at first to have no clear scalar derivation, but this is a ruse. In fact, the ascending bass line is constructed from four octatonic tetrachords that "modulate" through all three scales: F–G♭–E♭–A♮ ([0,1,3,4], from Scale B); B♭–C–D♭–E♭ ([0,2,3,5], from Scale A); G–A♭–B♭–B♮ ([0,1,3,4], from Scale C); and C–D–E♭–F ([0,2,3,5]), returning to Scale B). Parenthetically, this is the passage (mentioned in Chapter 4) that had so had fascinated Jules Pasdeloup when Polignac played it for him in 1884.[13] As the phrase reaches its zenith, Pilate makes his momentous decision. At his words, "Ecce Rex vester, Accipite eum vos et crucifigite! Innocens ego sum a sanguine justi hujus [*sic:* Polignac has reversed the two previous words]: vos videristis" (Here is your king, take him and crucify him! I am innocent of the blood of this just man whom you see before you), the music "resolves" and stabilizes in collection A (mm. 169–191, not shown).

This climactic moment marks the halfway point in the work. Most of the remainder consists of further interchanges between Pilate and the chorus, using the scriptural text in Latin, and appropriating Scale B, modal collections along the lines of those used in measures 69–135, and occasionally even a whole-tone collection. The chorus's final cries for the release of Barabbas and the crucifixion of Jesus (mm. 328–343, not shown) turn to Scale C, thus marking the inclusion of the third and last of Polignac's octatonic collections in the work. The passage is cross-metric ($\frac{2}{4}$ in Barabbas's solo, the choral voices, and the flutes against $\frac{3}{4}$ in the oboes); the ostinato duple-meter sixteenth-note tetrachord (0,2,3,5) played by the three flutes, accompanied by a bass line foregrounding the tritone (not shown) would be re-employed in later octatonic compositions (for a similar example, see "Danse du Serpent," Ex. 9.15). But the end holds a surprise: suddenly the chorus transmogrifies from an angry crowd to a humble band of pious supplicants, who intone, now in French rather than Latin, a prayer (the text by the composer):

O doux vainqueur, ô Roi des cieux!
De tes bourreaux la face se voile!
Ta croix est notre étoile!
Force du faible, agneau radieux!

(O sweet victor, O King of heaven!
From your executioners one hides one's face!
Your cross is our star!
Strength of the weak, radiant lamb!)[14]

Even more astonishing, the music at the end turns to the "purified" diatonic radiance of C major, replete with functional chord progressions, and an absolutely conventional closing V^7–I cadence, even including a $\hat{4}$–$\hat{3}$–$\hat{2}$–$\hat{3}$ suspension figure on the final tonic triad.

Incidental Music to *Salammbô* (1886–88)

In 1886, Edmond de Polignac conceived of a series of pieces to be used as incidental music to accompany a reading or dramatization of Gustave Flaubert's novel *Salammbô*. In a series of notes, housed among the Polignac family papers, the composer outlines an eight-movement schema, of which the "Chant à la lune" is the first (the "Danse du Serpent," written later, is not included in this group).[15] Polignac wrote that this music would be "a musical production in new strains, not a pastiche, having its historical, ethnological, and literary place." The title character herself would be represented musically by "a voice that soars above a movement from the lowest depths of the accompaniment (taken from act 1 of *Tristan,* the arias of the two lovers)."[16] The orchestration for the incidental music would consist of "8 violas, 8 violins (in unison, both with mutes, in the high registers), 3 flutes, 3 upright pianos, 2 cellos (to replace the effect of the contrabass or doubled with the bass notes of the piano), 1 harp."

A. "Chant à la lune"

While the complete, fully orchestrated version of the "Chant à la lune" does not survive in the family's papers or elsewhere, two versions of the 82-measure-long work are extant. The first source is an autograph manuscript of the vocal line, with occasional bits of accompaniment sketched in. A second autograph manuscript includes approximately half the vocal line, with different accompanying figures from those in the first manuscript; however, these sketches are less worked out, and are frequently illegible.[17] In Source 1 (the first page of which is transcribed in Example. 9.9, mm. 1–12 of the work), Polignac writes out the "scale of sounds employed" for the entire work: this is Scale C, in its half-step/whole-step version, beginning on D♭. According to a note in the composer's hand at the top of the first page, Polignac planned to score the work for an ensemble of eight to ten violas (muted), two pianos (muted [i.e., played with the soft pedal down throughout]), harp, and three flutes (apparently Polignac had abandoned the initial idea of including violins and cellos). Another note (left side of the page) indicates that the composer intended to "finish with several chords (in ordinary harmony) in the violas, flying through the night and swaying, like an echo, in the style of the middle of the overture to [Carl Maria von Weber's opera] Euryanthe."[18]

Pour 8 ou 10 altos   deux Pianos droits d'Erard   une Harpe   (3 Grandes Flûtes)
     sourdines   sourdines

(terminer par quelques
accords (harmonie
ordinaire) aux altos
s'envolant dans la nuir en
balancement comme un
écho - genre milieu de
l'ouvert[ure] d'Euryanthe)

Salammbô

Example 9.9. "Chant à la lune," incidental music to *Salammbô* (1886), mm. 1–12

Although a meter of $\frac{2}{4}$ is given, the work has an improvisatory feeling, as the composer sets the incantation of the "sacred names" ("Baalet, Tanit, Astoreth, Derceto, Mylitha, Astarte, Rabettna") to a monody with irregular phrase rhythms, long melismatic passages, frequent directives to accelerate and slow down, and absences of textual and melodic stresses on strong beats. The eighty-two measures can be broken into three sections. Section 1 ("Lent, recit. ad libit:" mm. 1–20) alternates ascending perfect fifths with a "patter"-style repetition of the sacred names in thirty-second notes on one repeated pitch. Here, Polignac has clearly used the synagogue chants encountered in his research as a model (see Ex. 9.1, p. 116).

The first seven measures contain only three pitch classes, D♭, A♭, and B♭, which are derived from a (0,2,3,5) tetrachord referable both to the Dorian and octatonic collections; D♭ is established as the centric pitch. The delay until measure 8 of the completing C♭ causes the long initial phrase to sound diatonic, especially in the climactic final gesture (mm. 6–7). A sinuous, descending cadenza containing all of Scale C's eight pitches (mm. 8–12) acts as a link to a second phrase (mm. 14–21, not shown), whose pitch content, D♮ and G♮, are derived from the collection's internal (0,1,3,4) tetrachord. While the length, melodic shape, and rhythmic content of this subsection form a parallel to the piece's opening phrase, the A♭ introduced in measure 18 causes the ascending major 6th heard in the first climax (m. 7) to be replaced by a diminished fifth in the second. This alteration not only establishes firmly the primacy of the octatonic collection for the rest of the piece, but also creates a polar relationship between the D♭ that opens Section 1 and the G♮ that concludes it.

In Section 2, "Hymne," ("Lent mesuré," mm. 22–58, not shown), the vocal line becomes ever more daunting, featuring tricky rhythms, virtuoso leaps, and long stretches of chromatic passagework, in which the tritone gains increasing prominence, all based on Scale C. The Dorian/diatonic "teases" of the first section have disappeared. The pitch content of the hymn's opening—a florid melisma on the words "Baalet, Tanit," where the tessitura mounts in each succeeding phrase—is essentially a partitioning of Scale C on the nodal points (0,3,6,9), with *fioriture*. The section reaches its climax in a fiendishly difficult, tritone-laden cadenza, which twice brings the vocal line up to B♭, the highest pitch in the piece (Ex. 9.10, mm. 42–48). Accompaniment figures first appear in measure 28 and reappear intermittently through the remainder of the work. In his 1886 letter to Robert Montesquiou, Polignac suggests his approach to the accompaniment by quoting directly from Flaubert's *Salammbô:* "'The sounds follow [the voice], muffled and hurried, like a buzzing of bees, and, becoming more and more sonorous; they fly in the night with the sobs of the waves and the shivering of the tall trees, at the summit of the Acropolis.' The nebel, here, will be replaced by a simple Pleyel [piano]."[19] In the manuscript, both the "nebel" (piano) and harp share the rapid, arpeggiated sixteenth-note figurations to echo the (0156) tetrachord of the vocal line. In order to create the "buzzing bee" sonority, Polignac directs the performers (m. 42, the first measure of Ex. 9.10) to "mess around" (fouillez)—presumably, "improvise"—on the notated pitches beneath the syllable "let" (from "Baalet"). In Source 2, Polignac writes in a note that the "arrow" figures (above the tied eighth notes in the vocal line) direct the singer to slow down through the length of the arrow—thus allowing the "nebel" player to "vary the figurations on these notes"—and then to return to the original tempo.[20]

Example 9.10. "Chant à la lune," mm. 42–48

The third and concluding section (mm. 58–82, not shown) recapitulates the elements of the preceding music, ending with expanded flourishes in the accompaniment (Ex. 9.11, m. 88) and a six-measure-long melisma in the vocal line that descends an octave and a half, on virtuosic thirty-second notes and arabesque-like figures, along Scale C.

Example 9.11. "Chant à la lune," mm. 74

B. "La Danse du Serpent"

Polignac's second piece of *Salammbô* music, "La Danse du Serpent," was written in late 1886. It received its first performance in May 1887 in the Jacquemart-André salon, in its version for chamber orchestra (two E-flat trumpets, two chromatic trumpets, four horns, three pianos, harmonium, and strings); the following month, a version for solo piano was published in *La Danse,* a special music album offered to its subscribers by the daily newspaper *Le Gaulois.*

Sources consulted for this study are: (a) a fair copy of the piano-vocal score; (b) separate orchestral parts; (c) Polignac, "La Danse du serpent," published in *La Danse: Album musical du Gaulois* (Paris: Le Gaulois, June 1888), 2:197.[21]

The composer's essentialist link of the octatonic collection and the Orientalist "nature" of the music is reaffirmed in the explanatory note at the conclusion of the work: "The desired systematic exclusion of every conventionally tonal harmonic device, throughout this piece, can be justified by a logical bias towards avoiding, when adapting a scene from the ancient Orient, our modern tonality, which took hold only after the fifteenth century of our era."[22] The note also includes a writing-out of two of the scales, C (beginning on G) and A (beginning on C) in ascending half-step/whole-step form (see Chap. 4, Fig. 4.2, p. 63); as previously noted, this is the first time that the scales appear in a printed source). Foreshadowing modernist procedure, Polignac introduces one of his newly invented key signatures—the one for Scale C: A♭ and C♯—at the start of the work, "giving us . . . the fixed scale of sounds employed to the exclusion of all others (from the beginning, marked [scale] C up to the letter A, [pitch-class] G being used here as an arbitrary point of departure or an imaginary tonic."[23]

Curiously, despite the composer's assertions, G functions as more than "an arbitrary point of departure or an imaginary tonic"; quite the contrary, among all of Polignac's octatonic works, "La Danse du Serpent" is the one that leans most heavily on pitch-centricity—and Scale C's initial pitch-class G functions, along with D, as the work's two centers; moreover, these pitches, which inevitably make reference to diatonic tonic-dominant relations, replace the tritone-related poles (0,6) that were featured in "Pilate." This, and the fact that the tonally referential tetrachord (0,2,3,5) is featured prominently, belies somewhat Polignac's assertion that the piece eschews "every conventionally tonal harmonic formula." Additionally, the composer's desire to remain within "fixed" collections notwithstanding, a linking section towards the end of the piece introduces a chord progression based on a whole-tone scale, whose pitch content necessitates—as Polignac acknowledges in his note—a jumping back and forth between Scales C and A.

The text (taken from chapter 10 of Flaubert's novel) gives the piece its form: each section begins with a line describing the action or mood. A paragraph preceding the music describes the scene in Salammbô's apartment, which is filled with the odor of incense burners filled with cardamon; behind the door a young servant plays a reed flute; the noise from the streets fade as purple shadows fall over the colonnade of the temples. In the opening chorale-like section ("far-off chants by the priests in the Temple of Tanit"), the dyads D/G, B/E, and G♯/C♯ progress in slow rhythmic values, parsing the collection in minor thirds (Ex. 9.12).

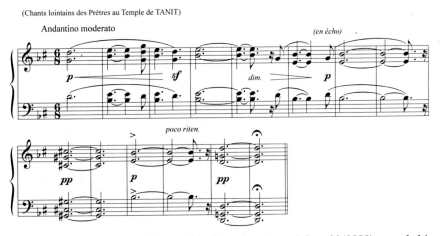

(Chants lointains des Prètres au Temple de TANIT)

Example 9.12. "La Danse du Serpent," incidental music to *Salammbô* (1888), mm. 1–14

The concluding dyad D/G signals the centricity of those two pitches in the contrapuntal, two-voice section that follows (Ex. 9.13, "Salammbô, with a swaying of her whole body, chanted prayers . . ."). The swaying scalar head motive (mm. 15–17) features the second half of the ascending Scale C on G, which features the "melodic" whole-step/half-step tetrachord D–E–F–G (0,2,3,5); the tail motive (two voices in contrary motion) begins in measure 4 in the upper voice with the "harmonic" half-step/whole-step tetrachord (0,1,3,4) that comprise the initial scale degrees of Polignac's Scale C. In effect, Polignac has created motivic contrast by pairing the two different pitch centers with the two different tetrachords.

SALAMMBÔ avec un balancement de tout son corps, psalmodiait des prières....

Example 9.13. "La Danse du Serpent," mm. 15–21

Example 9.13.—*(cont'd)*

The melody that concludes the section ("the cithara and the flute, both at once, begin to play," mm. 1–3 of Ex. 9.14) is a variation of the head motive, set in three voices; it ascends from A♭, moves sequentially to resting points on minor-3rd-related pitch-classes B and D, and reaches a climax on F.

Example 9.14. "La Danse du Serpent," mm. 28–35

The same melody becomes the principal theme in the main 6/8 section, "La Danse du python" (Andantino animato scherzando), a gigue-like dance that projects the octatonic collection in both the melody and the bass.[24] In the first half of the section, the D-centered melody weaves in rapid rhythmic patterns around the tetrachord (0,2,3,5), and is accompanied by a sixteenth-note ostinato whose lowest pitches outline the same tetrachord on pitches B♭–A♭–G–F. As the dance builds towards its climax ("The music continued . . . ever the same, hurried and frenzied; the strings grated, the flute blew"), the tempo shifts, by means of a metric modulation, into a $\frac{2}{4}$ "Marcato furioso" (mm. 88–104; Ex. 9.15, below, reproduces mm. 97–104), featuring the (0,2,3,5) ostinato tetrachord in the treble voice, set against a bass accompaniment of successive ascending fourths (which, according to the composer's directive, are to be "accentuated pompously"), the lower note of each fourth progressing sequentially through (0,3,6,9), the diminished seventh chord A♭–B♮–D–F.

Example 9.15. "La Danse du Serpent," mm. 97–104

While Polignac is no Stravinsky, one nonetheless easily recognizes a primitive foreshadowing of Stravinskian procedures. The piece concludes with a fragmentation of the "python" motive and a variation of the opening chorale.

"Exercice pour orgue" (1893)

The first (undated) sketch of the "Exercice pour orgue" appears in tiny, almost illegible handwriting in one of Polignac's sketchbooks. Composed almost exclusively on octatonic scales, it is preceded by a note in Polignac's hand: "Major thirds, Beautiful Effect." In January 1893, Polignac wrote the twenty-three-measure piece out onto full-size staff paper and presented it to his future wife, Winnaretta Singer, who was a talented organist. The original sketch of the "Exercice pour orgue" is found in one of EP's composition notebooks, labeled "Cahier No. 3"; it is untitled and undated. The autograph manuscript is dated "20 janvier 1893."[25]

Written over a C pedal, the four-measure scalar motive of the "Exercice," set contrapuntally in a predominantly three-voice texture—including an eight-note "cantus firmus" in the bass voice—traverses the three octatonic collections B, A, and C, respectively. At the bottom of the first page of the manuscript (reproduced in Fig. 9.1, p. 140), Polignac writes out the pitch content of each of the three scales, and, in a note, informs the reader/performer that "Any [scale] degree taken, in each series, as a point of departure [allows for] enharmonic substitutions, as the case arises." The opening tetrachord of the first iteration of the cantus firmus, C–D–F–E♭ (mm. 1–2 of Ex. 9.16), makes obvious reference to Mozart's frequently-used "Credo" motive (C–D–F–E), featured most prominently in the last movement of the "Jupiter" Symphony, K. 551. In keeping with Polignac's "major thirds" idea, each half note of the cantus firmus is paired with an augmented triad in the middle voice (for example, C–E–G♯ accompanies the opening pitch C); the roots of these triads (C–B♭–A–G) are an inversion of the (0,2,3,5) tetrachord that makes up each half of the cantus firmus. Augmented triads cannot be formed by the notes of an octatonic collection; therefore, Polignac must insert additional pitches to create (048) triads.

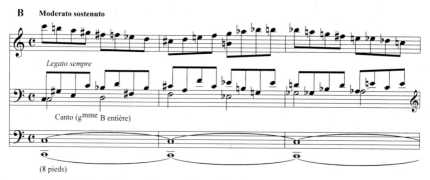

Example 9.16. "Exercice pour orgue," mm. 1–4

Example 9.16.—(cont'd)

The return to collection B in measure 13 (not shown) features a four-voice harmonization of the "cantus firmus," followed by an incomplete statement of the motive on Scale A. At this point, the composer (in his own words in the manuscript) "[abandons] the progression, whose limit is reached in the formidable aggregation of a chord (à la Schola) of five [sic: Polignac means four] minor thirds stacked up so as to end at the upper octave of the note with which the circular chain began."[26] Polignac has acknowledged the recursive aspect of the scales that eventually would cause Messiaen to name them among the "modes of limited transposition." It is this very quality of limitation (self-imposed by the composer) that makes this "exercise" less interesting than Polignac's other octatonic forays. As in "Ruine du Temple" and "Pilate livre le Christ," the composer concludes the work by reverting in the coda ("maestoso") to a diatonic collection—in this case, to the key of C minor. This return to diatonicism seems necessary from a dramatic standpoint: Polignac's experiment, throughout the body of the work, in the juxtaposition of two symmetrical elements—the repeating, minor-third-based scales in the highest voice, and the augmented triads in the middle voice—results in a sonority that is turgid rather than tension-filled; the building towards climax through rising tessitura and textural filling-out is not supported by tension in the pitches themselves, which are stuck in symmetry.

Interestingly, in the manuscript, Polignac precedes the music with two Latin aphorisms that allude to his thoughts on the meaning of the scales and octatonicism. The first, "Ablatâ petrarum unâ, Tota corruit Ædes" ("When one stone is taken away, the whole edifice collapses"), surely refers to the "collapse" of tonality resulting from the reordering of whole steps and half steps; the second, "Auditû primum Stupente stridorem, jam lenitam, Tonorum in unum compellere Gregem" (He hears first an astonishing screech of sounds, [which] then [sound] gentler, forming together in one group), undoubtedly expresses the composer's hope that the gritty "screech" of octatonicism will eventually be accepted and find a wider audience. One final Latin phrase, from Virgil, is cited just underneath a spelling-out of the three scales, at the bottom of the first page (Fig. 9.1): "Numero Deus impare Gaudet" ("God loves odd numbers.")[27]

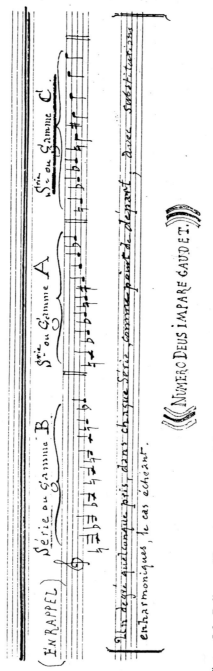

Figure 9.1. Polignac, "Exercice pour orgue" (manuscript), bottom of first page, with the three octatonic scales spelled out and explained, followed by a Latin phrase from Virgil, "God loves odd numbers"

Afterword

The "discovery" of the octatonic scale by Edmond de Polignac—and, later, by Alexandre de Bertha—entirely independent of the collection's earlier applications by German and Russian composers, can be attributed in part to a logical development in a tonal system that was rapidly becoming chromaticized. However, it may also speak to a deeper cultural need. If we look back on the history of another art form, for example, the first photograph was taken in 1826, but photography as a science was not invented until 1839. The imagination that wanted photography was ready for its reification only when it had reached a certain state in its technical advancement. Similarly, the Romantic musical imagination that dared to break the mold of conventional diatonic procedures, moving gradually into the realm of mediant-related harmonic progressions, would have to wait until 1867 for the scale governing some of those procedures to be reified, and another dozen years until that scale was theorized.

In the musical realm, a similar process of "evolutionary" revolution in musical composition was surely at work as well. The time that has passed between Rimsky-Korsakov's first version of *Sadko*—the tone poem, Op. 5 (1867), which introduces Rimsky's first octatonic scale—and the second version—the full-length opera of the same name (1897), whose second scene is based, in large part, upon triads drawn exclusively from Scale C—is a full thirty years. And, as Allen Forte has demonstrated, Franz Liszt experimented with proto-octatonic thirds-related constructions as early as 1858, but it was not until the composer's very late period (1880–83), when he was writing highly atonal experimental works, that, according to Forte, "[Liszt's] conscious manipulation of such structural properties seems incontrovertible." At the end of the manuscript of one such experimental work, *Ossa arida* (1879), Liszt wrote the following postscript: "Professors and apostles of the conservatories most strongly disapprove of the dissonance of the continuous thirds-construction of the first twenty bars, which is not yet customary. Nevertheless, so has he written. Liszt (Villa d'Este, 18–21 October 79)."[1] The year 1879 also marks the period of Polignac's octatonic discovery: by then, the idea was unquestionably "in the air."

It is not inconceivable that the early French modernists might have been influenced by Polignac's music and theories. The public debates and articles surrounding Polignac's "octatonic wars" with Bertha would surely have been followed with interest by composers who read *Le Figaro* and the leading journals of music and culture. Claude Debussy, an octatonic composer (of the "fortuitous" type, according to Taruskin), was introduced to the Prince and Princesse de Polignac in 1894 by musical salon hostess Marguerite de Saint-Marceaux, and subsequently frequented the Polignac salon; an 1895 letter to Pierre Louÿs attests to Debussy's interest in—and implied admiration of—Polignac's music.[2] Maurice Ravel (in Taruskin's terms, a "true" octatonic composer) began to attend the musical gatherings in the late 1890s, in the company of his teacher Gabriel Fauré. While both composers—especially Ravel—were influenced by the Russians, both would also have had many occasions to hear Edmond de Polignac holding forth on "his" scales. It is impossible to prove Polignac's influence with absolute certainty, but what is certain is that Debussy and Ravel can be placed in the Polignac salon—in Ravel's case, well before the date of his first octatonic essays; therefore this indigenous source of influence cannot be ruled out.

In any event, Polignac's octatonic compositions and treatise (transcribed, translated, and analyzed in part two), and Bertha's subsequent writings on the same subject, must now take their place in the history of the theoretical recognition of the collection. While Rimsky-Korsakov's 1867 description of the "half-step, whole-step" scale will remain its first written reification, the first published description of the octatonic scales, originally attributed to Berger in 1963, must now be moved backwards to 1888, and attributed to Edmond de Polignac.

Part Two

Edmond de Polignac's
Octatonic Treatise

Prince Edmond de Polignac, ca. 1890. Collection of the author.

Preface to Polignac's Octatonic Treatise

> For many authors the actual writing of the manuscript . . . is a means of composition, not an end.
>
> —Philip Gaskell

> I played this number for Pasdeloup, who seemed very interested in hearing the effect. Perhaps he'd be willing to have it performed, if I pushed him a bit, but I'm not very good at pushing others; I have enough trouble pushing myself.
>
> —Edmond de Polignac

General Remarks

Edmond de Polignac's treatise-sketchbook, "Étude sur les successions alternantes de tons et demi-tons (Et sur la gamme dite majeure-mineure)," in English: "A Study on the Sequences of Alternating Whole Steps and Half Steps (and on the Scale Known as Major-Minor)," is a fascinating document. It offers modern music scholars what are apparently the first full-length attempts to classify and organize the theoretical and compositional elements of octatonic theory, and it provides copious musical examples to demonstrate those elements. As an important precursor of the work of Berger, Van den Toorn, and Taruskin, the treatise is an astonishingly "modern" document. But the "modern" aspects of this nineteenth-century document created no end of complexities and problems for its twenty-first-century editors: personal (as regards the man writing the document), material, aesthetic, theoretical, historical, philosophical, and editorial.

First, as we have seen in the biographical chapters, Polignac's attitude toward his own creativity and what to do about it and with it is one of ambivalence. Here we have a man who believes he has created something truly revolutionary and forward-thinking in music, and he is confident that his ideas and his compositions will alter music forever. And yet, as the above quote from Polignac attests, he has self-promotion issues: he has trouble pushing himself. This led us to the question: what purpose was the document intended to serve? Was its writing meant to be, as Gaskell suggests, "a means of composition, not an end"—or was it meant eventually to be shared with an enlightened and adventurous musical readership, or published in a music magazine like *Le Ménestrel,* or perhaps even published as a book? It is not clear.

This brought us to the second problem: how to deal with the material of the autograph manuscript, specifically the manner in which Edmond de Polignac wrote out his ideas and compositional sketches. Some pages—especially those concerned with theoretical exposition—are written in ink, in the confident hand of a pedagogue intent on teaching. However, many others—especially the compositional sketches—are written in pencil; these frequently represent the spontaneous, off-the-cuff jottings of a composer in the act of composing. Many of these jottings are little better than "chicken scratches," almost impossible to read; their illegibility rendered transcription a nightmare. Additionally, it is clear that neither the overarching theoretical framework nor the order of the musical examples was completely thought out before being committed to paper. Sometimes Polignac will start an idea and pick up on it again several or many pages later; or the inverse will happen: Polignac will start writing down an idea, run out of room on the page, and cram the rest of the musical thought onto any staff of any page with some unused space left on it, sometimes fifty or so pages earlier.

The third problem was Edmond de Polignac's sloppy approach to notation, which became apparent as soon as the first draft rendered the document legible. To put it mildly, the composer had an extremely casual attitude regarding the way he wrote his music: the notation of noteheads and rhythms in the musical sketches is often slovenly, and Polignac's approach to the notation of accidentals throughout is, alternatively, erratic, erroneous, and redundant. In some cases, this might have indicated compositional indecision. Fortunately, at the top of most of the examples, the composer supplies a marking of "Scale A (or B or C)," therefore leaving no doubt as to the pitch content of the any given example.

In preparing the transcription and analysis of the treatise, we were confronted with the question of what kind of "scholarly" edition was to be published: would this be a "warts-and-all" edition, with every omitted flat, every misplaced notehead accounted for and footnoted? Or would it be more beneficial to create a corrected, "socialized" edition—one in which missing accidentals were supplied to allow for easy reading at the piano, in which understanding of the theory's and the music's meaning was editorially guided through a clean presentation on the page?

At the same time, we recognized problems inherent in the translation of Polignac's French texts. Chief among these were the tensions created 1) between the music-theoretical and the music-historical aspects of the document, and 2) between the nineteenth-century vocabulary that Polignac, with no precedent to guide him, used to describe his findings, and the twentieth- and twenty-first-century vocabulary of music-theoretical concepts and terminology with which any knowledgeable music scholar brings to a reading of this book. Even though, to this day, the theory of octatonicism is still being developed, we nonetheless have a working vocabulary with which to describe and address its constituent elements: we use terms like "pitch classes" and "pitch-class sets," "collections," "partitioning," "tritone axes," and "non-functional triads." In his treatise, Polignac frequently uses terms associated with diatonicism and tonality to describe these same elements— terms like "second inversion," for example. (These terms will be discussed in detail in the "Notational Unorthodoxies" section that follows, p. 152.) Translating these terms literally would have created confusion and no end of musical mixed metaphors; at the same time it would have been impossibly anachronistic to put twenty-first-century terms like "collection" and "partitioning" into the mouth of a nineteenth-century musician. It was often a struggle for us to determine a theoretical point of view and to arrive at an English translation that would both respect Polignac's authorial voice and the historical time and place of the document *and* render the translation comprehensible and meaningful for twenty-first-century readers, particularly those already knowledgeable in octatonic theory.

We cannot know either Polignac's authorial intentions as regards the disposition of the document's contents or whether he hoped ever to have it published. However, in the interests of posthumously presenting the composer and the theorist in the best light, we have chosen to "socialize" the document to the extent possible. Therefore, editorial intervention is considerable; the decision to do a thorough clean-up of the musical examples—including the addition throughout of all missing accidentals and other missing apparatuses—was made in the hopes of facilitating the legibility of Polignac's thought and music through an uncluttered presentation on the page and, thus, rendering the treatise's meaning more comprehensible to a scholarly readership.

Chronology

The autograph manuscript, the unique copy of the treatise, bears no date. Based on external evidence (documented elsewhere in this study), the date of its writing has been determined to be 1879. That Polignac revisited the document and added more text and musical examples at a later date is confirmed by a sketch, squeezed into a small empty space on a stave (on treatise-page [henceforth, tr-p.] 33), with the commentary "arrangement for harp as heard in London July 85," indicating that at least part of the treatise content was added post-1885. Polignac wrote a substantial number of octatonic sketches in the late 1890s, so it is possible that these addenda date from the same period.

Source Description

Polignac's 98-page manuscript is contained in a black oblong notebook, 100 pages of 8-stave paper, 13.5 x 21.5 cm. On the inside front cover, in the left-hand corner, part of a white label is visible containing the text "Maison L—LT, P—IE [or RE]." The missing words may be "Maison LARD-ESNAULT, PAPETERIE [Paris]." This label has been covered with another, smaller label: "Papeterie CHARTIER, 25, Faub. St Honoré." A price marking of "1f25" is visible. The first (non-stave) page, verso, contains "Signes d'Abbréviations." The title page, on the first piece of 8-stave paper, is marked in black ink, "Étude sur les successions alternantes de tons et demi-tons (Et sur la gamme dite majeure-mineure)." Roughly one-third of the pages are written in black ink; the other two-thirds are written in pencil. Pages are sporadically numbered by Polignac. The last (non-stave) page, recto, has a postscript, "Essais— Expériences—non-faite pour plaire au public"; on the reverse side, Polignac has added an ad-hoc "Table du cahier."

The manuscript is housed in a private collection. Permission was granted by the manuscript's owner for the reproduction and translation of this material.

General Characteristics

While the treatise does not break down into discrete sections per se, there are general groupings of subject matter, albeit with interruptions. Henceforth, to distinguish treatise pages from pages of this book, we shall refer to tr-p. or tr-pp., treatise-page(s).

The first quarter of the book is primarily concerns with an exposition of general octatonic theory. First Polignac spells out what he calls "Series A, B, and C," using the ascending half-step/whole-step form of the scale, beginning respectively on the semitones C/Db, B/C, and C♯/D (tr-p. 3). Next, still using the version of the scale beginning with a semitone, Polignac shows that the collection generates major and minor triads (in French theoretical parlance, *accords parfaits*—that is, triads whose root and fifth form a perfect fifth) on scale degrees Î, 3̂, 5̂, and 7̂ (tr-p. 5). On tr-p. 6 the three collections A, B, and C are given the name the "chromatico-diatonic scales." A few pages later Polignac offers a harmonic progression using Scale A (tr-p. 11), and he then notes (at the bottom of the same page) that the collection can be broken into two tetrachords a tritone apart— (0,1,3,4) tetrachords if the scale begins with a semitone, (0,2,3,5) tetrachords if it begins with a whole tone: C–Db–Eb–E♮/Gb–G♮–A–Bb, or E–F♯–G–A/Bb–C– Db–Eb in Scale A. [Note: for the most part, we will limit the use of pitch-class notation to these two sets: (0,1,3,4), indicating the octatonic tetrachord beginning with a half step, and (0,2,3,5), indicating the octatonic tetrachord beginning with a whole step.] On tr-p. 12 Polignac introduces key signatures applicable to the three different collections; on tr-pp. 16–17 and tr-p. 19 he mines the collections for their interval content. He then begins to experiment with melodic and contrapuntal figures, as well as harmonic progressions, derivable from the scale, even including "modulations" from one form of the scale to another (tr-pp. 15, 18). Toward the end of the section, Polignac starts applying his theories directly to composition, ascribing specific affects to certain chords progressions (e.g. the example on tr-p. 21 is described as having a "noble, mournful character").

From tr-p. 23 through tr-p. 34 (with a few interruptions), Polignac begins an exploration of what he calls the "major-minor" scale, today known as a "heptatonia secunda" mode. Explained most simply, the scale is a white-key C scale with a flatted third degree (Eb); it therefore contains a "minor" tetrachord (0,2,3,5) and a "major" tetrachord (0,2,4,5). In its various rotations it takes on qualities of the other white-key modes (transposed to start on F, for example, the initial tetrachord evokes the "Lydian" mode because of the tritone between the intial F and the B♮ on the fourth scale degree). The scale differs from the traditional white-key modes in that it contains two tritones (if starting on C, for example, Eb–A and F–B). The mode was sometimes used by Béla Bartók,[1] and has been the subject of various inquiries by modern scholars.[2] On tr-p. 23, Polignac takes the scale through six rotations. From that point on, for the next ten or so pages, he explores the collection's compositional possibilities, writing long musical sketches (he is particularly attracted to the "Phrygian" rotation of the scale, beginning with pitch-classes B and C).

In the next dozen or so pages, Polignac alternates experiments with sequences of intervals (alternations of [0,2,3,5], which produces a span of a perfect 4th, and [0,1,3,4], which produces a span of a major 3rd) and the trying-out of harmonic progressions. He experiments with "simulations" of cadences from "conventional tonality" using chord movements in mediant-relationship to each other (C to Eb, C to Ab, for example). On tr-p. 38, he lists melodies and motives from diatonic compositions (including an aria from Mendelssohn's *Elijah*) that prominently feature (0,1,3,4) tetrachords.

In the second half of the treatise, Polignac becomes increasingly preoccupied with the relationship of his octatonic theories to his musical settings of the Gospel texts, including the unfinished "Caiaphas" music from the missing "First Notebook of Scales A, B, C." Table 1.1 documents the number of musical sketches that may be related to this ongoing project, sketches that are meant to evoke Orientalism/exoticism, described as "Judaic" or "Hebraic," "pagan" or "Greek."

By the end of the treatise's 98 pages, Polignac has reached an impressively detailed and complex level of compositional application of the octatonic collection. It bears noting that literally half of the musical examples in the treatise are written on Scale A—no doubt because, as is the case with so many other pedagogical music texts, the model scale begins on pitch-class C.

In both his theoretical explanations and his musical examples, Polignac almost always uses the semitone/tone (0,1,3,4) form of the octatonic collection. He is more interested in exploring the collection's minor-3rd-related constructions than consideration of melodic activity. He alludes only in passing to the "diatonic qualities" that resulting from the utilization of the tone/semitone (0,2,3,5) form of the collection.

Table 1.1. Sketches with Titles Referring to Orientalist/Exotic or Biblical/Hebraic Subject Matter

Page	Subject matter	Description of the music	Scale
15	At Caiaphas's palace	Pompous "French overture" motive with dotted-8th, 16th rhythm	A
27	Theme for the Passover [the last Supper]	Progression of mediant-relation chords	A/C/B Maj/min
31–32	Phalanxes of harps and cherubim/vision of Christ/celestial spaces	4 "harmonic progressions" using the major-minor scale	A
39	Scene from "Dante's Inferno"—large celestial choir, Catholic-style	Alternating dom. 7th and minor chords, chorale-style;	B/A
45	Ave Rex to ornament the distant Jewish "Orientale"	Broken-chord "oom-pah" accompaniment and sinuous melody in "Jewish/Oriental" style	B
50	Crowd and Hebraic March/proposition "à la Zigane"/"biblical phrase"	Allegretto pesante; syncopated accompaniment in 3rds; sinuous melody	B
51	Character: sad, Judaic fervor	Moderato grave; ascending motive set over a pedal point	A/B/C
60–61	Sort of a prelude to the scene at Caiaphas' palace	$\frac{6}{8}$ meter; "French overture" motive in dotted rhythms from tr-p. 15; movement from scale to scale and progressions from "major" to minor"; internal pedal point	
62	Kind of Hebraic disorder	$\frac{6}{8}$ meter; contrapuntal texture; cross-rhythms; alternation of octonic tetrachords	C

67–68	Effects of stinging harmonies (perhaps for Greek music)	"stinging" juxtapositions of major and minor 3rds	A
72	Motive of a march to the Calvary	Contrapuntal motives grouped in 3-measure phrases; a second motive in 5 beats denotes "the fatigue created by the weight of the cross"	A
73–75	Genre Grand Pontiff (Caiaphas) / genre *Écho judaïque*	"Pompous" arioso bass motive, accompanied by ostinato tritone motive	A/C
86	Motive incited by the melody of Pilate—sickly, sad, desolate	Imitative melodic movement with arpeggiated accompaniment	A
89	Pagan harmony	Two-voice texture "without 3rds"	C

Editorial Principles

As we mentioned in the General Remarks, our first concern has been legibility and clarity: we have determined that the editorial intervention necessary to produce a comprehensible document supersedes issues of "authenticity."

Throughout, added accidentals and missing clefs have been notated in gray; corrections of other small errors and omissions have been tacitly incorporated. In instances when the pitch content was unclear, we relied on the indication of the Scale (A or B or C), usually written by Polignac above the first measure of the sketch.

Asterisks (*) indicate that Polignac wants to add some explanation or commentary *to his own text*. Occasionally he used plus signs (⁺) or x's in the examples as well as asterisks.

Plus signs (⁺), added editorially in the text, are used to point out one particular word or concept in Polignac's text, which is then explained in the comments.

Editorial comments are placed in the treatise, indented, and marked with a ❧.

Notational Unorthodoxies

Polignac devised and designed a number of original figured-bass markings, accidentals, and other indications, many of these very fanciful. These have been faithfully reproduced on a page of "Abbreviation Signs" that precede tr-p. 1. It should be noted that Polignac does not actually end up using all these signs in the treatise.

In most cases, we have adhered to Polignac's notation of stem direction, even in instances where this produces divergence from standard notational practice.

Throughout the treatise, Polignac makes reference to "figured-bass notation" (Fr. "chiffrage"), using two different kinds of 6's for major and minor triads; "first inversions" (Fr. "1ers renversements"); and other diatonic harmonic nomenclature. He is not bothered by the use of diatonic terminology to describe triad structures within an octatonic context. We have retained the eccentric paradox, and have left this terminology unchanged.

Unorthodoxies of Terminology and Nomenclature: A Glossary

In the treatise Polignac frequently uses diatonic/tonal terminology and nomenclature to name or describe octatonic terms or procedures. We therefore offer a glossary to define, describe, or explain Polignac's often complex terminology.

1. *Ambitus* (Lat.). This archaic theoretical word, meaning "the course of a melodic line," used pervasively in the study of Gregorian chant, has been translated here as "range." Polignac probably came across the word in his

studies of early music. In the treatise, he generally uses the term when discussing the octatonic pitch content that fills in the "range" of an interval.

2. *Dessin* (Fr.). A term used by Antoine Reicha and others to denote the smallest unit of melodic construction. We have translated it here as "pattern" or "model pattern."

3. *Dominant* (Fr. *dominante*). Polignac uses the French "dominante" in three conventional diatonic ways, to mean:

(a) a scale degree ($\hat{5}$);

(b) a harmony (a dominant chord in a diatonic system);

(c) a chord part, i.e., the fifth of a triad.

However, Polignac also gives the word "dominante" a specific meaning within the octatonic system; it denotes:

(d) scale degrees $\hat{2}$, $\hat{4}$, $\hat{6}$, and $\hat{8}$, the pitches that furnish the jumping-off point for datonically referential tetrachords (0,2,3,5), the "melody tetrachords." To distinguish between diatonic and octatonic uses of the word, we have italicized *dominant* when it is being used to refer to one of the nodal points. *Tonic* (see below) and *dominant* are often presented in antecedent-consequent-like phrases, an allusion to diatonic contrapuntal practice.

4. *Membre* (Fr.). Like *dessin,* this term, also used by Reicha, denotes a small unit of melodic construction. We have translated it here as "segment."

5. *Processus* (Lat.). The *New Grove Dictionary of Music and Musicians* defines *processus* as a synonym of *ambitus,* that is, to mean "the course of a melodic line." However, Polignac uses the two words in different contexts. In translating *processus* here as "progression," we acknowledge the "process" aspect of the term.

6. *System* (Fr. *système*). The organizational principals around a particular scale; today, we would use the word "collection." We have retained the word *system* in italics, to distinguish it from the other musical term, "system," which means the linking of two or more staves with a brace or double-barline.

7. *Tonic* (Fr. *tonique*). As with "dominante," Polignac uses the French "tonique" in three conventional diatonic ways, to mean:

(a) a scale degree ($\hat{1}$);

(b) a harmony (a tonic chord in a diatonic system);

(c) a chord part, i.e., the root of a triad.

In the octatonic system, Polignac also uses the word "tonique" to mean:

(d) scale degrees $\hat{1}, \hat{3}, \hat{5}$, and $\hat{7}$ in the (0,1,3,4) form of the scale. These are the four pitches in an octatonic scale upon which major and minor chords can be constructed (for example, in Scale A, in the [0,1,3,4] form of the scale, these pitches would be C, E♭, F♯, and A, the pitches that partition the collection symmetrically into [0,3,6,9]). Taruskin calls these pitches "nodal points." As with *dominant,* we have italicized *tonic* when it is being used to refer to an octatonic event.

Inclusive Pages

Some of Polignac's musical examples extend over more than one page. The following "inclusive" list indicates these examples:

Tr-pp. 24–25 (following tr-p. 27)
Tr-pp. 28–29
Tr-pp. 29–30
Tr-pp. 31–32
Tr-pp. 34–35
Tr-pp. 41–42–43
Tr-pp. 45–46
Tr-pp. 48–49
Tr-pp. 54–55
Tr-pp. 55–56
Tr-pp. 57–58 [top system]
Tr-pp. 60–61
Tr-pp. 63–64
Tr-pp. 64–65
Tr-pp. 67–68
Tr-pp. 68–69
Tr-pp. 73–74
Tr-pp. 82–83
Tr-pp. 85–86
Tr-pp. 87–88

"Displaced" Material

As we indicated earlier, Polignac would sometimes write down an idea and pick up on it again several or many pages later, cramming the rest of the musical thought onto any page with some unused space; in other instances, he would return to a musical idea and make reference to the page where the idea had first appeared. Sometimes he would invent imaginative little signs to indicate where the idea returned. The following list indicates the various instances of "displaced material":

Tr-p. 4 has been moved to follow tr-p. 5
Tr-p. 22: material from tr-p. 51 (bottom) has been moved to tr-p. 22
Tr-pp. 23, 24, and 25 have been moved to follow tr-p. 27
Tr-p. 37: material from tr-p. 92 has been moved to tr-p. 37 at the "moustache" sign
Tr-p. 37: material from tr-p. 40 has been moved to the bottom of tr-p. 37
Tr-p. 88: material from tr-p. 90 has been moved to the bottom of tr-p. 88

Edmond de Polignac

A Study on the Sequences of Alternating Whole Steps and Half Steps (and on the Scale Known as Major-Minor)

Translation and edition: Sylvia Kahan
Transcription and edition of the musical examples: David Smey

Abbreviation Signs

L loco: place and exact limit of a motive or accompanying figure

L.S. ou *L.inf.:* high limit or low limit

D means *dominant*

T means *tonic*

Figured bass:

⁴ means   Scale A

The same in the two other scales B and C

"Tritone" [is] indicated by ♈ or 𝟝

"up until" [is indicated] by ∽

"Entry of a motive or an instrument" [is indicated] by ▾ ▴

Continuation of an accompaniment above or below a motive [is indicated] by
Segue

One or two gestures at each bar line of the measure

or above the bar line

The figured bass **6** means 1st inversion of a minor chord (3)

The figured bass **6** means 1st inversion of a major chord (5)

The figured bass **Ɛ** means two major 3rds one on top of the other with one note in common

Abbreviation Signs [continued]:

For a [musical] stroke traversing one of the scales A, B, or C:

that is to say, the letter of the scale in which the piece is written replacing the notes of a line with an arrow indicating the arrival note of the line

α means the scale of six notes in whole steps beginning on C or any other degree

β means the same thing beginning on G♮ or F♮

Pariter, or *Par* means repetition of the same pattern in sequences and with other notes

> ~ Approximately half the abbreviation symbols never appear in any of the sketches. However, Polignac frequently employs the figured-bass numbers.

[- - - - -]

[tr-p. 1]

Theoretical Exposé

The natural series of whole steps and half steps, such as it is adopted today to make up our musical scale, can be built in *three different series* of whole steps and half steps (major 2nds and minor 2nds) alternating regularly between them.

Ex: V.S.

[- - - - -]

[tr-p. 2] [blank page]

[- - - - -]

[tr-p. 3]

Table of the 3 series A, B, C.

Ex.:

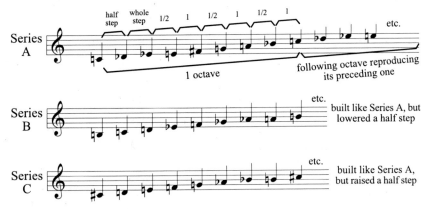

Taking any note in one of the 3 series (A, B, or C) as a point of departure, we can see that it reappears an octave higher at a distance of eight scale degrees. We can also see that, in Series A, for example, the scale from C to C is not made up the same way as from D♭ to D♭, in that, starting from C, the first degree is a half step, while, starting from D♭, it is a whole step.

❧ [Tr-p. 4 has been moved to follow tr-p. 5 in the translation.]

[- - - - -]

[tr-p. 5]

Harmonic elements that characterize each of these three series or scales

The triads that can be formed in Scale A are

major or minor

The triads that can formed in Scale B are

major or minor

The triads that can be formed in Scale C are

major or minor

> ✎ The pitches in the above examples, scale degrees $\hat{1}$, $\hat{3}$, $\hat{5}$, and $\hat{7}$ in the (0,1,3,4) form of the octatonic scales, are what Taruskin refers to as "nodal points," the notes upon which major and minor triads can be constructed. Polignac's term for these pitches is *tonics* (*toniques*), but he does not yet introduce the term; it will appear for the first time on tr-p. 9.

[- - - - -]

[tr-p. 4]

Remarks on the triads that occupy corresponding places in the different scales A, B, and C

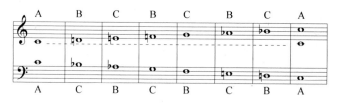

Roots of major and minor triads, starting with C and moving up or down by the same distance, produce roots belonging to the scales marked by the letters B or C.

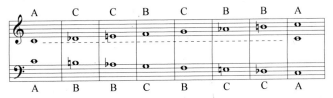

We can see that the triads on A♭ and E♮ are the most closely related because of the common tones E (third of C), C (third of A♭), and A♭ (G♯) (3rd of E).

> ❧ It is not clear how Polignac came to choose the pitches that comprise the above studies. The first study appears to be a precursor of the "major-minor" scale that will be discussed beginning on tr-p. 23. In alternating pitches from Scales B and C in mm. 2–7, Polignac inadvertently demonstrates the symmetrical quality of the scales.
>
> The second sketch demonstrates two tetrachords that share the same pattern, ½–1½–½. These studies may illustrate the possibility of accessing pitch content outside any given scale by "modulation" to one of the two other collections.

[-----]

[tr-p. 6]

Notes

We will designate each of the 3 series, according to the notes that make it up, by the names of scale A or B or C, or *system*[+] A, B, or C (see the table on tr-p. 3).

> ❧ +Here, in the original French, Polignac refers to "gamme A, B, C ou système A.B.C." Since, later on in this document, we make references to a "system" in the context of its traditional musical definition, that is, two or more statves connected by means of braces or bar lines, we have italicized this iteration of "system," which, in twenty-first-century parlance, would be referred to as a "collection."

Everything that will be said about scale A (as far as its constituent elements or its harmonic progressions are concerned) will be applicable to the two other scales, a fact that necessarily follows from their identical formations. These series will also be called "chromatico-diatonic" scales.

Remark: Each scale is composed of 4 whole steps and four half steps. In series A, the 8 notes, in ascending sequence from C to B♭, could be considered as being the superimposition of two similar segments, the range of each of which is a major third.

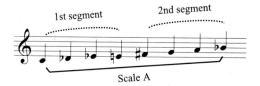

But in ascending from D♭ to C you proceed by superimposed fourths without encountering a major third in either of the separate segments.

❧ Polignac has identified the different ranges of the two tetrachords (0,1,3,4) and (0,2,3,5), respectively.

[- - - - -]

[tr-p. 7]

Major triads (with figured bass) [that can be constructed] from scale A

from whence it follows that in scale A, the interval content is comprised of four majors 3rds, which are

as well as four perfect 5ths, built on C, E♭, G♭, and A; eight minor 3rds (one on each scale degree); four perfect 4ths (inversions of the four perfect 5ths);

8 tritones (one on each scale degree); four half steps, four whole steps; four minor 6ths, and eight major 6ths (the inversions of the major and minor 3rds); four major 7ths, four minor 7ths (inversions of the whole or half steps); four minor 9ths, and four major 9ths.

> Here we see Polignac thinking as a composer as well as a theorist: he is mining the scale for its interval content in order to apply the sonorities to composition. As indicated in the "abbreviations," the figured-bass number "5" refers to a major chord in root position.

[- - - - -]

[tr-p. 8]

Continuation of the remark

But an interval of a tritone always cuts the octave of nine notes into two equal parts, whether the first degree is a whole step or half step.

Ex.: Scale A

or Scale A

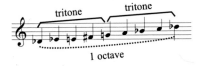

> Polignac illustrates a fundamental principle of octatonicism: the subdivision of the collection at the tritone (0,6).

[- - - - -]

[tr-p. 9]

In considering the major chords in Scale A, we see that the notes

are the roots[+] [of triads]; the notes

are the thirds [of triads]; and the notes

are the fifths [of triads].

Additionally, the notes

are the minor 7ths above the same roots, and

and

are the minor 9ths above the same roots,

producing the chords

7+

or

♭9+

etc. on each of the 4 *tonic* scale degrees.[++]

We can see that the major or minor triad on C is related by a tritone to the major or minor triads on F♯/G♭, and that this is also true for the major/minor triads on E♭ and the major or minor triads on A♮. The major 9th chord cannot be formed in these scales.

> 🐟 In its first iteration here ([+]), we have translated the French word "tonique" as "[triad] root." Polignac is showing the constituent parts—root, third, and fifth—of the major triads that can be built on Î, 3̂, 5̂, 7̂, the four *tonics* (nodal points) in the ascending form of an octatonic scale (C, E♭, G♭, and A♮ in Scale A). However, in the second iteration ([++]), Polignac intends "toniques" to mean "nodal points," i.e., pitch classes Î, 3̂, 5̂, 7̂, upon which major and minor triads can be constructed. See the Glossary in the Preface to the Treatise (pp. 154–55).

[- - - - -]

[tr-p. 10]

Continuation of the notes and remarks

In the chromatico-diatonic scales, if the first degree is a whole step, the range of the seven notes, before reaching the octave, is a major 7th; if the first degree is a half step, the range is only a minor 7th.

Ex.

Scale B   Scale A

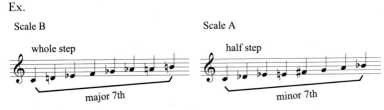

The reader will notice that every note in a scale that is not a *tonic* is a *dominant* of one of the four tonics.

Example: *tonics*[+] of collection A:

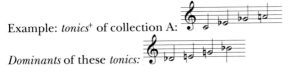

Dominants of these *tonics:*

When the point of departure is one of the four *dominants* in the succession of notes in a collection, the first degree is a whole step, and a half step when the point of departure is one of the four *tonics* (see the example above.)

> ❧ [+]Here Polignac makes explicit the partitioning of the octatonic collection at (0,3,6,9) that forms a diminished 7th chord. He also makes explicit the fact that any music that ascends on pitch-classes $\hat{1}, \hat{3}, \hat{5}, \hat{7}$ will start with a half step and that any music that ascends on $\hat{2}, \hat{4}, \hat{6}, \hat{8}$ will start with a whole step.

[- - - - -]

[tr-p. 11]

Various harmonic progressions[+] *within Scale A*

Scale A
Progression using minor triads

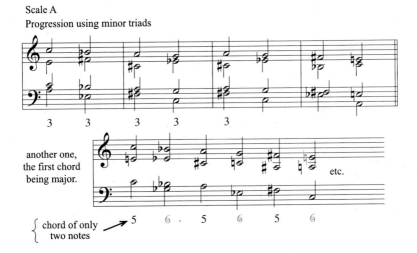

❧ †Here, and elsewhere in the treatise, we have translated the French word "processus" as "progression." According to the *New Grove Dictionary of Music and Musicians,* the term *processus* derives from the theory of Gregorian chant. It was used by later theorists such as Tinctoris and Aaron to mean "ambitus," that is, the "course" of a melodic line, or the range of a voice, instrument, or piece. Polignac's choice of this word surely reflects its use in harmony and counterpoint classes at the Conservatoire in the mid-nineteenth century.

Polignac introduces the concept of new figured basses, but he uses them erratically. In the "abbreviations" table, the figured-bass number "3" refers to a minor chord in root position, and Polignac uses it here as indicated in the table. However, the figured-bass number "6" is meant to signify a *major* chord in first inversion, while the symbol 6 is intended to signify a *minor* chord in first inversion; therefore, Polignac is using his own symbols erroneously.

Throughout the treatise, Polignac mixes octatonic and diatonic contexts and their respective terminologies, especially when discussing major and minor chords. The reference here to a "first inversion" chord is but one example.

Polignac harmonizes descending (0,2,3,5) tetrachords, both sequential and scalar, with the bass moving in sequences of descending tritones. The mediant-related harmonies resemble the "false progressions" on minor 3rds included in Rimsky-Korsakov's harmony text, some of which are reproduced in Taruskin's *Stravinsky and the Russian Traditions* 1:304–6.

Figuring of the scale beginning on one of the notes of the four [major and minor] chords.

From the C-major chord

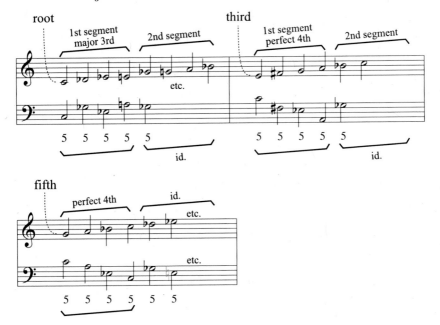

〜 Here we see an example of Polignac thinking simultaneously diatonically and octatonically. In the first measure of this example, the Scale-A collection is subdivided at the tritone into two ascending (0,1,3,4) tetrachords. The right-hand pattern is then rotated twice to form ascending (0,2,3,5) tetrachords, beginning on the 3rd and 5th of the C-major triad that can be formed from Scale A. In the bass clef, the first tetrachord always begins on C, thus harmonizing (diatonically) one of the C-major chord parts (C–E–G); the second tetrachord always begins on Gb, thus both affirming the subdivision of the collection at the tritone *and* harmonizing (diatonically) the Gb-major chord parts (Gb–Bb–Db).

[- - - - -]

[tr-p. 12]

Figured basses and key signatures

Each minor chord will be indicated by a 3, to distinguish it from a major chord 5.

Actually, in scale A, taking [the pitch] C as the point of departure, we encounter neither F♮, nor B♮, nor D♮. E♮ and G♮ can be flatted in the course of a piece, and the C and the A can be sharped.*

The same remarks are applicable to Scale B, if we take F as a point of departure, and in Scale C if we take G.

*If a piece is conceived in minor it will be good to note the key by a flat or a natural depending on the case. Thus, in scale A, E♭ for C minor, A♮ for F♯, G♭ for E♭ minor. It would be the same thing in the cases of pieces in which major chords frequently appear—for example, writing C♯ for the A major chord, etc.

> ❧ Polignac introduces the concept of new key signatures, but he uses them rarely and erratically. As in previous pages, Polignac mixes diatonic and octatonic contexts. Here, he creates special octatonic key signatures for the three collections, and yet thinks to add additional accidentals to identify pieces as being "major" or "minor."

> [- - - - -]

[tr-p. 13]

Harmonic sequences with inversions

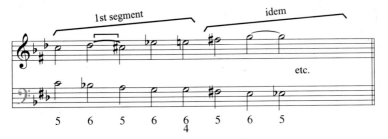

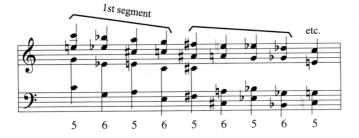

Major and minor chords mixed together

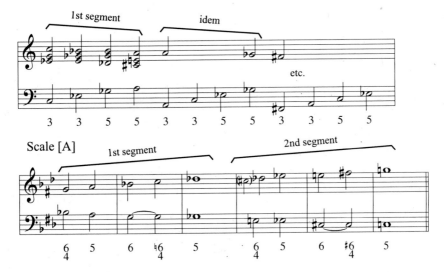

another:

> ❧ We have translated the French word "member" as "seg-ment." According to *New Grove*, the term was first used by Antoine Reicha and others to denote a small unit of melodic construction.

[- - - - -]

[tr-p. 14]

Remarks (continued)

Studies on the harmonic structure of the chords derived from a collection.
In building chords above a given root (for example, C in Scale A), it is possible to produce a minor 9th chord.

The first chord tone (above the C), that is to say E♮ (a third above C), is also a 5th above A♮ (one of the four *tonics*), a minor 7th above F♯ (another *tonic*), a minor 9th above E♭* (another *tonic*) and, finally, a third above C. Similar descriptions can be made for the other notes making up this chord.

From whence the following analytical figures:

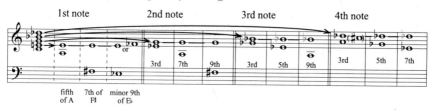

*E♮ is considered as F♭.

> ❧ Here, Polignac examines the way that each pitch-class in a collection fits into the nodal-point structure. He pulls each

tone out of the $C\flat^9$ chord and attempts to discover common tones, intervals, and closely related harmonies that can be gleaned from the initial extended chord. He is examining the way the meanings of tones change; in this way, he finds ways of establishing both a sense of harmonic stability within the dominant-9th structure and the mutability associated with diminished 7th chords.

[-----]

[tr-p. 15]

Harmonic sequences with inversions (continued)

Scale A

Segments of scale A in inversion, forming minor harmonies

      ❧ Polignac introduces the symbol for a first inversion of a minor triad, **6**.

Analogous segment with bass notes in root position (very somber character and retaining a diatonic feeling)

or again, in four parts throughout. The two treble parts proceed by sequences of 4ths and major 3rds

(At Caiaphas's palace)

This whole harmonic ensemble supports a stepwise bass.

> ❧ The last musical example ("At Caiaphas's palace") is an addendum to the musical material on tr-pp. 60–61; apparently written as an afterthought, it is jammed into the last system of tr-p. 15. The (*) symbol at the beginning of the first and third examples indicates that the four half notes in the first measure of the first example here are intended to serve as accompanying chords for each of the four measures of the third example. As discussed in chapter 3, the reference to "Caiaphas" indicates that Polignac began writing the treatise contemporaneously with or shortly after he composed "Pilate livre le Christ" and "Ruine du Temple prédite" in 1879.
>
> It is on this page that Polignac begins a practice that becomes increasingly prevalent through the treatise manuscript: he becomes sloppier in his notation of accidentals.

[- - - - -]

[tr-p. 16]

Table of interval sequences in two voices (included within an octave)
proceeding by neighboring degrees taken from the same scale (taking,
for this example, [the pitch] C as a point of departure)

Scale A

1. Sequence of alternating major and minor 2nds

whose inversions give

or [a] sequence of alternating major and minor 7ths.

2. Sequence of minor 3rds

whose inversions give

or [a] sequence of major 6ths.

3. Sequence of alternating major 3rds and perfect 4ths

whose inversions give

or [a] sequence of alternating minor 6ths and perfect 5ths.

4. Sequence of tritones

whose inversions give these same intervals,

[a] sequence identical in type [i.e., tritones].

> ❧ Following up on the discussion of the interval content of the collection (tr-p. 7), Polignac here spells out the intervals that might be mined from the octatonic scales. He is becoming progressively more "composerly," thinking about what principles could be applied to actual composition.

[- - - - -]

[tr-p. 17]

Relationships of the intervals to each other in the replication of melodic patterns in the same scale

In scale A, for example: When the replication is made at a distance of a minor 3rd, a tritone, or a major 6th, the intervals are reproduced identically in the two patterns.

Example:

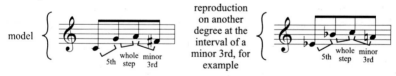

The same thing happens at another degree at the interval of a tritone or a major 6th.

> ❧ Here Polignac clarifies that replication of melodic patterns at the four nodal points will result in exact transposition of the interval content.

[- - - - -]

[tr-p. 18]

Passages offering an example of the connection among the 3 scales

Ascending line

Descending line

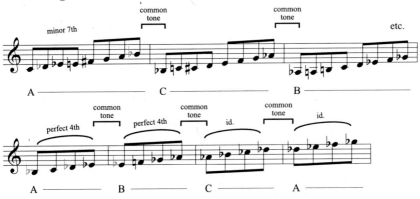

> ✍ Polignac indicates that one of the pairs of four common pitch-classes between any two collections (D♭, E, G, B♭ in Scales A and C, or C, E♭, G♭, A in Scales A and B, for example) can be used as a pivot between one collection and another.

By interval of a tritone

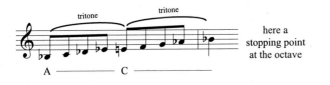

here a
stopping point
at the octave

Andante: Minor progression (scale A), very languorous character

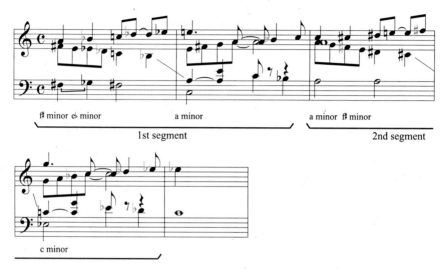

or another use

❧ Here, for the first time, Polignac ascribes specific affects (languorous, plaintive) to certain kinds of music.

[- - - - -]

[tr-p. 19]

[Relationship of intervals, cont.] But when the replication of the model pattern takes place on a degree at a distance from the point of departure of a half step, a whole step, a major 3rd, a perfect 4th, a perfect 5th, a minor 6th, a minor 7th, or a major 7th, then the half step becomes a whole step, the whole step becomes a half step, the minor 3rd doesn't change, the major third becomes a 4th, the 4th becomes a major third, the 5th becomes a minor 6th, the minor 6th becomes a 5th, the minor 7th becomes a major 7th, and the major 7th becomes a minor 7th, the minor 9th becomes a major 9th.

Table to show the replication

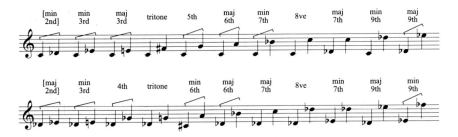

One can make other tables, from a major 2nd or whole step, major 3rd etc. (see the above text), from whence derive the following examples:

model   reproduction at the 5th   return of the model composed of the same intervals, here at the interval of a minor third

❧ Polignac is saying that reproduction of a pattern along different scale degrees does not result in reproduction of the same interval, whether in terms of arithmetic distance, quality, or spelling. Albeit elliptically, he affirms the principle that an exact transposition of interval content can take place only at the nodal points ($\hat{1}, \hat{3}, \hat{5},$ or $\hat{7}$, or 0,3,6,9) and that transpositions beginning on $\hat{2}, \hat{4}, \hat{6}, \hat{8}$ will result in changes in the interval content. A curious aspect of Polignac's thinking is that he still thinks of C–E as a major 3rd in terms of quality, but as a "4th" insofar as the relationship of scale degrees is concerned.

[- - - - -]

[tr-p. 20]

Practical arrangement of a table to facilitate melodic repetitions

„ Here Polignac spells out the consequence of transposition at $\hat{2}, \hat{4}, \hat{6}$ or $\hat{8}$: the tetrachords change from $(0,1,3,4)$ to $(0,2,3,5)$.

The major and minor 9ths are produced by the series of whole steps and half steps in carrying them to the next higher octave.

model pattern   reproduction at the major 3rd

[- - - - -]

[tr-p. 21]

Continuation of the studies on the harmonic sequences in the same scale (see also page 92)

Scale A

Sequence of tritones

Sequence of minor 3rds

another (the same thing with inversion of the voices):

double sequence of tritones in contrary motion

double sequence of diminished 5th chords; the same thing for a sequence of diminished 7ths

Harmonization of Scale A
Noble, mournful character

This measure can be harmonized by spilling
◇ into A minor (6).

(φ see also page 91)

another accompaniment of scale A

[- - - - -]

[tr-p. 22]

Minor sequences

Third [*sic:* second] inversion of the two chords E flat minor and A minor with alternation at the interval of a tritone.

Scale A

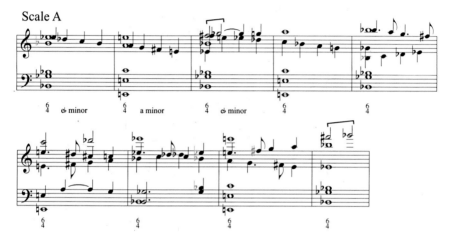

Major and minor sequences (alternating figures 5 and 6 [root position chords and $^6_4$ chords])

Scale A

The same thing with appoggiaturas

❧ In the preceding examples, with his reference to second inversions, Polignac continues to mix diatonic and octatonic systems.

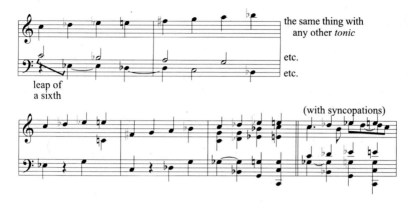

the same thing with
any other *tonic*

etc.

etc.

leap of
a sixth

(with syncopations)

Great third [i.e., tenth]

Can be used with the same bass on the four *tonics*.

tonic

tonic

leap of
a 7th

on a *dominant*

sad effect

dom.

leap of
a sixth

△ This voice can be doubled in tritones or major 6ths [with] syncopations.
(♺ see page 51, tenor [voice])

❧ The bottom of tr-p. 51 has been moved here.

[Cross-reference to p. 22]

The same melody or [a] scale with syncopations [in the upper voice].
Beginning on a *dominant* with a leap of a 7th in the Bass and beginning on [a]
tonic.

This example provides sketches or counterpoint and a crescendo through accel-
eration and complexity in the voices.

> ❧ In the preceding studies, Polignac stabilizes each example
> by establishing a tritone axis.
> ❧ Tr-pp. 23, 24, and 25 have been moved to follow tr-p. 27.

[- - - - -]

[tr-pp. 26–27]

Study or example of the effect of a series of mixture of the three collections A, B, C, with a cadence on a succession of three chords built on tonics, each [tonic] belonging to one of the three collections

❧ On this page and the next, Polignac explores cadences within an octatonic context. In this example he illustrates various ways that mediant-related harmonic movements at cadential points can create within an octatonic environment the same sense of "rest" or "arrival" as traditional diatonic cadences in tonal music. Thus, in the next-to-last measure of the example, a C–A♭ progression is meant, perhaps, to approximate a conventional I–IV cadence; the last measure may be an octatonic substitute for a I–V–I cadence.

Polignac seems to be searching for terms other than the conventional word "cadence" to denote cadential events. (Later on in the treatise, he will use the term "cadence" in sketches that end with leaping Î–5̂ or 4̂–Î figures—*faux* dominant-tonic or plagal motions—in the bass; see, for example, tr-pp. 33, 52, 65, 90, and 91.)

In the French language, the word *repos*—which we translate as "resting point"—can substitute for *cadence.* However, Polignac's intent in his deployment of the word *crochet*—which we translate simply as "cadence"—is less clear. A *crochet* can be defined as "sudden turn" or "detour." Perhaps Polignac was searching for a term that could signify a "deceptive cadence."

The discussion of cadential "theory" introduced on this page is continued briefly on tr-p. 34.

[- - - - -]

[tr-p. 27, cont.]

(Effect—character)

These cadences on successive chords, changing from one collection to another, take on a feeling of repose, of a solution, or a faraway echo. They can serve also as a solemn vow pronounced as a refrain, or they can be used in a theme like the one for the Passover [the last Supper].

(*) (Remarks on the cadences [resting points] in the three keys)

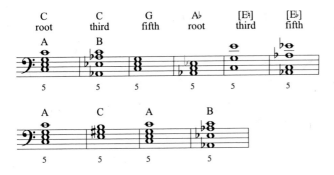

Connection of these cadences from [scale] A to [scale] B, that is to say, from C major to A flat major creates a feeling of repose, as it would from C to F in descending motion by a 5th in the bass, [or as it would when moving] from [scale] A to [scale] C, that is to say from C major to E major, creating a feeling of interrogative superimposition like from C to G in ascending motion by a 5th in the bass.

See tr-p. 26.

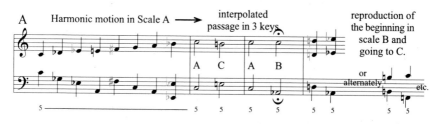

❧ As densely worded as Polignac's "remark" might be, it is one of the most revelatory in the entire treatise. The inspiration for the "remark" may come from his teacher Henri Reber's *Traité d'harmonie* (1862), Chapter 3, Article 1, p. 62. Here, Reber writes about "the relative tonal influence of consonant chords," explaining that "when several different chords follow each other, the result is a relationship of sounds that determine more or less promptly a 'tonal sensation' which, however, is only complete when the ear is able to recognize the 'tonic' chord that this succession of chords confirms or prepares." Applying this general concept to octatonic music, Polignac is saying that the octatonic cadential figure C major to A flat major creates the same "feeling of repose"—or sense of arrival—as a diatonic perfect-authentic cadence (C major to F major, with descending bass motion) and that the octatonic cadential figure C major to E major creates the same "questioning" affect as a diatonic half cadence (C major to G major, with ascending bass motion).

Progressively, Polignac returns to developing ideas for the musical settings of the Gospels that he had begun in the missing "First notebook of Scales A, B, C." The reference to "the Passover (the last Supper)" [la Pâque] signals Polignac's return to these ideas in this treatise notebook.

[- - - - -]

[tr-p. 23; moved to here]

Study on the scale called "major-minor" (its easiest key signature is an E♭ or a C♯) or Hypolydian scale, whose sixth degree (lowered by a half step) creates a minor 6th with the tonic

Type

with C as tonic

········ belongs to the ordinary F minor scale.

with G as tonic

belongs to the ordinary C minor scale.

with D as tonic

belongs to the G minor scale.

with A as tonic

belongs to the D minor scale.

belongs to the A minor scale.

etc.   etc.

Remark: from whence it follows that in the scale that has only one flat, that is to say E♭, we encounter three pitches upon which major or minor chords can be constructed from the other constituent pitches of the scale.

These are G for the major chord

C for the minor chord

and D for the minor chord

It is the same for the scale that carries only one sharp, [that is] a C♯, we find the three chords

❧ The "major-minor" scale is the subject of tr-pp. 23–34. Called in current theoretical parlance the "heptatonia secunda," the scale is explained in the Preface to the treatise (p. 149).

[- - - - -]

[tr-pp. 24–25]

Tests and results (in the major-minor scale) (scale established on the 5th degree of the tonic G, or on the 2nd degree of the usual tonic of C minor)

Two-part harmony

This [soprano] voice alone is comprised of the notes of the major-minor scale

Same example with the scale in the top voice, and the harmony [also] taken from the notes of the scale, the whole thing [above] a bass pedal of a perfect 5th.

Same example with pedal on the dominant replaced in the highest voice (like a faraway path shown by a star . . .)

Harmonic Progression (second degree of A minor)

Tonic pedal

Return to the point of departure four octaves away

[- - - - -]

[tr-p. 25]

Same example with ornamentation

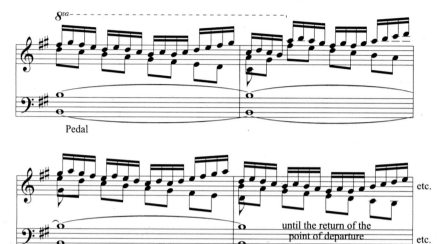

Pedal

until the return of the
point of departure   etc.

etc.

Same example with another pattern

col 8ᵛᵃ high voice sempre

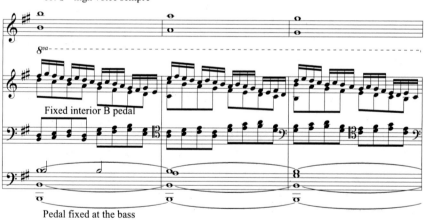

Fixed interior B pedal

Pedal fixed at the bass

 Continues on tr-p. 28.

[- - - - -]

[tr-pp. 28–29; continuation of tr-p. 25]

[p. 28]

same pattern following the progression

terminus

End of the
musical
journey

(*) Link to connect to what follows

v.s.

[- - - - -]

[tr-p. 29]

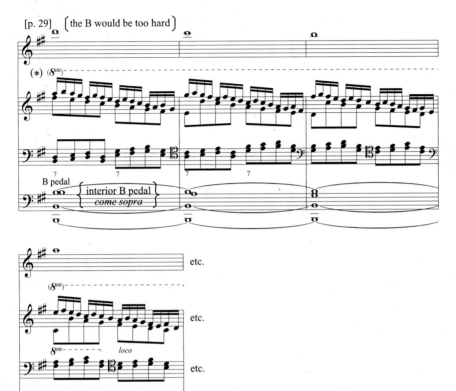

(*) New aggregation that produces a very rich harmony, leading to, on each strong beat, a chord with four voices with figured-bass number 7 instead of a chord with three voices with figured-bass number 5.

[- - - - -]

[tr-pp. 29, cont.–30]

This same progression can be simplified and reduced, as in the following example:

[p. 30]

{ Journey of an octave
return to the point of departure }

(end of the
B pedal)

etc.

etc.

etc.

[16 foot and 32. *Grosse Basse*
delayed by one beat]

[- - - - -]

[tr-p. 30]

[-----]

[tr-pp. 31–32]

Continuation of various examples using the major-minor scale

Harmonic progressions with Basses progressing alternately by 4ths, 5ths, or whole steps. (character: celestial spaces, phalanxes of harps and cherubim. Can serve for "the vision" of Christ)

Another example (Character: phrase of very great tension)
(↘ sign to mark the entrances)

[-----]

[tr-p. 32, cont.]

Another cadence on the tonic E

(Major-minor scale) on the 2nd degree of the major-minor tonic

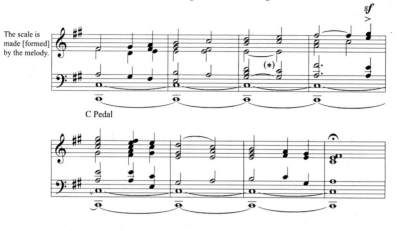

The scale is made [formed] by the melody.

C Pedal

(*) variant

[- - - - -]

[tr-p. 33]

(Continuation of the remarks on the major-minor scale)

Other resolutions by the following cadences: on E♮ or B minor

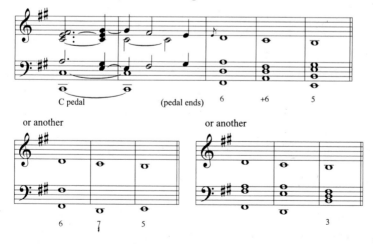

C pedal   (pedal ends)   6   +6   5

or another   or another

6   7   5   3

Major/minor scale Dominant of E

To establish the harmony

Another ending

or with bass line

Another form of the major-minor scale

Harmony [based on] "rule of the octave" of the ordinary (G) minor scale (arrangement for harp as heard in London July '85)

G minor

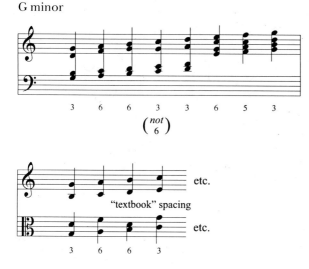

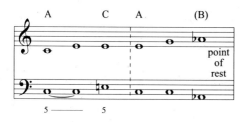

❧ Polignac makes reference to *la règle de l'octave,* a harmonization of major and minor ascending and descending scales popularized in France by François Campion in 1716; it was reproduced widely in most eighteenth-century thoroughbass and composition treatises. This short passage has been squeezed into a small passage at the bottom of tr-p. 33. The reference to the G minor scale on a page otherwise devoted to the "major-minor" scale makes the question of accidentals unclear and, thus, accidentals have not been added. The reference to music "heard in London [in] July 1885" confirms that Polignac added material to his notebook many years after he first began to write his "study."

[- - - - -]

[tr-pp. 34–35]

Theory from whence follows the "going and coming back" cadence, with a resting point [created by the movement] from scales A to scale C and from scale A to scale B

Thus a *dominant* from scale A in the treble voice [illegible] on a *tonic* in scale B

❧ By "going and coming back" cadence (*cadence d'aller et retour*), Polignac presumably refers to conventional diatonic cadential formulas, such a half cadence followed by a perfect authentic cadence.

Good pattern of counterpoint in the major-minor scale

(∗) Ornamented:

Or more elegant:

Another one

to figure out

❧ This is the last sketch that contains one of Polignac's new key signatures; from this point forward, he writes in the accidentals, although he is extremely erratic in his notation.

A progression simulating tonic and dominant basses in standard harmonic practice. These progressions use all the notes of the different scales A, B, and C.

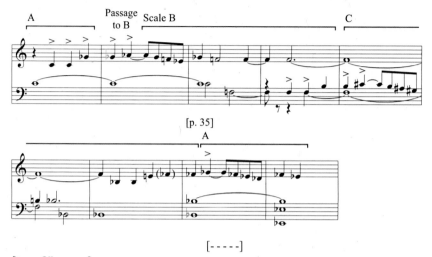

[p. 35]

[tr-p. 35, cont.]

Motive affirming the "key" of [scale] A

Scale A

Scale B

[alternate for mm. 12-14]

Harmonic résumé of the 2 preceding examples [i.e., the subject and its response]

etc.

Etc. and by progression of descending 5ths: C–F, B♭–E♭, A♭–D♭ etc.

❧ These sketches, whose progressions "simulate tonic and dominant basses from standard harmonic practice," illustrate well Polignac's dual octatonic/diatonic approach to imitative writing. In the second example, the subject, derived on Scale A, opens with an ascending tritone G–D♭; it is answered at the interval of a perfect 4th higher (or, in Polignac's conception, a perfect 5th lower) by the pitches C–G♭, which derive from Scale B. Thus, by means of "modulating" (using common tones) from one octatonic scale to another, Polignac retains the traditional intervallic relationship of P4/P5 in the subject-response material.

[- - - - -]

[tr-p. 36]

Studies of the sequences of [perfect] 4ths and major 3rds in Scale A

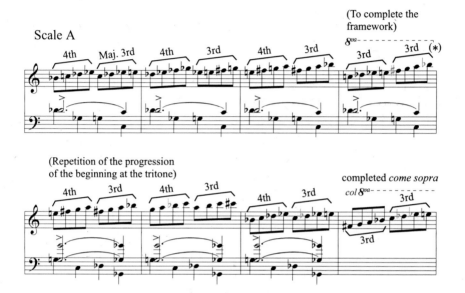

(To complete the framework)

(Repetition of the progression of the beginning at the tritone)

completed *come sopra*

Leap to the other tritone, E♭–A

(This arrangement [is]
gentler than having already
heard the E♭)

(∗) One can add the other superimposition of the major third
from one of the tritones

etc.

Another harmony with a slight modification in the melody as in the example above

Key of C affirmed by the pedal C

Example of a motive where the major and minor 3rds above a *tonic* are alongside each other

❧ Here, Polignac writes a motive that explores the diatonic reference created by pitches C–E–G, scale degrees $\hat{1}$, $\hat{4}$, and $\hat{6}$ in Scale A.

[- - - - -]

[tr-p. 37]

Form rich in contrapuntal voices

Scale A

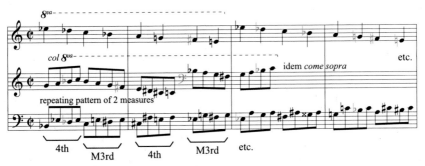

(cycle of 4 measures in the bass, progression of 4ths and major 3rds)

Another ornamentation on the same progression in 4ths and major 3rds in the bass.

Melody of caressing and sad expression

Condensation of the middle voice

Condensation of the bass voice

> ❧ The "condensation" alluded to above refers to a paring-down from four to three notes in each half measure of the alto and bass voices.

At the Sign ⌣ on p. 92 another version

> ❧ The example below has been moved here from tr-p. 92.

⌣
Scale A

> ❧ Polignac returns to tr-p. 37 for the material below.

Progressions with basses simulating the tonal processes of traditional harmony

Scale A

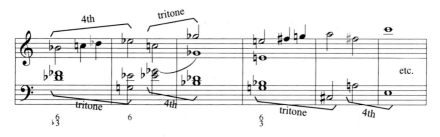

Another progression

(∗) variant

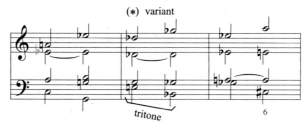

❧ Material from tr-p. 40 has been moved here.

Another cycle

Another progression as above

Better connection for moving through the tonal range

[- - - - -]

[tr-p. 38]

List of motives naturally reproduced by the pitches making up scales A, B, and C

Aria from *Elijah* by Mendelssohn

Scale B

leaving B,
entering A

"Le Curé de Pomponne"

Scale A

etc.

"Le Roi Don Juan"

A

Quoi vous ne me dites rien   "Que tout se fasse jeune et beau"
jadis c'était différent   (*Noël* from my *Douze Mélodies*)

"La Marseillaise," especially the phrase

A

Harmonic forms of the *Plaintes de Medora*

A

V.S.

❧ Polignac makes reference to a passage from Mendelssohn's oratorio *Elijah*, mm. 32–33 of the tenor aria "So ihr mich von ganzem Herzen suchet." The pitch classes in the original [F♯–G–A–B♭–C–D–E♭], are referable to scale B. The other examples refer to music that strongly feature the tetrachord [0,1,3,4].

[- - - - -]

[tr-p. 39]

Air from "La Diligence qui part pour Mayence" (approximate)

Example of a key with a minor "feeling" created by a sequence of [alternating] dominant 7th chords and minor chords (serious, noble, sad character, mixed with fright, good for Dante's *Inferno*)

Scale A

(∗) Variant in the continuation of the progression

This example could also be employed for a large celestial choir, Catholic style, because of the dominant 7ths that have none of the Hebraic or Oriental character.

> ❧ Polignac implies that dominant 7th chords "have none of the Hebraic or Oriental character" because they are too firmly grounded in a Western tonality that progresses through circles of fifths, whereas the "chromatico-diatonic" (octatonic) system features progressions that move through circles of thirds.

[- - - - -]

[tr-p. 40]

Remarks on the preceding examples

The minor chord could be ornamented thus by a melody.

Variant as on the preceding page

Grosse basse in major in
Wagner's *Tristan and Isolde*

〜 The reference to Wagner's *Tristan and Isolde* is obscure.
〜 Material from the bottom of this page has been moved to
tr-p. 37.

[- - - - -]

[tr-pp. 41–42–43]

[tr-p. 43, cont.]

Harmonization of Scale A (model could be syncopated in three voices)

Scale A

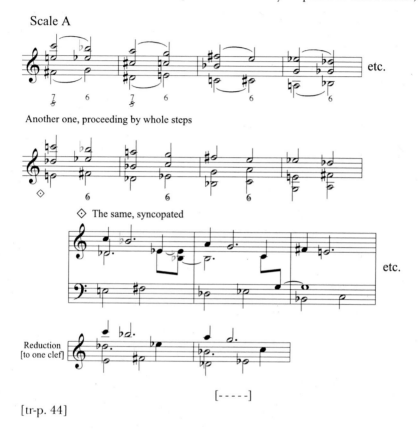

Another one, proceeding by whole steps

◇ The same, syncopated

etc.

Reduction [to one clef]

[-----]

[tr-p. 44]

Progression (development in minor)

Scale C

Another mixture of scales

(C - - - - -)   (A - -)   (B - - - - ·)

or in abridged form

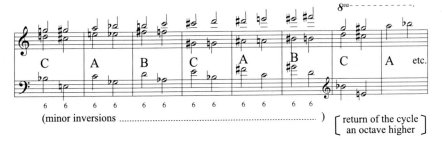

(minor inversions ....)   ⌈ return of the cycle ⌉
                                                                                          ⌊ an octave higher ⌋

Minor progression (far-off, plaintive)

Scale C

▪ In the Table of Contents, Polignac titles tr-p. 44: "Romantic effect of sad complaints to develop." The above page demonstrates Polignac's continued dual octatonic-diatonic thinking, as he apparently ascribes an affective meaning to a preponderance of minor triads in an example.

[- - - - -]

[tr-pp. 45–46]

Remark on the harmonic relations tying together the two scales A and B

Melody beginning and finishing on a note common to the two scales A and B, the harmony made by two notes common to the two scales

Ave Rex (to ornament the distant Jewish "Orientale")

(traveling through [scale] B)

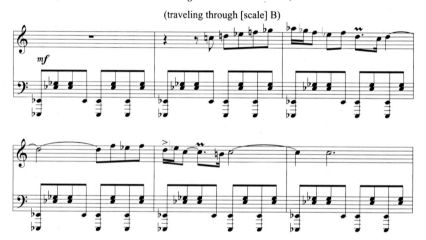

Reprise of the melody in [scale] A a whole step lower.

❧ The "Jewish 'Orientale'" apparently refers to the broken chord "camel walk" in the accompaniment.

Example of appoggiaturas, very sad

Scale B

appog.

[p. 46]

cresc. molto

marcato

the melody should end at the tonic E♭

response and reprise of the melody
a half step higher in Scale A

etc.

according to example X (below)

[- - - - -]

[tr-pp. 46, cont.]

Segment ⟨X⟩ belonging to [scale] B and
leading to the rest on the tonic of E♭ minor

Segment belonging to A with rest on the
dominant of E♭ minor.

(D♯ [is the]
leading
tone of E♭)

(A♯ [is the]
leading tone
of B♭)

❧ Even within the octatonic system, Polignac retains the concept of the "sighing" appoggiatura.

In the preceding examples, the harmony of two notes ⟨3̖⟩ and ⟨5̖⟩ could be represented in the higher regions

Example of two segments of different scales placed side by side

forming a mirror

From whence the subjects on the reverse side of the page [tr-p. 47]: V.S.

[- - - - -]

[tr-p. 47]

Minor progression Scale A

[tr-p. 48–49]

Minor progressions (without change of scales)

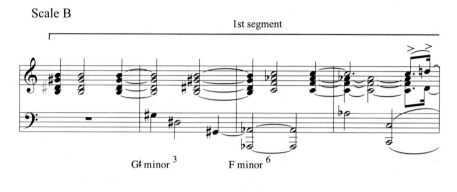

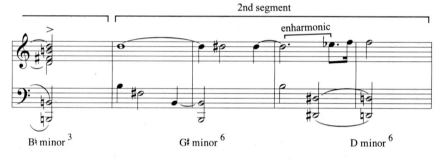

Remark: In a minor chord, all the notes contained between a high 3rd and the 5th [below it] lend themselves well to the melody on this chord.

Sequence that can move in two resting points of 4ths

These four notes are the points of rest of the sequence.

Example of notes making a melody, same harmonic sequence

Example of the major or minor model—to be avoided (frequent pitfall in a melodic line)

D harmony in
two parts

[p. 49]

(*)
the only measure with a
chord of three [tones]

[- - - - -]

[tr-p. 49, cont.]

Another minor progression

Another minor progression

Another minor progression

Good primitive treatment of a minor progression:

>  In the middle of the 1st system below, Polignac writes a numeric shortcut (notated below) and labels it "chant" (melody); it has been transcribed as follows:

Scale B

This harmony can be varied here by the melody and by simple ritards [i.e., augmentations] or doubled by minor 3rds.

 "ritard" = augmentation
"simple" = single line

[- - - - -]

[tr-p. 50]

Crowd and Hebraic March

Proposition "à la Zigane" on the notes F and A (crowd and Hebraic progression)

(*) Here [one could] perhaps insert this more biblical phrase in response—a slower rhythm, syncopated

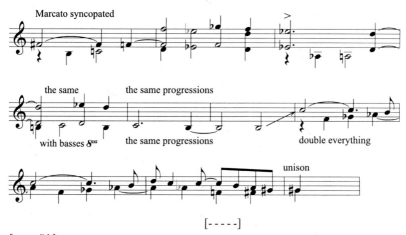

[tr-p. 51]

(Minor progressions)
(Character: crescendo, sad, Judaic fervor)
Scale B

❧ The remainder of the page, a continuation of the ideas and musical examples of tr-p. 22, is included with tr-p. 22 (p. 184–85)

❧ Once again, in this sketch, meant to evoke "Judaic fervor," Polignac returns to developing ideas for the musical settings of the Gospels.

[- - - - -]

[tr-p. 52]

This high voice supports ritards [i.e., augmentations] in appoggiatura.

Scale B

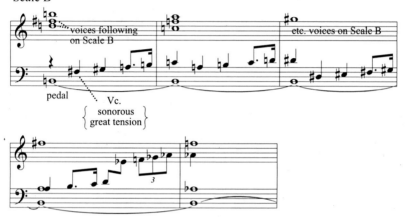

Comparison of cadences, customary formulas or phrases of an ordinary [i.e., diatonic] major scale and scales A, B, C, with progressions of the note from a [diatonic] dominant-to-tonic movement in the bass voice

Scale A

(*) Another harmony, more *concertante*

Easier with appoggiatura

❧ Polignac uses the term "appoggiatura" somewhat convolut-
edly, but essentially means that the four *tonics* of Scale A (C,
E♭, F♯, A) stand out better when approached by an upper
neighbor tied over the barline (the tied D♭ to C in mm. 1–2,
for example).

[-----]

[tr-p. 53]

Passage from A minor to F minor to D♭ minor/C♯ minor

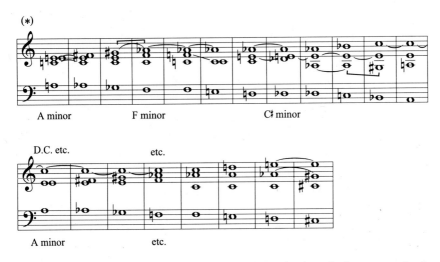

(*)Remark: The highest voice has gone through the whole-tone scale from

 to

Bass voice:

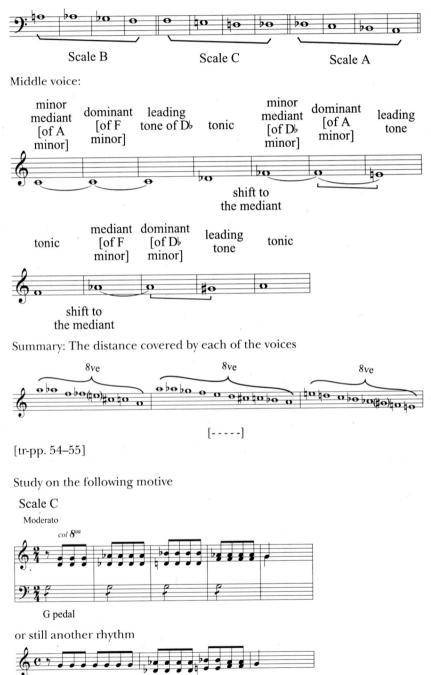

Scale B   Scale C   Scale A

Middle voice:

minor mediant [of A minor]   dominant [of F minor]   leading tone of D♭   tonic   minor mediant [of D♭ minor]   dominant [of A minor]   leading tone

shift to
the mediant

tonic   mediant [of F minor]   dominant [of D♭ minor]   leading tone   tonic

shift to
the mediant

Summary: The distance covered by each of the voices

8ve   8ve   8ve

[- - - - -]

[tr-pp. 54–55]

Study on the following motive

Scale C

Moderato

col 8va

G pedal

or still another rhythm

the inversions of which are

etc.

Examples with minor arrangements

another richer arrangement

[Scale C]

(∗) the C♯ [is] very biting against the min. 3rd

[p. 55]

with G interior pedal

[- - - - -]

[tr-p. 55, cont.–56]

Remark {downplay the D–F 3rd of the upper part to avoid the shocks of the notes that intermingle harshly}

Harmony by contrary motion
Exchange of notes

Scale C

etc. in contrary motion

One can carve out a melody on this sequence of notes—similar to the songs of the Dervishes of Cairo
(*)

Scale C

(*) could also be accompanied in this manner:

Harmonic arrangement [that is] rich, sonorous, violent, martial

Scale C

[- - - - -]

[tr-p. 56, cont.]

Homophonic remark: after establishing for the ear a Scale C (for example) in a melody restricted to a major 3rd from a G *tonic* (for example), then extending to to F below the G, having the following range:

Jump to the D♭ tritone that is part of Scale A, and after the figure that is in Scale A, [arriving] on the F♯ that doesn't belong to Scale C and that characterizes well the tritone of Scale A. The effect is more violent unharmonized.

[- - - - -]

[tr-p. 57: top system]–[tr-p. 58: top system]

❧ The following sketch is written directly across the two facing tr-pages 57 and 58.

Scale B

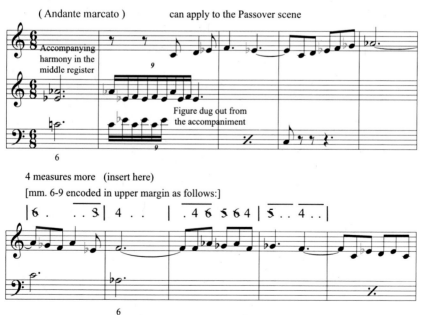

4 measures more (insert here)

[mm. 6-9 encoded in upper margin as follows:]

❧ With the allusion to "the Passover scene" at the beginning of the musical sketch (tr-p. 57, top system), Polignac indicates that he is once more preoccupied with musical settings of Gospel texts. Sketches for these settings predominate the next portion of the notebook, through tr-p. 74.

[- - - - -]

[tr-p. 57; bottom system]

From C [major] to F♯ [minor] and from E♭ [major] to A [minor], etc.

Scale A

[- - - - -]

[tr-p. 58; bottom system]

Example of a simulated tonality

Scale A

{[Yet] to find: the basses and the harmony, the tritone (inverted or not) simulating the dominant of ordinary tonality}

> ❧ On the downbeats of mm. 1 and 2, Polignac "simulates" a (functionally) dominant chord—or more correctly, a diminished 7th chord—from "ordinary tonality." But he doesn't attempt to solve the problem inherent in the octatonic system: because the system is tritone-based, the "dominant" cannot lead to a "tonic."

[- - - - -]

[tr-p. 59]

Example of a counterpoint in imitation [at the octave] on every scale degree

[Scale] A

C pedal

This subject can be broken up, and gives a good crescendo and stringendo. A good thrust on the pedal.

Melodic genre of "Le Roi Don Juan un jour chevauchant"[+]

Scale B

reprise of the bass

> ❧+ Polignac makes reference to the first line of "Ballade de l'Abencérage," a poem by François-René Chateaubriand. The poem was set to music by several French composers in the 1830s. It is not clear which version Polignac used for his octatonic melodic model.

[- - - - -]

[tr-pp. 60–61]

Example of a harmonic progression between the first inversions of the minor chords

The *tonics* of Scale A are written in the following order: E♭ min, F♯ min, A min, C min.

(+)   etc.

6   6   6

(+)   [insertion] of an additional measure,
       rendering the form more melodic

6 ─────────────────────────────────── 6

❧ The next 15 pages are concerned with a working-out of material for the "Caiaphas" movement first undertaken in the "first notebook of Scales A, B, C," apparently no longer extant. None of the sketches are complete, but we are given a glimpse of some of Polignac's first octatonic sketches. Even in incomplete form, the music manages to convey Caiaphas's pomposity and arrogance in the dotted-eighth-sixteenth figures and the tension that mounts as Jesus faces the insults and blows delivered by Caiaphas's entourage.

Sort of Prelude to the scene at Caiaphas's palace, already started on in the first notebook of Scale A, page 35

Scale A

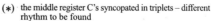

p *quasi mysterioso*   a sort of eruption in the basses

(∗) the middle register C's syncopated in triplets – different
     rhythm to be found

(Scale C) —————————— (Scale B) —— A ——— C ———

Entry motive from the notebook that
prepares the musical architecture

[p. 61]

motive

responses

B ——————— A

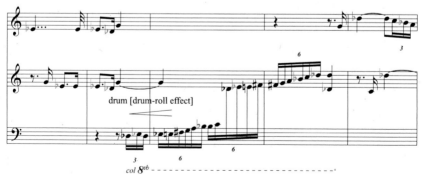

drum [drum-roll effect]

col 8ᵛᵇ -

come sopra
inverted rhythm

later, the
minor
progression

[- - - - -]

[tr-p. 62]

Scale A: harmony without 3rds

Scale A

chordal fifths
in the bass
$\frac{6}{4}$

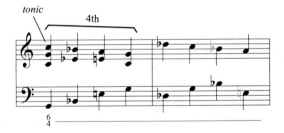

With the range of a 4th

tonic
4th

$\frac{6}{4}$

≋ Here, the French word "dominante," which appears twice in the first measure, signifies two different things. In the treble clef, the appellation "*dominant*" refers to the pitch-classes G, D♭, B♭, and E♮ ($\hat{6}$, $\hat{2}$, $\hat{8}$, and $\hat{4}$, respectively) that open all the measures except the seventh. The indication "basses en dominante" refers to chordal 5ths; in other words, every chord is written in second inversion.

Kind of Hebraic disorder

The bass motive alternates the (0,2,3,5) and (0,1,3,4) tetra-chords. The elevated degree of dissonance contributes to the sense of "disorder," which reaches a climax on the first beat of the eighth measure, when five of the eight pitch classes (0,2,3,5,8) are sounded simultaneously.

[- - - - -]

[tr-pp. 63–64]

Another sketch

Scale C

dominant   tonic   dominant

end of
cycle

Descent by minor 9ths

Scale A

9+   7+   9+5   9+

9+5

Allegro molto—passionate, in thrust with [the] swaying [figure]

Scale A

bass added

imitation of the beginning in the bass

[p. 64]

loco

C.B.

end of
cycle,
traversing
3 octaves

etc.

Return to the first note that
begins the bass line.

❧ One senses Polignac's frustration with the limitations of
the octatonic collection. After two iterations of the motive,
the composer has exhausted the pitch collection. In the two
sketches that follow, he varies the motive in such a way as to
create more opportunities to open up the range.

[- - - - -]

[tr-pp. 64, cont.–65]

Another bass

Same example

Scale A

[Below,] a curious example of passing tones in a harmonic progression coming from two *tonics* a tritone apart, incorporating into one chord both the major and minor 3rd above the triad root.

(*) One can suppress the G [minor] half note (root pitch of G minor) for this first measure

> The reference to the "major and minor thirds above the triad" refers to the dual (non-diatonic) thirds above the nodal roots in triads referable to the octatonic collection. This example illustrates that in the (0,1,3,4) form of a scale beginning on G, both B♭ and B♮ are present; likewise with E♮ and E♯ (here, spelled, enharmonically, as F) in the scale beginning on C♯.

Progression in the style of the entrance of Tristan

> Polignac makes reference to the orchestral introduction to Act 1, scene 5 of Wagner's *Tristan und Isolde,* in which the first three phrases ascend sequentially through minor-3rd-related pitch centers (F, A♭, B♮), before arriving—at the moment of Tristan's entrance—on D.

[- - - - -]

[tr-p. 65, cont.]

Example of a harmony in 3 parts

(Example: Succession of 4ths and 5ths in the top two voices)

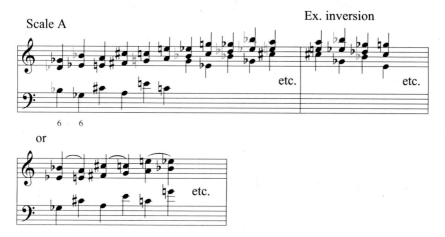

or

Ascending line combining the 3 scales A, B, C with basses moving by 5ths

Example simulating the usual B♮ scale

The melody [is built on] Scale A

To be constructed with the intent of keeping the three upper voices in the form of a first-inversion chord.

Cadences establishing one key

Scale A

❧ Polignac makes reference to "the three upper voices," but the alto and tenor voices are missing. Nonetheless, the figured bass indicates that Polignac was aiming for a "fauxbourdon" setting of the melody.

[- - - - -]

[tr-p. 66]

Allegro moderato appassionato (chords appoggiaturas on the inversions of G dominant 7th).

Modern, sonorous march

Rule: In Scales A, B, C, each consecutive figure having a range of a 4th and beginning (if it is ascending), necessarily, on one of the 5ths or 3rds above a *tonic*, is accompanied in contrary motion and note for note by a range of a major 3rd.

The two figures are always invertible; the notes [illegible] no dissonances; the resulting intervals are unisons or octaves, minor 3rds or their inversions (major 6ths), and augmented fourths or tritones, which are invariable in the inversions.

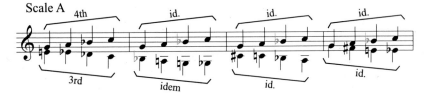

The same thing in inversion

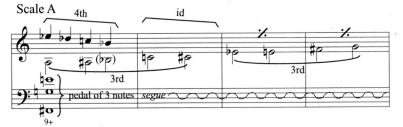

   ❖ The descending (0,2,3,5) quarter-note tetrachord beginning on E♭ juxtaposed with the ascending (0,1,3,4) half-note tetrachord beginning on A♭ is reminiscent of the contrary motion–augmentation/diminution schema of Contrapunctus VII in J. S. Bach's *Art of the Fugue*.

[- - - - -]

[tr-pp. 67–68]

(Rich and dissonant harmony)

Example of the harmonic shock of the major and minor mediant B♮ and B♭ (form in the aria from Mendelssohn's *Elijah*)

Scale C

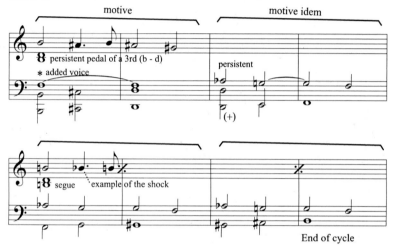

Very sonorous in this form

very sonorous

Could also resolve like this:

end of the example

Same example with the bass doubled in 10ths

More elegant, especially if [the tenor] voice is echoed in the high registers

Another analogous harmonic progression

Scale C

Moderato

C.B. (more elegant to make the contrabass
enter on [the next] note a whole step
from the preceding degree)

Another arrangement

etc. in minor 3rds

[p. 68]

return to the position of the beginning

[- - - - -]

[tr-pp. 68, cont.–69]

Another arrangement

Double shock of the mixture of major and minor

Scale A

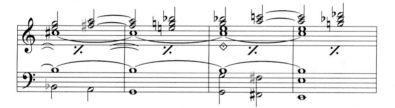

(*)here the [chord formed by] the internal pedal is augmented by a B♭
(◇ here, by a C♯)

The same, with regard to Scale A above

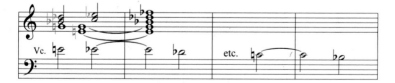

❧ From Table of Contents: "Effect of stinging harmonies (perhaps for Greek music)"

Scale C

[illegible] of E

in Scale C

D.C. *rinforzando*

ritard più pesante a tempo primo

[- - - - -]

[tr-p. 70]

Another motive

Scale A

doubles the bass

etc.

Minor and major sequences (noble, sad, mournful)

Scale A

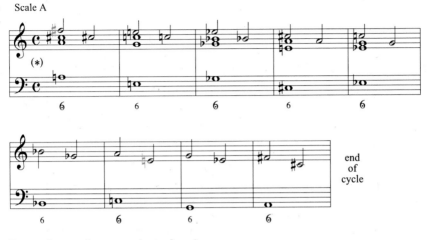

end
of
cycle

From whence [one can derive] various patterns

etc.

or

Scale A

Patterns on these harmonies

plaintive, affectionate

Scale A

(*)Application and [a] better arrangement of this harmony

❧ This last example (*) refers to the opening of the "Minor and major sequences (noble, sad, mournful)" in the seventh system above this one (marked "Scale A," with the same bass line).

[- - - - -]

[tr-p. 71]

Contrapuntal studies in contrary motion

Note-for-note accompaniments covering the same ranges [i.e., P4 and M3]

Scale A

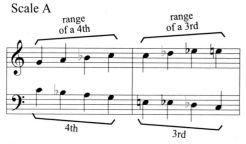

Examples of possible dissonances [hard sonorities] are marked with an x

Scale A

or

A preliminary preparation of the counterpoint for the motive on the next page

Scale A

Preparing the entry of the mob.

[- - - - -]

[tr-p. 72]

Motive of a march to the Calvary, already tried

(taken from the first notebook of Scale A, B, C, page 34)

Scale A (Rhythm of 3 measures)

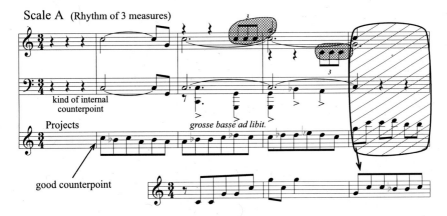

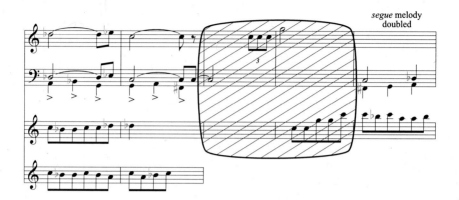

❧ From the Table of Contents: "Study on 'March to the Cal-vary' with Rhythm etc." It is not clear whether Polignac means "triple meter," or a hypermeter of three-measure phrases (an allusion to *ritmo di tre battute* in the Scherzo of Beethoven's Ninth Symphony)

another rhythm:

Scale A

Allegro moderato animato

One can also use a 5-beat rhythm for the project for the march to the Calvary. This rhythm imitates well the fatigue created by the weight of the cross.

Scale A

[tr-p. 73]

Scale A

realization of the figured bass

[tr-pp. 73–74–75]

Genre Grand Pontiff (Caiaphas)

[the symbol ◇ that appears in the second measure of the first system and in the first and second measures of the eighth system refers to the motive on tr-p. 21]

Scale A

[p. 75]

🫠 From the Table of Contents: "Example of a passage from Scale A to Scale C (genre *Écho judaïque*)"

The ◇ denotes the return of the Caiaphas theme.

This sketch features a tritone axis D♭–G, which serves as both an agent of stability and a point of departure for imitation.

[- - - - -]

[tr-p. 75; cont.]

Scale A

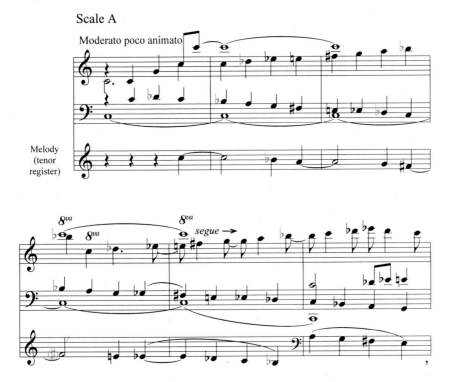

Theoretical remark: In the chromatico-diatonic scales, in order to facilitate movement (especially ascending) by consecutive degrees within the span of an octave, and principally when the harmony is created by a first-inversion major chord, one can alter the chromatico-diatonic scale by replacing the 2 notes that separate a *tonic* from its major 3rd by a note at the distance of a whole step from the aforementioned *tonic;* the other notes of the chromatico-diatonic scale do not undergo any change.

> ❧ The "major 3rd" of the *tonic* is the 4th scale degree. Polignac wants to have his cake and eat it, too: he wants the melodic quality of the whole step as well as the ability to harmonize it with major and minor triads. It is significant that Polignac is willing to include non-octatonic scale tones in order to realize the musical thought.

Example for Scale A

becomes

whose root is the so-called major-minor scale

or the traditional [melodic] minor scale starting on G and with the same notes

> ❧ The major-minor scale—or the "heptatonia secunda" scale—was first introduced on tr-pp. 23–24. Discussion of this scale continues on tr-p. 77.

[- - - - -]

[tr-p. 76]

Example of a *tonic* in a scale (C for example) becoming a *dominant* in Scale A

Scale C

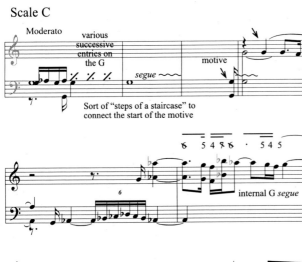

❧ In this example, by shifting the role of pitch-class G from a *tonic* in Scale C to a *dominant* in Scale A, Polignac transforms G from the starting pitch of a bassline ostinato (0,1,3,4) to one pitch in a melodic, diatonically referential tetrachord (G–F–E–D, or [0,2,3,5]).

Typical figure from a chromatico-diatonic scale

Example:

Scale B

etc.

A comparable example, in syncopation

cont.

D.C.

end of
cycle

V.S.

[- - - - -]

[tr-p. 77]

Same idea:

Scale B

Poco maestoso (ferocious character)

Scale A
(Heavy, *moderato*)

effect of *Plein air* – Plainchant

same sonic principle (effect)

variant

Type

Theory (reference to [tr-]p. 75)

Frequently heard form of the progression in question

Ascending   Descending

❧ Here, Polignac creates an approximation of a traditional melodic minor scale, employing the "major-minor" scale in the ascent and the octatonic scale in the descent.

[- - - - -]

[tr-p. 78]

[×] Effects of appoggiaturas on a major 7th (principle of a sad, romantic effect)

Scale B

Syncopated counterpoint, always good

Scale B

A different pattern, beginning on a *dominant*

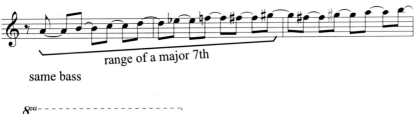

range of a major 7th

same bass

❧ These studies are among the very few in which Polignac begins with the (0,2,3,5) form of the scale.

Octaves with the melody are tolerable; can be avoided by raising the cello line a minor 3rd, that is to say G♭ instead of E♭; or in replacing the D of the melody or beginning of the next measure with an F.

[- - - - -]

[tr-p. 79]

Phrase with tension (example of a higher note making a minor 3rd with the bass at the same time as a major third)

Scale B

Continuation of the preceding: fearsome effect

Effect of appoggiaturas on major chords (character: sad, hard, biting, grand)

Scale B

[- - - - -]

[tr-p. 80]

(This example lends itself to a motive "tempo passato" from *Francesca di Rimini* in Dante)

To develop: Progression of a "Sarnian" Romanticism resulting from the nobility of the diatonic elements of Scale C.

Scale C

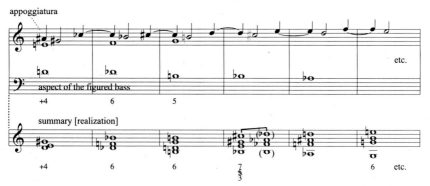

❧ Polignac's allusion to the "diatonic elements of Scale C" refers to the fact that Scale C includes five pitch classes from the D melodic-minor scale (D–E–F–G–B–C♯) and, in the (0,2,3,5) form, resembles most closely a diatonic scale.

In other words, the 3 voices in the right hand [shown in the summary and the following example] progress in Scale C, ascending, while the bass voice descends in Scale C as well.

The following form is suitable for Pathos

This same harmony in contrary motion can be carried out in the following ranges

Scale C

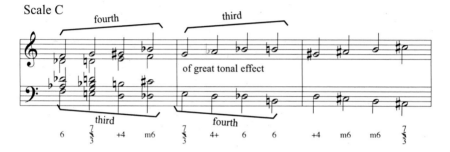

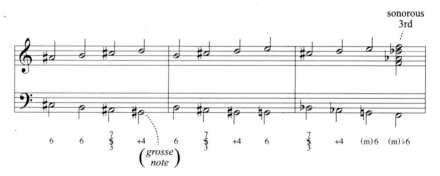

[- - - - -]

[tr-p. 81]

Sketch

drone in the bass is paired against a sequentially ascending tetrachord countersubject in the tenor that begins on a *dominant* B (m. 1) and moves up to C♯ (m. 2), thus creating dual tritone axes with the bass F and G, respectively. Each measure of the soprano line outlines a diminished 7th chord, connected by octatonic passing tones and concluding with a tritone. Tritone relations are intensified in the second sketch with the addition of an additional countersubject that pits an F–B axis in the tenor and bass against a C♯–G axis in the alto and soprano.

Same figure with two countersubjects

ending up at C♯, and more biting

End of cycle

[- - - - -]

[tr-pp. 82–83]

Remark concerning counterpoint in Scales A, B, C (leading toward an endpoint at the tritone at the termination of two phrases in counterpoint)

Scale B

leading to the accompaniment of E♮ by this technique

[- - - - -]

[tr-p. 83, cont.]

Studies for orchestral movements, passionate with tension

Scale B

Sequences of chords with expansion of the voices, taken from the 3 scales

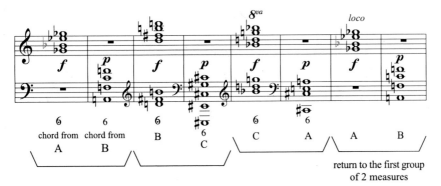

chord from chord from   B   C   A   A   B
A   B

return to the first group
of 2 measures

Another arrangement

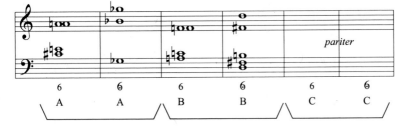

6   6   6   6   6   6
A   A   B   B   C   C

Another sequence

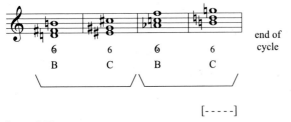

6   6   6   6
B   C   B   C

end of
cycle

[- - - - -]

[tr-p. 84]

Succession of major 6ths (harmonizing Scales A, B, C)

Scale B

Reduction in inversions [of major chords]

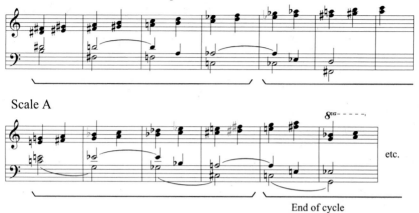

Scale A

etc.

End of cycle

Example in one of the 3 scales A, B, C of a tearing-away from ordinary modern tonality through a mutation.

Another counterpoint from the preceding example

Scale C

❧ In these sketches, the sustained B♭ (one of the *tonics* in Scale C) and the pervasive (0,2,3,5) tetrachords hold forth the possibility of "ordinary modern tonality." However, the sense of centricity and stability created by the internal pedal B♭ and the diatonic subset is undermined by a subject that outlines a diminished triad E–G–B♭ and a countersubject that alternates (0,2,3,5) tetrachords that enter, respectively, on F and B, two of Scale C's *dominants*. Thus, Polignac "tears away from tonality" by pitting (0,1,3,4) against (0,2,3,5).

[- - - - -]

[tr-pp. 85–86]

From whence the root of the following cycle

Scale C

The F to finish with the chord

for one can begin building on the tritone E♮

A new figure

coming to an end; restitution to finish with B♭–D–B♭

Minor progression: the same can be done in Scale B [using major chords]

Scale B

Example of Scale B in major, with a point of rest on an augmented chord Ɛ

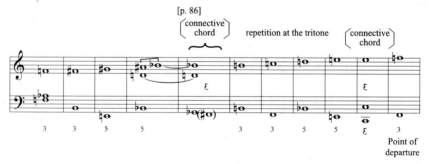

[- - - - -]

[tr-p. 86, cont.]

Type of motive incited by the melody of Pilate—sickly, desolate, sad

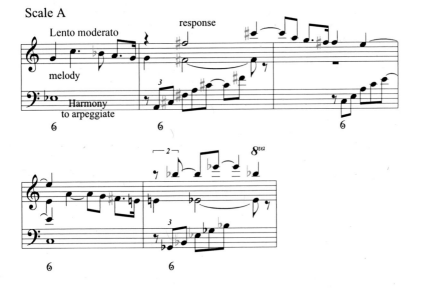

Scale A

❧ The above motive and its three imitative repetitions each feature one of the four *tonics* of Scale A: C, F♯, A, and E♭, respectively. The motive is derived from "Pilate livre le Christ," a passage from Pilate's recitative on the text "Innocens ego sum," marked "A little more solemn, but sad" (mm. 201–207). The arpeggiated accompaniment in the above sketch is unique to the treatise, and in no way resembles the spare accompaniment in the oratorio movement. Polignac's comment seems to allude to an already-completed piece of music, which further suggests that the treatise was written after the composition of "Pilate."

Rich, moving accompaniment, the highest voice is climbing

Scale B

Moderato

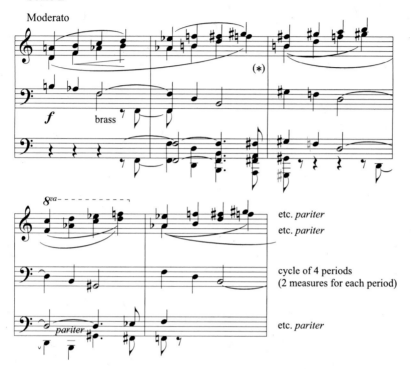

etc. *pariter*

etc. *pariter*

cycle of 4 periods
(2 measures for each period)

etc. *pariter*

(*) The descent of a 2nd from G♯ to F♯ is better than leaping to C♮ (one measure later) to return, via the perfect 5th F–C, to the regularity of the [melodic] pattern.

[- - - - -]

[tr-p. 87–88]

Tryouts of counterpoint (breaking-up and inverting of an arranged figure or scale)

Scale B

❧ Here, we have translated "jeu sur le triton" as "play" (as in "riffing") on the tritone. The French word also connotes "ritual," as in the "Jeu de rapt" (ritual of seduction) movement of Stravinsky's *Sacre du printemps*.

The above example goes across tr-pp. 87–88, and the explanation continues on tr-p. 87.

[- - - - -]

[tr-p. 87, cont.]

Remark: the *tonic* notes of scales A, B, and C are produced as the heads of groups of 2, 4, or 6 notes when the line proceeds by step (the same in descending lines, and for the *dominants*)

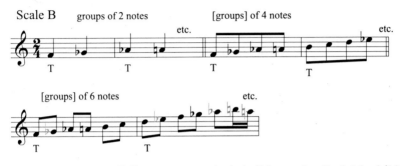

🍂 Polignac progressively builds up the diminished 7th chord (0,3,6,9) through motives constructed at the minor 3rd, the (0,1,3,4) tetrachord, and the (0,1,3,4,6,7) hexachord.

[-----]

[tr-p. 88, cont.]

Principle of simple harmonic arrangement to harmonize a range of a 4th followed by a range of a major 3rd

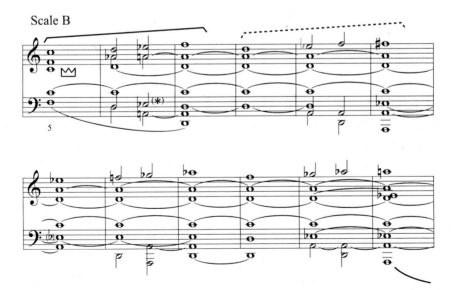

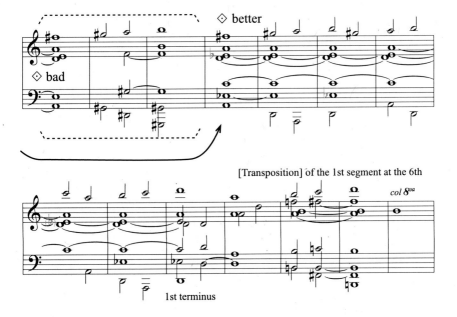

[Transposition] of the 1st segment at the 6th

1st terminus

To avoid between two neighboring voices a relation resulting in the too-rich interval of the major or minor 3rd

(*) This part can also do:

and the F whole note at this last reprise in place of the D whole note would be too rich, leading to the chord (example)

F whole note

⋈ If the 2nd segment should echo the 1st at the tritone, it would be better to begin thus avoiding the key of F (5):

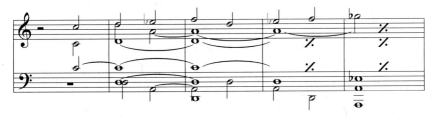

See tr-p. 90✣

❧ The following example has been moved from tr-p. 90.

✣Reference to page 88, response at the tritone for the second segment

Scale B

etc.

D.C.

unison

❧ From the Table of Contents: "Arrangement spaced by a harmonization of Scale B upon which the melody proceeds by ranges of 4ths or neighboring major 3rds (a curious example)."

[- - - - -]

[tr-p. 89]

Example of patterns in voice parts (bumpy, diatonic), in the style of the rocking bassline of the Symphony with Chorus, simulating the effects of the organ bass at the moment of the chorus's prayer—with winds and brass [*caisse d'harmonie*] in consonant 3-part harmony.

❧ From the Table of Contents: "Effect of a cathedral organ (in the genre of the Symphony with Chorus the second movement)"

In this passage, Polignac describes potential orchestration of the treble and bass voices, which function in a kind of voice exchange. The "Symphony with Chorus" is surely Beethoven's Ninth Symphony, and Polignac imagines the bass voices here evoking the recitative passage for low strings in the fourth movement of the Beethoven symphony. He imagines the three treble voices being played by a "caisse d'harmonie," a brass and wind band.

Pagan Harmony without a 3rd, in which the tonic and the 5th are played simultaneously, spanning the four *tonics*.

Scale C

Moderato

[- - - - -]

[tr-p. 90]

Testing-out of an assimilation at the resolution in conventional tonality of the dominant 7th leading to a major triad

Conventional tonality

Scale A

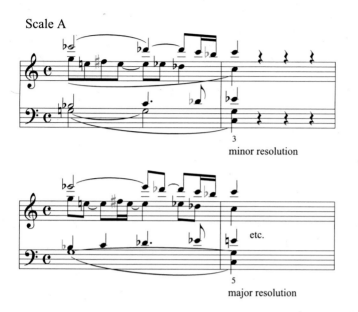

minor resolution

major resolution

❧ Here, Polignac first presents a "conventional tonal" V⁷–I cadence, followed by an example whose pitches are drawn from Scale A, but whose melodic and bass motion mimic the tonal model.

Harmonic principle on scales A, B, C

Scale A

and can be inverted, ex:

Can also be doubled like this:

from which emanate especially these intervallic formations

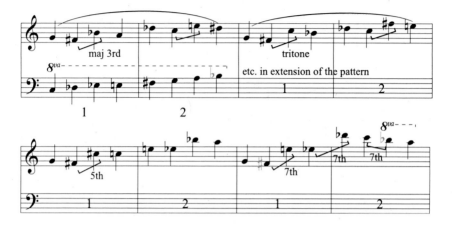

✹ Material from the bottom of tr-p. 90 has been moved to tr-p. 88.

[- - - - -]

[tr-p. 91]

Relations of minor chords in the same scale

Scale A

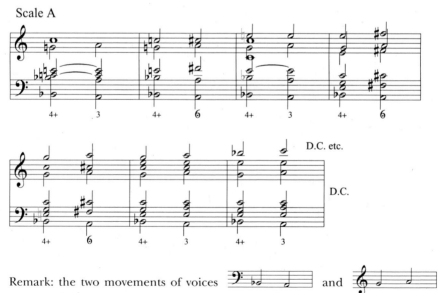

Remark: the two movements of voices [notation] and [notation] are perpetual.

Reference [to here] from the sign ✠ on [tr-p.] 21.

Cadence on C major brought by the harmonization of Scale A, for example

Scale A

Another law for the movement of the basses

Scale A

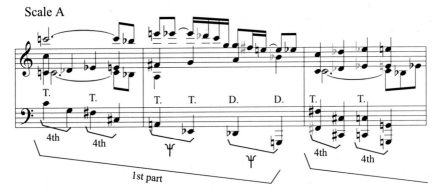

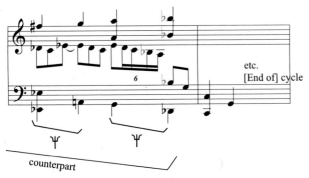

❧ T. stands for *tonic;* D. stands for *dominant;* Ⴤ is Polignac's symbol for a tritone. [T. and D. are in the middle of the staff.]

Polignac once again mimics tonal practice by featuring a bass line of sequentially descending perfect 4ths followed by the octatonic augmented 4th.

[- - - - -]

[tr-p. 92]

Cross-reference from page [i.e., tr-p.] 21. (By similar movements): accompaniment of the notes:

Scale A

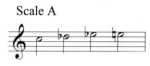

1. Scale A

2.

3.

4.

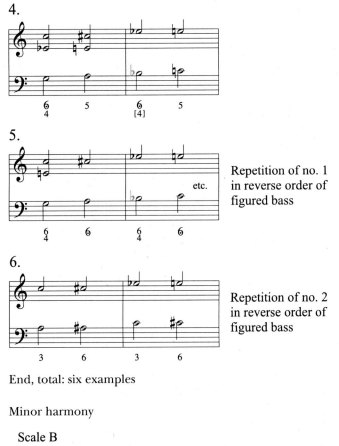

5.

Repetition of no. 1
in reverse order of
figured bass

6.

Repetition of no. 2
in reverse order of
figured bass

End, total: six examples

Minor harmony

Scale B

D minor $^6_4$ to A♭ minor [in root-position]

An example from this page has been moved to page 37 at
the sign

[- - - - -]

[tr-p. 93]

Arrangement of the voices on a harmonic scale permitting a doubling of the bass voice by a higher voice, with a harmony in the extreme highest voice and an internal pedal

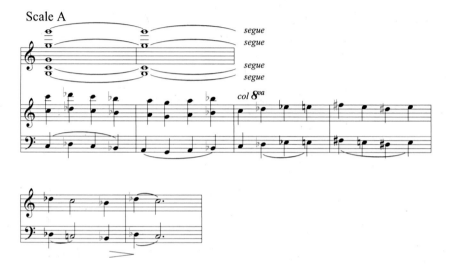

Scale A

❧ In the autograph manuscript, the first verticality comprises eight voices. In the interest of clarity, we have separated out the sustained voices. The "internal pedal" consists of the trichord G3–C4–G4 and the "harmony in the extreme highest voice" consists of an octave G5–G6.

Counterpoint on the span of a tritone

variant - better

etc.

and also in the bass

❧ The descending scalar subject beginning on pitch-class A is subdivided over the barline at the tritone; the second iteration is completed by the pedal-point on A in the lowest voice. The highest voice also outlines spans of a tritone, albeit in a less regular manner.

[- - - - -]

[tr-p. 94]

another harmony

[End of] cycle
D.C. an octave higher

[- - - - -]

[tr-p. 95]

Forms

Scale C   (Subject on the *tonic*)

A voice that can be added to complete the four parts

(Response on the *dominant*)

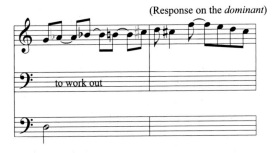

to work out

❧ No clef was indicated by Polignac for the lowest voice ("the voice that could be added to complete the four parts"). Taking into account the preexisting accidentals in the score, we have added a bass clef, as it best corresponds with Scale C and produces harmonies that best complement the two other voices.

Scale C

Poco agitato (perplexing effect)

End of the cycle for repetition at the octave

[- - - - -]

[tr-p. 96]

(In music) Tests—Experiments—not done to please the public

Today, since the [advent of the] Sunday concerts, one can try anything: invasion of the critical spirit [to influence] the impact felt by the public; a philosophical, ethnographic view of souls and of things, substituted for the lyrical visions of yesteryear (Vogüé). Additionally, an attempt to bring to the public the personal impressions of the individual, [without filtering them through] the prism of "the School"; the microcosm, phenomenon of mental intussusception.

Attempts [to create] a new musical art for those tired of hearing conventional 4-part music.

Technical advice: Be careful to leave some room in the accompaniment that will allow the melodic line to include an ornament or figuration, and to sweep clear the spot in the scale that the melodic line is occupying, so that it can be sung clearly and be heard distinctly without being hidden.

(Table of contents: see the other side of the page)

[- - - - -]

[tr-p. 97]

TABLE of Contents of this Notebook

Edmond de Polignac

Étude sur les successions alternantes de tons et demi-tons
[Et sur la gamme dite majeure-mineure]

(Transcription of the Original French Text)

Editor's note: In the transcription many of Polignac's abbreviations have been filled in to create complete words:

acc or accd has become accord
acct or accmpt = accompagnement
Allo = allegro
Alletto = allegretto
altern = alternante
Andte = Andante
c.a.d. = c'est-à-dire
chrom-diat = [gamme] chromatico-diatonique
dom or domin = dominante
ex = exemple
Gme or Gmme = Gamme
m.m. = maj.min.
Modto = Moderato
renvt = renversement
stacc. = staccato
ton = tonique
tron = tronçon
uniss = unisson

On the other hand, standard musical abbreviations have been left as written:

accel (accelerando)
cresc (crescendo)
maj (majeur)
min (mineur)

The treatise pages are indicated, as they are in the English translation, by the abbreviation tr-p. for a single page and tr-pp. for multiple pages.

The musical examples are not included here; their placement in the original is indicated by the symbol ▲. They can be found in the English translation.

Some of Polignac's musical examples extend over more than one page. These are not indicated in the transcription provided here, but are listed in the Preface to the English translation, p. 154. As we indicated earlier, Polignac would sometimes write down an idea and pick up on it again several or many pages later, cramming the rest of the musical thought onto any page with some unused space; in other instances, he would return to a musical idea and make reference to the page where the idea had first appeared. These shifts are not indicated here.

Etude sur les successions alternantes de tons et demi-tons (Et sur la gamme dite majeure-mineure)

Signes d'Abréviations

L. loco: lieu et limite exacte d'un motif ou d'un dessin d'accompagnement

L. S. ou L.-inf: limite supérieure ou limite inférieure

D signifie "dominante"

T signifie "tonique"

Le chiffrage

♃ ▲ signifie gamme A Brodé par ré♭ ▲ Brodé par la♮

idem dans les deux autres gammes B et C

le chiffrage ♭6 signifie 1er renversement d'un accord parfait min (3)

le chiffrage 6 signifie 1er renversement d'un accord parfait maj (5)

le chiffrage Ɛ signifie deux 3^{ces} majeures superposées avec une note commune

"Triton" indiqué par ↟ ou ⸔

"jusqu'à" par ∾

"Entrée d'un motif ou d'un instrument" par ⬆ ou ⬇

Continuation d'un accompagnement au-dessous ou au-dessus d'un motif
par Segue

ou par deux traits à chaque Barre de mesure ▲

ou en-haut de la mesure ▲

Signes d'abbréviations

Pour un trait parcourant une des gammes A.B.C. ▲

c'est-à-dire la lettre dans laquelle le morceau est écrit remplaçant les notes
du trait avec une flèche indiquant la note d'arrivée du trait

α signifie la gamme de six tons entiers partant de ut ou tout autre degré

β▲ signifie idem pour tons de sol♮ ou fa♮

Pariter . . . ou Par signifie reproduction du même dessin en progressions
avec d'autres notes

[- - - - -]

Exposé Théorique

La série naturelle, des tons et demi-tons, telle qu'elle est adoptée aujourd'hui pour constituer notre échelle musicale peut être divisée en *trois séries* différentes de tons et demi-tons (2des majeures et 2des mineures) alternants régulièrement entre eux.

Ex: v.s.

[- - - - -]

[tr-p. 2: blank page]

[- - - - -]

[tr-p. 3]

Tableau des 3 séries A.B.C.

Ex.

Série A   ▲ octave suivante reproduisant sa précédente
Série B   ▲ constituée comme la série A, mais baissée d'un ½ ton
Série C   ▲ constituée comme la série A, mais haussée d'un ½ ton

Si l'on prend, dans une de ces 3 séries (A B ou C) une note quelconque comme point de départ, on remarquera qu'elle se représente à son 8^{ve} après un parcours de huit degrés; on remarquera également que, dans la série A par exemple, la gamme d'ut à ut n'est pas constituée [continuation p. 5]

[- - - - -]

[tr-p. 4]

Remarques sur les accords parfaits qui occupent une place correspondante dans les différentes gammes A B C

Toniques d'accords parfaits s'écartant de la tonique "ut" par degrés égaux supérieures et inférieurs et donnant des toniques appartenant aux gammes marquées par leurs lettres B ou C. ▲
autre exemple ▲

On remarquera que les accords parfaits de la♭ de ut et de mi♮ sont les plus apparentés à cause de la note commune mi (médiante d'ut) ut médiante de ré♭ et la♭ (sol♯) médiante de mi

[- - - - -]

[tr-p. 5]

[continuation de la p. 3]

semblablement à cela de ré♭ à ré♭ en ce que, en partant d'ut, le premier degré est un demi-ton tandis qu'en partant de ré♭ il est d'un ton.

Eléments harmoniques qui caractérisent chacun de ces 3 séries ou gammes.

Les accords parfaits formés par la Gamme A sont ▲ majeurs ou mineurs
Les accords parfaits formés par la Gamme B sont ▲ majeurs ou mineurs
Les accords parfaits formés par la Gamme C sont ▲ majeurs ou mineurs

[- - - - -]

[tr-p. 6]

Notes

Nous désignerons chacune de ces 3 séries, suivant les notes que la constituent, par les noms de gamme A ou B ou C, ou système A B ou C (voir au tableau page 3)

Tout ce qui sera dit sur la gamme A (en ce qui concerne ses éléments constitutifs ou ses progressions harmoniques) sera applicable aux deux autres gammes, fait qui découle nécessairement de leur formation identiquement similaire. Ces séries recevront également l'appellation de gamme "chromatico-diatoniques."

Remarque: chaque gamme est composée de 4 tons et 4 demi-tons. Dans la séries A les 8 notes, par succession ascendante, de ut à si♭, peuvent être considérées comme étant la superposition de 2 tronçons semblables dont l'ambitus est pour chacun d'une tierce majeure. Ex. ▲ 1er tronçon ▲ 2me tronçon Gamme A

Mais de ré♭ à ut vous procédez par quartes superposées sans rencontrer dans aucun des tronçons séparément, une 3^{ce} majeure. Ex. ▲ 1er tronçon ▲ 2de tronçon Gamme A

[- - - - -]

[tr-p. 7]

Chiffrage en accords parfaits de la gamme A (au chant) ▲

d'où il suit que dans la gamme A on rencontre 4 tierces majeures qui sont / ▲ / de même 4 quintes justes prise sur do, mi♭, sol♭ et la♮.

8 tierces mineures, une sur chaque degré; 4 quartes justes qui sont ▲ étant les renversements de 4 quintes justes.

8 tritons, un sur chaque degré de la gamme—4 demi-tons, 4 tons, 4 sixtes mineures, 8 sixtes maj. (renversements des tierces maj. et min), 4 7èmes maj., 4 7èmes min (renversements des tons et ½ tons), 4 9èmes min; et 4 9èmes majeures.

[- - - - -]

[tr-p. 8]

Suite du remarque

mais un intervalle de triton coupe toujours l'octave de neuf notes en deux parts égales soit que le 1er degré soit un ton ou qu'il soit un demi-ton.
Ex gamme A ▲ triton / triton / 1 octave / ou gamme A ▲ triton / triton / 1 octave

[- - - - -]

[tr-p. 9]

Par suite des accords parfaits constitutifs de la Gamme A nous remarquerons que les notes ▲ sont des notes toniques; ▲ des notes médiantes, et ▲ des notes de dominantes; de plus les notes ▲ seront les 7èmes mineures des toniques ▲ et ▲ les 9èmes mineures des mêmes toniques, donnant les accords ▲ ou ▲ etc sur chacun des 4 degrés toniques. On remarquera que l'accord parfait d'ut est en rapport de triton avec l'accord parfait de sol♭ ou fa♯, et qu'il en est de même entre l'accord parfait de mi♭ et l'accord parfait de la♮. L'accord de 9ème majeure ne peut pas être formé sur ces gammes.

[- - - - -]

[tr-p. 10]

Suites des notes et remarques

Dans les gammes chromatico-diatoniques si le premier degré est d'un ton l'ambitus des 7 notes, avant de retomber sur l'octave, est d'une 7ème majeure; si le premier degré est d'un ½ ton, l'ambitus n'est que d'une 7ème mineure.

Ex: Gamme B   Gamme A
1 ton ▲ 7ème majeure ½ ton ▲ 7ème mineure

On remarquera que toute note qui n'est pas une tonique dans une gamme est dominante d'une des 4 toniques.

Ex: toniques du système A ▲ dominantes de ces toniques ▲. Lorsque le point de départ est une dominante dans la succession des notes d'un système, le 1er degré est d'un ton et seulement d'un ½ ton lorsqu'on part d'une tonique (voir Ex: plus haut).

[- - - - -]

[tr-p. 11]

Diverse marches d'harmonie dans la Gamme A

Gamme A processus mineur ▲ / autre le 1er accord étant maj ▲ / accord de 2 notes seulement /
Chiffrage de la Gamme en partant d'une des notes d'un des 4 accords parfaits de l'accord d'ut / tonique / ▲ 1er tronçon 3^{ce} maj / 2^d tronçon / médiante / ▲ 1er tronçon 4te juste / 2^d tronçon / dominante / ▲ 4te juste idem

[- - - - -]

[tr-p. 12]

Chiffrages et armures

tout accord parfait mineur sera chiffré par un 3, pour le distinguer de l'accord 5. armure de la gamme A ▲ armure de la gamme B ▲ armure de la gamme C ▲

En effet dans la gamme A, en prenant ut comme point de départ, on ne rencontre ni fa♮, ni si♮, ni ré♮; le mi♮ et le sol♮ peuvent être bémolisés au courant du morceau, tout aussi bien que l'ut et le la peuvent être diésés. (*)

Les mêmes remarques sont applicables à la Gamme B, en prenant Fa comme point de départ et dans la Gamme C en y prenant sol.

(*) Si, un morceau est conçu en mineur il sera bon de marquer à la clef par un Bémol ou un Bécarre suivant le cas. Ainsi en Gamme A, mi♭ pour ut min, la♮ pour fa♯ mineur, sol♭ pour mi♭ mineur—idem pour les cas de fréquence de l'accord parfait majeur, alors ut♯ pour l'accord de la maj. par exemple etc.

[- - - - -]

[tr-p. 13]

Successions harmoniques avec renversements

▲ 1ᵉʳ membre idem ▲ 1ᵉʳ membre etc
accords maj. et min mélangés ▲ 1ᵉʳ membre idem etc
Gamme [A] ▲ 1ᵉʳ membre 2ᵈ membre / autre ▲

[- - - - -]

[tr-p. 14]

Remarques (suite)

Etudes de la constitution harmonique des accords d'un système.
Sur une tonique en prenant successivement les notes de la gamme qui s'y prêtent ou rencontre sur la tonique ut par exemple de la Gamme A l'accord de 9ᵉᵐᵉ min:

Ex ▲ la 1ᵉʳᵉ note faisant harmonie (à partir de l'ut note inférieure) c'est-à-dire mi♮ (médiante d'ut) se trouve être dominante de la♮ (une des 4 toniques) septième min. de fa♯ (autre tonique) 9ᵉᵐᵉ min. de mi♭ (*) (autre tonique) et enfin médiante d'ut etc pour les autres notes constituant cet accord; d'où la figure analytique suivante ▲ 1ᵉʳᵉ note / ▲ dominante de la/ ▲ 7ᵉᵐᵉ de fa♯ / ▲ 9ᵉᵐᵉ mineure de mi♭ / 2ᵈᵉ note ▲ 3ᶜᵉ / ▲ 7ᵉᵐᵉ / ▲ 9ᵉᵐᵉ / 3ᵉᵐᵉ note ▲ 3ᶜᵉ / ▲ dominante / ▲ 9ᵉᵐᵉ / 4ᵉᵐᵉ note ▲ 3ᶜᵉ / ▲ dom / ▲ 7ᵉ /

(*) mi♮ étant considéré comme fa♭.

[- - - - -]

[tr-p. 15]

Successions harmoniques avec renversements (suite)

Gamme A ▲ /
Tronçons de la Gamme A avec renversements et Harmonies mineures ▲ /
Tronçon analogue avec les fondamentales à la basse (très sombre de caractère et gardant un aspect diatonique ▲) / ou encore régulièrement à 4 parties ▲ / ces deux parties procèdent par succession de 4tes et 3^{ces} majeures/ (*) (Chez Caïphe) ▲ tout cet ensemble harmonique supporte une basse par degrés

[- - - - -]

[tr-p. 16]

Tableau de successions d'intervalles à 2 parties (compris dans une 8^{ve}) procédant par degrés conjoints pris sur la même gamme (en prenant pour cet exemple ut comme point de départ.)

Gamme A
1 Succession de 2des min. et 2des maj. alternantes ▲
dont renversements donnent ▲ etc / ou successions de 7èmes maj. et min. alternantes.
2 Succession de tierces mineures ▲ etc
dont les renversements donnent ▲ etc / ou succession de sixtes majeures
3 Successions de 3^{ces} maj. et 4tes justes alternantes ▲ etc
dont les renversements donnent ▲ etc ou succession de sixtes min et de 5tes justes alternantes
4 Succession de tritons ▲ etc
dont les renversements donnent les mêmes intervalles ▲ etc succession identique au type.

[- - - - -]

[tr-p. 17]

Rapports des intervalles entre eux dans la reproduction de dessins mélodiques sur la même gamme

Dans la Gamme A par ex Quand la reproduction se fait à distance d'une 3^{ce} mineure, d'un triton ou d'une 6te majeure les intervalles se reproduisent identiques dans les deux dessins/

Ex modèle ▲ 5te 1 ton 3^{ce} min

reproduction sur un autre degré à un intervalle de 3^{ce} min par exemple ▲ 5te 1 ton 3^{ce} min/

idem sur un autre degré à distances d'un triton ou d'une sixte majeure.

[- - - - -]

[tr-p. 18]

Traits offrant un exemple de liaison entre les 3 gammes

Trait ascendant/ septième min ▲ / si♭ note commune à [la gamme] A et à [la gamme] C / idem ▲ / idem ▲ / 3ce maj ▲ / 3ce min ▲ / idem ▲ /
Trait descendant/ 7ème min ▲ / note commune ▲ / note commune ▲ / etc. /
4te juste ▲ / note comm. / 4te juste ▲ / id. ▲ / id. ▲ /
Par intervalle de triton/ Triton ▲ / Triton ▲ / ici point d'arrêt à l'octave
And[an]te Processus mineur (gamme A) caractère très langoureux/ fa♯ min
bécarre ▲ 1er membre/ la min ▲ / 2^{d} membre/ la min fa♯ min ▲ ut min ▲ /
Renvoi de la page 15 (forme plaintive) ▲ ou autre emploi ▲

[- - - - -]

[tr-p. 19]

mais lorsque la reproduction du dessin modèle est faite sur un degré distant du point de départ d'un ½ ton, d'un ton, d'une 3^{ce} maj, d'une 4te juste, d'une quinte juste, d'une 6te min, d'une 7ème min. ou d'une 7ème maj.

Alors le ½ ton devient ton, le ton demi-ton, la 3^{ce} min. ne change pas, la tierce maj. devient 4te, la 4te tierce maj, la 5te devient 6te min, la 6te min. devient 5te, la 7ème min. devient 7ème maj, et la 7ème maj devient 7ème min, la 9ème min devient 9ème maj.

Tableau pour servir à la reproduction à la seconde min:

3^{ce} min	3^{ce} maj	triton	5te	6te maj	7ème min	8^{ve}	7ème maj	9ème min	9ème maj
▲	▲	▲	▲	▲	▲	▲	▲	▲	▲	▲

3^{ce} min	4te	triton	6te min	6te maj	7ème maj	8^{ve}	7ème min	9ème maj	9ème min
▲	▲	▲	▲	▲	▲	▲	▲	▲	▲	▲

On peut tracer d'autres tableaux d'où la seconde maj ou ton entière, 3^{ce} maj etc (voir au texte plus haut) d'où l'Ex suivant modèle / ▲ modèle/ reproduction à la 5te ▲ / retour du modèle composé des mêmes intervalles étant à un intervalle de tierce mineur ▲ /

[- - - - -]

[tr-p. 20]

Disposition pratique d'un tableau pour servir aux reproductions mélodiques

7ème min ▲ 7ème maj
5te juste plus haut ▲ 6te min
3ce maj plus haut ▲ 4te
1 ½ ton plus haut ▲ ton
Echelle modèle Gamme A ▲

(Renvoi) les 9èmes maj ou min sont produites par la série des tons et ½ tons en les remportant à la 8ve supérieure.
Dessin modèle ▲/ reproduction à la 3ce maj ré♭ pour ut♯

[- - - - -]

[tr-p. 21]

Suite des études sur les successions harmoniques prises dans la même gamme/(voir aussi page 92)

Gamme A
succession de tritons ▲ etc / succession de 3ces mineurs / etc
(idem avec renversement des parties)
autre ▲ double succession de tritons par mouvement contraire etc
▲Double succession d'accords de quinte diminuée
idem pour une succession de 7èmes diminuées
Harmonisation de la Gamme A ▲ caractère noble douloureux (ɸ voir aussi page 91)
▲ Cette mesure peut être harmonisée en versant en la mineur
▲ autre renversement de la Gamme A / ▲ V.S.

[- - - - -]

[tr-p. 22]

Successions mineures
(3èmes renversements des deux accords mi♭ et la min avec *alternances par intervalle du triton.*)
Gamme A ▲ / Gamme A Successions maj. et min. alternants chiffrages 5 et 6 alternants ▲ / idem avec appogiatures ▲ / idem avec toute autre tonique ▲ / saut de 6te
Gamme A ▲ (avec syncopes) ▲ / Grande tierce

Practicable avec la même basse sur les 4 toniques▲

tonique ▲ saut de 7ème/ tonique ▲ / sur une dominante/ dominante ▲

saut de 6te ▲

effet triste ▲ /

△ Cette partie peut être doublée en tritons ou sixtes maj. syncopés

♉ (voyez page 51, ténor)

[- - - - -]

[tr-p. 23]

Etude sur l'Echelle dite "majeure-mineure" (son armure la plus simple est un ♭ sur le mi, ou un ♯ sur l'ut)

Type

Avec ut pour tonique ▲ appartient à la Gamme min ordinaire de jeu/ou gamme Hypolydienne

dont le sixième degré (baissé d'un ½ ton) fait sixte min. avec la tonique

avec sol pour tonique ▲ appartient à la gamme min. ordinaire d'ut.

avec ré pour ton. ▲ appartient à la gamme min. de sol.

avec la pour ton. ▲ appartient à la gamme min. de ré.

▲ appartient à la gamme de La min. etc. etc.

Remarque. D'où il suit que dans l'Echelle qui ne porte qu'un ♭, c'est-à-dire mi♭, on rencontre trois toniques naturelles sur lesquelles peut se construire un accord parfait (maj. ou mineur).

Ce sont sol pour l'accord majeur ▲ ut pour l'accord mineur ▲ et ré pour l'accord mineur ▲

De même pour l'Echelle qui ne porte qu'un ♯ ou ut♯ on trouve les 3 accords ▲

[- - - - -]

[tr-p. 24]

Essais—Effets (dans la gamme maj-min) [gamme établie sur le 5ème degré de la tonique sol, ou sur le 2^{d} degré de la tonique habituelle d'ut mineur]

Harmonie à 2 parties/ Cette partie seulement fait les notes de la gamme m.m. ▲

Même exemple avec la gamme au chant, et l'harmonie prise dans les notes de la gamme, le tout avec pédale inférieur en quinte ▲

Même exemple avec pédale de la Dominante réparentée à la partie supérieure (comme un chemin lointain montré par une étoile) ▲ violi sourdine

Marche harmonique (2^{d} degré de la min)

▲

[- - - - -]

[tr-p. 25]

▲ retour au point de départ à 4 8^ves de différence
Même Ex. avec broderie ▲ / etc jusqu'au retour du point de départ / même
Ex. avec un autre Dessin ▲ /
col 8va supérieure sempre ▲ / Si pédale fixe intérieure ▲ / Pédale Fixe à la B^se
▲ / idem suivez la marche/ suivez page 27 /

[- - - - -]

[tr-p. 26]

Etude ou Ex. à effet d'une série de mélanges des 3 systèmes A.B.C,
avec repos ou crochet sur une succession de trois accords de toniques
appartenant chacun à un des 3 systèmes

Système A / ▲ / Rythme / Maestoso / Gamme ou Système A ▲ /Repos ou crochet ▲ / tonique A / tonique B / A / tonique C / tonique A / Repos ou crochet ▲ /
(*) Crochet des 3 tonalités ▲ /

[- - - - -]

[tr-p. 27]

(Effet—Caractère)

Ces repos périodiques sur des accords successifs, changeants de système, pren-
nent le caractère d'un repos, d'une solution, ou d'un écho lointain. Ils peuvent
servir aussi comme d'un serment solennel prononcé comme refrain. En tirer
parti dans une thème comme celle de la Pâque. /
(*) Remarque sur le crochet des 3 tonalités▲ /
Do tonique / do médiante / sol dominante / la♭ tonique / mi♮ médiante /
Dominante ▲
Exemple de cadence / ▲ /
Connection de ces cadences de A à B c'est-à-dire d'ut maj. à la♭ maj sentiment
de repos comme de ut à fa par marche descendante de quintes à la de quintes
à la basse; ou [gamme] A à [gamme] C, c.a.d. [i.e., c'est-à-dire] de ut maj à mi.
Sentiment de suspension interrogative comme de ut à sol par marche ascen-
dante de quinte à la basse / voir page 26 /
Parcours Harmonique de la Gamme A crochet des 3 tonalités. ▲ / Reproduc-
tions du début ▲ / Parcours de la Gamme B et allant à [la gamme] C ▲ / ou
bien

[- - - - -]

[tr-p. 28]

Suite de la page 25 ▲ / même dessin suivez la marche ▲ / terminus / Fin du Parcours (*) / (*) raccord pour enchaîner la suite ▲ / V.S.

[- - - - -]

[tr-p. 29]

(*) ▲ / (le si serait trop dur) / (Si Pédale intérieure come sopra) Si Pédale / (*) Nouvelle agrégation qui produit une harmonie très riche, en amenant à chaque temps fort un accord de 4 tons chiffré 7 au lieu d'un accord de trois sons chiffré 5 /
Cette même marche peut être simplifiée et résumée comme dans l'Ex. suivant ▲ /

[- - - - -]

[tr-p. 30]

Parcours d'une octave / retour au point de départ
16 pieds et 32 grosse Basse / en retard d'un temps.

[- - - - -]

[tr-p. 31]

Suite des exemples divers avec la Gamme Maj. min.

[successions harmoniques avec Basses progressant alternativement par quartes, quintes ou tons entiers] / (caractère: Espaces célestes, phalanges de Harpes et chérubins. Peut servir à "la vision" du Christ) ▲ / mi tonique ▲ / autre exemple (caractère, Phrase de tension grandiose) ▲ / maestoso moderato / signe pour marquer les entrées ▲ / Parties chantantes—entrées successives ▲ / Cette partie en 3ᶜᵉ double la partie supérieure. /

[- - - - -]

[tr-p. 32]

Autre cadence sur la tonique mi / (Gamme maj.min.) sur le 2ᵈ degré de la tonique maj. min. / La gamme est faite par le chant. ▲ / ut pédale ▲ / Variante(*) ▲ / V.S.

[- - - - -]

[tr-p. 33]

(Suite des remarques sur la gamme m: min.)

autres résolutions par les cadences suivantes: sur mi♮ ou si min. / ▲Do pédale /
▲ Pédale cesse / ou encore ▲ / ou encore ▲ /
Gamme maj. min. Dominante de mi / Harmonie à établir / autre terminaison
▲ /
autre forme même gamme ▲ /
Harmonie Règle d'octave de la Gamme majeure ordinaire (disposition pour la
Harpe comme entendu à Londres juillet 85 / sol min. ▲ / disposition d'école ▲ /

[- - - - -]

[tr-p. 34]

renvoi de la page 26 / Théorie d'où suit la cadence d'aller et retour avec repos
de [gamme] A à [gamme] C et [gamme] A à [gamme] B ▲ / repos / Donc une
dominante de [gamme] A à la / partie supérieure [illegible] / sur une tonique
de [gamme] B.
Bon dessin de contrepoint en gamme maj.min ▲ / au plus élégant / (*) Brodé
▲ / etc. / autre ▲ / à trouver
Marche simulant les Basses de toniques [?] et dominantes / dans le cours
d'Harmonie usuel
[Gamme] A / passage à [gamme] B / gamme B / [gamme] C / V.S.

[- - - - -]

[tr-p. 35]

Gamme A ▲ / Ces marches supportent toutes les notes des différentes gammes
A.B.C. / Gamme A motif affirmant la tonalité de A ▲ / Gamme B ▲ / Variant /
Résumé harmonique des 2 Exemples précédents ▲ / etc. / par marche de 5tes
descendantes $\overline{\text{do fa}}$ $\overline{\text{si♭ mi♭}}$ $\overline{\text{la♭ ré♭}}$ etc

[- - - - -]

[tr-p. 36]

Etudes sur les successions de 4tes et de 3^{ces} maj dans la Gamme A

Gamme A ▲ / Pour la carrure resumé▲ / Reprise de la marche sur le triton du
début ▲ / Résumé come sopra ▲ / Saut à l'autre triton mi♭ la ▲ / cette disposition plus douce que de faire entendre déjà le mi♭ ▲ / (*) on peut ajouter
l'autre superposition de la tierce majeure d'un des tritons ▲

Autre harmonie avec légère modification au chant ▲ / comme à l'ex cy dessus▲ / tonalité d'ut affirmée par la pédale ut ▲ / fin / Ex. de motif ou la 3^{ce} maj et min de la tonique se côtoient ▲ /

[- - - - -]

[tr-p. 37]

Forme riche de parties en contrepoint ▲ / Gamme A / Dessin continu de 2 mesures / (circulus de 4 mesures à la Basse/ processus de 4te et 3^{ce} maj)/ idem come sopra/ autre Broderie sur le même processus en 4tes et 3^{ces} maj à la Basse / chant d'expression caressante triste ▲ etc / 3^{ce} de la maj. / circulus de 4 mesures aux 2 parties / même Basse qu'à l'Ex précédant / [come sopra] condensation de la partie intermédiaire ▲/ condensation de la Basse voir page 92 au signe ∿/ autre version/
Marches Gamme A/ Avec Basses simulant le processus tonal de la tonalité usuelle
autre marche ▲/ (x) variant ▲/ (voir page 40)

[- - - - -]

[tr-p. 38]

Liste de motifs naturellement reproduits par la constitution des gammes ABC

Air d'Elie de Mendelssohn / Gamme B ▲/ sortie de B entrée en A / Le curé de Pomponne / Gamme A ▲/ Le Roi Don Juan (A) ▲/ Quoi vous ne me dites rien jadis c'était différent / "Que tout se fasse jeune et beau" (Noël de mes 12 mélodies)/ La Marseillaise surtout la phrase A: ▲/ Formes harmoniques des Plaintes de Médora ▲/ V.S.

[- - - - -]

[tr-p. 39]

Air de "la Diligence qui part pour Mayence" (approximatif) A ▲ /
Exemple d'une tonalité d'aspect mineure formée par une succession d'accord 7+ et d'accords parfait mineurs/ (caractère grave noble douloureux, mêlé d'effroi, bon pour l'Enfer de Dante)/
Lento / Chant ajouté / Gamme A ▲/
(*) chant / variante dans la suite de la progression ▲ / etc
Cet exemple peut aussi être employé pour un choeur céleste large style catholique à cause des accords de 7ème dominante (7+) qui n'ont point le caractère hébraïque, ou oriental.

[- - - - -]

[tr-p. 40]

Remarques sur l'ex. précédant

A (Lento) / Chant ▲ / l'accord min peut-être agrémenté ainsi par un chant /
pour ré♯ / note de passage ▲ /
variante comme à la page précédente ▲ / Grosse Basse à la Wagner /
Tristan et Isolde /
renvoi de la Page 37 autre circulus ▲ /
autre parcours come sopra ▲ / meilleure agraffe [sic] pour parcourir l'ambitus
tonal ▲ /

[- - - - -]

[tr-p. 41]

(Plein air et Plainchants) (Sorte de Pleinchant [sic] hébraïque procession pay-
sanne aux champs
avec agrafe entre B et C par les 3 notes communes fa si et ré) ▲
chœur ave rex / Gamme C / pédale de fa avec triton s'établissant peu à peu
▲ / pédale fa segue / gamme B / (Entrée dans la gamme B par le mi♭) ▲ /

[- - - - -]

[tr-p. 42]

jeu sur le triton ▲ / segue pédale ▲ / Pédale tient ▲ /

[- - - - -]

[tr-p. 43]

Gamme A / Harmonisation de la Gamme A (modèle pouvant être syncopé aux
trois parties) ▲ /
autre procédant par tons entières ▲ / idem (syncopé) ▲ / Carcasse ▲ /

[- - - - -]

[tr-p. 44]

Marche (Processus mineur)/ Gamme C Lento ▲ / autre mélange des gammes
▲ / ou en abrégé ▲ (renversements mineurs) / etc / retour au circulus à l'8va /
Processus mineur (Lointain—plaintif) ▲ /

[- - - - -]

[tr-p. 45]

Remarque sur les rapports harmoniques reliant deux gammes A et B

Chant commençant et finissant par une note commune aux deux gammes A et
B, Harmonie faite par deux notes communes aux 2 gammes. /
Ex. Ave Rex (d'agréer la Orientale juive) lointaine ▲ / (Parcours B) ▲ / ex ▲
/ reprise / du chant en A un ton plus bas ▲ / Ex d'apogiature [*sic*] très douloureux / Gamme B ▲ / appog[iature] /

[- - - - -]

[tr-p. 46]

[▲, cont.] le chant doit aboutir à la tonique mi♭ / réponse et reprise du chant
un ½[-ton] plus haut en gamme A / d'après l'exemple ⊠ cy-dessous / ⊠ Tronçon appartenant à B et amenant le repos sur la tonique de mi♭ min / ré♮ intervalle sensible de mi♭
Tronçon appartenant à [gamme] A avec repos sur la dominante de mi♭ min
(la♮ sensible de si♭)
Dans les exemples précédents l'harmonie des 2 notes ꙅ et ꙅ peut se représen-
ter dans les régions supérieures
Exemple de 2 tronçons de gammes différentes se colés [*sic*] ▲ / Formant
miroir
Ex ▲ d'où sujets au verso: V.S.

[- - - - -]

[tr-p. 47]

(Quasi maestoso) gamme A ▲ gamme B ▲
Variante à la basse ▲ / autre variante à la partie supérieure ▲ / gamme B /
Meilleure forme Plus régulière comme marche▲ /
Gamme A / Processus mineur Gamme A ▲ / gamme B / etc.

[- - - - -]

[tr-p. 48]

Progressions mineurs (sans changement de gammes) / Gamme B ▲
1er membre ▲ / 2d membre ▲ / ⌐‾‾‾⌐ indique enharmonique▲ /
Remarque / Dans un accord mineur toutes les notes comprises entre une médiante supérieure et la quinte se prêtent au chant sur cet accord /gamme B / ▲
médiante min. / 5te / succession qui peut se sucéder [*sic:* succéder] en deux
repos de 4tes / Ex. ▲ / ces quatre notes sont les points de repos de la succession //Exemple de notes faisant un chant, même succession harmonique ▲ /
recitando lento / etc. / Exemple de la modalité maj ou min. éviter (écueil

fréquent dans un trait mélodique ▲ / Harmonie de ré à 2 parties▲ / (*) seul mesure d'accords de 3 sons

[- - - - -]

[tr-p. 49]

autre progression mineure ▲ / gamme B / médiante / etc. / autre progression mineure ▲ /
Bonne disposition primitive de processus mineur / Gamme B / chant ▲ /
variante comme [illegible] / apogiature [*sic*] /
(*) Cette harmonie peut être variée ici par le chant et par les retards simples ou doubles par 3es mineures /

[- - - - -]

[tr-p. 50]

(foule et marche Hébraïque)

Allegretto Pesante / Gamme B / Proposition à la Zigane sur les notes fa la ▲ /
[illegible] troublé ▲ / tierce troublée des syncopes ▲ / tronçon écho de voix (paroles) Ave Rex (*) / etc. doublez le chant/ etc. doubles / tron. Echo / si lâche au 3ème temps et monte avec chant / fa♯ toujours seul / doublez toujours /
(*) Ici peut être intercalée cette phrase plus Biblique en réponse—Rythme plus large / syncopé ▲ / etc doublez /
Syncope marcato ▲ / idem ▲ / avec Basses 8ve ▲ / idem marche ▲ / idem marche ▲ / doublez tout / unis.

[- - - - -]

[tr-p. 51]

(Progressions mineures) Moderato Grave (Caractère cresc. de ferveur doulou-reuse judaïque) / Gamme B ▲ / Chant
Renvoi de la page 22 Début sur un Dominante avec saut de 7ème à la Basse—et Début sur tonique / le même chant ou gamme avec syncopes supérieurs ▲ / pouvant fournir des Dessins ou contrepoint et un crescendo par accélération et complication des parties

[- - - - -]

[tr-p. 52]

cette partie supérieure supporte des retards en appogiature [*sic*] / Gamme B ▲ / Parties suivant la Gamme B / V. c. {sonore Grande tension} / Pédale / etc. parties en gamme B

Comparaison des cadences, formules ou phrases habituelles à la gamme ordinaire maj. et les gammes A.B.C. avec processus de la note de dominante à la tonique dans la partie de Basse

Gamme A ▲
(*) Autre harmonies plus concertantes ▲ / plus facile avec apogiature [*sic*] ▲ / bonnes septièmes ▲ /

[- - - - -]
[tr-p. 53]

Passage de la min. à fa min. à ré♭ ou ut♯ min / (*) Remarques. La partie supérieure a parcouru la gamme de tons entiers de E♮ à E♮ / Notes de la Basse ▲
Gamme B / Gamme C / Gamme A /
Partie intermédiaire ▲ / médiante min / dominante / sensible de ré♭ / tonique / saute à la médiante / médiante min / dominante. / sensible / tonique / saute à la médiante /
médiante / dominante / sensible / tonique /
Résumé Parcours de chacune de parties

[- - - - -]
[tr-p. 54]

(Etude sur le motif suivant) col 8^ve / Moderato / Gamme C ▲ Sol Pédale / ou encore autre Rythme / dont les reversements ▲ / Exemples avec dispositions mineures▲ / autre disposition plus riche▲ / (*) l'ut♯ très mordant contre les 3^ce ré fa♮

[- - - - -]
[tr-p. 55]

Gamme C ▲ / avec sol pédale intérieure ▲ / Remarque (éloigner la 3^ce ré fa du dessin supérieur pour éviter les chocs de notes qui s'entremêlent avec dureté) / Harmonie Gamme C par m[ouvemen]t[s] contraires ▲ / Echanges de notes ▲ / etc. en sens contraire / (on peut découper un chant sur cette succession de notes—semblables aux chants des Derviches du Caire) Ex. ▲ /
Disposition Harmonique riche sonore violente martiale/ Moderato energico / Gamme C / Trompette / tutti ff / (*) peut aussi l'accompagner ainsi ▲ / Bonne 2de comme choc / même basse

[- - - - -]

[tr-p. 56]

poco più pesante / Remarque Homophonique après l'établissement pour l'oreille d'une gamme C par exemple en un chant borné à une tierce maj d'une tonique sol (par ex.) puis s'étendre au fa♯ sous le sol, ayant l'ambitus suivant / jouer sur la 3^{ce} maj ▲ / Gamme A / Sauter au triton Ré♭ que fait partie de la Gamme A et après le dessin qui est en gamme A tomber sur le fa♯ qui n'appartient pas à la Gamme C et caractérise bien le triton de la gamme A / L'effet est plus violent non harmonisé

[- - - - -]

[tr-p. 57; top]

Gamme B / (Andante marcato) / pouvant s'appliquer à la scène de la Pâque / Harmonie acct. dans la région moyenne ▲ / dessins fouillés de l'accompagnement ▲ / 4 mesures en plus (insérer ici) ▲ /

[- - - - -]

[tr-p. 58; top]

D.C. transposé / ré 5 sans tierce ▲ etc. etc.

[- - - - -]

[tr-p. 57; bottom]

Ex: de ut^5 à Fa♯^{3} et de mi♭^{5} à la^3 / etc ▲ / Gamme A

[- - - - -]

[tr-p. 58; bottom]

Ex. d'une tonalité simulée Gamme A ▲ /
▲ {à trouver les Basses et l'harmonie: le triton (en renversement ou non) simulant la dominante de la tonalité ordinaire.}

[- - - - -]

[tr-p. 59]

Exemple d'un contrepoint en imitation etc sur tous les degrés ▲ / [Gamme] A / Do pédale ▲ / Ce sujet peut se morceler et donne un bon crescendo et stringendo / une bonne poussée sur pédale / genre mélodique du "Roi Don Juan un jour chevauchant" ▲ / Gamme B ▲ / ornement ▲ / Renversements mineurs ▲ / reprise de la Basse

· [- - - - -]

[tr-p. 60]

Exemple d'un enchaînement harmonique entre les 1ers renversements des accords mineurs des toniques de la gamme A

dans l'ordre suivant: mi♭ min–fa♯ min–la min–ut min. ▲ / etc (+) audition d'un mesure de plus rendant la forme plus mélodique ▲ / Sorte de Prélude à la scène chez Caïphe déjà entamée au 1er cahier de Gamme A Page 35 ▲ / quasi mysterioso sorte de poussée des Basses / (*) les ut medium syncopés en triolets rythme différente à trouver/
(nu)/ (Gamme C) ▲ / (Gamme B) ▲ A–C–B–A ▲ / etc. / V.S.

[-----]

[tr-p. 61]

Entrée motif du 1er cahier à préparer avec carrure / motif ▲ / Réponses ▲ / tambour ▲ / col 8^v Basse / come sopra Rhythme inverse / plus tard le processus mineur ▲ /

[-----]

[tr-p. 62]

Gamme A / Harmonies sans tierces/ Dominante/ ambitus de 3^{ce} ▲ / idem / idem / idem / idem / idem /
Basses en Dominante ▲ / avec l'ambitus de 4te ▲ / tonique ▲

Sorte de désordre Hébraïque

Gamme C ▲ / 1er membre / tonique / 2de / irrégulier mais meilleur / dom. / tonique / sorte de contrepoint à vérifier et fixer / le ré descend à l'ut♯ et revient au ré. ▲ / Fin du circulus

[-----]

[tr-p. 63]

Gamme C (autre dessin)
Dom ▲ / Tonique ▲/ Dom ▲/ Fin du circulus
Descente par 9èmes min.
Gamme A ▲ /
Allegro molto / passionné en poussée avec rallentando / Gamme A /
Basse ajoutée ▲ / 1er membre / 8va Bassa / imitation du début de la Basse▲ /

[-----]

[tr-p. 64]

Fin du circulus parcours de 3 octaves / etc /
retour à la note du début de la Basse ▲ /
autre Basse ▲ /
même exemple / Gamme A ▲ / Fin du circulus /
Curieux exemple de notes de passage sur le processus harmonique revenant de deux toniques en triton amenant dans un accord la même médiante à la fois majeure et mineure / Gamme C / Andante ▲ (*) / (*) on peut supprimer le Sol-3-blanche (tonique de sol min) pour cette 1ère mesure. / Progression style de l'entrée de Tristan / Gamme C ▲ /

[- - - - -]

[tr-p. 65]

Ex.: Harmonie à 3 parties / (Ex. succession de 4tes et de 5tes à la 1ère et 2de parties) / Ex.: reversement ▲ ou ▲ /
Echelle de combinaison des 3 gammes avec Basses par 5tes ▲ / Ex. simulant Gamme usuelle de si♮ ▲ / au chant Gamme A ▲ / à construire en tâchant de garder aux 3 parties
supérieures la forme 6 /
cadences établissant une tonalité ▲ /

[- - - - -]

[tr-p. 66]

Allegro moderato appassionato (accords appogiatures sur les renversements de (sol 7+) / Marche moderne sonor [sic] / Gamme C ▲ / puis jouer sur l'accord ▲ se résolvant sur ▲ /
Règle / Dans les gammes A.B.C. tout dessin conjoint ayant un ambitus de 4tes et partant (s'il est ascendant) nécessairement d'une des dominantes ou médiantes de tonique, s'accompagne par mouvement contraire et note pour note par un ambitus de 3ce majeure.
Les deux dessins sont toujours renversables; les notes [illegible] aucune dissonance; les intervalles amenés sont: uniss[on] ou 8ve, 3ce mineur ou son renversement la 6te. maj. et la 4te augmenté ou Triton, invariable dans des renversements. / Gamme A ▲ / idem avec renversement Ex ▲ etc /
Gamme A ▲ / pédale de 3 notes / segue /

[- - - - -]

[tr-p. 67]

(Harmonie riche et dissonante)

Exemple du choc harmonique de la médiante maj. et min si♮ et ♭ (forme à l'air d'Elie de Mendelssohn) / Gamme C ▲ / Pédale de tierce (si ré) persistante ▲ / partie ajoutée ▲ / segue ▲ /exemple du choc ▲ / fin du circulus / pouvant se résoudre ainsi ▲ / très sonore dans cette forme ▲ / très sonore ▲ / fin de l'exemple / Même Exemple avec la Basse doublée en 10èmes ▲ / Plus élégant surtout si cette partie est repercutée dans les régions hautes ▲ / Autre Marche harmonique analogue / Gamme C Moderato. ▲ / CB (plus élégant de faire entrer la C.B. sur le degré distant d'un ton du degré précédent) ▲ / autre disposition / etc. en 3^{ces} mineures ▲

[- - - - -]

[tr-p. 68]

Retour à la position du début ▲ / autre disposition ▲ / En 3^{ces} min segue / etc / Gamme A / double choc de la méd. maj. et mineur ▲ / Pédale segue ▲ / (*) ici la Péd. interne s'augmente d'un si♭ ▲ ◇ ici d'un ut♯ ▲ / idem, avec regard à la dessus ▲ /
Allegro pesante / Gamme C / Pédale intérieur / harmonie pauvre / Gamme C ▲ / etc double le chant / Segue

[- - - - -]

[tr-p. 69]

[▲ segue / segue dessin à l'8^{ve} /
▲ / mi segue / ce mi cesse / accel poco a poco ▲ / col Basso /
segue / segue pédale ♮ mi ▲ / passage en Gamme A ▲ / [illegible (2 words)] de mi ▲ / en Gamme C ▲ / D.C. renforcé ▲ / retenez plus pesant à tempo 10 /

[- - - - -]

[tr-p. 70]

Autre motif / Gamme A ▲ / double la basse ▲ /
successions mineures et majeures (nobles, tristes, douloureux) /
Gamme A ▲ / fin du circulus /
D'où divers dessins ▲ / ou encore / Gamme A ▲ /
Dessins sur ces harmonies [Plaintif, caressant] ▲ /Andantino / Echo / Lent /
(*) application et meilleure disposition de cette harmonie ▲ /

[- - - - -]

[tr-p. 71]

Etudes de contrepoints par Mouvement[s] Contraires

Gamme A / Exemple de duretés possibles marquées par une x̄ ▲ / Accompagnement note pour note par le même ambitus à rebours / (x) mauvais ▲ / Bon ▲ / ou encore ▲ / Préparation à peu près du contrepoint pour le motif de la page suivante ▲ / préparant l'entrée de la foule ▲ /

[- - - - -]

[tr-p. 72]

Motif d'une marche au Calvaire déjà essayé (pris du 1er cahier des gammes A.B.C. page 34)

Gamme A (Rythme de 3 mesures) ▲ / Segue le chant doublé ▲ / 3 mesures / Espèce de contrepoint interne ▲ / grosse basse ad libit. ▲ / etc.
Projets ▲ / Bon contrepoint ▲ / 3 mesures
Gamme A / autre Rythme /Allegro moderato animato ▲ / On peut aussi exploiter le Rythme à 5 temps pour le projet de marche au Calvaire ▲ / Ce Rythme imitant bien la fatigue du poids de la croix. ▲ /

[- - - - -]

[tr-p. 73]

Gamme A ▲ / réalisation du chiffrage ▲ /
Genre Grand Pontife (Caïfe) / moderato molto / troublé sur sol♮ ré♭ / syncopes ▲ / approche lointaine ▲ / ascension sur le triton ▲ / motif: "Que tout se fasse jeune et beau" ▲ / Boulangère tronçon ▲ / réponse au triton ▲ /

[- - - - -]

[tr-p. 74]

triton ▲ / jeu sur les 4 quartes ▲ / motif doublé à l'8va alta ▲ / cresc ▲ / voir au signe ▲ / tritone cesse ▲ /
uniss[on] (entrer en [gamme] C) / pesante / staccato / très sonore/ très sonore ▲ / reprise du triton sol ré♭ ▲ / reprise du motif cette fois en C ▲ / réponse au triton ▲ / V.S.

[- - - - -]

[tr-p. 75]

Gamme A / moderato poco animato ▲ / Chant (Ténor registre) ▲ /
Remarque Théorique. Dans les Gammes Chromo-diatoniques, pour faciliter
le mouvement (surtout ascendant) par degrés conjoints dans l'ambitus d'un
octave, et principalement quand l'harmonie se chiffre par un 6 renversante
de l'accord 5, on peut altérer l'échelle chromo-diatonique en remplaçant les
2 notes qui séparent une tonique de sa tierce majeure par une note à distance
d'un ton entier de la dite tonique; les autres notes de l'échelle chromo-diatonique ne subissent aucun changement: / Ex / pour [gamme] A ▲ / devient
▲ / dont le radical est (dit gamme maj. min) ▲ / ou la gamme min usuelle en
partant de sol et avec les mêmes notes. ▲ /

[- - - - -]

[tr-p. 76]

Exemple d'une tonique tenue dans une gamme (C par Ex) devenant dominante
en Gamme A / Gamme C / Moderato / diverses entrées successives sur le sol
▲ / Sorte de marches d'Escaliers pour accrocher l'entame du motif / motif
▲ / Segue Sol interne ▲ / Reprise de la phrase en gamme A / Gamme A ▲ /
Dessin typique de Gamme chromatico-diatonique / Ex. Gamme B ▲ / etc / de
comparable ainsi en syncopes ▲ / D.C. / fin du circulus / V.S.

[- - - - -]

[tr-p. 77]

même esprit / Poco maëstoso (caractère de Férocité) / Gamme B ▲ /
(Lourd modéré) / Gamme A ▲ / Effet de Plein-air—Plainchant / variante ▲ /
même principe sonore (d'effet) ▲ /
Type ▲ / Théorie (renvoi de la page 75) / forme fréquente de la succession
dont il s'agit ▲ / forme ascendante ▲ / forme descendante ▲ /

[- - - - -]

[tr-p. 78]

✕ Effets d'appogiaturas par une 7ème maj (principe d'effet douloureux romantique) ▲ / Gamme B / Contrepoint syncopé toujours bon ▲ /
(Début sur Dominante) autre dessin (ambitus de 7ème majeure) ▲ / même Basse /
(Début sur une Tonique) ▲ / Tonique ▲ / (Ambitus de 3ce maj.) / Tonique
▲ / Tonique autre ▲ / tonique ▲ /
(8ves avec le chant tolérables; peut être évité en exhaussant la V.C. d'une 3ce
min—c'est-à-dire sol♭ au lieu de mi♭; ou en remplaçant le ré du chant au commencement de la mesure suivante par un fa /

[- - - - -]

[tr-p. 79]

Phrase à tension (Exemple d'une note supérieure faisant 3^{ce} min. avec la Basse en même temps que la 3^{ce} maj) Gamme B / Poco animato ▲ /
Suite du précédent / Effet redoutable / saut à la gamme C ▲ / triton 2♮ motif ▲ / segue ▲ / etc
Gamme B / Effets d'appogiatures sur des accords parfaits maj. ▲ / (caractère triste, dur, mordant, grand) ▲ /

[- - - - -]

[tr-p. 80]

(se prêtant au motif "tempo passato" de Françoise di Rimini dans Dante) / Gamme C ▲ / à exploiter (Progressions d'un Romantisme de "Sarniatisé" par la noblesse des éléments diatoniques de la Gamme C) / appogiature ▲ /aspect de chiffrage / La Forme suivante s'approprie Pathétiquement / Résumé ▲ / c'est-à-dire que 3 parties à la main droite progressent en Gamme C./ ascention-nellant [*sic*] tandis que la Partie de la Basse descend en Gamme C également/ mod[era]to ▲ / Cette même harmonie en sens contraire peut se pratiquer sur les ambitus suivants/ Gamme C ▲ / quarte ▲ / tierce ▲ / tierce ▲ / quarte ▲ / d'un grand effet tonal / (grosse note) ▲ / 3^{ce} sonore ▲ / Fin du circulus /

[- - - - -]

[tr-p. 81]

Dessin / Gamme C▲ / Ambitus de 6te maj / col 8^{ve} / contresujet / Pédale ▲ / segue cresc poco a poco ▲ / contresujet ▲ / segue ▲ / Analyse du contrepoint cy-dessus / ambitus de 4 ▲ / triton ▲ / idem de 3^{ce} ▲ / irrégularité / plus élégante ▲ / autre contresujet ▲ / même dessin avec 2 contresujets ▲ / autre contresujet / aboutissant à do♯ et plus mordante ▲ / idem ▲ / Fin du circulus /

[- - - - -]

[tr-p. 82]

Remarque pour contrepoint dans les Gammes A B C (tendre vers un aboutisse-ment au triton à la terminaison de deux phrases en contrepoint) /
Gamme B / moderato / Dim. / col 8^{ve} / più risoluto ▲ / col 8^{ve} B[as]se ▲ / loco ▲ / Solo / col 8^{ve} Basse / 8^{ve} / trombones ▲ / stringendo ▲ / sortie de la Gamme B ▲ / dolce ▲ / V.S. / dim ▲ / menant à l'accompagnement de mi♮ par cette gamme▲ /

[- - - - -]

[tr-p. 83]

Etudes mouvements d'orchestre passionnels à tension

Gamme B animato (un peu retenu) ▲ / Successions d'accords avec élargissement des parties, pris aux 3 gammes ▲ / accord de A ▲ / accord de B ▲ / retour au 1ᵉʳ groupe de 2 mesures ▲ /
autres dispositions ▲ / pariter ▲ / autre succession ▲ / fin du circulus

[- - - - -]

[tr-p. 84]

Succession de sixtes majeures (harmonisant les gammes ABC) ▲ / Gamme B ▲ / réduction en renversements ▲ / Gamme A ▲ / Fin du circulus / etc.
Ex: dans une des 3 gammes ABC d'un déchirement de la tonalité moderne ordinaire par un [*sic*] mutation / contresujet / Gamme C ▲ / {ultérieurement d'abord le motif seul} ▲ / segue (si♭ tenue) ▲ / (moderato lento automatico) / (répétition au triton) ▲ / segue pédale si♭ ▲ / Gamme C ▲ / autre contrepoint de ex cy-dessous.

[- - - - -]

[tr-p. 85]

d'où racine du circulus suivant / Gamme C ▲ / basso continuo ▲ / segue pédale (si♭) ▲ / Fin du circulus / Le fa pour finir par l'accord ▲ / car on peut amorcer sur le triton mi♮ / un nouveau dessin ▲ / come sopra au triton / come sopra / etc come sopra/ etc (come sopra Basso continuo) / Finissant ▲ / Restitution pour finir en si ré si / Gamme B / Processus min: le même peut être dit dans la Gamme B maj ▲ / chant ▲ / Fin du circulus / Exemple Gamme B en maj. avec repos sur un accord Ɛ ▲ /

[- - - - -]

[tr-p. 86]

boucle ▲ / répétition au triton ▲ / boucle ▲ / point du départ
Type de motif incité du chant de Pilate / chétif, désolé, triste / Gamme A / Lento moderato ▲ / chant / Harmonie à arpéger ▲ /
Accompagnement riche Pathétique / la partie supérieure est rampante. / Gamme B ▲ / cuivres ▲ / etc pariter / etc pariter / circulus de 4 Périodes / (2 membres pour chaque Période) / (*) le saut de seconde de sol♯ à fa♯ est meilleur que si l'on sautait à ut♮ (une mesure plus loin) pour reprendre par la quinte de fa–ut la régularité de la marche.

[- - - - -]

[tr-p. 87]

Essais de contrepoint (morcellement et renversement d'un trait disposé en gamme)

Gamme B
Allegro moderato ▲ / Jeu sur le triton ▲ / Basse analogue ▲ /
Remarque: les notes toniques des gammes A.B. et C. se reproduisent en tête de groupes de 2 de 4 de 6 notes lorsque le trait procède par degrés conjoints (idem) en descendant, et pour les Dominantes) / Ex. / Gamme B / groupes de 2 notes ▲ / de 4 notes ▲ / de 6 notes ▲ / etc.

[- - - - -]

[tr-p. 88]

Loi de disposition harmonique sobre pour harmoniser un ambitus de 4ᵗᵉ suivi d'un Ambitus de 3ᶜᵉ majeure

▲ / Eviter entre deux parties voisines un rapprochement amenant l'intervalle trop riche de la tierce maj. ou mineur ▲ / mauvais ▲ / meilleur ▲ / 1ᵉʳ terminus ▲ / Répercussion du 1ᵉʳ membre à la 6ᵗᵉ ▲ /
᛭ Si le 2ᵈ membre doit répercuter le 1ᵉʳ au triton, il vaut mieux commencer ainsi, évitant la tonalité de Fa (5) ▲ /
Voir p. 90 ⌽ / (*) cette partie peut aussi faire ▲ / et le fa ronde à cette dernière reprise au lieu du ré ronde serait trop riche amenant l'accord / ex / fa ronde ▲ /

[- - - - -]

[tr-p. 89]

Exemple de dessins des parties (cahoté diatonique) style de la Basse troublée de la Symphonie avec Chœur simulant les effets de basses d'orgue au moment de la prière du chœur—avec caisse d'harmonie à 3 parties consonantes /
Gamme C / Allegro moderato ▲ / pédale segue / cresc. molto / très gros d'effet ▲ / col 8ᵛᵉ / loco CB / col 8ᵛᵉ ▲ / Harmonie Païenne (sans tierce frappée avec la tonique et la 5ᵗᵉ) et parcourant les 4 toniques ▲ / rall.

[- - - - -]

[tr-p. 90]

Essai d'une assimilation à la résolution dans la tonalité usuelle de la + sur 5 / tonalité usuelle

▲ / Gamme A ▲ / résolution mineure ▲ / résolution majeure ▲ / etc.
Règle d'harmonie sur les Gammes A.B.C. / Gamme A / avec doublure à l'octave
▲ / etc. et peut se renverser / Ex: ▲ / peut aussi se doubler ainsi ▲ etc. / d'où
sortent ces formes ▲ / 3ᶜᵉ maj. ▲ / triton ▲ / etc. par extension du dessin ▲ /
5ᵗᵉ ▲ / jusqu'à cette limite ▲ / 7ᵉᵐᵉ ▲ / 7ᵉᵐᵉ ▲ / 7ᵉᵐᵉ ▲ / Renvoi de la page
88 ⌽ / réponse au triton pour le second membre / Gamme B ▲ / etc. / D.C. /
unisson

[- - - - -]

[tr-p. 91]

relations d'accords min. dans la même gamme / Gamme A ▲ / Remarque: les
deux mouvements de parties ▲ et ▲ sont perpétuels / D.C. / etc. / D.C. / Renvoi de la [page] 21 au signe ⌽ /
Cadence sur ut maj. amenée par l'harmonisation de la Gamme A par Ex. ▲ /
acc. sans quintes ▲ / autre loi pour le mouvement de Basses / Gamme A ▲ /
T[onique] ▲ / T. ▲ / T. ▲ / T. ▲ / D[ominante] ▲ / D. ▲ / T. ▲ / T. ▲ /
4ᵗᵉ ▲ / 4ᵗᵉ ▲ / 4ᵗᵉ ▲ / 4ᵗᵉ ▲ / etc. Circulus / 1ᵉʳᵉ partie / contrepartie /

[- - - - -]

[tr-p. 92]

Renvoi de la Page 21 (par mouvement semblable) accompagnement des notes /
Gamme A ▲ / 1° Gamme A ▲ etc. / 2° ▲ / 3° ▲ / 4° ▲ / 5° ▲ répétition du
no 1 en ordre inverse de chiffrage / 6° ▲ répétition du no 2 en ordre de chiffrage inverse / fin / total: six exemples /
Harmonie mineure Gamme B ▲ / de ré min 6/4 à la♭ min 3 / Renvoi de la
page 37 au signe ⌣ / autre disposition / Gamme A ▲

[- - - - -]

[tr-p. 93]

Disposition des Parties sur une Echelle Harmonique permettant un redoublement du chant de la Basse par une partie supérieure, avec harmonie à la partie haute extrême et pédale intérieure

Ex Gamme A ▲ / segue / segue / col. 8va ▲ / segue / segue / Gamme A / contrepoint sur l'ambitus de triton ▲ / trait disjoint ▲ / variante / meilleur ▲ / etc et aussi à la basse ▲ /

[- - - - -]

[tr-p. 94]

▲ / autre harmonie ▲ / circulus DC une 8^{ve} plus haut ▲ /

[- - - - -]

[tr-p. 95]

Formes / Gamme C (sujet à la tonique) ▲ / (réponse à la Dominante) ▲ / Gamme C / poco agitato (effet perplexe) ▲ / Fin du circulus pour répercussion à l'octave / Partie qui peut s'ajouter pour compléter les quatre parties.

[- - - - -]

[tr-p. 96]

(En musique) Essais—Expérience—non faite pour plaire au public

Aujourd'hui depuis les concerts du Dimanche, on peut tout tenter. Envahissement de l'esprit critique dans l'impression éprouvée par le public;—La vue philosophique, ethnographique des âmes et des choses, substituée aux visions lyriques d'autrefois (Vogué). De plus la tentative d'apporter au public, les impressions personnelles de l'individu sans l'aide du prisme de l'Ecole. Le microcosme, phénomène de l'intussusception mentale.

Essais—: nouvel art musical pour les fatigués des 4 parties concertantes consacrées.—

Avis technique—Avoir soin de laisser un vide dans l'accompagnement pour ménager à un trait ou ornement du chant sa place, et déblayer son point d'occupation de l'échelle, pour qu'il chante nettement et s'entende distinctement sans être masqué.
(TABLE voyez au verso)

[- - - - -]

[tr-p. 97]

TABLE de ce cahier

Notes

Introduction

1.   Arthur Berger, "Problems of Pitch Organization in Stravinsky," *Perspectives of New Music* 2, no. 1 (1963): 11–42.

2.   In post-tonal music theory, a collection is defined as a group of notes—also called pitch classes—that are considered without regard to their order, the duplication of their content, or the implications of that content.

3.   Pieter C. van den Toorn, *The Music of Igor Stravinsky* (New Haven: Yale University Press, 1983), 50–51; idem, "Octatonic Pitch Structure in Stravinsky," in *Confronting Stravinsky*, ed. Jann Pasler, 130–56 (Berkeley and Los Angeles: University of California Press, 1986); and Richard Taruskin, "Chernomor to Kashchei: Harmonic Sorcery; or, Stravinsky's 'Angle,' " *Journal of the American Musicological Society* 38, no. 1 (1985): 72–142; revised and repr. as chap. 4 of Taruskin, *Stravinsky and the Russian Traditions: A Biography of the Works through "Mavra,"* 2 vols. (Berkeley and Los Angeles: University of California Press, 1996), 1:255–306.

4.   Nicolai Rimsky-Korsakov to Mily Balakirev, 1 August 1867, as quoted in Rimsky-Korsakov, *My Musical Life,* trans. Judah A. Joffe, ed. Carl van Vechten (London: Eulenberg, 1974), 78.

5.   The passage from the composer's *Sadko* is reproduced in Taruskin, *Stravinsky and the Russian Traditions* 1:268, ex. 4.12. *Sadko* (1867) was first a symphonic poem; after revising the work in 1869 and 1891, Rimsky-Korsakov wrote an eponymous "opera-legend" (1898), based on the same story.

6.   Taruskin cites an earlier work, Glinka's 1842 opera *Ruslan and Ludmila,* as the first Russian Composition to feature a whole-tone scale. Ibid. 1:261.

7.   According to Taruskin (ibid. 1:268), Roman Vlad, in his *Stravinsky,* 3rd ed. (London: Oxford University Press, 1978, p. 17), finds an example of octatonicism in Carl-Maria von Weber's 1812 Piano Concerto No. 2. Allen Forte discusses octatonic writing in Webern in "An Octatonic Essay by Webern: No. 1 of the *Six Bagatelles for String Quartet,* Op. 9," *Music Theory Spectrum* 16 (1994): 171–95.

8.   Olivier Messiaen, *Technique de mon langage musical,* 2 vols. (Paris: Leduc, 1944).

9.   Allen Forte, "Debussy and the Octatonic," *Music Analysis* 10 (1991): 125–69; Richard S. Parks, *The Music of Claude Debussy* (New Haven: Yale University Press, 1989); Steven Baur, "Ravel's 'Russian' Period: Octatonicism in His Early Works, 1893–1908," *Journal of the American Musicological Society* 52, no. 3 (1999): 531–92; Roy Howat, "Modes and Semitones in Debussy's Preludes and Elsewhere," *Studies in Music* [University of Western Australia] 22 (1988): 81–104; idem, "Ravel and the Piano," in *The Cambridge Companion to Ravel,* ed. Deborah Mawer, 71–96, 271–73 (Cambridge: Cambridge University Press, 2000); and Mark McFarland, "Debussy and Stravinsky: Another Look at Their Musical Relationship," *Cahiers Debussy* 24 (2000): 79–112.

10. The absence of any extensive theoretical writing on octatonicism by Rimsky-Korsakov enabled his most famous student, Stravinsky, to declare, famously, "I was guided by no system whatever in *Le Sacre du Printemps*. . . . Very little tradition lies behind *Le Sacre du Printemps* . . . and no theory. I had only my ear to help me. . . . I am the vessel through which *Le Sacre* passed." See Stravinsky and Robert Craft, *Expositions and Developments* (Garden City, NY: Doubleday, 1962), 147–48.

11. Taruskin, *Stravinsky and the Russian Traditions* 1:268.

12. Ibid. 1:269.

13. Similar obscurity clouds the history of the early use of the octatonic scale in jazz performance (in jazz, the scale is called the "diminished scale") and the subsequent development of jazz harmonic theory. In an e-mail exchange with the author (14 August 2006, 7 September 2006), jazz scholar Andy Jaffe identifies octatonically derived extended chords in early Duke Ellington and Charlie Parker solos of the 1940s, but asserts that the scale's conscious use doesn't occur until certain John Coltrane solos in 1957. Jaffe discussed the subject by telephone on 7 September 2006 with renowned jazz musician Yusef Lateef, who performed extensively with Coltrane. According to Jaffe, neither he nor Lateef could pinpoint when the term "diminished scale" became a commonly used term in jazz circles.

14. An in-depth examination of the many cultural, political, and artistic forces in play at the time of the Paris 1878 World's Fair would be a wonderful "prequel" to the outstanding study done by Annegret Fauser in her 2005 monograph, *Musical Encounters at the 1889 Paris World's Fair* (Rochester, NY: University of Rochester Press, 2005).

15. N. A. Rimsky-Korsakov, *Polnoye sobraniye sochineniy; literaturniye proizvedeniya I perepiska,* vol. 4: *Uchebnik garmonii* (Moscow: Murgiz, 1960), 222–24; transcribed and reproduced in Taruskin, *Stravinsky and the Russian Traditions* 1:304–6.

16. Forte, "Debussy and the Octatonic," 126.

17. Ibid., 127. In his 1999 article "Ravel's 'Russian' Period," Steven Baur examines in detail Forte's application of set-theory to octatonicism (pp. 536–39 and note 21); he points out that every example cited by Forte can be attributable to mediant relations.

18. Forte, "Debussy and the Octatonic," 153–55.

19. In his 1990 article "Pitch-Class Set Analysis: An Evaluation," George Perle writes that his rejection of Forte's pitch-class analysis of atonal music "is based . . . on the fact that I find the system irrelevant to my experience as a composer, to my perceptions as a listener, and to my discoveries as an analyst." *Journal of Musicology* 8, no. 2 (Spring 1990): 151–72. In retrospect, this position seems extreme. However, the tension between what is understood and absorbed intellectually from the classification of music and what is understood and absorbed sensorily from listening to music seems pertinent in the discussion of octatoncism.

20. Joseph N. Straus, *Introduction to Post-Tonal Theory,* 3rd ed. (Englewood Cliffs, NJ: Prentice Hall, 2005).

21. Taruskin, *Stravinsky and the Russian Tradition* 1:256.

Chapter One

1. "Un jour nous le trouvâmes enfoui dans son fauteuil, le chef couvert d'un béret tricoté. Il se chauffait les pieds mélancoliquement. . . . 'Je suis le dernier né, le fond du vase . . . toutes les saletés ancestrales je les ai . . . Eczéma, goutte, V. [vérole] . . . ! très probablement. 'Saluez! Pourri Mon cher Prince . . . tu ne me crois pas, blagueur! comme les autres! imitait les gestes des amis qui venaient le voir, et résumait ainsi la situation:

parlant bref, à la cantonade, avec les gestes les plus drôles, 'Mais cela va très bien: Bonne mine, fort comme Hercule, Allons, ne vous tracassez pas . . . tiens! il est mort!'" Melchior de Polignac, unpublished "Souvenirs," 60, private collection.

2.   Jules de Polignac's condemnation to *mort civile* was exceptional: this form of legal punishment was partially abolished during the French Revolution, and completely abolished in 1854.

3.   Sir Horace Rumbold, *Recollections of a Diplomatist,* 2 vols. (London: Arnold, 1903), 2:156.

4.   Stendhal, *Racine et Shakespeare: Études sur le romantisme* (Paris: Michel Lévy Frères, 1854), 32–33.

5.   Pierre Robin-Harmel, *Le Prince Jules de Polignac, Ministre de Charles X: Sa vie de 1829 à 1847* (Paris: Maison Aubanel Père, 1950), 212.

6.   EP to LP, [undated, ca. 1840], private collection.

7.   Robin-Harmel, *Le Prince Jules de Polignac,* 212.

8.   Ibid., 211.

9.   Melchior de Polignac, "Souvenirs," 57, private collection.

10.   EP learned piano and harmony from the most popular instruction book of that era, August Eberhard Müller's *Fortepiano Schule.*

11.   Pianos scores inscribed with the name "Miss Parkyns" are still extant in the Polignac family music library.

12.   Melchior de Polignac, "Souvenirs," 2, private collection.

13.   Rumbold, *Recollections of a Diplomatist* 1:46.

14.   CP to EP, various letters, 1854–1865, private collection; CP to LP, 21 September 1847, private collection.

15.   EP's music library contains, for example, among other of Handel's works, Novello's "centenary edition" (undated, presumably 1837) of the oratorio *Israel in Egypt.*

16.   First written in the eighteenth century, French *romances,* usually published in groups of six, were settings of strophic texts with amorous stories to simple, unadorned, sentimental melodies and equally simple accompaniments that included a piano introduction/ritornello.

17.   For a number of years during the mid-nineteenth century, Alphonse Thys was a member of the editorial board of the weekly magazine *Le Ménestrel,* which published a number of his compositions. In 1851, he cofounded, with Ernest Bourget, the SACEM (Société des auteurs, compositeurs, et éditeurs de musique), the organization that to this day oversees the administration and dissemination of payment of rights to creative musicians.

18.   EP's "Chœur de buveurs" (1851) is in a notebook of early compositions; his "Romance pastorale" (1852) was privately printed (Imprimerie Guillet, Paris); both works are housed in a private collection.

19.   Philippe Gumplowicz, *Les Travaux d'Orphée: 150 ans de vie musicale amateur en France; Harmonies, chorales, fanfares* (Paris: Aubier, 1987), 55.

20.   Ibid., 88–89.

21.   EP's notebook of early compositions (1851–56), private collection.

22.   Ibid. Before its association with the piano, the "nocturne" genre denoted a vocal duet whose lines were written in thirds and sixths and which was accompanied by a homophonic piano part.

23.   Henri Reber's *Traité d'harmonie* (Paris: Colombier, E. Gallet) was first published in 1862; an expanded and corrected second edition appeared in 1870. Generations of Conservatoire students learned harmony from Reber's work, including the young Claude Debussy.

24. EP's undated notebook, "Cours d'Harmonie (Conservatoire—Classe de Mr Reber)" [presumably begun in 1855], is housed in a private collection.

25. The two manuscripts are extant in the Polignac family archives.

26. "Prière à la Mecque" was included in a collection of works published during the 1900 World's Fair. See chap. 8, note 8.

27. Ludovic de Polignac (1827–1904) rose to the rank of lieutenant-colonel in the French Army. He participated in the colonization of Algeria.

28. ChP to LP, 8 March 1857, 9 September 1857, 29 October 1857, private collection.

29. ChP to LP, January 1858, private collection.

30. ChP to LP, 12 April 1858, private collection.

31. ChP to LP, February 1858, private collection.

Chapter Two

1. CaP to EP, New York, 21 October 1859, private collection.

2. Alphonse de Polignac (1817–63) is known today as the creator of "de Polignac's conjecture," also known as the theory of twin primes.

3. Ryno, "Le Prince Alphonse de Polignac, souvenirs intimes," *L'Étoile de France,* 21 November 1886.

4. "Nouvelles," *RGMP* 27, no. 24 (10 June 1860): 213.

5. Jules Lovy, "Semaine théâtrale," *Le Ménestrel* 27, no. 36 (29 July 1860): 276.

6. Prince Josef Poniatowski (1816–1873) was a Polish composer and tenor.

7. "Nouvelles," *RGMP* 27, no. 10 (22 April 1860): 154; Richard Wagner, *My Life,* trans. Mary Whittall, ed. Martin Gregory-Dallin (New York: Da Capo Press, 1992), 303.

8. "Nouvelles," *RGMP* 27, no. 10 (22 April 1860): 154.

9. The members of the Société des Derniers Quatuors de Beethoven (otherwise known as the Maurin Quartet) were Jean-Pierre Maurin (1st violin), J.-B. Sabatier (2nd violin), Joseph Louis Marie Mas (viola), and Pierre-Alexandre Chevillard (cello), founder of the society with Maurin.

10. EP's Second String Quartet in F Major (1860) was published by S. Richault in 1864. It is housed in the BnF-Mus under shelf number K. 5093. EP's "first" string quartet has been lost. The manuscript of an Andante movement from a Third String Quartet is housed in a private collection.

11. Thirty-five years later, Marcel Proust would be impressed by the pizzicato section of the Scherzo of EP's quartet. See chap. 7; see also Proust's third letter in Sylvia Kahan and Nathalie Mauriac Dyer, "Quatre Lettres inédites de Proust au Prince de Polignac," *Bulletin Marcel Proust* 53 (December 2003): 17–18.

12. "Richard Wagner et la musique de l'avenir," *Le Ménestrel* 27, no. 9 (29 January 1860): 65–67.

13. Wagner, *My Life,* 176. According to Proust biographer George Painter, the Comte (later the Marquis) d'Osmond was the great-nephew of the Comtesse de Boigne, whose memoirs (5 vols., 1837–66), describe her part in social and political life under Napoleon, Louis XVIII, Charles X, and Louis-Philippe. Osmond inherited her memoirs and her wealth. He appears in *À la Recherche du temps perdu* under his own name and as the Marquis de Beausergent and the young Duc de Guermantes.

14. Wagner, *My Life,* 176.

15. Ibid.

16. Ryno, "Le Prince Alphonse de Polignac, souvenirs intimes," *L'Étoile de France,* 21 November 1886.

17. EP's *Six Mélodies,* including Roger de Beauvoir's "Notre Dame au peigne d'or" were published by Flaxland in 1860. Curiously, the works were released under the names of two different composers: one series under Polignac's name and another under the pseudonym "Mariaweldt."

18. EP to LP, 3 September 1860, private collection; *Le Ménestrel* 27, no. 35 (29 July 1860): 276.

19. Alfred Beaumont served as director of the Opéra-Comique from 19 June 1860 to 27 January 1862. See Nicole Wild, *Dictionnaire des théâtres parisiens au XIXe siècle: Les théâtres et la musique* (Paris: Aux amateurs de livres, 1989), 330.

20. EP to LP, 3 September 1860, private collection.

21. Patrick Barbier, *Opera in Paris, 1800–1850, a Lively History,* trans. Robert Luoma (Portland, OR: Amadeus Press, 1995), 162.

22. EP to LP, 3 September 1860, private collection.

23. ChP to LP, 18 July 1860, private collection.

24. Alfred Beaumont to EP, written on letterhead from the "Théâtre Impérial de l'Opéra-Comique, Cabinet du Directeur," 9 November 1860, private collection.

25. EP, *Un Baiser de duchesse,* manuscript and libretto, private collection.

26. ChP to LP, 13 February 1861, private collection.

27. ChP to LP, 30 June 1861, private collection.

28. *Le Ménestrel* 29, no. 10 (2 February 1862): 75; "Théâtre Impérial de l'Opéra-Comique: Changement de direction," *RGMP* 29, no. 5 (2 February 1862): 33. Émile Perrin (1814–1885), a painter, art critic, and theatrical set designer, first served as director of the Opéra-Comique from 1848 to 1857, and, again, after Beaumont's dismissal from the post, for a brief period between February and December 1862. Named director of the Paris Opéra from December 1862 to March 1871, he then served as Administration of the Comédie-Française from 1871 until his death.

29. In March 1861 Camille de Polignac (1832–1913) offered his services on behalf of the South to Confederate General Beauregard, for whom he would serve as staff officer. CaP arrived in New York in June 1861; by January 1863 he had been promoted to brigadier general, and took command of an infantry brigade in Texas. He led in battles in Louisiana in 1864 and at Mansfield in the first major action of the Red River campaign. CaP was eventually promoted to major general, leading his division through the end of 1864. In 1865 he returned to France to request intervention by Napoleon III on behalf of the Confederacy, but the war ended soon thereafter. See Roy O. Hatton, "Prince Camille de Polignac and the American Civil War, 1863–1865," *Louisiana Studies* 3 (Summer 1964); and Jeff Kinard, *Lafayette of the South: Prince Camille de Polignac and the American Civil War* (College Station: Texas A&M University Press, 2001).

30. CaP to EP, 20 December 1862, private collection.

31. "How Mires [*sic*] Was Arrested," *Harper's Weekly,* 31 March 1861, 199.

32. EP's music library includes pocket scores of two of Mendelssohn's oratorios, published by the London publishing house Novello and Ewer: *Elijah,* published in 1863, and *Saint Paul,* published in 1864. It is likely that the score into which EP inserted the pencil sketch was hot off the presses.

33. ChP to LP, 7 May 1864, private collection. On 31 July 1864, CaP wrote to his cousin Elizabeth Ann Levinge, "I know [Edmond] is in quest of a better half . . . thro' you I learn that he is now trying to poach up the Game in English warrens," private collection.

34. ChP to LP, 7 May 1864, private collection.

35. EP, "Martha et Marie" (Paris, édition privée, 1863), BnF-Mus, M, D. 16971

36.   Henri Heugel, "Paris et Départements," *Le Ménestrel* 31, no. 8 (24 January 1864): 63. The score of EP's choral work "Les Dryades" is now lost. The other "modern" works on the program were the overture to Auber's opera *Le Dieu et la Bayadère,* a symphonic movement by Hector Salomon, Aristide Hignard's choral work, "O Tahiti," and the "Wedding March" from Wagner's *Lohengrin.* The second half of the program consisted of symphonic works by Beethoven, Weber, and Haydn.

37.   Gumplowicz, *Les Travaux d'Orphée,* 76.

38.   Ibid., 88.

39.   Ibid.

40.   "Concours de l'Orphéon de Paris,"*RGMP* 32, no. 5 (5 March 1865): 73–74.

41.   The score of EP's choral work "Le Myosotis" has been lost.

42.   "Concours de l'Orphéon de Paris,"*RGMP* 32, no. 5 (5 March 1865): 73–74.

43.   "Orphéon: Séances solennelles des 14 et 21 mai," *RGMP* 32, no. 22 (28 May 1865): 164, 173.

44.   Victor Foucher, "Séance solennelle de l'Orphéon sous la direction de M. François Bazin," *L'Art musical* 5, no. x (18 May 1865) :195.

45.   "Concours de l'Orphéon de Paris," *Le Ménestrel* 35, no. 12 (16 February 1868): 93. EP's "L'Abeille" (Paris: S. Richault, 1867) is housed at the BnF-Mus, D. 16892. Delibes and Massenet won first and second prizes, respectively, for their settings of the texts "C'est Dieu" and "En Avant."

46.   Emmanuel Mathieu de Monter, "Séance solennelle de l'Orphéon de Paris," *RGMP* 35, no. 19 (10 May 1868): 146–47.

47.   Elizabeth Ann Levinge to LP, undated (late May or June 1865) and 3 August 1867, both letters in a private collection.

48.   In addition to EP, the other eleven men portrayed in James Tissot's *Le Balcon du Cercle de la rue Royale* include the Marquis de Lau, the Comte de Ganay, Baron Rodolphe Hottinguer, the Marquis (later General) Gallifet, Gaston de Saint-Maurice, and Charles Haas (Marcel Proust's eventual prototype for Charles Swann).

49.   Georges Bizet to Paul Lacombe, in Georges Bizet, "Lettres inédits de Georges Bizet," in *Portraits et Études; Lettres inédites de Georges Bizet,* ed. Hugues Imbert (Paris: Fischbacher, 1894), 173. Imbert dates the letter as early April 1867 (177n1).

50.   "Concours ouverts aux théâtres lyriques impériaux: Rapport et programme." *Le Ménestrel* 34, no. 37 (11 August 1867): 289–90.

51.   "Le Concours d'opéra," *Le Ménestrel* 35, no. 21 (19 April 1868): 161–62. Both Blau and Gallet went on to successful careers as librettists. Gallet, in particular, wrote numerous librettos for major composers, including Massenet, Bizet, Saint-Saëns, and Gounod.

52.   The folder "Concours d'Opéra," AN-AJ13 450/1, lists the numbers of the competitors' opera scores and their epigraphs. The ms. of EP's score of *La Coupe du Roi de Thulé,* in three volumes, is housed in a private collection.

53.   Winton Dean, *Bizet,* 3rd ed. (London, 1975), 77–78.

54.   "Concours de Grand Opéra," *Le Ménestrel* 36, no. 52 (28 November 1869): 413.

55.   Ibid.

56.   Ibid.

57.   Eugène d'Harcourt, "Un Prince musicien," *Le Figaro,* 9 August 1901, 1.

58.   For reviews of Diaz's opera, see Bénédict, "Opéra: La Coupe du Roi de Thulé," *Le Figaro,* 14 January 1873, 3; Paul Bernard, "Théâtre National de l'Opéra: *La Coupe du Roi de Thulé," RGMP* 40, no. 2 (12 January 1873): 9–11.

59.   Three of EP's *mélodies,* "Lamento," "Cavatina," and "Remembrance," were published by the Paris house Georges Hartmann, and bear the catalogue numbers 370, 394, and 395,

respectively. Only the score of "Cavatina" has a publication date, 1870; it is in the BnF, Vm. 7 côte 91144. "Lamento" remained in the Hartmann catalogue through the late 1880s.

60.   Duc Jean-Héracle de Polignac, *La Maison de Polignac: Étude d'une évolution sociale de la noblesse* (Le Puy: Éditions Jeanne d'Arc, 1975), 67.

61.   Théophile Gautier's "Lamento" (incipit: "Connaissez-vous la tombe blanche") was also set by Duparc and Berlioz; the latter included it in his cycle *Les Nuits d'été* under the title "Au Cimetière."

62.   See above, note 57. Another song from this period, "Prière à l'indigent" (composed in 1872, text by Lamartine) was published in 1886 by Henri Heugel under the auspices of *Le Ménestrel*.

63.   EP's "Remembrance" bears the dedication "To Adelina Patti, respectfully inscribed," private collection.

64.   "Les Premières: La Coupe du Roi de Thulé," Le Figaro, 12 January 1873, 3.

65.   Clipping from unspecified newpaper in Polignac family archives, hand-dated "17 avril 1873."

66.   "Les Adieux de Deïdamia" was published by the reputable house J. Maho (the score is undated; presumably the publication took place in the early 1870s); when Maho's catalogue was acquired by J. Hamelle in 1877, "Les Adieux" was re-released in a corrected, revised version.

67.   "Nouvelles des Théâtres Lyriques," *RGMP* 41, no. 23 (7 June 1874): 182.

68.   Ludovic de Polignac married Princesse Gabrielle de Croÿ. The marriage was not a happy one, and when LP took up his post as Chief of Military Officers in Constantine, the couple separated. Camille de Polignac married Marie-Adolphine Langenberger, a distant relative of Goethe's and a fine violinist. She died in 1876 shortly after giving birth to the couple's daughter, Armande. Camille remarried in 1883, to Marguerite Elizabeth Knight, and fathered three more children.

69.   EP, in an undated letter to RM ("ce mardi" [July 1888], BnF-Mss, NAfr 15140, 17–18), recalls the memories evoked by looking through a 1874 program of the Handel Festival, and describes the Festival as "l'Elysée des éternelles musiques où les peuples chantent, comme dans 'Zadock' le sublime God save the King avec la Frange lumineuse brodée par les soprano, et plus tard les volutes prodigieuses où s'enroulent les Basses."

70.   Preface to "Adieu, France!" in *Le Journal de musique*, 2 December 1876, which published EP's song in a version for voice and piano.

71.   EG to Baron Denys Cochin, 22 December 1921, writing after the death of RM, AN-AP101(II)/77.

72.   Edgar Munhall, *Whistler and Montesquiou, The Butterfly and the Bat* (New York: The Frick Collection, 1995), 35.

73.   George Painter, *Marcel Proust*, 2 vols. (New York: Vintage, 1978), 1:127.

74.   Ibid. 1:132–33.

75.   ". . . de Cannes, à Menton, avec leurs routes trop jaunes, leurs montagnes trop violettes, leur Méditerranée trop bleue, mer peu familière, sans flux ni reflux, prude qui ne permet point l'accès de son lit à l'ensemble de ce pays trop dur, trop rude et trop cru, et trop cruel, et trop accrédité aux contours délimités, quasi plombés comme dans les vitraux, et pareil de la faïence faite par une demoiselle mé-expérimentée." RM to EP, 24 February 1886, private collection.

76.   "J'ai revu nos promenades à Cannes, par les routes extraites entre deux murailles basses de jardins, près de la mer, et vous m'êtes revenu comme alors, en veste à carreaux: c'était notre premier rencontre, vous me lisiez des passages des 'Lettres d'un voyageur.'

Vous me sembliez comme perdu dans un monde étranger, et aussi un peu comme un abandonné." EP to RM, Paris, 19 November 1892, BnF-Mss, NAfr 15113:91–2. EP makes reference to Georges Sand's *Lettres d'un voyageur,* twelve articles in letter form published in the *Revue des deux mondes* (1834–36).

77.   Victoria Thompson, in "Creating Boundaries," in *Homosexuality in Modern France,* ed. Jefrrey Merrick and Bryant T. Ragan, Jr., 102–27 (New York and Oxford: Oxford University Press, 1996), discusses the mid-nineteenth-century perception of homosexuality in France as a danger to the social order. Thompson writes, "Public scandal and financial ruin, the consequences of homosexual sex, could only be avoided if homosexuals created and maintained a way of differentiating between public and private life. . . . According to a variety of sources from the Second Empire, men risked social ostracism and financial ruin if they crossed lines of class, gender, and sexuality" (116–17).

78.   Painter quotes writer André Germain, a great friend of Montesquiou's as saying, "He was not an invert, but merely an introvert" (*Marcel Proust* 1:129).

79.   EP to LP, 5 April 1878, private collection.

80.   EP to RM, "ce vendredi," [28 January 1886], BnF-Mss, NAfr 15269:44–45.

81.   EP to RM, undated telegram [late April 1875], BnF-Mss, NAfr 15112:128. I date this telegram by EP's reference to the performance of the vocal quartet from *La Coupe du Roi de Thulé* will take place on "Samedi (1 May)." EP's other guest for this performance was Charles Haas, Marcel Proust's model for Charles Swann in *À la Recherche du temps perdu.*

82.   Jean-Alexandre Talazac (1851–1896) was a leading tenor at the Théâtre-Lyrique. He created many roles, including those of Gérald in Delibes's *Lakmé,* Des Grieux in Massenet's *Manon,* and the tile role in Offenbach's *Contes d'Hoffmann.* The other singers in the Polignac work were Madame Boidin-Puisais and M. Carroul; the evening's conductor was A. Vinchon.

83.   "Nouvelles des Théâtres Lyriques," *RGMP* 44, no. 48 (2 December 1877): 381.

Chapter Three

1.   "Je continue toujours à rêver à quelques travaux en musique. Je commence à fixer d'après les Evangiles les belles et dramatiques scènes de la Passion. J'en ai déjà achevé presque deux numéros, l'un complétant 'Pilate livre Jesus—tolle! crucifigatur etc.' J'ai joué ce numéro à

Pasdeloup, qui serait très désireux d'en entendre l'effet; peut-être serait-il disposé à le faire exécuter, en le poussant un peu; mais, je ne suis pas fort pour pousser les autres, j'en ai assez de me pousser moi-même. Je compte faire aussi la scène chez Caïphe, le grand prêtre; mais il me faudra judaïser et arabiser ferme; je tâcherai d'amener une fugue farouche sur le 'Prophetiza' quand les injures et les coups pleuvent de toutes parts." EP to LP, 18 April 1879, private collection. The "Prophetiza" mentioned by EP makes reference to Matthew 26:64–68, in which the high priest Caiaphas and other chief priests are looking for "evidence" with which they can bring charges against Jesus. When Jesus makes an allusion to the "Son of Man," Caiaphas and the others charge him with blasphemy and strike and slap him.

2.   See the Introduction, pp. 1–5.

3.   In 1868–69, Pasdeloup directed numerous performances of Wagner's *Rienzi* at the Théâtre Lyrique.

4.   Richard Taruskin points out, in *Stravinsky and the Russian Traditions* 1:290, that, in act 2, scene 1 of Wagner's *Siegfried,* "the 'tonic' [is] a tritone (C and G♭/F♯) and [the] key signature [is] perpetually oscillating between those of F minor and B minor." In his

treatise (see tr-p. 64), Polignac models one of his sketches on the passage based on mediant-related keys in the orchestral introduction to act 1, scene 5 of *Tristan und Isolde.*

5. Lizst, *Des Bohémiens,* 288–89.

6. Ibid., 298.

7. Ibid., 301. The fact that there is a *pair* of Gypsy scales creates an interesting parallel to the threesome of octatonic scales.

8. L[ouis]-A[lbert] Bourgault-Ducoudray, *Trente mélodies populaires de Grèce & d'Orient* (Paris: H. Lemoine, 1876).

9. Louis Niedermeyer (1802–1861), composer and musicologist. He was the founder, in 1853, of the famed École Niedermeyer, a conservatory that emphasized the study of plainchant, a subject rarely touched upon in conventional French music education. The school's influence on one of its first and most famous pupils, Gabriel Fauré, can be found in the strong emphasis on modal writing in Fauré's works. Niedermeyer's 1856 *Traité de plain-chant,* written in collaboration with Joseph d'Ortigue and published one year later (Paris: E. Repos, 1857), provided the first exposure to Gregorian melody and theory to many nineteenth-century composers and musicians.

10. Since 1833 Don Prosper Guéranger (1805–1875) had made a cornerstone of his directorship of the abbey the reintegration of the "authentic" practices of eighth-century Gregorian worship into modern worship. In 1860 Guéranger had expanded his quest for authenticity by charging two younger monks, Dom Jausions and Dom Pothier, to commence a paleographic study of the original Gregorian manuscripts and codices. Pothier's treatise, *Les Mélodies grégoriennes d'après la tradition* was published in 1880; three years later, a *Liber Gradualis,* the authoritative edition of plainchant was released. For a fascinating study of the Solesmes practices, scholarship, and publications, see Katherine Bergeron, *Decadent Enchantments: The Revival of Gregorian Chant at Solesmes* (Berkeley and Los Angeles: University of California Press, 1998),

11. Bergeron, *Decadent Enchantments,* 21–23.

12. The first of Monter's articles for *RGMP* on the 1878 World's Fair, "Exposition universelle: L'inauguration," appeared on 5 May 1878 (45, no. 18, pp. 137–38); the last, "Laboramus!" was published on 3 November 1878 (45, no. 44, pp. 353–54). Monter, who had written a similar series about the 1867 World's Fair for the same journal, provided coverage on the music of thirty-one nations, as well as related topics such as foreign instrument manufacture and educational methods.

13. EP, sketch dated "July 94," "après des airs arabes entendus chez la Belle Fatma," private collection. For an interesting discussion of Rachel Bent-Eny, "La Belle Fatma," see Fauser, *Musical Encounters at the 1889 Paris World's Fair,* 227, 237, 239, 345; a photograph of the dancer appears on p. 228. According to Fauser, at the time of the 1889 Paris World's Fair, La Belle Fatma was so celebrated that she moved out of the Grand Théâtre into her own space, the Concert Tunisien.

14. Nicolai Rimsky-Korsakov to Mily Balakirev, 1 August 1867, as quoted in Rimsky-Korsakov, *My Musical Life,* 78.

15. See the Introduction, note 4 (p. 335).

16. Taruskin cites an earlier Russian work, Glinka's 1842 opera *Ruslan and Ludmila,* as the first work to feature a whole-tone scale. Ibid. 1:261.

17. César Cui, "La Musique en Russie," *RGMP* 45, no. 19 (12 May 1878): 145–47. Subsequent articles by Cui were published on 10, 17, and 24 November 1878, and 8 and 29 December 1878.

18. In the 8 December installment of "La Musique en Russie," Cesar Cui, in his discussion of Glinka's *Ruslan and Ludmila,* specifically mentions the Introduction and

Chernomor's leitmotif in act 1 "written on a scale in whole tones." *RGMP* 45, no. 49 (8 December 1878): 393–95).

19. André Schaeffner, "Debussy et ses rapports avec la musique russe," in *Variations sur la musique* (Paris: Fayard, 1998), 269.

20. D. Kern Holoman, *Berlioz* (Cambridge, MA: Harvard University Press, 1989), 316–17.

21. Emmanuel-Mathieu de Monter, "Exposition universelle de 1867: La Russie," two-part article, *RGMP* 34, no. 32 (11 August 1867): 253–5, and no. 34. (25 August 1867): 269–71.

22. Monter, "Concert russe," *RGMP* 45, no. 37 (15 September 1878): 298; see also A. Landély Hettich's article in *L'Art musical* 17, no. 37 (12 September 1878): 390–91, where Hettich writes, "La musique est certainement une des manifestations les plus curieuses du développement intellectuel dans ce pays. . . . Nous aimons, pour notre part, cet état demi-sauvage, nous nous intéressons à la fougue de cette sève qui frémit dans tout un people. Nous nous plaisons même à croire que la vieille écorce ne se déchirera pas complètement sur la civilisation qui bourgeonne. . . . Que la Russie mûrisse lentement, qu'elle ne mûrisse pas complètement, tel est le meilleur souhait que nous puissions faire pour ses grandeurs."

23. *RGMP* 45, no. 39 (29 September 1878): 314; *Le Ménestrel* 44, no. 44 (29 September 1878): 356.

24. *RGMP* 45, no. 48 (1 December 1878): 391; "Concerts populaires," *L'Art musical* 17, no. 49 (5 December 1878): 389.

25. *RGMP* 46, no. 1 (5 January 1879): 7.

26. "Bibliographie musicale: *Mélodies populaires russes,* recueillies et harmonisées par Rimsky-Korsakoff," *RGMP* 46, no. 47 (23 November 1879): 381.

27. The class rosters of the Paris Conservatoire housed in the Archives nationales (AJ 37/91) indicate that both Polignac and Bourgault-Ducoudray were among Reber's seventeen harmony students during the academic year 1859–60.

28. Bourgault-Ducoudray, *Trente mélodies populaires,* 11–22. See also Samuel Baud-Bovy, "Bourgault-Ducoudray et la musique grecque ecclésiastique et profane," in "Les Fantaisies du voyageur: Variations Schaeffner" [*festschrift* for André Schaeffner], *Revue de musicologie* 68, no. 1–2 (1982): 153–63.

29. See L[ouis]-A[lbert] Bourgault-Ducoudray, *Études sur la musique ecclésiastique grecque: Mission musicale en Grèce et en Orient janvier–mai 1875* (Paris: Hachette, 1877); and idem, *Souvenirs d'une mission musicale en Grèce et en Orient,* 2nd ed. (Paris: Hachette, 1878).

30. According to *L'Art musical* 17, no. 36 (5 September 1878): 287, Bourgault-Ducoudray demonstrated the ancient-Greek hypophrygian, major, Dorian, Phrygian, and "Oriental chromatic" [the Hungarian *kalindra*] modes.

31. "Bourgault-Ducoudray: Conférence-audition; Modalité dans la musique grecque," *RGMP* 45, no. 37 (15 September 1878): 298.

32. "La Modalité dans la musique grecque: Conférence de M. L.-A. Bourgault-Ducoudray," *Le Ménestrel* 44, no. 43 (22 September 1878): 346–47.

33. Elaine Brody and Richard Langham-Smith, "Bourgault-Ducoudray, Louis (Albert)," in *The New Grove Dictionary of Music and Musicians,* 2nd ed., ed. Stanley Sadie and John Tyrrell (London: Macmillan, 2001), 4:111.

34. Cesar Cui, "La Musique en Russie," *RGMP* 45, no. 19 (12 May 1878): 145–47; Charles-Émile Ruelle, "Histoire de notre gamme," *RGMP* 45, no. 19 (12 May 1878): 147–48. Subsequent installments of Cui's article appeared in *RGMP* (see above, note 18) and were published together in a monograph, *La Musique en Russie* (Paris: Fischbacher, 1880).

35. Charles-Émile Ruelle, "Histoire de notre gamme (suite)," *RGMP* 45, no. 25 (23 June 1878): 195–97; Émile-Mathieu de Monter, "Exposition universelle: La Russie," *RGMP*

45, no. 25 (23 June 1878): 193–95; idem, "Les Tziganes de Moscou," *RGMP* 45, no. 25 (23 June 1878): 198.

36. "Concert russe," *RGMP* 45, no. 37 (15 September 1878): 298; "Bourgault-Ducoudray: Conférence-audition: Modalité dans la musique grecque," *RGMP* 45, no. 37 (15 September 1878): 298.

37. Bourgault-Ducoudray, *Souvenirs d'une mission musicale, 17.*

38. EP's "Fantaisie-Tanz" is No. 5 in the collection *Pièces diverses pour piano à 2 et 4 mains* (Paris: Ménestrel/Heugel, 1884). It is housed in the BnF-Mus, D. 9795.

39. The Greek Dorian mode to which EP refers corresponds with the medieval and modern Phrygian mode; however, with the inclusion of G♯, EP has altered the traditional scale, which would consist of the "white key" pitches E–F–G–A–B–C–D–E.

40. "La constitution de cette nouvelle Gamme peut l'apparenter à celle du mode Dorien (grec) dans laquelle le sixième degré est exhaussé d'un demi-ton; mais elle s'écarte de ce mode par sa tonalité plus moderne, et qui prendra un aspect facilement bizarre, déboîté, quasi macabre." Edmond de Polignac, Preface to "Fantaisie-Tanz," date of composition unknown (probably late 1870s), published in 1884 in *Pièces diverses* (Paris: Heugel, 1884).

41. This scale conforms neither to the *verbunkos* nor the *kalindra* models mentioned in the earlier discussion of Hungarian gypsy scales on pp. 39 and 43.

42. Messiaen, *Technique de mon langage musical.* The octatonic scales are Messiaen's second mode, described as "[divisible] into four groups of three notes each. It is transposable three times, like the diminished seventh chord."

43. For an overview of French nineteenth-century representations of Orientalist music, see Fauser, *Musical Encounters at the 1889 Paris World's Fair,* 146–65.

44. Pietro Bianchini, ed., *Chants liturgiques de l'Église arménienne, traduits en notes musicales européennes* (Venice: Congrégation des pères mekhitaristes, 1877).

45. *Chants en usage dans les Temples Consistoriaux Israëlites de Paris* (Paris, 1879). In nineteenth-century Republican France, Jews referred to themselves as "Israelites."

46. "Je commence à fixer d'après les Évangiles les belles et dramatiques scènes de la Passion. J'en ai déjà achevé presque deux numéros, l'un complétant 'Pilate livre Jesus—tolle! crucifigatur etc.'" EP to LP, 18 April 1879, private collection.

47. EP's "Ruine du Temple prédite" was published in 1906 by Édition Mutuelle, Paris; it is in the collection of the BnF-Mus, K. 15698.

48. "Une bonne oeuvre et une belle oeuvre," *Le Gaulois,* 17 May 1894, 1.

49. See note 1 in this chapter for the original French and an explanation of the allusion to "Caiaphas."

50. Polignac, "Étude sur les successions alternantes de tons et demi-tons" [1879], private collection. It will henceforth be referred to in the notes simply as "Treatise." Page numbers will be identified as "tr-p."; plural pages will be identified as "tr-pp." References to the "Cahier de Gammes A. B. C." (tr-pp. 60 and 72), a scene "at Caiaphas's palace" (tr-pp. 15, 60, and 73–74), and the "March to the Calvary" (tr-p. 72) are reproduced.

51. Polignac, Treatise, tr-p. 39.

52. Polignac's conviction that the octatonic collections were well suited to the representation of ancient "Hebraic" and "Judaic" music will be discussed at length in Chapter 9 and the Preface to Polignac's Octatonic Treatise in part two.

53. EP, Treatise, tr-p. 96.

54. EP makes reference to the Berlioz Festival that took place took place at the Hippodrome on 8 March 1879, commemorating the tenth anniversary of the conductor's

death. The event was organized and conducted by Ernest Reyer, and featured a long list of celebrated soloists. See *RGMP* 46, no. 11 (16 March 1879): 83–84.

55. "Berlioz est très en goût depuis quelques temps, chez notre public de Paris. Un festival en sa mémoire, pour de l'anniversaire de sa mort, a été monté à l'Hippodrome, et a eû [*sic*] grand succès. Le beau Septuor des "Troyens" a été bissé. Ce morceau respire une poësie des plus élevées. Mais que de défaillances ailleurs, quelle confusion, quels inextricables mauvais goûts. On s'explique malgré ce succès posthume, comment il a eû [*sic*] tant de peine à se faire jouer de son vivant; enfin le voilà arrivé; et il paraît, qu'ici bas on arrive que quand on s'en va." EP to LP, 18 April 1879, private collection.

Chapter Four

1. EP to LP, 3 January 1880, private collection.

2. EP to LP, 30 July 1880, private collection. EP makes reference to the 1879 discovery by Italian astronomer Giovanni Schiaparelli (1835–1910) of a remarkable network of narrow dark lines intersecting the so-called Martian "continent." The "canals" nomenclature ultimately proved misleading and controversial, but Schiaparelli's detailed map of the Martian landscape became a standard reference in planetary cartography.

3. Melchior de Polignac, unpublished "Souvenirs," 59, private collection.

4. Princesse Henri de Polignac, unpublished memoirs (1906), private collection.

5. EP to RM, undated [mid-February 1886], BnF-Mss, NAfr 15347:59–60.

6. Anna de Noailles, *Le Livre de ma vie* (Paris: Mercure de France, 1976), 248–51.

6. Poet Paul Collin, critic for *Le Ménestrel*, thought highly of Polignac's music. Reviewing the concert given at the Cercle on 20 April 1883 (*Le Ménestrel* 49, no. 22 [29 April 1883]: 174–75), Collin found especially worthy of praise, "amidst the riches of an admirably put-together program," the "Queen's Aria" from Polignac's *La Coupe du Roi de Thulé*. The critic hailed as "powerful" Polignac's *Don Juan et Haydée*, performed at the Cercle in May 1885. *Le Ménestrel* 51, no. 23 (10 May 1885): 184.

7. A note by EP written on telegram paper and included in a "Dossier pour gammes A.B.C." (private collection) mentions Pasdeloup's perusal of "Pilate livre le Christ" in April 1884.

8. Henri Heugel to EP, 25 February 1884, private collection.

9. For an in-depth study of the Greffulhe salon, see Jann Pasler, "Countess as Entrepreneur: Negotiating Class, Gender, and Nation, in *Writing Through Music: Essays on Music, Culture, and Politics* (New York: Oxford University Press, 2008), 285–317.

10. EG to her mother, Princesse Marie de Caraman-Chimay, 27 July 1884, AN-AP101(II)/40.

11. Ibid.

12. On 25 July 1884, EG wrote to her mother, "It's true that Henry promised [Polignac] Colonne and his orchestra for this winter. That will cost a lot of money, I think. I'm delighted by it, for [Polignac] is wildly happy" (AN-AP101[II]/40). In September, Marie de Caraman-Chimay wrote to her nephew Robert de Montesquiou, "Polignac played us some of what Colonne will have us hear. I was struck by how pretty [the music] is." (25 September 1884, BnF-Mss, NAfr 15115:31). The project appears not to have materialized.

13. EP to EG, 7 August [1884], AN-AP101(II)/106.

14. EG to Princesse Marie de Caraman-Chimay, 19 November 1884, AN-AP101(II)/40.

15. EG to Princesse Marie de Caraman-Chimay, undated [20 November 1884], AN-AP101(II)/40.

16. EG to Princesse Marie de Caraman-Chimay, 26 November 1884, AN-AP101(II)/40.

17. "Merci d'avoir pensé à moi qui pense si souvent à vous, dans mes très précieuses et choisies réceptions cérébrales, alors que vous apparaissez en beau costume de vision qui passe, seule, alors, sans la gangue obturatrice des mondanités insensés, et, ainsi, facile aux conseils heureux et épanchements réparateurs." EP to EG, undated [probably Spring 1887], AN-AP101(II)/106.

18. Most of the twelve autograph poems sent by RM to EP (private collection) eventually appeared in the numerous published collections of RM's poetry. I am grateful to Caroline Szylowicz of the Kolb-Proust Archive for Research for helping me locate the published editions of RM's poetry.

19. "La musique parfois me prend comme une mer." RM to EP, 1 March 1885, private collection.

20. "Munde Edmunde, n'avez-vous pas pris au sérieux mon engagement Wagnérien? C'est pour le commencement de la semaine prochaine. Répondez-moi, vite afin que je me munisse d'un autre compagnon au défaut de mon Edmonde monde. Tuus meus, MF." RM to EP, 9 March 1885, private collection.

21. EP to LP, "ce Dimanche" [5 Juillet 1885], private collection.

22. Henry James to RM, undated [Wednesday, 24 June 1885], BnF-Mss, NAfr 15335:45; James McNeill Whistler, two undated cards [end of June 1885], BnF-Mss, NAfr 15335:42–43. John Singer Sargent, who had painted Dr. Pozzi's portrait and knew "the unique extrahuman Montesquiou," had sent a letter of introduction to Henry James, asking him to direct the Frenchmen towards the studios of London's "aesthetic" artists. The text of Sargent's letter is quoted in Munhall, *Whistler and Montesquiou,* 58–60.

23. Munhall, *Whistler and Montesquiou,* 60. Montesquiou subsequently commissioned Whistler to paint his portrait. The full-length portrait of Montesquiou can be viewed today at the Frick Museum, New York City.

24. Marcel Proust, "Le Salon de la Princesse Edmond de Polignac," *Le Figaro,* 6 September 1903, 3.

25. EP to RM, "Dimanche" [late September 1886], BnF-Mss, NAfr 15140:17–18.

26. Théophile Gautier's poem "Affinités secrètes (Madrigal Panthéiste)" first appeared in the collection *Émaux et Camées* (Paris: Charpentier, 1872).

27. EP to RM, undated [late March 1886], BnF-Mss, NAfr 15343:76–77.

28. EP to RM, 4 November [1885], BnF-Mss, NAfr 15113:95.

29. Baronne Annette de Poilly to RM, undated, BnF-Mss, NAfr 15115:40.

30. The manuscript of EP's "Litanie de Notre Dame" for soprano, tenor, and piano/organ is dated 9 June 1886; it is housed in a private collection.

31. EP to RM, undated [spring 1886], BnF-Mss, NAfr 15241:45.

32. Edmond Vergnet (1850–1904) was a celebrated tenor at the Paris Opéra; he created the roles of John the Baptist in in Massenet's *Hérodiade* and Admeto in Catalani's *Dejanice.*

33. Émile Bourgeois, a *répétiteur* at the Paris Opéra, was one of the pianists. Coincidentally, he was also the piano instructor of Singer sewing machine heiress Winnaretta Singer—who, in 1893, would marry Edmond de Polignac.

34. Printed programs of the all-Polignac concert are housed in the Greffulhe Papers, AN-AP101(II)/135, and in the Montesquiou Papers, BnF-Mss, NAfr 15115:217.

35. Marcel Proust, "Le Salon de la Princesse Edmond de Polignac," *Le Figaro,* 6 September 1903, 3.

36. Marquis Guy de Polignac to LP, 12 October 1886, private collection.

37. EP to RM, undated [late September 1886], BnF-Mss, NAfr 15271:19–22. Polignac writes, "Nothing good or conclusive to announce to you with respect to the goal of my 'campaign' . . . nothing there for me but one more 'Rosa mystica' to add to my 'Rosary of Love.'" Polignac makes reference to his recently composed work for choir, *Rosa mystica.*

38. Marcel Proust [Echo], "La Comtesse de Guerne," *Le Figaro,* 7 May 1905, reprinted in Proust, *Contre Sainte-Beuve . . . Essais et articles* (Paris: Gallimard, 1971), 504–5. Of Comtesse Marie-Thérèse de Guerne née Ségur, Proust wrote, "Hers is probably the unique example of a voice without physical essence—a voice not merely pure, but so spiritualized that it seems to be some kind of natural harmony, begging comparison not to the sighs of a flute, but to a reed in the wind. . . . Neither music, nor even diction, interferes with the delivery of the emotional meaning, conveyed here by the impressive quality of the sound."

39. Henri Troyat, *Flaubert,* trans. Joan Pinkham (New York: Viking Penguin, 1992), 184–85.

40. Edward W. Said, *Orientalism* (New York: Vintage, 1979), 185, 188–90. For Said, Flaubert's *Salammbô* is *the* prime example of Western Orientalist literature and its title character the very embodiment of escapist sexual fantasy.

41. For a discussion of the fashion for using Oriental and Arabic subjects as the basis of composition, see Ralph P. Locke, "Cutthroats and Casbah Dancers, Muezzins and Timeless Sands: Musical Images of the Middle East," in *The Exotic in Western Music,* ed. Jonathan Bellman, 104–36, 326–33 (Boston: Northeastern University Press, 1998), and a fuller version in *19th-Century Music* 22 (1998): 20–53; and Fauser, *Musical Encounters at the 1889 Paris World's Fair,* chaps. 4 and 5.

42. Eventually Flaubert sought out Berlioz's protégé Ernest Reyer to write an opera on *Salammbô.* Camille du Locle wrote the libretto after Flaubert's novel. The work received its Brussels premiere on 10 February 1890, and was performed by the Opéra de Paris in 1892.

43. An envelope marked "Salambo Textes Mementa divers," housed in APEP, contains an autograph transcription, in Polignac's hand, of four pages from chapter 3 of Flaubert's *Salammbô;* a description of the work's "incitations," including the "musical production" passage quoted; a description of the music, in seven sections, to accompany the text; and eight pages of musical sketches.

44. The *Harvard Dictionary of Music,* ed. Don Michael Randel (Cambridge, MA: Harvard University Press, 2003), defines a nebel (called a psaltery in English Bibles) as "a stringed instrument of ancient Israel, probably a small, triangular harp."

45. The Pleyel piano was the standard concert instrument in Paris during the nineteenth century. The piano firm Pleyel et Cie was founded in 1807 by composer Ignaz Pleyel and continued by his son, piano virtuoso Camille Pleyel; the firm provided pianos to, among others, Frédéric Chopin, who performed on the instruments for his Paris concerts.

46. "J'ai écrit pour elle, et presque terminé, une Prière à Tanit . . . priant la nuit sur la terrasse du Palais des Barea, prosterné devant la Lune. Taanach, sa servente-nourrice, l'accompagne sur le Nébal: 'Les sons se succéderaient sourds et précipités, comme un bourtonnement d'Abeilles et de plus en plus sonores, ils s'envolaient dans la nuit avec les plaintes des flots et le frémissement des grands arbres, au sommet de l'Acropole.' Le nébal, ici sera remplacé par un simple Pleyel.

"La voix, portée sur les noms sacrés: 'Tanit, Baalet, Rabbetna, Derceto, Mylitta' etc, tantôt se traine plaintive, étouffée lointaine, tantôt terrible éclate déchirante, en une monodonie (empruntée à mes gammes) qui n'a *rien de la tonalité usuelle* [italics added]." EP to RM, "Dimanche" [late September 1886], BnF-Mss, NAfr 15140:20.

47. The undated manuscript of Polignac's monody, "Chant à la lune" is housed in a private collection.

48. "Mme de Guerne, étonnée d'abord et désarçonnée n'a pas tardé à plier sa voix flexible et implacablement juste, aux intervalles durs et distants de mon canvas musical, qu'elle ornera brillement et illustrera bientôt." EP to RM, dated "dimanche" (Sunday) [late September 1886], BnF-Mss, NAfr 15140:20.

49. EP to RM, 10 November 1886, BnF-Mss, NAfr 15235:59–60.

50. Polignac's sketches for the "Chant à la lune," including the unfinished orchestration of the vocal line, are found in a notebook in the archives of Prince Edmond de Polignac; various pages are dated 22 December [1886], 7 February 1887, 12 April 1887, and August 1887. There is no documentation that the Comtesse de Guerne ever performed the work in a public or salon venue.

51. The program of the Polignac-Fauré-Harcourt program is housed in the Montesquiou Papers, BnF-Mss, NAfr 15115:17–18.

52. Adam de La Halle (1220–1287) was a *trouvère*, or poet-composer. His pastoral play, *Le Jeu de Robin et Marion,* was written for the French court at Naples, and is considered the first French play with music on a secular subject.

53. Claude Debussy expressed the same yearnings to create "la musique en plein air" in an article (bearing that phrase as its title) that appeared in *La Revue blanche* on 1 July 1901; the article is reprinted in *Debussy on Music,* collected by François Lesure, ed. and trans. Richard Langham Smith (New York: Knopf, 1977), 40–42. In the article, Debussy writes, "I envisage the possibility of a music especially written for the open air, flowing in bold, broad lines from both the orchestra and the voices. It would resound through the open spaces and float joyfully over the tops of the trees, and any harmonic progression that sounded stifled within the confines of a concert hall would take on a new significance. Perhaps this is the answer to the question of how to kill off that silly obsession with overprecise 'forms' and 'tonality,' which so unfortunately encumber music." Debussy met Polignac in 1894; perhaps the younger composer was influenced by the prince's ideas on the same subject.

54. Marcel Proust, "Le Salon de la Princesse Edmond de Polignac," *Le Figaro,* 6 September 1903, 3. Proust mentions that the Comtesse Greffulhe had organized a concert of Polignac's music "en plein air," thus fulfilling a lifelong wish to hear his music played outdoors. Whether the concert in question was the one held at the "Châtaigneraie" cannot be ascertained.

55. Gabriel Fauré to EG, 16 August [1887] and undated [29 September 1887], AN-AP101(II)/131, in Gabriel Fauré, *Correspondance,* ed. Jean-Michel Nectoux, 126, 131–32; and in *Gabriel Fauré, His Life through His Letters,* ed. Jean-Michel Nectoux, trans. J. A. Underwood (New York: Boyars, 1984), 125, 130–31.

56. Jacques-Émile Blanche, *La Pêche aux souvenirs* (Paris: Flammarion, 1947), 205.

57. Gabriel Fauré to EG, 5 December 1887, AN-AP101(II)/131, in Fauré, *Correspondance,* 136–37; and in *Gabriel Fauré, His Life through His Letters,* 136.

58. Durand-Schoenewerk to EP, 21 December 1887, private collection.

59. EP to RM, 13 February 1888, BnF-Mss, NAfr 15271:55–58.

60. In an 1888 "bleu" (telegram) addressed to "Mme la Vicomtesse Greffulhe," EP writes, "Dear Madame, I have received a note from Fauré. He tells me that you have spoken to him about the Requiem, but he was afraid to make any allusion to the ways and means, and he asks if he can arrange everything for Friday and would be grateful if I could give him a prompt response. The costs come to 300 francs. I'm contributing 100 francs. May I tell him that the rest has been guaranteed? Your very devoted EP." ("Chère Madame, Je reçois un mot de Fauré. Il me dit que vous lui avez parlé du Requiem, mais qu'il n'a osé faire aucune allusion aux voies et moyens, il me demande aussi s'il peut

tout ordonner pour Vendredi et me serait reconnaissant lui donner prompte réponse. La dépense s'élève à 300 fr. Je souscrit pour 100 fr, puis-je lui répondre que c'est affaire conclue? Votre tout dévoué EP.") (AN-AP101(II)/106). The letter probably dates from April 1888, and the "Friday" mentioned in the letter is probably Friday, 4 May 1888, the date of the second performance of the Requiem.

61. The André mansion and its art collection is now home to the Musée Jacquemart-André, Boulevard Haussmann.

62. "Nous aurons trois Pianos et une vingtaine d'instruments à cordes. L'orchestre est constitué d'après mes intentions. . . . Fauré tiendra un des Pianos et nous donnera de ses compositions. Eug. d'Harcourt se charge de recruter les exécutants parmi les jeunes élèves du Conservatoire. . . . [N]ous pouvons voir dans ces réunions hebdomadaires le point de départ de curieuses expressions musicales." EP to RM, 13 February 1888, BnF-Mss, NAfr 15271:56.

63. While the conductor's score has not been found, the individual vocal and instrumental parts of the 'Marche des Pasteurs d'Ephraïm"—"Danse du Serpent" are housed in the archives of Prince Edmond de Polignac. The composer's decision to exclude wind instruments from his orchestration is notable, especially when compared to the "exotic" music of future modernist composers, such as Debussy, Ravel, and Stravinsky, who relied so heavily on the particular orchestral color of woodwinds to evoke the ancient and the Eastern. On the back covers of the instrumental scores, two of the octatonic scales are written out (Scale C, beginning on G♭, and Scale A, beginning on C) in red crayon.

64. Martin Gregor-Dellin, *Richard Wagner, His Life, His Work, His Century,* trans. J. Maxwell Brownjohn (San Diego: Harcourt Brace Jovanovich, 1983), 422, 424. Wagner had brought part of the hostility against him and his music by the French upon himself: in 1871, just at the moment when anti-German sentiment was running highest in France, Wagner, still bitter after the *Tannhäuser* debacle, had published a satirical article called "A Capitulation," in which he scathingly derided the French and their musical culture.

65. RM to EP, 23 February 1888, private collection.

66. "Vos observations sur le danger à courrir en faisant executer la Marche Teutonica sont très sensées et judicieuse, J'y ai pensé mais passé outre . . . J'ai déjà à moitié fini mon travail d'arrangement trop conscieusement mené à bien pour que je'en ai pas le bénéfice de l'audition. Et quand on voit près le travail d'orchestre Wagnérien on reste confondu de la logique et de la sincérité de ce travail . . . et que de clarté en cette Richesse . . ." EP to RM, undated [late February 1888], BnF-Mss, NAfr 15233:70.

67. "Etincelle" (author), "Mondanités," *Le Figaro,* 17 May 1888, 1. The columnist makes reference to French novelist and naval officer Pierre Loti (1850–1923), who was renowned for his picturesque romances. Loti's sensual, opulent writing style was well suited to descriptions of the exotic spots to which he traveled, especially those in the Far East. The columnist's reference to Polignac's "original art" is probably a backhanded compliment: The French word "original" is often intended to connote eccentricity.

68. Alfred de Lostalot, "Concerts," *Gazette des Beaux-Arts* 37, no. 2 (1 June 1888): 506–9.

69. *La Danse,* a special collection of piano pieces offered by the daily newspaper *Le Gaulois* to its subscribers, was published in June 1888. It includes the works of thirty-eight composers, most of whom were French, with the exceptions of Johann Strauss and Moritz Moskowski. The dance forms employed by the various composers range from rigaudons and menuets to waltzes. Polignac's "La Danse du Serpent" is published in vol. 2, 191–97.

70. Preface (author unknown) in vol. 1 of ibid.

71. Polignac, "La Danse du Serpent," ibid. 2:197.

72.   Ibid.

73.   "Si vous allez au Handel-Festival, pensez au vieux Camarade de concerts. Je crois qu'il serait de rigueur d'aller entendre, dans le "Messie," "L'Alleluia," monolithe musicale, dont tant esprit comme le vôtre, ouverts aux vastes Horizons, doit aller prendre les gigantesque triangulations . . .

"Votre présent séjour n'aura sans doute rien de l'optique de l'ancien; pourtant, au milieu de vos impressions actuelles, nouvelles mais réflexes, vous vous rappellerez sans doute, nos joints-conjoints et nos soirées à l'hôtel et vos longs récits de la vie de collège, et nos joyeuses rencontres des femmes esthétiques, tous ces faits qui me sont rappelés par votre départ en une douce évocation. Les souvenirs, en s'éloignant, se poëtisent, et vous aurez peut-être réçu un Album musical publié par le Gaulois, en effet un étrenne à ses abonnés. . . . Depuis, j'ai appris par Fauré que sa Pavane y figurait avec vos paroles, je suis donc heureux que nous nous rencontrions pour la première fois dans les mêmes pages." EP to RM, 24 June 1888, BnF-Mss, NAfr 15187:20–22.

Chapter Five

Epigraph.

I was sad and pensive when I met you;
I feel less today my obstinate torment.
Oh tell me, were you the unhoped-for woman
And the ideal dream vainly pursued?
Oh, passer-by with gentle eyes, were you then the friend
Who brought happiness to a lonely poet,
And will you shine upon my hardened soul,
Like the native sky on an exile's heart?

This is the first stanza of Charles Grandmougin's poem "Rencontre," set by Gabriel Fauré as the first song in the cycle *Poème d'un jour,* Op. 21.

1.   In his memoirs, *L'Œuvre de Maurice Barrès* (Paris: Au Club de l'Honnête Homme, 1965–68), 20:137, Barrès wrote of his Boulangism: "France was living under the idea of a Caesar-philosopher, of a prince-Napoléon. That was the idea behind my Boulangism . . . I walked with hope."

2.   Anna de Noailles, *La Livre de ma vie,* 251.

3.   Marcel Proust, *Correspondance,* ed. Philip Kolb, 20 vols. (Paris: Plon, 1970–93), 2:11.

4.   Maurice Barrès to EP, undated [before July 1889], private collection.

5.   The "Cahier No. 3" and the various sketches on loose pieces of staff paper and notepaper are housed in a private collection. "Cahier No. 3" contains twenty-four pages of music and two pages of "signes—abbréviations": an additional page of "Termes pour indications de mouvement—Chiffrage" is pasted onto the inside cover. A label, "Papeterie Chartier, 109, Faubourg-St.-Honoré," as well as a price marking in pencil of 1f25, is affixed to the left-hand corner of the inside front cover. A few of the musical sketches in the notebook are dated: the earliest is July 1890 and the latest is June 1894.

There are roughly one hundred loose pages of musical sketches. written on staff paper, graph paper, and note paper; some of these are in envelopes and some were inserted into the pages of Cahier No. 3. A number of the sketches, jotted down on tiny scraps of white paper or graph paper, consist of only a "number code" of composition used frequently by

Polignac. Only half of the sketches are dated, and some pages contain sketches that date from different years. (Polignac often "recycled" staff paper by writing new musical ideas on old pages with empty staves.) It is impossible to determine the exact dates of compositions of the undated sketches. However, there are clear links, both musical and chronological, between Cahier No. 3 and the earliest of these loose sketches, which bears a date of May 1890: both reveal Polignac's preoccupation with the "Pan" project and the "harmonies of fourths and fifths." These ideas continued to interest him until close to the end of his life: the last "Pan" sketch is dated August 1899, and the very last of the loose sketches, dated April 1900, is entitled "Exemple d'effets de 4 et 5 d'accords par A.B.C."

6.   The envelope "Harmonies de 2 sons de 5tes et 4tes, Genre 'Grecques'—Thrénies PAN Orgiastiques et processus Hébraïque" and its contents are housed in a private collection.

7.   The translations of Achille de Lauzières, Marquis de Thèmines (1800–1875), include translations of Gounod's *Faust,* Meyerbeer's *Le Pardon de Ploërmel,* Verdi's *Don Carlo,* and Flotow's *L'Esclave de Carmoëns.* He wrote over four hundred articles for the music journal *L'Art musical* on subjects such as the influence of Italian music in Egypt, the role of the orchestra in opera, the administration of lyric theaters, Lully and the recitative, nationalism in the works of Verdi and Wagner, and the letters of Haydn.

8.   Marquis Achille de Lauzières de Thémines to EP, 5 May 1890, private collection. According to the letter, Lauzières was paid 600 francs.

9.   In 1886, the membership of the Société Nationale de Musique split into contentious factions over the issue of the inclusion of non-French music in its programs. As a result, the organization's conservative founder, Camille Saint-Saëns, resigned as president; in the subsequent elections, César Franck, a progressive, was voted president, d'Indy and Ernest Chausson were elected secretaries. When Franck died in November 1890, d'Indy was elected president.

10.   Vincent d'Indy to EP, 11 February 1891, private collection.

11.   "Cher ami, Je n'osais vous demander l'amical service d'accompagner la romance. J'ai été très touché . . . dirai-je même un peu ému (ce sont décidément les premières atteintes du gâtisme et gaga-isme qui s'avance). Je n'ai repris *tous* mes esprits qu'à la pensée de toutes les décorations au piano et j'ai trouvé le spectacle vraiment majestueux et merveilleusement rastaquouëre!!! Donc merci, vous serez le poisson qui fera passer ma mauvaise sauce. J'en reste très touché et honoré." EP to Gabriel Fauré, undated [February 1891], NLa 3:200. "Rastaquouère" is a slang French word from the 1880s meaning "social intruder, upstart, especially one of exaggerated manners and dress."

12.   Michel Duchesneau, *L'Avant-garde Musicale à Paris de 1871 à 1939* (Sprimont, Belgium: Mardaga, 1997), 251.

13.   Julien Tiersot, "Revue des grands concerts: Société Nationale," *Le Ménéstrel* 57, no. 12 (22 March 1891): 94.

14.   After hearing the "Hallelujah Chorus" at London's 1888 Handel Festival, RM wrote to EP (24 June 1888, BnF-Mss, NAfr 15187:20–21) that he found the work to be "a brutal brine. But isn't that its mission? Isn't it destined [to create] beautiful masses and geysers of sound?" He was amused by the notion of Baroque representations of "those Hebrews who dance the gavotte and the pavane, the menuet and the passacaglia and the passé-pied under their wigs."

15.   Documents related to the founding, administration, and concert programs of the Société des Grandes Auditions Musicales de France, AN-AP101(II)/128 and 129. See also "Les Compositeurs français en France," *Le Figaro,* 10 April 1890, 1; Anne de Cossé-Brissac, *La Comtesse Greffulhe* (Paris: Perrin, 1991), 85–88; Pasler, "Countess Greffulhe as Entrepreneur," 302–8.

16.   Andrew Thomson, *Vincent d'Indy and His World* (Oxford: Clarendon, 1996), 80–81; Katherine Ellis, *Interpreting the Musical Past: Early Music in Nineteenth-Century France* (Oxford: Oxford University Press, 2005), 105–11.

17.   "Cette nature droite *gobait* très facilement les personnalités bluffeuses, et il fut souvent victime de sa droiture et de sa crédulité. C'est ainsi qu'il mangea peu à peu sa petite fortune *en excellente placement* conseillés par les gens *les plus forts.*" Melchior de Polignac, "Souvenirs," unpublished ms, private collection.

18.   EP to Comte Guy de Polignac, 30 January 1892 and 6 February 1892, private collection.

19.   "Mais rien—silence et zéro, pas même la plus vague allusion au milieu de mes fatigantes luttes et injustes tracas; par exemple quantité de plongeons en eau bénite de cour, ou appels d'attention, sans tact, sur leur luxe par le 'mes aises passent avant vos besoins' durement souligné. . . . Il avaient dû ou devraient comprendre cependant que plus qu'eux je faisais honneur à mon nom, par moi-même, et en y ajoutant." EP to Comte Guy de Polignac, 30 January 1892, private collection.

20.   MP, "Souvenirs," private collection, 58.

21.   Ibid.

22.   EP to Comte Guy de Polignac, 6 and 8 February 1892, private collection.

23.   EP to Comte Guy de Polignac, 24 March 1892, private collection.

24.   Ellis, *Interpreting the Musical Past,* 105–11.

25.   Ibid.

26.   Most of the information on Winnaretta Singer in the current study can be found in my *Music's Modern Muse: A Life of Winnaretta Singer, Princesse de Polignac* (Rochester, NY: University of Rochester Press, 2003); see also "Memoirs of the Late Princesse Edmond de Polignac," *Horizon* 12, no. 68 (August 1945): 110–40.

27.   WSP, "Memoirs," 118.

28.   These canvasses, signed Winnaretta Singer, were exhibited in the Salon des Beaux-Arts in the years 1886, 1887, 1889, and 1890.

29.   According to the December 1883 listings in *Le Ménestrel,* a typical program by the Concerts du Conservatoire, for example, featured the music of Mendelssohn, Weber, Beethoven, Lenepveu, Gluck, and Wagner. Lenepveu was the only French composer among the six.

30.   The correspondence of WSP and Gabriel Fauré is housed in the FSP, Paris.

31.   WSP, "Memoirs," 122.

32.   Ibid.

33.   Ibid. See also Francis Poulenc, *Emmanuel Chabrier* (Paris: La Palatine, 1961), 82.

34.   "A travers Paris: Dans le monde," *Le Figaro,* 16 and 24 May 1888.

35.   An undated letter to WS from the Artistic Committee of the Société Nationale de Musique [probably 1889, FSP], signed by Franck, Chabrier, Fauré, d'Indy, Benoit, and Bréville, asks her "to consent to take under your special protection our Society and to encourage the efforts that we continue to make for an exclusively artistic goal." A subsequent letter from Fauré to WS, also undated [early April 1889, FSP] asks WS to grant an appointment to the Committee members of the Sociéte Nationale de Musique so that they can thank her personally for her support.

36.   Vincent d'Indy to WS, 19 July 1889, FSP.

37.   WS to Marguerite Baugnies, undated [September 1891], Archives Saint-Marceaux, Paris.

38.   Greffulhe's recollections of her meeting with EP are recounted in a one-page document. "Pour servir aux mémoires de la comtesse Greffulhe," AN-AP101(II)/149.

39.   Ledger entitled "Administration" in a carton of documents concerning the Société des Grandes Auditions Musicales de France, Greffulhe Papers, AN-AP101(II)/129.

40.   WS to Marguerite Baugnies, undated [24 July 1891], Archives Saint-Marceaux.

41.   Printed program of the Greffulhe soirée of 21 July 1891, Fonds Montesquiou, BnF-Mss, NAfr 15038:117. The concert consisted of a J. S. Bach violin sonata, arranged for orchestra by Polignac; Fauré's *Pavane, Berceuse,* and "Chanson" from *Shylock;* Wagner's *Siegfried Idyll; Chanson d'autrefois,* an orchestral work by Greffulhe protégé Xavier Perreau; Polignac's *Robin m'aime;* and recitations, by Charles Le Bargy of the Comédie française, of Montesquiou's poems "Le Bulbul" and "Éloge de la nuit." Maurice Bagès was the tenor soloist. According to a note in Montesquiou's hand at the bottom of the printed program, the same concert was given at a soirée (date unknown) in the Comte's home at 8, Rue Franklin.

42.   Marcel Proust [Horatio], "Le Salon de al Princess Edmond de Polignac: Musique d'aujourd'hui, Échos d'autrefois," *Le Figaro,* 6 September 1903.

43.   EG, "Pour servir aux mémoires de la comtesse Greffulhe," AN-AP101(II)/149.

44.   EP to RM, BnF-Mss, NAfr. 15032:130–31.

45.   EP is describing the not at all unique musical devices of augmentation and diminution.

46.   EP makes reference to the A natural-minor scale.

47.   "Je m'empresse de vous faire parvenir la carte d'entrée pour le concert de demain mardi, très heureux que vous veuillez bien m'honorer de votre bienveillante présence.... Je me permets de vous envoyer le morceau que vous entendrez, chanté par Mme Caron. C'est là une version primitive qui j'ai dû agrémenter de broderies, à l'accompagnement, selon l'esprit du jour. Il y a, notamment, à la troisième strophe: "Les Belles de Nuit demi-closes" un artifice que je crois presque unique au Littérature Musicale consistant à faire entendre sous le chant, le motif initial, aux choeurs (bouche fermé) et à l'orchestre simultanément, en . . . quatre valeurs différentes:

"Ainsi qu'il convient aux suggestives et simples paroles, la couleur musicale s'implante plus tôt du Diatonique Oriental Latin, que du chromatisme romantique Germain, lequel est peut-être trop exclusivement pratiqué aujourd'hui et égale distance kilométique le Diatonique Latin portera toujours d'avantage. Excusez, Madame, cette très pédantesque digression. Je risque de passer auprès de vous pour un 'Professional' comme je vous sais les éviter." EP to WS, 4 April 1892, FSP.

48.   WS to RM, undated [between 13–16 May 1892], BnF-Mss NAfr 15168:177.

49.   RM to WS, 5 June 1892, FSP.

50.   WS to RM, undated letter [November or December 1892], BnF-Mss, NAfr 15115:59.

51.   EP, "thrénie greco-orientale" and "thème funèbre (un peu Egyptien)," in "Cahier No. 3," private collection.

52.   The manuscript of EP's "Exercice pour orgue," dated 20 January 1893 is housed in a private collection. A first draft of the work can be found in "Cahier No. 3."

53.   EP to RM, télégramme bleu adressé au 8, rue Franklin, 9 April [1892], BnF-Mss, NAfr 16113:90.

54.   Robert de Montesquiou, "Effusions," in *Le Chef des suaves odeurs* (Paris: Georges Richard, 1893), 315–16.

55.   "Vous me flattez outre mesure en me décernant cet exceptionnel brevet de Bonté; je ne sais si je le mérite, peut-être préférais-je une pointe de perversité toujours moins bannale; maintenant c'est peut-être vous qui me l'inspirez cette bonté, en tous cas je désire fermement que vous sachiez et sentiez près de vous (au milieu des torrents et ravins, des lacs bleus où des fêtes mondaines et à travers les temps et les distances) toujours le souvenir d'un attachement (*raisonné* et irraisonné) que rien ne pourra atténuer." EP to WS, 27 September 1893, FSP.

56.   WS to EG, 9 November 1893, BnF-Mss, NAfr 15115:60.

57. Marcel Proust to his mother, 31 August 1901, in *Correspondance 1896–1901* 2:445.

58. Duchesse Isabelle Decazes to WS, undated [November or December 1893], private collection.

59. "A travers Paris," *Le Figaro*, 16 December 1893.

60. Blanche, *La Pêche aux souvenirs*, 249.

61. Edmond and Jules de Goncourt, *Journal 1894–1895*, Vol 20 (Monaco: Éditions Imprimerie Nationale, 1956), 26.

62. Ibid.

63. "Je constate que l'envoi qui vous était adressé a été mis par la personne chargée des expéditions. Je tiens à vous informer de fait au *plûtot*, pour que vous n'y puissiez supposer aucun négligence de ma part et que vous en recevrez, ainsi qu'il convient et me convient, l'assurance de tous mes regrets." EP to RM, 18 January 1894, BnF-Mss, NAfr 15115:49–50.

64. André Germain, "Robert de Montesquiou," typed text numbered "33" with accompanying autograph by André Germain, 15–16, private collection.

65. Comtesse Edmond de Pourtalès to RM, BnF-Mss, NAfr 15112:126.

66. RM, "Vinaigrette," portrait satirique, extrait de *Quarante bergères*, 3e série, No. 20 (private printing). For the autograph, see BnF-Mss, NAfr 15115:54.

67. RM, *Les Pas effacés: Mémoires*, 3 vols. (Paris: Émile-Paul, 1923), 2:243.

68. Proust [Horatio], "Le Salon de la Princesse Edmond de Polignac," 3.

69. LMLV, *Le Figaro*, 27 February 1896, 2; Marguerite de Saint-Marceaux, journal entry of 25 February 1896, in Saint-Marceaux, *Journal, 1894–1927*, ed. Myriam Chimènes (Paris: Fayard, 2007), 129.

70. For an in-depth study of the Polignac salon, see my *Music's Modern Muse: A Life of Winnaretta Singer, Princesse de Polignac*.

71. "Courrier des Théâtres," *Le Figaro*, 9 January 1894.

72. *Le Ménestrel*, 59, no. 44 (15 October 1893): 351.

73. Charles Darcours, "Notes de musique," *Le Figaro*, 7 February 1894; 3 articles: "Revue des grands concerts: Concerts d'Harcourt, *Le Ménestrel* 60, no. 2 (14 January 1894): 13; 60, no. 3 (21 January 1894): 21; and 60, no. 4 (28 January 1894): 30.

74. "Courrier des Théâtres," *Le Figaro*, 21 March 1894.

75. Saint-Marceaux, journal entry of 25 February 1896, in *Journal*, 129.

76. EP to LP, 1, rue Cortambert, n.d. [early June 1894].

77. François Magnard, whose son Albéric was a gifted composer, was predisposed to reporting musical events. His first report of the Polignac salon appeared in the column "A travers Paris," *Le Figaro*, 5 June 1894, 2. After Magnard's death in November 1894, Gaston Calmette, who succeeded him as chief editor, prominently featured the Polignac salon in *Le Figaro*'s new society column "Le Monde et La Ville (LMLV)." During the years 1894–1901, no fewer than fifty mentions of the Polignac salon—including numerous full-length articles—appeared in the *Figaro*'s society pages.

78. LMLV, *Le Figaro*, 18 June 1895, 2.

Chapter Six

1. Alexandre de Bertha, "Un Système de gammes nouvelles," *La Nouvelle Revue* 86 (1 January 1894), 125–37.

2. An announcement of Bertha's lecture, entitled "Essai d'un système de gammes nouvelles," appeared in *L'Art musical 32, no. 27* (30 December 1893): 95. An announcement

of the publication of the lecture text (Paris: private edition, H. Eymieu, 1893) appeared in *Le Monde musical 5, no. 15* (15 December 1893): 254.

3. Alexandre de Bertha, *Essai d'un système de gammes nouvelles* (Paris: P. Mauret [no publication date, probably late 1893]), 16 pp. A copy of the monograph is housed in the Bibliothèque nationale de France, Music Department, L.9.382.

4. "Franz Liszt: Étude musico-psychologique," article in 3 parts, *Mercure musical et Bulletin français de la S.I.M.* 3, no. 9 (15 September 1907): 957–79; 3, no. 10 (15 October 1907): 1046–63; 3, no. 11 (15 November 1907): 1160–84.

5. *In April 1871, Liszt conducted a concert that included Bertha's Wedding March, which, according to Bertha, "his" (Liszt's) critics ripped to shreds.*

6. Alexandre de Bertha, "La Musique bohémienne" and "La Musique hongroise, " in *Encyclopédie de la musique,* vol. 1, ed. Alfred de Lavignac (Paris: Delagrave, 1922), 2597–2613 and 2613–45, respectively. Bertha also wrote "La Musique hongroise et les tsiganes," an article in the *Revue des deux mondes* 28 (1878): 909–20.

7. Approximately two dozen of Bertha's short piano works, published between 1867 and 1899, are housed in the Music Department of the Bibliothèque nationale de France.

8. See, for example, Bertha's "Czardas" (1887) and "Kolping" (1894), both housed in the Département de la Musique, Bibliothèque nationale de France. The "Hungarian scale" is discussed in chap. 3, pp. 39, 43, 44 and p. 344n30.

9. Bertha, "De la Possibilité de nouvelles combinaisons harmoniques," part one, *Le Ménéstrel* 61, n0.28 (14 July 1895): 219–20.

10. Bertha, "Un Système de gammes nouvelles," 127–28.

11. The translation of the first two paragraphs of Fig. 6.1:

"We count five whole steps and two half steps in a diatonic major scale and three whole steps, an augmented 2nd and three half steps in a diatonic [harmonic] minor scale. Now, if we divide each of these whole steps into two half steps, and the augmented 2nd into three [half steps], we obtain for each scale a total of twelve half steps, which are found all together in the chromatic scale.

"The division of this total into equal parts has been, for a long time, in common use in harmony, as evidenced by the diminished 7th and augmented 5th chords, the first having a quotient of three and the second of four half steps. The result is that each note contained in each chord can be considered as a root, taking into account enharmonic changes. [Comprised of] identical [pitch classes] in several keys, there are only three [different] forms of the first chord and only four of the second.

"With such precedents, if we accept the possibility of symmetrical scales, we can't be accused of aberration [i.e., we can't be accused of "pushing the envelope"]. For having the tempered [equal-distanced] half steps entirely at our disposition—as it was stated above—thanks to the facility of our players and the perfection of our instruments, and recognizing that their current repartition has nothing regular about it, what prevents us from grouping them in an arithmetic progression, alternating the single half-steps with the putting-together of two half steps into a whole step and vice versa—that is to say:

$$\tfrac{1}{2} + 1 + \tfrac{1}{2} + 1 + \tfrac{1}{2} + 1 + \tfrac{1}{2} + 1$$
$$\text{or } 1 + \tfrac{1}{2} + 1 + \tfrac{1}{2} + 1 + \tfrac{1}{2} + 1 + \tfrac{1}{2}$$

combinations, which also give a total of twelve half steps?"

12. "Prise une à une, elles présentent les particularités suivantes:

"La *première*—avec le binôme de ½ + 1 ton pour la progression arithmétique—contient une seconde mineure, la médiante et la dominante, et manque au contraire de sous-dominante et de note sensible. Au lieu de cette dernière, nous rencontrons sur son septième degré la *septimème mineure*, que les tubes sonores produisent en note naturelle et dont la présence n'a pas pu être justifiée jusqu'ici dans le système des gammes diatoniques; . . .

"La *seconde*—avec le binôme de 1 + ½ ton pour la progression arithmétique—contient la note sensible et la sous-dominante et manque au contraire de médiante et de dominante. Sa seconde est majeure, correspondant en renversement à la septième mineure de la gamme précédente, et comme il sort aussi des tubes sonores en note naturelle, elle témoigne également en faveur de notre découverte." Ibid., 129–30.

13. Ibid., 129.

14. "Or, je tiens à faire valoir mes droits d'absolue priorité à l'invention et à l'application de ces mêmes gammes en rappelant que l'Album musical du *Gaulois* de 1888 a publié un morceau de moi, intitulé Danse du Serpent, composé en ces sortes de gammes. Une note explicative, à la suite du morceau, donne en deux exemples notés leur mode de formation et leur désignation par lettres romaines (A. B. C.), désignation empruntée à des cahiers d'études sur la théorie de ces gammes et leur application, études remontant à une date bien antérieure à la publication du *Gaulois*. D'autre part, ainsi que le confirme la *Gazette des Beaux-Arts* du 1er juin 1888, dans sa *Chronique musicale*, signée: A. de Lostalot, j'ai fait entendre en divers concerts l'emploi de ces gammes et juge, de ce fait, le public suffisamment informé." EP, "Boîte à lettres," *Le Figaro*, 28 February 1894.

15. "C'est par des combinaisons arithmétiques que j'ai trouvé les gammes enharmoniques et je ne connaissais nullement le morceau du signataire. Mon ignorance a été du reste partagée par MM. Ambroise Thomas, Marmontel père, Joncières, Pougin, Mangeot, Marchesi, de Dubor, etc., qui m'ont fait l'honneur d'assister à ma conférence du 27 novembre 1893, ainsi que par MM. Diémer, Eymien, Lavignac et Soubie [*sic*], auxquels j'en ai fait part antérieurement à la publication.

"Il eût été étrange qu'aucun musicien ne se soit aperçu avant moi de la possibilité de disposer symétriquement les tons et les demi-tons. C'est un fait qui est à la portée de tout le monde.

"Autre chose est d'en déduire un système complet, déterminant les ressources que cette nouvelle disposition des intervalles fournit à la mélodie, à l'harmonie et au contrepoint. Je n'ai pas sous les yeux l'album du *Gaulois* ni l'article cité de M. de Lostalot, mais je suis sûr que rien de semblable ne s'y trouve; car ceci ne peut être fait que dans un travail spécial n'entrant dans le cadre ni d'un album mondain, ni d'un article de journal. Or, mon essai . . . est consacré particulièrement et est le fruit de plusieurs mois de recherches.

"Donc, si le signataire de la lettre en question a eu la chance de reconnaître la possibilité d'une nouvelle disposition des intervalles dès 1888, j'en suis très fier, puisque cela prouve que je ne me suis pas trompé. Mais il doit m'accorder aussi que le système des gammes enharmoniques m'appartient entièrement et que j'ai le droit d'en faire la propagande comme il avait le droit de ne pas donner de suite à son inspiration de 1888." Alexandre de Bertha, "Boîte à lettres," *Le Figaro*, 1 March 1894, 3.

The eminent musicians to whom Bertha alludes in his letter to *Le Figaro* are, in order of citation: Ambroise Thomas (composer and Conservatoire director); Antoine François Marmontel (pianist and pedagogue); Victorin de Joncières (composer and critic); Arthur Pougin (music critic); Édouard Mangeot (piano manufacturer and founder of the journal *Le Monde* musical); Salvatore Marchesi (baritone, vocal pedagogue and professor at the Vienna Conservatory); Georges de Dubor (writer and poet); Louis Diémer (pianist); Henry Eymien (composer); Albert Lavignac (music scholar); and Albert Soubies (music historian).

16. The Académie des Sciences's *Comptes rendus* is considered even today to occupy a place of choice among scientific journals; because of its biweekly publication, it assures

the possibility of presenting rapidly new scientific ideas and discoveries to an international community.

17. Alexandre de Bertha, "Acoustique musicale: Sur un système de gammes nouvelles," presented 21 May 1894, *Comptes rendus des Séances de l'Académie des Sciences* 18 (January–June 1894): 1137–39. The text of his report is in the library of the Académie des Sciences, Paris.

18. Edmond de Polignac, "Acoustique: Sur un système de gammes chromatico-diatoniques," presented 18 June 1894, *Comptes rendus des Séances de l'Académie des Sciences* 18 (January–June 1894): 1412. A rough draft of the text, in a folder marked "Dossier polémique relative aux gammes A.B.C.," is housed in a private collection. The folder contains an unsigned note from CaP, who, after reading the first draft of the report that EP intended to present to the Académie des Sciences, suggested that EP point out at the very beginning of his presentation that Bertha's designation of the octatonic scales as "enharmonic" was "incorrect according to the commonly accepted meaning" of the word. "That way," wrote CaP, "you deal an immediate blow to your plagarist and his so-called invention" (private collection).

19. Alexandre de Bertha, "Acoustique musicale: Sur un système de gammes nouvelles," presented 2 July 1894, *Comptes rendus des Séances de l'Académie des Sciences* 19 (July– December 1894): 56.

20. *Le Figaro,* 17 May 1894, 2.

21. *Le Figaro,* 16 and 18 May 1894. The other works on the program were Janequin's "La Bataille de Marignan," Fauré's Requiem (the "second" version, with all seven movements and expanded orchestra), excerpts from Wagner's *Die Meistersinger,* and EP's "Les Adieux de Deïdamia." The vocal soloists were the Comtesse de Guerne and Madame Grammacini, and Messieurs Auguez, Leneuve, and Pierron; the Chanteurs de Saint-Gervais were conducted by Charles Bordes.

22. "A travers Paris," *Le Figaro,* 18 May 1894, 2.

23. Gabriel Fauré to WSP, n.d. [September 1894], FSP, in Gabriel Fauré, *Correspondance,* 225–26; and in *Gabriel Fauré: His Life through His Letters,* 228–29.

24. EP, sketch entitled "D'après et surtout après des airs arabes entendus chez la Belle Fatma," dated July 1894, private collection.

25. The manuscripts and scores of the three movements of the *Échos de l'Orient judaïque* (privately published, 1894) are extant and housed in a private collection.

26. Bertha, "De la Possibilité de nouvelles combinaisons harmoniques," article in 3 parts, *Le Ménestrel* 61, no. 28 (14 July 1895): 219–20; 61, no. 29 (21 July 1895): 229–31; 61, no. 31 (4 August 1895): 245–46.

27. Bertha, "De la Possibilité de nouvelles combinaisons harmoniques," part two, 229–31.

28. Bertha, "De la Possibilité de nouvelles combinaisons harmoniques," part 3, 245.

29. "Nécrologie," *Le Ménestrel* 78, no. 48 (30 November 1912): 383.

Chapter Seven

1. For a discussion of the curious pairing of J. S. Bach and Richard Wagner in some critical writings in late 19th-century France, see Katherine Ellis, *Interpreting the Musical Past,* 102–7.

2. Charles Bordes to EP, undated letter [1893 or 1894], private collection. In the letter, Bordes writes, "My dear Prince, d'Harcourt gets our project off the ground, or pretty much. What a man!" See also Ellis, *Interpreting the Musical Past,* 106.

3. "Paris et départements," *Le Ménestrel* 60, no. 26 (8 July 1894): 216.

4. The first officers of the Schola Cantorum, elected on 15 June 1894, were Alexandre Guilmant, president; Bourgault-Ducoudray, Ferdinand de La Tombelle, and André Pirro, vice presidents (with Polignac); Bordes and G. de Boisjelin, secretaries; and d'Indy, treasurer. His signature is included along with the other members of "Le Comité de la Schola Cantorum" addressed to the Cardinal of Paris, 30 November 1894 (Archives Historiques de l'Archevêché de Paris). The letter outlines the goals of the Schola that "second the views of the Church," and asks the Cardinal to agree to be a patron of the new organization. I am grateful to Catrina Flint de Médicis for calling this letter to my attention.

5. Charles Bordes to EP, three undated letters [1894–96], private collection; Vincent d'Indy to EP, 23 January 1895, FSP.

6. Vincent d'Indy to EP, FSP.

7. LMLV, *Le Figaro*, 4 and 22 April 1895; *Le Gaulois*, 24 April 1895. A printed program of the Schütz-Rameau performance in the Polignac salon is housed in the BnF-Mus.

8. Hedwige de Polignac, *Les Polignac* (Paris: Fasquelle, 1960), 252–5.

9. WSP, "Memoirs of the Late Princesse Edmond de Polignac," 120.

10. Colette, "Un Salon en 1900," from *Journal à Rebours*, ed. Robert Laffont (Paris: Fayard, 1989), 53.

11. Claude Debussy to Marguerite de Saint-Marceaux, undated [30 January 1894], in *Claude Debussy, Correspondance. 1872–1918*, ed. François Lesure and Denis Herlin (Paris: Gallimard, 2005), 188–89. WSP, "Memoirs of the Late Princesse Edmond de Polignac," 126.

12. Marguerite de Saint-Marceaux, journal entry of February 1894, in *Journal 1894–1927*, 77.

13. See my *Music's Modern Muse*, 106–7.

14. Baur, "Ravel's 'Russian' Period," 531–92.

15. Colette, "Un Salon en 1900," 53.

16. Ibid.

17. Marguerite de Saint-Marceaux, diary entry of 21 May 1894, in *Journal 1894–1927*, 85.

18. Kahan and Mauriac-Dyer, "Quatre Lettres inédites de Proust au Prince de Polignac," 9.

19. Proust to Madame Jean Hennessy, in Proust, *Correspondance* 16:322.

20. Proust to EP, n.d. [6 or 7 February 1895], private collection. The French text is published in Kahan and Mauriac-Dyer, "Quatre Lettres inédites de Proust," 13.

21. While Polignac's song bears no resemblance, musically speaking, to Henri Duparc's more celebrated setting of the same poem, it evokes in its own way, and just as successfully, the feeling of a medieval ballad.

22. Proust's name is mentioned among the listing of the audience members in the Polignac salon in articles in *Le Gaulois*, 24 April 1895 and 18 June 1895.

23. Proust [Horatio], "Le Salon de la Princesse Edmond de Polignac," 3.

24. Ibid.

25. *Le Roi Chilpéric* (1868) is an opérette with a book by Paul Ferrier and music by Hervé (1825–92). Hervé was instrumental in establishing the vogue of French operetta.

26. Claude Debussy to Pierre Louÿs, 23 February 1895, in Debussy, *Lettres*, ed. François Lesure (Paris: Hermann, 1980), 73. (My translation.)

27. "Revue des grands concerts," *Le Ménestrel* 61, no. 9 (3 March 1895): 69. In addition to Polignac's *Robin m'aime*, the program of the Société National de Musique also included performances of works by Fauré, Georges Huë, Rimsky-Korsakov (*Conte féerique*), Chausson (*Viviane*), Guirard, and Joseph Erb.

28. *Le Siècle,* 26 February 1895.

29. Guigues Talaverney, *Le Monde musical,* 24 February 1895.

30. André Gresse, in *Le Journal,* 24 February 1895.

31. *Le Mot d'Ordre,* 26 February 1895.

32. Charles Bordes to EP, n.d. [June 1895], private collection.

33. Ibid.

34. LMLV, *Le Figaro,* 15 June 1895, 2.

35. EP to WSP, St-Gervais, n.d. [summer 1895], FSP.

36. "J'ai lu les premières pages, les très belles premières pages de votre lettre; au risque de vous paraître ridicule, j'en ai été très ému, et, plein de foi, j'ai baisé le dernier mot qui termine cette partie de votre lettre ainsi: "Je vous écris mes pensées dans les examiner et les refroidir,—je sais que vous les comprendrez et les respecter. . . . Good bye, ma bien-aimée et chère unique Amie. Je vous embrasse bien tendrement et mets dans ce baiser tout ce que le sort m'a repris de joie, et tout ce que je trouve de bonheur enfin sur le tard de ma vie, à vous Edmond." EP to WSP, St-Gervais, n.d. [summer 1895], FSP.

37. Ernest Chausson, diary entry, 25 February 1896, in Ernest Chausson, *Choix et Présentation des écrits inédits,* ed. Jean Gallois and Isabelle Brétaudeau (Monaco: Éditions du Rocher, 1999).

38. Charles Bordes to EP, undated [1896], private collection; Vincent d'Indy, "La Schola Cantorum en 1925," in d'Indy et al., *Le Schola Cantorum, son histoire depuis sa fondation jusqu'en 1925* (Paris: Librairie Bloud et Gay, 1927), 8.

39. Eugène Gigout to EP, 4 March 1896, private collection.

40. "Paris et Départements," *Le Ménestrel* 62, no. 15 (5 April 1896): 112.

41. LMLV, *Le Figaro,* 13 May 1896, 2.

42. Reynaldo Hahn to EP, Jeudi [n.d., 14 May 1896], private collection.

43. LMLV, *Le Figaro,* 7 August 1896. See also Albert Lavignac, *Le Voyage artistique à Bayreuth* (Paris: Delagrave, 1897), 571–78.

44. EP to WSP, St-Gervais, 17 July 1896, FSP.

45. Marguerite de Saint-Marceaux, diary entry of 14 August 1896, in *Journal, 1894–1927,* 143; Gabriel Fauré to his wife Marie, Bayreuth, 4 August 1896, in Fauré, *Lettres intimes,* ed. Philippe Fauré-Fremiet (Paris: Grasset, 1951), 15.

46. Marguerite de Saint-Marceaux, *Journal, 1894–1927,* 144; Fauré, *Lettres intimes,* 17.

47. EP to LP, Paris, 22 February 1897, private collection. See also LMLV, *Le Figaro,* 16 November 1896, 2.

48. WSP, "Memoirs," 117.

49. EP, it may be recalled (see chap. 4, p. 55), had visited Morris's studio in London with Montesquiou in 1885, and had also gone to see an exhibition of his fabrics in Paris [BnF-Mss, undated, NAfr 15343:66].

50. D'Indy et al., *Le Schola Cantorum,* 228.

51. Armande de Polignac, excerpt from "Winnaretta Singer," an homage delivered at a memorial for WSP, n.d. [1944], private collection; CP to EP, Podwein, Austria, 18 August 1897, private collection.

52. Armande de Polignac, "Winnaretta Singer," private collection.

53. CP to EP, three letters sent from Podwein, Austria, 18 August 1897, 24 August 1897, and 30 September 1897, private collection.

54. CP to EP, 30 September 1897, private collection.

55. CP to EP, 12 November 1897, private collection.

56. EP's octatonic sketches from July through December 1897 are written on loose pieces of score paper, and are housed in a private collection.

57. LMLV, *Le Figaro*, 22 June 1898, 2.

58. Marcel Proust to EP, 25 June 1898, private collection. For the complete text, see Kahan and Mauriac-Dyer, "Quatre Lettres inédites de Proust au Prince de Polignac," 15–17.

59. Proust [Horatio], "Le Salon de la Princesse Edmond de Polignac," 465.

60. Fauré subsequently arranged the Incidental Music from *Pelléas et Mélisande* into a Suite. The work, which became the composer's Opus 80, was dedicated to the Princesse Edmond de Polignac.

61. LMLV, *Le Figaro*, 9 July 1898. See also d'Indy, et al., *La Schola Cantorum*, 228.

62. "Au-dessus de moi des millions de mouches bourdonnent dans les hautes cimes baignées par le soleil et remplissant la Forêt d'une note tenue perpétuelle, invariable un 'do,' comme posée sur la corde d'un immense violon invisible." EP to WSP, n.d., FSP.

63. Printed program for a lecture-recital given on 9 February 1899 at an unspecified location, Archives de l'Institut Catholique de Paris. The program identifies EP's work as "O Rives du Jourdain!" I am grateful to Catrina Flint de Médicis for bringing this program to my attention.

64. LMLV, *Le Figaro*, 19 May 1899, 2.

65. LMLV, *Le Figaro*, 23 March 1899, 2. The violist in the quartet performances was the young Pierre Monteux.

66. See Proust's third letter to EP, in Kahan and Mauriac-Dyer, "Quatre Lettres inédites de Proust," 17–18.

67. Marcel Proust, *Le Prisonnier* (vol. 3 of *À la Recherche du temps perdu*), 762 and 755, respectively.

68. *La Presse*, 4 September 1899, 2.

69. Abel Hermant, *Souvenirs de la vie mondaine* (Paris: Hachette, 1935), 220, 223.

70. Ibid., 223.

71. Marcel Proust to his mother, Évian, 11 September 1899, in *Correspondance* 2:308.

72. EP's sketch, "Schema rythmique du Choeur PAN," dated August 99, is housed in a private collection. The sequential use of intervals derived from the octatonic collection continued to preoccupy EP through the remainder of the year. Several sketches dated December 1899 (private collection) are entitled "melodic sketches in succession of 4ths and 3rds." EP's last extant octatonic sketch, dated April 1900 (private collection) is entitled "Exemple d'effets de 4 et 5 d'accords par A.B.C." (Example of effects of accompaniments [built on] 4ths and 5ths [from] Scales A.B.C.).

Chapter Eight

1. Barrès, *L'Œuvre de Maurice Barrès* 20:148. See also Princesse Hélène de Caraman-Chimay to Augustine Bulteau, undated letter [after August 1901], Fonds Bulteau, BnF-Mss, NAfr 17473:151.

2. EP to EG, 7 January 1900, Fonds Greffulhe AN-AP101(II)/106.

3. Gabriel Fauré to EP, undated [January 1900], FSP. Fauré wrote, "You know how much I can't wait to hear the *Imprécations,* and how much I will participate with joy!"

4. See Kahan, *Music's Modern Muse*, 108–10, 376–77.

5. Program of a musicale given at the home of the Comtesse Greffuhle on 29 June 1900, private collection. See also Pasler, "Countess Greffulhe as Entrepreneur," 299.

6. EP's quip, the wordplay of which gets lost in translation, comes from the typescript of a speech given by Comtesse Jean de Polignac at a memorial gathering organized for the Princesse de Polignac in 1944 (private collection). The French verb "bander" means "to get an erection." More of EP's witticisms are quoted in Ronald Storrs, *Orientations* (London: Ivor Nicholson and Watson, 1937), 117; and Claude Mignot-Ogliastri, *Anna de Noailles: Une amie de la Princesse Edmond de Polignac* (Paris: Fondation Singer-Polignac and Méridiens Klincksieck, 1986), 111.

7. The Polignac music library (private collection) contains a score of "Pilate livre le Christ," with two notes at the top of the cover page, in EP's handwriting: "Avec corrections 1899 et 1901" and "Partition ayant servi à Chevillard."

8. I am grateful to M. Pierre Vidal of the Bibliothèque de l'Opéra, Paris, for calling my attention to this collection, classed as "Autographes, Exposition Universelle de 1900," collected by Charles Malherbe.

9. "Departs: La princesse de Polignac à Venise," Le Figaro, 13 April 1900, 6.

10. Mignot-Ogliastri, *Anna de Noailles*, 112.

11. Marie Dujardin, "Marcel Proust à Venise," *Le Figaro*, 10 October 1931, 7. Dujardin erroneously identifies Proust's visit to Venice as taking place in Spring 1901.

12. EP to Augustine Bulteau, 19 May 1901, NAfr 17554:3.

13. WSP, "Memoirs," 129.

14. WSP to Bulteau, 1, rue Cortambert, [n.d. early January 1901], BnF-Mss, NAfr 17554:11; LMLV, *Le Figaro*, 25 January 1901; Montesquiou, Diary-scrapbook, Fonds Montesquiou, BnF-Mss, NAfr 15115:47. See also Kahan, *Music's Modern Muse*, 112–13.

15. Montesquiou, Diary-scrapbook, Fonds Montesquiou., BnF-Mss, NAfr 15115:48.

16. Excerpt from Théophile Gautier, "Affinités secrètes," *Emaux et camées*, copied in Montesquiou, Diary-scrapbook, Fonds Montesquiou., BnF-Mss, NAfr 15115:48.

17. LMLV, *Le Figaro*, 23 June 1900, 2. EP to WSP, 4 July 1900, FSP.

18. "Je tiens à verser une part (minime il est vrai) dans le prix que sera payé le tableau, une part de deux-mille francs. Ce sera toujours un allègement d'autant en effort commun. . . . Ainsi que je vous le dois et le dois à moi-même. Voilà bien des embarras pour vous dire que je veux contribuer pour ma quote-part à l'honneur de la décoration de nos Palais futurs." EP to WSP, "Dimanche matin" [n.d. 8 July 1900], FSP.

19. An article in LMLV, *Le Figaro* (15 March 1901, 2) states that the program on 27 March would include the compositions of Prince Edmond de Polignac, Marquis d'Ivry, René de Bosideffre, Alixis de Castillon, and Comte H. de Fontenailles, and the poems of Comtesse Mathieu de Noailles, Baronne de Baye, Vicomte de Guerne, Comte Robert de Montesquiou, and Comte Jacques de Briey. However, in *Le Figaro*'s subsequent review on the event (28 March 1901), Montesquiou's name is missing from the list of participants.

20. The program given on 18 April 1901 in the Polignac salon consisted of songs by Fauré, accompanied by the composer; choral works by Handel (excerpts from *Alexander's Feast*); Fauré (the "Pavane" and "Madrigal"); Brahms (a set of *Liebeslieder-Walzer*); and three of Polignac's unaccompanied choruses, "Chœur de buveurs," "Ave Maris Stella," and "Aubade." The choral ensemble "L'Euterpe" was best known for giving the French premiere of Brahms's *German Requiem* in the Chapel of the Versailles Palace on 24 March 1891. For an accounting of the Polignac's 18 April 1901 *soirée* and the "back-story" regarding the hiring of L'Euterpe in place of the Chanteurs de Saint-Gervais, see my *Music's Modern Muse*, 113.

21. LMLV, *Le Figaro*, 19 April 1901, 2.

22. The reporter from *La Vie parisienne* makes reference to the song "Comme tout le monde" by C. Dubreuil and H. Prévost.

23. *La Vie parisienne,* 27 April 1901.

24. Charles Joly, "Les Œuvres du Prince Edmond de Polignac au Conservatoire," *Le Figaro,* 17 May 1901, 1.

25. Among the congratulations sent to EP after his concert at the Conservatoire are letters from journalist Augustine Bulteau, conductor Camille Chevillard, painter Maurice Lobre, and poet Anna de Noailles; all, except Noailles's letter, are dated 17 May 1901, and are housed in a private collection.

26. Proust to EP, "Saturday" [18 May 1901], private collection. See the fourth letter in Kahan and Mauriac-Dyer, "Quatre Lettres inédites de Proust au Prince de Polignac," 19–21.

27. Ibid.

28. René Lara, "Notre Page musicale," *Le Figaro,* 18 May 1901, 2. *La Chanson de Barberine,* poem by Musset, music by Edmond de Polignac, appeared in the same issue on p. 6.

29. Isadora Duncan, *My Life* (New York: Liveright, 1955), 82.

30. LMLV, *Le Figaro,* 19 and 24 May 1901. See also my *Music's Modern Muse,* 116–17.

31. *Le Figaro,* 12 June 1901, 1; LMLV, *Le Figaro,* 25 June 1901, 2.

32. "Une Fête au hameau de Marie-Antoinette," *Le Figaro,* 12 June 1901, 1.

33. "La Vie de Paris: Une berquinade à Trianon," *Le Figaro,* 28 June 1901, 1.

34. LMLV, *Le Figaro,* 27 June 1901, 2.

35. Proust to his mother, 31 August 1901, in *Correspondance de Marcel Proust* 2:445n622.

36. Proust to his mother, 31 August 1901, in ibid. 2:445.

37. Ibid.

38. Ibid.

39. Ibid.

40. EP's will and other documents pertaining to the settling of his estate are housed in the Archives nationales, shelf number MS ET/LXXXIV/1383–1445.

41. "Mon maître et ami . . . vient de mourir. . . . Il a suivi pas à pas l'évolution musicale de ce dernier demi-siècle. Toujours en quête de nouveauté, il avait inventé une gamme, une succession de tons, à laquelle on peut reprocher une certaine dureté, mais qui donne à ses œuvres une étonnante originalité . . . il s'intéressait à toute idée neuve et s'appliquait à être artiste, dans quoique branche que ce fût." Eugène d'Harcourt, "Un Prince musicien," *Le Figaro,* 9 August 1901, 1.

42. LMLV, *Le Figaro,* 13 August 1901, 2.

43. Fauré to WSP, 12 August 1901, FSP.

44. Fauré to WSP, Bagnères-de-Bigorre, [n.d. September 1901], FSP. EP also left a bequest of 10,000 francs to painter Maurice Lobre, "in memory of a great and vibrant sympathy." Both bequests are in EP's will, housed in the Archives nationales.

45. Proust [Horatio], "Le Salon de la Princesse Edmond de Polignac."

46. LMLV, *Le Figaro,* 14 August 1901, 2. EP's desire to be buried in Torquay is included in a codicil to his will, Archives nationales, Paris.

47. WSP, "Memoirs," 132.

48. The founding or Édition Mutuelle, in February 1902, was based on an idea of Charles Bordes. It was launched by René de Castéra, Secretary General, then President of the press. See Guy de Lioncourt, "La Schola depuis 1900," in Vincent d'Indy et al., *Le Schola Cantorum, son histoire depuis sa fondation jusqu'en 1925,* 91, 105. Édition Mutuelle published music until 1919; after its dissolution, the plates of EP's publications were turned over to Édition Henn (Geneva).

49. Letters from Blanche Selva to René de Castéra, 11 April, 14 April, 21 April, 5 May, 2 June, and 13 June 1903, private collection.

50. These ten works were: *Chant de Blanche Flor, Lamento* (orchestral version and piano-vocal reduction), *Robin m'aime* (orchestral version and reduction), *Échos de l'Orient judaïque* ("Christ à Gethsémani," "Ruine du Temple prédite," "Pilate livre le Christ"), "Madrigal," "Salve Regina," *Mireïo aux Saintes-Maries, Martha et Maria,* "Ave Maris Stella," and "Aubade." Subsequently, Polignac's *Am Thuringerwald, Imprécations, Le Vallon,* and *Effet de lointain* were also released by Édition Mutuelle.

51. Letters from the Comtesse du Jouffroy-Bérard to Gabriel Astruc, Paris, 25 June 1905, and from the Princesse Edmond de Polignac to Gabriel Astruc, Venice, 1 August 1905, Fonds Gabriel Astruc, AP409/35, Archives nationales, Paris.

52. Letters concerning the "Fondation Edmond de Polignac," as well as a draft of its charter, are in the Fonds Gabriel Astruc, AP409/35, Archives nationales, Paris.

53. Text of a letter to the subscribers of the Société des Grandes Auditions Musicales de France, undated [spring 1903], Archives Greffulhe AN-AP101(II)/138.

54. WSP thought originally about multiple performances of "Pilate." In a letter to EG, (AN-AP101[II]/106, n.d. [late October 1902]), she writes, "I would like to speak with you about my plans for performances of Pilate in Paris and in London, at Queen's Hall." EG responded, "I would very much like to hear Pilate and other works of the Prince de Polignac. I am convinced that with a judicious choice one could put together a very interesting program. Perhaps in a church rather than in concert. I find that there is in all his works a very deep *religious and sad* feeling" (late October 1902, private collection).

55. Blanche Selva to René de Castéra, 14 April 1930, private collection.

56. *Le Ménestrel* 71, no. 17 (23 April 1905): 133–34. Polignac's work was included in a program that also comprised d'Indy's *Symphonie sur un chant montagnard français,* conducted by the composer with Cortot at the piano; Roussel's *Vendanges; La Sulamite* by Chabrier; and Bach's Brandenburg Concerto No. 2.

57. Fauré began to write music reviews for *Le Figaro* in March 1903, continuing through much of the next eighteen years. See Nicole Labelle, "Gabriel Fauré: Music Critic for *Le Figaro*" in *Regarding Fauré,* ed. Tom Gordon, 15–42 (Newark, NJ: Gordon and Breach, 1999).

58. "La condition sociale du prince de Polignac lui eût facilité les plus immédiats comme les plus constants succès, pour peu qu'il s'y fut prêté. Son culte pour l'art véritable lui inspira, au contraire, la volonté de gravir les sommets; comme sa conscience lui commanda de parler son langage propre, même au prix non seulement de n'être pas compris tout de suite, mais aussi d'être quelque peu raillé. Sans découragement, il entreprit des oeuvres considérables par les proportions, considérables par la pensée, considérables par la hauteur du but. . . .

"Dans le nombre de ces oeuvres, il n'en est pas cependant qui caractérisent plus vivement son éloignement du "facile" et du "convenu" ni qui fassent rassortir plus brillamment la valeur de ses conceptions personnelles que ces ECHOS DE L'ORIENT JUDAIQUE dont s'honorait hier, parmi des oeuvres des plus illustres, le programme des Concerts-Cortot. . . .

"[I]ci, l'éloquence du texte et l'émotion des scènes sont enveloppés dans un atmosphère vraiment lointain, teint avec une couleur vraiment orientale. . . .

"De cette musique qui raconte si bien, qui traduit avec une justesse si saisissante et qui fait naître, au même temps avec si vivantes images, se dégage une impression trop réelle pour qu'on y puisse s'échapper." Gabriel Fauré, *"Échos de l'Orient judaïque* du Prince Edmond de Polignac," *Le Figaro,* 19 April 1905, 5–6.

59. See, for example, LMLV, *Le Figaro*, 2 February 1905, 3; 5 and 12 March 1906; 10 and 13 April 1907; and 11 June 1911.

60. See my *Music's Modern Muse*, chap. 9.

61. Ibid., 265.

62. Ibid., 173.

63. "A la mémoire chère et vénérée du Prince Edmond de Polignac. Hommage de celui à qui il témoigna tant de bonté et qui admire encore, dans le recueillement du souvenir, la singularité d'un art et d'un esprit délicieux." Proust to WSP, undated [September 1918], in Proust, *Correspondance* 17:350–54.

64. Proust to WSP, undated [September 1918], in ibid. 17:358–60.

65. This story was recounted to me, in different versions, by various members of the Singer family.

66. WSP to Comte Jean de Polignac, 23 October 1923, private collection.

Chapter Nine

1. The "Cahier No. 3" and the loose sketches are housed in a private collection. For additioinal information on these sources, see chap. 5, note 5.

2. Taruskin, *Stravinsky and the Russian Traditions* 1:269.

3. In post-tonal music theory, a collection is defined as a group of notes—also called pitch classes—that are considered without regard to their order, the duplication of their content, or the implications of that content.

4. Taruskin, *Stravinsky and the Russian Traditions* 1:269; Arthur Berger, "Problems of Pitch Organization in Stravinsky," *Perspectives of New Music* 2, no. 1 (1963): 11–42; Pieter C. van den Toorn, *The Music of Igor Stravinsky* (New Haven, CT: Yale University Press, 1983).

5. It is impossible to determine the order of the movements intended by the composer. If the story of the Passion were told in scripturally chronological order, the movements—including the incomplete "Caiaphas" should be organized in this order: 1. "Ruine du Temple prédite"; 2. ["Caiaphas" movement]; 3. "Pilate livre le Christ." Ultimately, Polignac wrote "Christ à Gethsemani" to replace the "Caiaphas" movement, and when Édition Mutuelle published the three pieces in 1906 as the oratorio *Échos de l'Orient judaïque*, the order of the movements was changed to the following: 1. Pilate; 2. Christ à Gethsemani: 3. Ruine du Temple.

6. A piano-vocal score of "Ruine du Temple prédite" (Paris: Édition Mutuelle, 1906) is housed in the Music Department of the Bibliothèque nationale de France, shelf no. K. 15698.

7. "Barouch Ata (Tafilat Agheschem)" from *Chants en usage dans les Temples Consistoriaux Israëlites de Paris* (Paris, 1879), Polignac family music library. A number of the chant titles in the index of the volume are marked with a slash, indicating that these held special interest for Polignac. "Barouch Ata" was marked with a double slash.

8. As Taruskin notes in *Stravinsky and the Russian Traditions* 1:273–75, Rimsky-Korsakov employs a procedure similar to Polignac's in his contrasting uses of diatonic and octatonic collections: in his 1897 opera *Sadko*, the composer (writes Taruskin) "[differentiates] the human and fantastic worlds by contrast between diatonic and chromatic harmony, the chromatic/fantastic being of the third-related kind (whole-tone or octatonic) to play off against the fifth relations of the human music."

9.   Anti-Semitic depictions of Jews in Orientalist music continued into the twentieth century. In a 2001 article, "Sensuous Pagans and Righteous Jews: Changing Concepts of Jewish Identity in Ernest Bloch's *Jézabel* and *Schelomo*" (*Journal of the American Musicological Society* 54 [2001]: 439–91), Klára Móricz describes how "the chromatic, augmented-second-ridden style" of *Schelomo* "fulfilled the expectations of Bloch's audiences by playing into stereotypes of Jewish music. (491). She also writes, "While the Oriental colors that most force fully connoted Jewish character to the audience distanced the Jews geographically by placing them East, the primitive, barbarous ostinatos that govern the music of *Schelomo* located the Jews in a historically distant past, thus identifying them with the ancient Hebrews" (483).

10.   All sources are housed in a private collection. Source (c) contains an erroneous B♭ on the first beat of the viola (upper bass clef) line, m. 6; this error was carried forward into the published piano-vocal score (g).

11.   "Une bonne oeuvre et une belle oeuvre," *Le Gaulois,* 17 May 1894, 1.

12.   Polignac, "Étude sur les successions alternantes de tons et demi-tons" [undated, 1879], 52, private collection.

13.   See Chap. 4, note 7.

14.   The words are adapted from a Latin text by Edmond de Polignac.

15.   A group of papers entitled "Salammbô, textes, mémentos divers" is housed in a private collection. The first piece, Salammbô's chant, was to be followed by seven more movements, including "a direct invocation by the piano" and several instrumental intermezzi, one of which was to be scored for "Nebel and orchestra."

16.   "Quelque chose de mal fait si vous voulez, mais ayant son lieu dans l'espace . . . une production musicale, d'accent nouveau, non un pastiche, ayant son lieu historique, ethnologique, littéraire. . . . Pour Salammbô: spéculer sur l'effet d'une tenue de la voix qui plane au-dessus d'un mouvement des bas fonds de l'accompagnement (tiré du 1er Acte de *Tristan* le airs des deux amants)." Ibid.

17.   The two partial manuscripts of EP's "Chant à la lune" (Source 1 and Source 2) are in a private collection.

18.   EP's reference to the Overture from Carl-Maria von Weber's 1823 opera *Euryanthe* is somewhat obscure. While the overture's central development section does feature a "swaying" triplet figure that moves through many keys, nothing in the music seems to resemble the "echo" referred to in EP's note.

19.   EP to RM, "Dimanche" [late September 1886], BnF-Mss, NAfr 15140:20. See Chap. 4, note 46 for the original French text. See Chap. 4, note 45 for information about the Pleyel piano.

20.   In Source 2, EP notes that arrows pointing to the right (not shown) direct the performer to "accelerate a bit and equally during the entire length of the arrow only." Arrows pointing to the left (those in Ex 9.10) direct the performer "to slow down, then return to the [first] tempo."

21.   Sources (a) and (b) are housed in a private collection; a copy of source (c) is housed in the Music Department, Bibliothèque nationale de France.

22.   Polignac, "La Danse du Serpent," *La Danse* (Paris: Le Gaulois, 1888), 2:197.

23.   Ibid.

24.   Contrapuntal octatonic motives in $\frac{6}{8}$ meter similar to those in the "Danse du Serpent" are found in the "Source 2" manuscript of "Chant à la lune," written between the opening and the "Hymne" sections. This suggests that EP originally intended these rapid, dancelike figures to contrast with Salammbô's slow, sultry chant. Apparently,

this idea was abandoned, and the motives were used instead for this second, separate movement.

25.   Both the sketch and the manuscript are housed in a private collection.

26.   "Abandon de la progression dont la limite tend à l'aggregation formidable d'un accord (à la Schola) de cinq tierces mineures superposées à la rencontre à l'octave du début du circulus." Note on the manuscript of Edmond de Polignac, "Exercice pour orgue," dated 20 January 1893 (private collection).

27.   All three Latin phrases cited by Polignac appear on the first page of the two-page manuscript (private collection).

Afterword

1.   Allen Forte, "Liszt's Experimental Idiom and Music of the Early Twentieth Century," *19th-Century Music* 10, no. 3, Special Issue: *Resolutions I* (Spring, 1987): 216.

2.   "Je n'ai pas pu, à mon grand regret, entendre *Chilpéric* [libretto by Paul Ferrier, music by Hervé], mais ce soir j'irai entendre la musique d'E. de Polignac [at a concert of the Société Nationale de Musique], que j'espère que ceci remplacera cela." Claude Debussy to Pierre Louÿs, Friday, [23] February 1895, repr. in Claude Debussy, *Correspondance 1884–1918,* 73.

Preface to Polignac's Octatonic Treatise

Epigraph 1. Philip Gaskell, *A New Introduction to Bibliography* (Oxford: Oxford University Press, 1972), 340.

Epigraph 2. EP to LP, 18 April 1879, private collection.

1.   A good example of Bartók's use of the heptatonia secunda mode can be found in his *Cantata Profana* (mm. 72–87), tenor solo and stretto string parts; here, the pitch content of the scale is D, E, F♯, G♯, A, B, C, D.

2.   See for example, Jody Nagel, "On Modes," http://www.jomarpress.com/nagel/articles/OnModes.html.

Bibliography

Primary Sources

Archive and Manuscript Sources

Archives de l'Institut Catholique de Paris
Archives Famille Saint-Marceaux
Correspondence of Marguerite Baugnies and Winnaretta Singer
Archives historiques de l'Archevêché de Paris
Archives nationales, Paris: Series AJ[13] (Opéra); AJ[37] (Conservatoire); AP (Archives privées comtesse Greffulhe)
Archives Prince Edmond de Polignac, private collection
Files of newspaper clippings concerning the Polignac family
Music manuscripts and copies and writings of Prince Edmond de Polignac
Association Blanche Selva, La Touche, France
Bibliothèque nationale de France (Manuscrits): NAfr: Fonds Bulteau, Fonds Montesquiou
Bibliothèque nationale de France (Musique): NLa: Fonds Gabriel Fauré, Programmes imprimés
Fondation Singer-Polignac, Paris: correspondence of Winnaretta Singer, Princesse Edmond de Polignac

Published Compositions by Edmond de Polignac

L'Abeille (Paris: S. Richault, 1867) - 2
Adieu, France! in *Journal de la musique* 1, no. 27 (2 December 1876)
Adieu Montagnes, chœur écossaise (Paris: S. Richault [n.d., 1867])
Les Adieux de Deïdamia (Paris: J. Maho, n.d.; J. Hamelle, n.d.)
Aubade (Paris: Édition Mutuelle, 1906)
Autographes, Exposition Universelle de 1900. Vol. 12 (Paris: Exposition Universelle, 1900): two facsimiles: 1. Prière à la Mecque (1857); 2. Aubade (1900).
Ave Maris Stella (Paris: Édition Mutuelle, 1906)
La Chanson de Barberine, "Supplément littéraire." *Le Figaro,* 19 May 1901, 6
Cinq Esquisses chorales (Paris: Édition Mutuelle, 1906): 1. Ave Maris Stella; 2. Effet de lointain; 3. Prière à la vierge; 4. Madrigal romantique; 5. Le Vallon

La Danse du Serpent, in *La Danse* (Paris: Le Gaulois, 1886)
2e Quatuor à cordes en Fa majeur (Paris: S. Richault, 1864)
Échos de l'Orient judaïque (Paris: Édition Mutuelle, 1906): 1. Pilate livre le Christ; 2.
    Christ à Gethsemani; 3. Ruine du Temple prédite
Hirondelles (Paris: Société musicale G. Astruc, 1905)
Lamento, piano-vocal score and orchestra score (Paris: Édition Mutuelle, 1906)
Martha et Maria (Paris: Édition Mutuelle, 1906)
Mélodies et pieces diverse (Paris: Heugel, 1884)
Pièces diverses, pour piano à 2 et à 4 mains (Paris: Heugel, 1884)
Respect à la vieillesse (Paris: S. Richault, 1865)
"Romance pastorale" (private printing, 1852)
Salve Regina (Paris: Édition Mutuelle, 1906)
Sur les Lagunes, Lamento (Paris: G. Astruc, 1905)

Newspapers and Periodicals (Paris)

L'Art musical (1892–93)
Le Courrier musical (1901)
Le Figaro (1873–1931)
Le Gaulois (1894–1901)
La Gazette de Beaux-Arts (1888)
Le Journal (1895)
Le Journal de musique (1876)
Le Matin (1895)
Le Ménestrel (1838–1923)
Le Mot d'Ordre (1895)
La Nouvelle Revue (1894)
La Revue des deux mondes (1834–36)
La Revue et Gazette musicale de Paris (1860–77)
La Vie parisienne (1901)

Books, Pamphlets, and Articles

Barrès, Maurice. *L'Œuvre de Maurice Barrès,* Vol. 20. Paris: Au Club de l'Honnête
    Homme, 1969.
———. *Scènes et doctrines du nationalisme.* Paris: Félix Juven, 1902.
Bertha, Alexandre. "Acoustique musicale: Sur un système de gammes nouvelles."
    Comptes rendus des Séances de l'Académie des Sciences 18 (January–June 1894):
    1137–39.
———. "Acoustique musicale: Sur un système de gammes nouvelles." *Comptes rendus
    des Séances de l'Académie des Sciences* 19 (July–December 1894): 56.
———. "Boîte à lettres." *Le Figaro,* 28 February 1894, 3.
———. "De la Possibilité de nouvelles combinaisons harmoniques." Article in 3
    parts, *Le Ménestrel* 61, no. 28 (14 July 1895): 219–20; 61, no. 29 (21 July 1895):
    229–31; 61, no. 31 (4 August 1895): 245–46.

———. *Essai d'un système de gammes nouvelles.* Paris: P. Mauret, n.d. [1893].

———. "Franz Liszt: Étude musico-psychologique." Article in 3 parts, *Mercure musical et Bulletin français de la S.I.M.* 3, no. 9 (15 September 1907): 957–79; 3, no. 10 (15 October 1907): 1046–63; 3, no. 11 (15 November 1907): 1160–84.

———. "La Musique bohémienne." In *Encyclopédie de la musique,* edited by Alfred de Lavignac. Paris: Delagrave, 1992, 2597–2613.

———. "La Musique hongroise." In *Encyclopédie de la musique,* edited by Alfred de Lavignac. Paris: Delagrave, 1992, 2613–2645.

———. "La Musique hongroise et les tsiganes." *Revue des deux mondes* 28 (1878): 909–20.

———. "Un Système de gammes nouvelles." *La Nouvelle Revue* 86 (1 January 1894): 125–37.

Bianchini, Pietro, ed. *Chants liturgiques de l'Église arménienne, traduits en notes musicales européennes.* Venice: Congrégation des pères mekhitaristes, 1877.

Bizet, Georges. "Lettres inédits de Georges Bizet." In *Portraits et Études; Lettres inédites de Georges Bizet,* edited by Hugues Imbert, . Paris: Fischbacher, 1894.

Blanche, Jacques-Émile. *La Pêche aux souvenirs.* Paris: Flammarion, 1947.

Bourgault-Ducoudray, L[ouis]-A[lbert]. *Études sur la musique ecclésiastique grecque: Mission musicale en Grèce et en Orient janvier–mai 1875.* Paris: Hachette, 1877.

———. *Souvenirs d'une mission musicale en Grèce et en Orient.* 2nd ed. Paris: Hachette, 1878.

———, comp. *Trente mélodies populaires de Grèce & d'Orient.* Translations by M. A. de Lauzières. Paris: H. Lemoine, 1876.

Chants en usage dans les Temples Consistoriaux Israëlites de Paris. Paris, 1879.

Chausson, Ernest. *Choix et Présentation des écrits inédits.* Edited by Jean Gallois and Isabelle Brétaudeau. Monaco: Éditions du Rocher, 1999.

Clermont-Tonnerre, Elaine de Gramont, Duchesse de. *Robert de Montesquiou et Marcel Proust.* Paris: Flammarion, 1925.

———. *Years of Plenty.* Translated by Florence and Victor Llona. New York: Cape and Smith, 1931.

Cocteau, Jean. *The Journals of Jean Cocteau.* Edited and translated by Wallace Fowlie. London: Museum Press, 1956.

Colette. "Un Salon en 1900." In *Journal à Rebours,* edited by Robert Laffont. Paris: Fayard, 1989.

Cui, César. *La Musique en Russie.* Paris: Fischbacher, 1880.

Daudet, Léon. *Souvenirs des milieux littéraires, politiques, artistiques et médicaux.* Paris: Nouvelle Librairie nationale, 1920.

Debussy, Claude. *Correspondance, 1872–1918.* Edited by François Lesure and Denis Herlin. Paris: Gallimard, 2005.

———. *Debussy on Music.* Collected and introduced by François Lesure. Translated and edited by Richard Langham Smith. New York: Knopf, 1977.

———. *Lettres.* Edited by François Lesure. Paris: Hermann, 1980. Published in English as *Letters.* Selected and edited by François Lesure and Roger Nichols. Translated by Roger Nichols. Cambridge, MA: Harvard University Press, 1987.

Delius, Frederick. *Delius: A Life in Letters 1862–1934.* Edited by Lionel Carley. 2 vols. London: Scolar Press in association with the Delius Trust, 1983–88.

Duncan, Isadora. *My Life.* New York: Liveright, 1995.

Fauré, Gabriel. "Les Concerts: *Échos de l'Orient judaïque* du Prince Edmond de Polignac." *Le Figaro,* 19 April 1905, 5.

———. *Correspondance.* Edited by Jean-Michel Nectoux. Paris: Flammarion, 1980. Translated into English by J. A. Underwood as *Gabriel Fauré: His Life through His Letters.* Edited by Jean-Michel Nectoux. New York: Marion Boyars, 1984.

———. *Lettres intimes.* Edited by Philippe Fauré-Fremiet. Paris: Grasset, 1951.

———. "Souvenirs." *La Revue musicale,* Numéro spéciale: Gabriel Fauré, 1924.

Gallet, Louis. *Notes d'un librettiste: Musique contemporaine.* Paris: Calmann Lévy, 1891.

Gaskell, Philip. *A New Introduction to Bibliography.* Oxford: Oxford University Press, 1972.

Gautier, Théophile. *Émaux et camées.* Paris: Charpentier, 1872.

Goncourt, Edmond et Jules de. *Journal 1894–1895.* Vol. 20 of *Mémoires de la vie littéraire.*Monaco: Éditions Imprimerie Nationale, 1956.

Hermant, Abel. *Souvenirs de la vie mondaine.* Paris: Hachette, 1933.

Indy, Vincent d,' et al. *Le Schola Cantorum, son histoire depuis sa foundation jusqu'en 1925.* Paris: Librairie Bloud et Gay, 1927.

Lavignac, Albert. *Le Voyage artistique à Bayreuth.* Paris: Delagrave, 1897.

Liszt, Franz. *Des Bohémiens et de leur musique en Hongrie.* Paris: A. Bourdillat, 1859. Revised and expanded edition, Leipzig: Breitkopf und Härtel, 1881. This later version was translated into English as *The Gipsy in Music* by Edwin Evans. London: William Reeves, 1926.

Messiaen, Olivier. *Technique de mon langage musical.* 2 vols. Paris: Leduc, 1944. Reprinted 2000.

Montesquiou, Robert. *Les Pas effacés: Mémoires.* 3 vols. Paris: Émile-Paul, 1923.

Niedermeyer, Louis (with Joseph d'Ortigue). *Traité de plain-chant* (1856), Paris: E. Repos, 1857.

Noailles, Comtesse Anna de. *Le Livre de ma vie.* Paris: Mercure de France, 1976.

Polignac, Alphonse de. "Six Propositions arithmologiques déduites de crible d'Ératosthène." *Nouvelles Annales de mathématiques* 8 (1849): 423–29.

———. "Mathématique." *Comptes rendus des Séances de l'Académie des Sciences, Paris* 29 (1849): 738–39.

Polignac, Edmond de. "Acoustique: Sur un système de gammes chromatico-diatoniques," *Comptes rendus des Séances de l'Académie des Sciences* 18 (January–June 1894): 1412.

———. "Boîte à lettres," *Le Figaro,* 24 February 1894, 3.

Polignac, Hedwige de. *Les Polignac.* Paris: Fasquelle, 1960.

Polignac, Duc Jean-Héracle de. *La Maison de Polignac: Étude d'une évolution sociale de la noblesse.* Le Puy: Éditions Jeanne d'Arc, 1975.

Polignac, Winnaretta Singer, Princesse Edmond de. *Lettres, 1888–1938.* Paris: Fondation Singer-Polignac, 1998.

———. "Memoirs of the Late Princesse Edmond de Polignac." *Horizon* 12, n0.68 (August 1945): 110–40.

———. "Mes Amis musicians." *La Revue de Paris 71* (August–September 1964): 97–105.

Pothier, Dom Joseph. *Les Mélodies grégoriennes d'après la tradition.*Tournai: Desclée Lefebvre, 1880.

Proust, Marcel. *Contre Sainte-Beuve . . . Essais et articles.* Paris: Gallimard, 1971.

———. *Correspondance.* Edited by Philip Kolb. 20 vols. Paris: Plon, 1970–93.

———[Horatio]. "Le Salon de la Princesse Edmond de Polignac: Musique d'aujourd'hui; Échos d'autrefois." *Le Figaro,* 6 September 1903.

Reber, Henri. *Traité d'harmonie.* Paris: Colombier, E. Gallet, 1862.

Rimsky-Korsakov, Nicolai. *My Musical Life.* Translated by Judah A. Joffe. Edited by Carl van Vechten. London and Boston; Faber and Faber, 1989.

———. *Polnoye sobraniye sochineniy; literaturniye proizvedeniya I perepiska.* Vol. 4, *Uchebnik garmonii.* Moscow: Murgiz, 1960.

Rumbold, Sir Horace. *Recollections of a Diplomatist.* 2 vols. London: Arnold, 1903.

Ryno. "Le Prince Alphonse de Polignac, souvenirs intimes." *L'Étoile de France,* 21 November 1886.

Saint-Marceaux, Marguerite de. *Journal, 1894–1927.* Edited by Myriam Chimènes. Paris: Fayard, 2007.

Saint-Saëns, Camille. *Harmonie et mélodie.* Paris: Calmann-Lévy, 1885.

Storrs, Sir Ronald. *Orientations.* London: Ivor Nicholson and Watson, 1937.

Stravinsky, Igor, and Robert Craft. *Expositions and Developments.* Garden City, NY: Doubleday, 1962.

Wagner, Richard. *My Life.* Translated by Andrew Gray. Edited by Mary Whittall. Translation of first authentic edition, edited by Martin Gregory-Dallin. New York: Da Capo Press, 1992.

Secondary Sources

Barbier, Patrick. *Opera in Paris, 1800–1850, a Lively History.* Translated by Robert Luoma. Portland, OR: Amadeus Press, 1995.

Baud-Bovy, Samuel. "Bourgault-Ducoudray et la musique grecque ecclésiastique et profane." In "Les Fantaisies du voyageur: Variations Schaeffner" [*festschrift* for André Schaeffner]. *Revue de musicologie* 68 (1982): 153–63.

Baur, Steven. "Ravel's 'Russian' Period: Octatonicism in His Early Works, 1893–1908," *Journal of the American Musicological Society* 52 (1999): 531–92.

Beach, Vincent W. *Charles X of France: His Life and Times.* Boulder, CO: Pruett, 1971.

———. "The Polignac Ministry: A Re-evaluation," University of Colorado Studies, Series in History 3 (January 1964): 87–146.

Beauchamps, Louis de. *Marcel Proust et le Jockey Club.* Paris: Émile-Paul, 1973.

Beaupuy, Anne de, Claude Gay, and Damien Top. *René de Castéra (1873–1955): Un compositeur landais au cœur de la musique française.* Paris: Séguier, 2004.

Berger, Arthur. "Problems of Pitch Organization in Stravinsky," *Perspectives of New Music* 2.1 (1963): 11–42.

Bergeron, Katherine. *Decadent Enchantments: The Revival of Gregorian Chant at Solesmes.* Berkeley and Los Angeles: University of California Press, 1998.

Bertrand, Antoine. *Les Curiosités esthétiques de Robert de Montesquiou.* Geneva: Droz, 1996.

Brandon, Ruth. *The Dollar Princesses: Sagas of Upward Nobility, 1870–1914.* London: Weidenfeld and Nicolson, 1980.

———. *Singer and the Sewing Machine, A Capitalist Romance.* London: Barrie and Jenkins, 1977.

Bribitzer-Stull, Matthew. "The A-flat–C–E Complex: The Origin and Function of Chromatic Major Third Collections in Nineteenth-Century Music." *Music Theory Spectrum* 28 (2006): 167–90.

Brody, Elaine. "The Russians in Paris, 1889–1914." In *Russian and Soviet Music: Essays for Boris Schwarz*, edited by Malcolm Hamrick Brown, 157–83. Ann Arbor, MI: UMI Research Press, 1984.

Brody, Elaine, and Richard Langham-Smith. "Bourgault-Ducoudray, Louis (Albert)." In *The New Grove Dictionary of Music and Musicians*. 2nd ed. Edited by Stanley Sadie and John Tyrrell, 4:112. London: Macmillan, 2001.

Chastenet, Jacques. *Histoire de la Troisième République*. Vol. 3, *La République triomphante, 1893–1906*. Paris: Hachette, 1955.

Chimènes, Myriam. *Mécènes et Musiciens: Du salon au concert à Paris sous la IIIe République*. Paris: Fayard, 2004.

Clément, Félix. *Dictionnaire des opéras*. Revised by Arthur Pougin. Paris: Larousse, 1905.

Cossart, Michael de. *The Food of Love: Princesse Edmond de Polignac (1865–1943) and Her Salon*. London: Hamish Hamilton, 1978.

Cossé Brissac, Anne de. *La Comtesse Greffulhe*. Paris: Perrin, 1991.

Dean, Winton. *Bizet*. 3rd ed. London: Dent, 1975.

Delahaye, Michel. "Marguerite de Saint-Marceaux (1850–1930)." In *Une Famille d'artistes en 1900: Les Saint-Marceaux*. Paris: Éditions de la Réunion des Musées nationaux, 1992.

Diesbach, Ghislain de. *Histoire de l'Émigration, 1789–1814*. Rev. ed. Paris: Perrin, 1984.

Duchesneau, Michel. *L'Avant-garde musicale à Paris de 1871 à 1939*. Sprimont, Belgium: Mardaga, 1997.

Duchen, Jessica. *Gabriel Fauré*. London: Phaidon, 2000.

Ellis, Katherine. *Interpreting the Musical Past: Early Music in Nineteenth-Century France*. New York and Oxford: Oxford University Press, 2005.

———. "Palestrina et la musique dite 'palestrinienne' en France au XIXe siècle." In *La Renaissance et sa musique au XIXe siècle*, edited by Philippe Vendrix, 155–90. Paris: Klincksieck, 2000.

Fauquet, Joël-Marie, and Antoine Hennion. *La Grandeur de Bach: L'amour de la musique en France au XIXe siècle*. Paris: Fayard, 2000.

Fauser, Anngret. *Musical Encounters at the 1889 Paris World's Fair*. Rochester, NY: University of Rochester Press, 2005.

Forte, Allen. "Debussy and the Octatonic." *Music Analysis* 10 (1991): 125–69.

———. *The Harmonic Organization of The Rite of Spring*. New Haven: Yale University Press, 2005.

———. "Letter to the Editor in Reply to Richard Taruskin." *Music Analysis* 5 (1986): 321–37.

———. "Liszt's Experimental Idiom and Music of the Early Twentieth Century." *19th-Century Music* 10, no. 3, Special Issue: *Resolutions I* (Spring 1987): 209–28.

———. "Musorgsky as Modernist: The Phantasmic Episode in 'Boris Godunov.'" *Music Analysis* 9, no. 1, A Musorgsky Symposium (March 1990): 3–45.

———. "An Octatonic Essay by Webern: No. 1 of the *Six Bagatelles for String Quartet*, Op. 9." *Music Theory Spectrum* 16 (1994): 171–95.

Fulcher, Jane F. *French Cultural Politics and Music: From the Dreyfus Affair to the First World War.* New York and Oxford: Oxford University Press, 1999.

Gavoty, Bernard. *Reynaldo Hahn, le musician de la Belle Époque.* Paris: Buchet-Chastel, 1976.

Gerhard, Anselm. *The Urbanization of Opera: Music Theater in Paris in the Nineteenth Century.* Translated by Mary Whittall. Chicago: University of Chicago Press, 1998.

Gossett, Philip. *Divas and Scholars: Performing Italian Opera.* Chicago: University of Chicago Press, 2006.

Gregor-Dallin, Martin. *Richard Wagner, His Life, His Work, His Century.* Translated by Maxwell Brownjohn. San Diego: Harcourt Brace Jovanovich, 1983.

Gumplowicz, Philippe. *Les Travaux d'Orphée: 150 ans de vie musicale amateur en France; Harmonies, chorales, fanfares.* Paris: Aubier, 1987.

Harvard Dictionary of Music. Edited by Don Michael Randel. Cambridge, MA: Harvard University Press, 2003.

Hatton, Roy O. "Prince Camille de Polignac and the American Civil War, 1863–1865." *Louisiana Studies* 3 (Summer 1964): 65–74.

Holoman, D. Kern. *Berlioz.* Cambridge, MA: Harvard University Press, 1989.

Howat, Roy. "Chopin's Influence on the *Fin de Siècle* and Beyond." In *The Cambridge Companion to Chopin,* edited by Jim Samson, 246–83. Cambridge: Cambridge University Press, 1992.

———. "Modes and Semitones in Debussy's Preludes and Elsewhere." *Studies in Music* [University of Western Australia] 22 (1988): 81–104.

———. "Ravel and the Piano." In *The Cambridge Companion to Ravel,* edited by Deborah Mawer, 71–96, 271–73. Cambridge: Cambridge University Press, 2000.

Huebner, Steven. *French Opera at the Fin de Siècle: Wagnerism, Nationalism, and Style.* New York: Oxford University Press, 1999.

Jullian, Philippe. *Robert de Montesquiou, A Fin-de-Siècle Prince.* Translated by John Haycock and Francis King. London: Secker and Warburg, 1967.

Kahan, Sylvia. *Music's Modern Muse: A Life of Winnaretta Singer, Princesse de Polignac.* Rochester, NY: University of Rochester Press, 2003.

———. "'Rien de la tonalité usuelle': Edmond de Polignac and the Octatonic Scale in Nineteenth-Century France." *19th-Century Music* 29 (2005): 97–120.

Kahan, Sylvia, and Nathalie Mauriac-Dyer, "Quatre Lettres inédites de Proust au Prince de Polignac," *Bulletin Marcel Proust* 53 (December 2003): 9–21.

Kinard, Jeff. *Lafayette of the South: Prince Camille de Polignac and the American Civil War.* College Station: Texas A&M University Press, 2001.

Labelle, Nicole. "Gabriel Fauré: Music Critic for *Le Figaro.*" In *Regarding Fauré,* ed. Tom Gordon, 15–42. Newark, NJ: Gordon and Breach, 1999.

Locke, Ralph P. "Cutthroats and Casbah Dancers, Muezzins and Timeless Sands: Musical Images of the Middle East." In *The Exotic in Western Music,* edited by Jonathan Bellman, 104–36, 326–33. Boston: Northeastern University Press, 1998. A fuller version appeared in *19th-Century Music* 22 (1998): 20–53.

———. *Musical Exoticism: Images and Reflections.* New York: Cambridge University Press, 2009.

McFarland, Mark. "Debussy and Stravinsky: Another Look at Their Musical Relationship." *Cahiers Debussy* 24 (2000): 79–112.

McGann, Jerome J. *A Critique of Modern Textual Criticism.* Charlottesville: University Press of Virginia, 1992.

Merrick, Jeffrey, and Bryant T. Ragan, Jr., eds. *Homosexuality in Early Modern France: A Documentary Collection*. New York and Oxford: Oxford University Press, 2001.

Mignot-Ogliastri, Claude. *Anna de Noailles: Une amie de la Princesse Edmond de Polignac*. Paris: Fondation Singer-Polignac and Méridiens Klincksieck, 1986.

Munhall, Edgar. *Whistler and Montesquiou, The Butterfly and the Bat*. New York: The Frick Collection, 1995.

Nectoux, Jean-Michel. *Gabriel Fauré: Les voix du clair-obscur*. Paris: Flammarion, 1990.

Painter, George. *Marcel Proust, A Biography*. 2 vols. New York: Vintage Books, 1978.

Parks, Richard S. *The Music of Claude Debussy*. New Haven: Yale University Press, 1989.

Pasler, Jann. "Countess Greffulhe as Entrepreneur: Negotiating Class, Gender, and Nation." In *Writing Through Music: Essays on Music, Culture, and Politics*. New York: Oxford University Press, 2008, 285–317.

Perle, George. "Pitch-Class Set Analysis: An Evaluation." *Journal of Musicology* 8 (1990): 151–72.

Poulenc, Francis. *Emmanuel Chabrier*. Paris: La Palatine, 1961.

Rees, Brian. *Camille Saint-Saëns: A Life*. London: Chatto and Windus, 1999.

Robin-Harmel, Pierre. *Le Prince Jules de Polignac, Ministre de Charles X: Sa vie de 1829 à 1847*. Paris: Maison Aubanel Père, 1950.

Russ, Michael. *Musorgsky, Pictures at an Exhibition*. Cambridge: Cambridge University Press, 1992.

Said, Edward W. *Orientalism*. New York: Vintage, 1979.

Schaeffner, André. "Debussy et ses rapports avec la musique russe." In *Variations sur la musique*. Paris: Fayard, 1998, 157–206.

Stendhal. *Racine et Shakespeare: Études sur le romantisme*. Paris: Michel Lévy Frères, 1854.

Straus, Joseph N. *Introduction to Post-Tonal Theory*. 3rd ed. Englewood Cliffs, NJ: Prentice Hall, 2005.

Tardif, Cécile. "Les Salons de musique à Paris sous la Troisième République." Master's thesis, Université de Montréal, 1994.

Taruskin, Richard. "Chernomor to Kaschei: Harmonic Sorcery; or, Stravinsky's 'Angle.'" *Journal of the American Musicological Society* 38.1 (Spring 1985): 72–142.

———. "Letter to the Editor." *Music Analysis* 5 (1986): 313–20.

———. *Stravinsky and the Russian Traditions: A Biography of the Works through "Mavra."* 2 vols. Berkeley and Los Angeles: University of California Press, 1996.

Thompson, Victoria. "Creating Boundaries." In *Homosexuality in Modern France*, edited by Jeffrey Merrick and Bryant T. Ragan, Jr., 102–27. New York and Oxford: Oxford University Press, 1996.

Thomson, Andrew. *Vincent d'Indy and His World*. Oxford: Clarendon, 1996.

Troyat, Henri. *Flaubert*. Translated by Joan Pinkham. New York: Viking Penguin, 1992.

Tuchman, Barbara W. *The Proud Tower: A Portrait of the World before the War, 1890–1914*. New York: Macmillan, 1966.

Tymoczko, Dimitri. "The Consecutive-Semitone Constraint on Scalar Structure: A Link between Impressionism and Jazz." *Intégral* 11 (1997): 135–79.

————. "Stravinsky and the Octatonic: A Reconsideration." *Music Theory Spectrum* 24 (2002): 68–102.

Vallas, Léon. *Claude Debussy, His Life and Works.* Translated by Marie O'Brien and Grace O'Brien. New York: Dover, 1973.

Van den Toorn, Pieter C. *The Music of Igor Stravinsky.* New Haven, CT: Yale University Press, 1983.

————. "Octatonic Pitch Structure in Stravinsky." In *Confronting Stravinsky,* edited by Jann Pasler, 130–56. Berkeley and Los Angeles: University of California Press, 1986.

Van den Toorn, Pieter C., and Dimitri Tymoczko. "Colloquy: Stravinsky and the Octatonic." *Music Theory Spectrum* 25 (2003): 167–202.

Vella, Christina. *Intimate Enemies: The Two Worlds of the Baroness de Pontalba.* Baton Rouge: Louisiana State University Press, 1997.

Vlad, Roman. *Stravinsky.* 3rd ed. London: Oxford University Press, 1978.

Wagstaff, John. *André Messager, A Bio-Bibliography.* New York: Greenwood Press, 1991.

Walsh, T. J. *Second Empire Opera: The Théâtre Lyrique, Paris 1851–1870.* London: J. Calder, 1981.

Wentworth, Michael. *James Tissot.* Oxford: Clarendon, 1984.

Wild, Nicole. *Dictionnaire des théâtres parisiens au XIXe siècle: Les theaters et la musique.* Paris: Aux amateurs de livre, 1989.

Wildenstein, Daniel. *Monet ou le triomphe de l'Impressionisme.* 4 vols. Cologne: Taschen, 1996.

Wood, Christopher. *Tissot: The Life and Work of Jacques Joseph Tissot, 1836–1902.* London: Weidenfeld and Nicolson, 1986.

Index

Page numbers in italics refer to figures or examples.

Eastman Studies in Music